Elite Parties, Poor Voters
How Social Services Win Votes in India

Why do poor people often vote against their material interests? This puzzle has been famously studied within wealthy Western democracies, yet the fact that the poor-voter paradox also routinely manifests within poor countries has remained unexplored. This book studies how this paradox emerged in India, the world's largest democracy. Tariq Thachil shows how arguments from studies of wealthy democracies (such as moral values voting) and the global south (such as patronage or ethnic appeals) cannot explain why poor voters in poor countries support parties that represent elite policy interests. He instead draws on extensive survey data and fieldwork to document a novel strategy through which elite parties can recruit the poor while retaining the rich. He shows how these parties can win over disadvantaged voters by privately providing them with basic social services via grassroots affiliates. Such outsourcing permits the party itself to continue to represent the policy interests of its privileged base.

Tariq Thachil is an assistant professor in the Department of Political Science at Yale University. Thachil's doctoral dissertation received the 2010 Gabriel A. Almond Award for best dissertation in the field of comparative politics from the American Political Science Association and the 2010 Sardar Patel Award for best dissertation on modern India in the humanities, education, fine arts, or social sciences from the University of California, Los Angeles. His articles have appeared in *American Political Science Review*, *Comparative Politics*, *Contemporary South Asia*, and *World Politics*.

For my parents
Ania Loomba and Suvir Kaul
for teaching me to love the world of ideas
And for my Nana
Satish Loomba
whose memory inspires these pages

Cambridge Studies in Comparative Politics

General Editor

MARGARET LEVI, University of Washington, Seattle

Assistant General Editors

KATHLEEN THELEN, Massachusetts Institute of Technology
ERIK WIBBELS, Duke University

Associate Editors

ROBERT H. BATES, Harvard University
STEPHEN HANSON, The College of William and Mary
TORBEN IVERSEN, Harvard University
STATHIS KALYVAS, Yale University
PETER LANGE, Duke University
HELEN MILNER, Princeton University
FRANCES ROSENBLUTH, Yale University
SUSAN STOKES, Yale University
SIDNEY TARROW, Cornell University

Other Books in the Series

Ben W. Ansell, *From the Ballot to the Blackboard: The Redistributive Political Economy of Education*

Leonardo R. Arriola, *Multi-Ethnic Coalitions in Africa: Business Financing of Opposition Election Campaigns*

David Austen-Smith, Jeffry A. Frieden, Miriam A. Golden, Karl Ove Moene, and Adam Przeworski, eds., *Selected Works of Michael Wallerstein: The Political Economy of Inequality, Unions, and Social Democracy*

Andy Baker, *The Market and the Masses in Latin America: Policy Reform and Consumption in Liberalizing Economies*

Lisa Baldez, *Why Women Protest: Women's Movements in Chile*

Stefano Bartolini, *The Political Mobilization of the European Left, 1860–1980: The Class Cleavage*

Robert Bates, *When Things Fell Apart: State Failure in Late-Century Africa*

Mark Beissinger, *Nationalist Mobilization and the Collapse of the Soviet State*

Nancy Bermeo, ed., *Unemployment in the New Europe*

Carles Boix, *Democracy and Redistribution*

Carles Boix, *Political Parties, Growth, and Equality: Conservative and Social Democratic Economic Strategies in the World Economy*

Catherine Boone, *Merchant Capital and the Roots of State Power in Senegal, 1930–1985*

(*Continued after the index*)

Elite Parties, Poor Voters

How Social Services Win Votes in India

TARIQ THACHIL

Yale University

CAMBRIDGE
UNIVERSITY PRESS

University Printing House, Cambridge CB2 8BS, United Kingdom

Cambridge University Press is part of the University of Cambridge.

It furthers the University's mission by disseminating knowledge in the pursuit of education, learning and research at the highest international levels of excellence.

www.cambridge.org
Information on this title: www.cambridge.org/9781107678446

© Tariq Thachil 2014

First published 2014
First paperback edition 2016

A catalogue record for this publication is available from the British Library

Library of Congress Cataloguing in Publication data
Thachil, Tariq.
Elite parties, poor voters : how Social Services win votes in India / Tariq Thachil,
Yale University.
    pages   cm. (Cambridge studies in comparative politics)
ISBN 978-1-107-07008-0 (hardback)
1. Political participation – India.   2. Marginality, Social – Political aspects – India.
3. Poor – Political activity – India.   4. Social service – Political aspects – India.
5. Political parties – India.   I. Title.
JQ281.T53 2014
324.954–dc23   2014009763

ISBN 978-1-107-07008-0 Hardback
ISBN 978-1-107-67844-6 Paperback

Additional resources for this publication at "http://www.tariqthachil.com"

Contents

Figures

Tables

Acknowledgments

I began working on this project in early 2005. Since then, I have spent more than twenty months in India, principally between 2007 and 2011, conducting research for this book. During this period, I have incurred a great many debts, none greater than to the many people who took the time to speak with me. I had the privilege of speaking to literally hundreds of politicians, activists, and ordinary citizens in Chhattisgarh, Kerala, Uttar Pradesh, and New Delhi. These informants were incredibly generous – answering my questions with candor and patience, sharing information and documents, and even allowing me to shadow them as they worked. They gave not only of their time but also of their homes – inviting me for meals, to stay with them, and to return as often as I liked. I do not know why they would be so kind to an outsider they did not know well, and the purpose of whose work remained unclear (I was frequently asked who would want to read a book about all this and had to confess I was myself unsure). I do know, however, that without their guidance, there would have been no book at all. I cannot ever repay my debts to them, but I do hope this work will prove to be worthy of their generosity. When I refer to these conversations in the pages that follow, I only provide the names of informants if an interview was expressly on the record and if the informant was an experienced interviewee (most often a high-ranking politician) who understood what this agreement meant. I have withheld the names of all ordinary citizens and low-ranking candidates and activists to protect their anonymity.

In New Delhi, the Center for the Study of Developing Society offered me a much needed institutional home in 2007. I am particularly grateful to Yogendra Yadav, Sanjay Kumar, and Himanshu Bhattacharya for generously sharing portions of their valuable National Election Study datasets (1996, 1999, and 2004). Without their generosity, this study would have been far more limited in its scope. Thanks also to Dhananjai Joshi for providing perceptive insights into Indian politics during many conversations in our shared office. My research in Chhattisgarh is indebted to Bupendra Sahu for his excellent assistance during the administration of the local surveys. I also benefited greatly from conversations with Baba Mayaram, Shashank Sharma, Sunil Kumar, Louise Tillen, and Mayank Tiwari. In Kerala, Sajad Ibrahim was exceedingly generous in recommending his excellent students N. T. Aneesh, Mohammad Shaan, and Shihab Koodal, without whose research assistance, perceptive criticisms, and translation skills my study of the state would have been infeasible. In Uttar Pradesh, I relied on the invaluable assistance of Mirza Asmer Beg and his students for conducting the Agra survey.

I also thank the librarians at the Nehru Memorial Library, National Archives, Parliamentary Library in New Delhi, and Deshbandhu Press Library in Raipur, all of whom went out of their way to help access materials for this project. In New Haven, special thanks go to Abraham Parrish at the Yale Map Library for the fantastic maps he made for this book.

This book began as a doctoral dissertation at Cornell University, where I benefited from the guidance of several scholars I admire deeply. Ronald Herring guided me through each stage of this project with his signature cocktail of encouragement, intellectual engagement, and much-needed plain speaking. Christopher Way was a thorough and constructive early reader, offering critical inputs on issues of research design and analysis. Ken Roberts provided valuable guidance on how to frame the dissertation theoretically, and his extensive knowledge of literatures on political parties and social movements proved essential for a project examining the nexus of the two. Thomas Pepinsky graciously agreed to read the entire dissertation on short notice and offered both incisive criticism and genuine excitement about the project, both of which were greatly appreciated.

Yale University has provided me with a stimulating and rigorous environment, which has proved to be the perfect setting in which to write my first book. My colleagues in New Haven deserve many thanks for engaging my work in such a sustained and supportive manner. Their feedback was crucial in helping me chart the difficult course for developing a dissertation into a book manuscript. While I was a graduate student, Steven Wilkinson's book on riots opened my eyes to what a comparative politics book about India could look like. Having him as a source of advice when writing my own book was a true privilege. Susan Stokes has been the most generous senior colleague one could ask for. She has read multiple drafts of this work and provided constant advice and encouragement at critical junctures. Ellen Lust kindly agreed to read the entire manuscript and offered very thoughtful feedback; Elisabeth Wood served as an extremely caring and conscientious faculty mentor. K. Sivaramakrishnan deserves thanks for his meticulous feedback and support, and also for creating a vibrant interdisciplinary community of South Asia scholars who provided an ideal environment in which to finish this book.

The manuscript also benefited from sustained feedback at a one-day workshop held in New Haven in 2012. I thank the external participants at the workshop, Melani Cammett, Kanchan Chandra, Herbert Kitschelt, and Steven

Levitsky, for making the time to read a lengthy manuscript in its entirety and offering such constructive criticism. It was a personal thrill to see this distinguished group of scholars engage with my work. Irfan Nooruddin and Emmanuel Teitelbaum read several chapters and offered incredibly detailed and valuable advice. I am also extremely grateful to Dan Slater, who has been a very generous friend and colleague, reading several drafts of this work, constantly pushing me to improve it, and offering me encouragement when I needed it most. Many thanks are also due to Madhavi Devasher for her excellent assistance in constructing the index.

For helpful discussions and comments, I also thank Amrita Basu, Harry Blair, Jennifer Bussell, Elisabeth Carlson, Samuel Decanio, Ana De La O, Thad Dunning, Devashree Gupta, Patrick Heller, Amaney Jamal, Sigrun Kahl, Stathis Kalyvas, Devesh Kapur, Atul Kohli, Adria Lawrence, Akshay Mangla, Kristin McKie, Steven Rosenzweig, Mark Schneider, Richard Snyder, Nandini Sundar, Ashutosh Varshney, Lisa Wedeen, and participants in seminars at Amherst, Brown, Columbia, Cornell, the School of Oriental and African Studies, the University of Pennsylvania, and Yale. Finally, my thanks to Lew Bateman, my editor at Cambridge University Press, and to Shaun Vigil, who ably shepherded the manuscript through many hoops. A special thanks to Margaret Levi for including my book in the Cambridge Studies in Comparative Politics series.

The research for this project was only possible because of the generous financial support of several institutions. The Social Science Research Council provided me with the opportunity to conduct extensive fieldwork in 2007–2008. At Yale, generous support from the MacMillan Center for International and Area Studies and the South Asian Studies Council permitted subsequent fieldwork trips in 2009, 2010, and 2011. Kenneth Scheve kindly agreed to fund a workshop for my manuscript through the Leitner Program in International and Comparative Political Economy he directed at the time.

In the many years I have spent working on this project, I have relied heavily on my friends and family to keep me (sort of) sane. The graduate student community in Ithaca was as warm as the winters were cold. Ameya Balsekar read every word, some many times over, and walked with me each step of the way. I very much miss the all-day picnics, costume parties, Slope Days, and late-night drinking (that inevitably devolved into interpretive dance sessions) with Philip Ayoub, Jamie Bleck, Namita Dharia, Don Leonard, Igor Logvinenko, Steven Nelson, Danielle Resnick, Idrissa Sedibe, and many others.

In New Haven, I was lucky to find a similarly wonderful group of friends who softened the harsh transition from graduate school to "real life," including Madhavi Devasher, Sahana Ghosh, Kasturi Gupta, Martin Mattson, Rohit Naimpally, Vivek Sharma, and the members of our infamous Scotch club – SubMaltern Studies – (you know who you are). Samuel Decanio's ability to calm my "on-the-clock" neuroses has been extremely necessary, as has the time he spent with me working at coffee shops, shooting hoops, or watching sports.

Frequent visits to Philadelphia to see Toorjo Ghosh and Kasturi Sen began and
ended in hysterical laughter, with doses in between for good measure, and were
simply essential. Radhika Govindarajan and Jayadev Athreya were housemates
who became family. As fellow gluttons, work counselors, pajama gossipers, bad-
TV addicts, and (extremely bad) punners, they redefined the contours of friendship for me.

In Delhi, Kaushalya Kaul and Urvi Puri provided ever-open homes, good
food, and near-telepathic logistical support. Bindia Thapar gave me a lifetime
of love, which made Delhi feel like home no matter how many years I spent
away from it. One of the great benefits of having this book in print will be seeing
the relief on Primla Loomba's face, as she worried each year about what was
taking me so long. She has been my harshest critic but always softens her blows
with *aloo ka paranthas* and warm hugs. In New York, Shishir and Sumita
Bhattacharya provided endless restorative hangouts on the pink sofa, coupled
with endless streams of girth-widening *kachoris* and *kathi* rolls. Romit
Bhattacharya has introduced me to the delight of having a younger brother,
not least because of the endless amusement his follies have provided me.

This book is dedicated to my parents. My father, Suvir Kaul, reads everything
I send his way, and his sharp red pen has made my "political science prose" at
least partially more readable. Far more crucially, he remains my one-stop crisis
management center and confidant, a constant reminder that reassurance is just a
phone call away. My mother, Ania Loomba, has made warm homes for me
across the world, while providing me with a model for how to think: sharply,
fiercely, but with compassion and a sense of the larger stakes of why we do what
we do.

It is difficult to express my gratitude to Piyali Bhattacharya in words. This
project – and indeed my hopes of becoming an academic – would have long since
perished were it not for her unflagging support, her irrepressible cheerfulness,
and her unerring ability to know whether I needed a hug or a swift kick in the
rear. She walked me through every step of the process: patiently reading drafts
and gently counseling against disastrous decisions. Even more importantly, she
rescued me from the grumpy vortex of book writing by filling our apartment
with people, laughter, and love; by making sure we kept our promise to see the
world; and by providing me with the eternal comfort of knowing that home is
not a place, but a person.

I

Introduction

Why do poor people often support political parties that do not champion their material interests? Disadvantaged voters have routinely cast their ballots in favor of parties that represent the policy interests of wealthier citizens. They have done so across a variety of political contexts – in rich and poor countries, in plurality and proportional electoral systems, and in parliamentary and presidential regimes. Such counterintuitive patterns of support have constituted an enduring puzzle for observers of political life. The prevalence of this paradox in advanced, industrial democracies has been particularly well documented. One recent study finds successful parties opposing redistributive economic policies "actually do about as well or better among the poor as among the rich" in several of these countries, including Belgium, France, Israel, Japan, Switzerland, and Portugal.[1] Another analysis finds similarly high support for right-of-center parties in Ireland, Bulgaria, and Canada.[2] In fact, the authors of this latter study note that in a number of the Western democracies they analyze, "large proportions of low-income voters ... support parties that favor lower taxes and redistribution, even though they doubtfully benefit from [these] economic policies."[3]

Scholars of American politics have wrestled with similar electoral puzzles, examining why the Republican Party has consistently won elections, despite advocating economically conservative policies that should not appeal to a majority of voters. Indeed, Bartels argues that an understanding of why so many poor Americans support a party whose policies have had a "startling negative impact" on their economic fortunes is fundamental to any satisfactory

[1] Gelman et al. 2008, p. 102.
[2] Huber and Stanig 2009.
[3] Ibid., p. 15.

account of the country's political economy.[4] This issue was perhaps most compellingly framed by Frank's well-known question, "What's the matter with Kansas?" prompted by the robust support he observed for Republicans among poorer residents of his native state.[5]

These patterns of support are seen as paradoxical because they cut against the expectations of both sociological and instrumental theories of party politics. In sociological accounts of European party formation, the organization of politics around deep social cleavages was understood to produce enduring class-based partisan divides. Lipset and Rokkan's definitive articulation of this perspective held that the economic and cultural shifts associated with the Industrial Revolution created "uniformly divisive" conflicts between employers and workers across Europe.[6] This division was entrenched by a wide range of organizations, most notably socialist parties and their affiliates, which mobilized poor working-class communities into loyal partisans of progressive politics.[7] Such stable class cleavages became, in the words of another influential account, "*the* standardizing element across the variety of Western European party systems."[8]

By contrast, instrumental models of democratic politics argue that underlying social divisions, collective solidarities, and party organizations are all of little importance in shaping electoral ties between parties and voters. Following Downs, this scholarship conceptualizes politicians as office-seeking entrepreneurs who craft policy positions solely to maximize their vote share.[9] Meanwhile, voters are defined as atomized, self-interested individuals who vote for party platforms that maximize their own welfare. Studies using this framework do not see the poor coalescing into a socially produced partisan collective. However, they still expect poor citizens to support progressive, redistributive parties, because the individual preferences of these voters more closely align with the latters' policy positions in any given election.[10]

Despite their obvious disagreements, sociological and instrumental theories of electoral politics both expect poor voters to support parties that advance their

---

[4] Bartels 2008, p. 3.

[5] Frank 2004.

[6] Lipset and Rokkan 1967, p. 21.

[7] The classic account on the workings of such mass parties is Duverger 1954. Converse provides a slightly different account of partisan stability. He argues that "the partisan stability of voting behavior tends to accumulate as an adult participates in the electoral process" (Converse 1969, pp. 142–3). Such individual-level processes aggregate over time to produce larger, stable, partisan collectives as a democratic political system matures.

[8] Bartolini and Mair 1990, p. 42, emphasis added. Lipset (1981, p. 230) similarly noted that the principal generalization that can be made of Western party politics is that "parties are primarily based on either the lower classes or the middle and upper classes."

[9] Downs 1957. See also Aldrich 1995.

[10] In an influential analysis in this vein, Meltzer and Richard (1981) show why extending the franchise to include more poor voters, thereby lowering the income of the pivotal median voter, increases overall political support for parties and candidates espousing redistributive agendas.

material interests.[11] The frequency with which this shared expectation is contradicted has understandably attracted a great deal of scholarly and popular attention.[12] After all, the willingness of many poor people to vote against their economic interests has significant political ramifications, enabling conservative parties to win popular majorities and moderating the redistributive pressures produced by economic inequality. Why do poor voters so often fail to improve their lot through their collective power at the ballot box?

Despite the global significance of this question, it has been investigated almost exclusively through the experiences of wealthy Western democracies. The prospect of equivalent puzzles existing outside these cases has scarcely been acknowledged, much less explored. Principally, this neglect stems from conventional views of how politics in the global south is organized. Countries in these regions are home to mostly poor and poorly educated electorates, limited technologies of communication and information, and weak party organizations.[13] Such contexts, we have believed, facilitate a politics that is centered on personalist- or ethnic group–based appeals and is heavily reliant on discretionary flows of patronage to win support. The traditional left-right spectrum of Western politics, premised on programmatic differences in policies of redistribution and regulation, is therefore not seen to order political life for most of the world.[14]

Yet, the reduced salience of such distinctions should not blind us to the possibility of broadly similar political puzzles arising in non-Western electoral arenas. After all, these regions are scarcely devoid of poor voters or of political actors who represent elite interests. However, when examining these cases, it is necessary to replace the restrictive terminology of "left" and "right" with the more flexible concept of *elite parties*. Following Gibson, I define these parties on the basis of the social composition of their core constituencies (the groups most influential in providing their electoral, ideological, and financial support, and in shaping their policy profile).[15] Put most simply, the core constituencies of elite parties are located within the upper strata of society.

Of course, the question of who these elites are has contextually specific answers. As Acemoglu and Robinson note, it is possible to acknowledge the varying ways in which elite identities are formed, without foreclosing opportunities to observe

---

[11] As Bartels (2008, p. 26) notes, mainstream majoritarian frameworks of political economy have "remarkable difficulty in explaining why the numerous in poor democratic political systems do not expropriate the unnumerous wealthy."

[12] This literature is too vast to review here, but specific strands will be detailed throughout this chapter. Influential analyses of the determinants of political preferences for redistribution have emphasized the importance of economic inequality (Meltzer and Richard 1981, Milanovic 2000, Boix 2003, Acemoglu and Robinson 2006), post-material values (Inglehart 1971, Inglehart and Flanagan 1987), religious values specifically (Roemer 1998, Frank 2004, De La O and Rodden 2008), and electoral institutions (Iverson and Soskice 2006).

[13] See Hagiopan 2007, Kitschelt and Wilkinson 2007.

[14] Linzer 2010.

[15] See Gibson 1996, p. 7. I prefer the term *elite* parties to Gibson's *conservative* parties, because the latter term still carries the connotations of left-right ideological divides.

general patterns about elite politics.[16] Examples can vary from landowners in nineteenth-century Chile, to crony capitalists in mid-twentieth-century South East Asia, to upper castes in postcolonial India, to educated urbanites in contemporary Egypt. In poorer countries, this privileged strata often includes the so-called middle classes, who are also defined in accordance with Western standards of consumption. The members of this "middle" class are therefore far closer to the top than the middle of their countries' income distribution.

Yet, even if we allow for contextual variation in defining elite communities, how can we then establish if they constitute a party's core base of support? I emphasize three main areas for isolating a party's core constituency: its internal composition, pattern of electoral support, and policy profile. Each of these dimensions is discussed in greater detail in later chapters, but they are worth briefly introducing here.

First, elite parties emerge out of privileged social communities and thus have organizational positions (such as legislative candidacies or internal party executive positions) dominated by members from these groups. Second, elite parties receive disproportionate, although not exclusive, electoral support from these privileged groups. Such disproportionality can be established through a variety of metrics. At a minimum, the percentage of elites who support the party should be consistently higher than the percentage of non-elites. In the cases closely examined in this book, I also focus on the composition of a party's partisan base, not simply those who voted for its candidates. To be successful, elite parties must necessarily win some support from non-elite voters in any given election. However, the composition of their most loyal supporters should still reflect an elite bias. Accordingly, these privileged citizens should constitute at least a plurality of those who identify as partisans of the party.

Third, and finally, elite parties seek to advance the economic and cultural interests of the elite constituencies they emerged to represent. What this means in practice can vary across the global south and need not be limited to the standardized set of tax and transfer issues focused on in advanced industrial settings. Elite parties can take positions that defend the interests of large landowners in limiting the redistribution or nationalization of landholdings (such as the Partido Acción Nacional [PAN] in Mexico in the 1940s or the Alianza Republicana Nacionalista [ARENA] in El Salvador in the 1970s), that support the demands of business communities in advancing particular market reforms (such as the Front Islamique du Salut [FIS] in Algeria, Unión del Centro Democratico in Argentina [UCEDE], Partido Liberal in Brazil, or Movimiento Libertad in Peru), or provide constituency services primarily used by the non-poor (the Muslim Brotherhood in Egypt).[17] Elite interests can also be expressed through the language of ethnicity

---

[16] Acemoglu and Robinson (2006, p. 15).

[17] On ARENA in El Salvador, see Paige 1996; on the UCEDE, see Gibson 1996; on the FIS, see Chhibber 1996; on the PAN, see Middlebrook 2001; on the Muslim Brothers, see Masoud 2010 (especially pp. 183–4); on the BJP, see Hansen 1996.

rather than of class, especially when economic asymmetries significantly overlap with ascriptive differences (as in the case of Hutus and Tutsis in Burundi, ethnic Chinese and Malays in Malaysia, upper and lower castes in India, or whites and blacks in South Africa and the United States).[18]

Acknowledging such variations across diverse settings should not, however, obscure the common challenges elite parties face. As political vehicles of the advantaged, these actors face electoral challenges comparable to their right-wing counterparts in wealthy democracies. Most parties face the general challenge of winning over new voters while retaining old supporters. Yet, the nature of this task is heavily informed by who is in that loyal base. In this respect, the obstacles facing elite parties are unique. Unlike parties with less privileged cores, the core constituencies of elite parties constitute a small slice of all voters, especially in poor countries. These parties therefore face particularly strong imperatives not only to expand but also to craft coalitions in which their cores comprise a numerical minority.

Yet, these small, privileged cores are also economically powerful and politically well organized. Consequently, elite parties are disproportionately constrained by their cash-rich, vote-poor base from pursuing expansionary strategies that may hurt the latter's interests. How then can elite parties appeal to the numerous poor without alienating their powerful core supporters? For their part, why would disadvantaged communities ever vote for parties that are run by and for more privileged citizens? These are the central questions that motivate this book.

The prior scholarship on political parties suggests three major strategic alternatives available to elite parties: redistributive programmatic shifts, patronage, or "distracting" appeals to a voter's moral values or social identity. I explain why each of these tactics is limited in its ability to explain elite party success, especially outside of wealthy Western democracies. Instead, I detail a novel electoral strategy through which elite parties can win over poor voters while preserving core support. I argue these parties can deploy an organizational division of labor, in which the party outsources the task of mobilizing poor voters to non-electoral affiliate organizations. The latter are tasked with recruiting the poor through the *private* provision of local public goods – mostly basic health and educational services. This arrangement leaves the party itself free to continue to represent the policy interests of the wealthy. A service-based electoral strategy is thus ideal for elite parties seeking to recruit the poor and retain the rich.

WHAT'S THE MATTER WITH CENTRAL INDIA?

I investigate the broad paradox of poor voters backing elite parties by studying how a particularly unlikely case of such support emerged within the world's

---

[18] Herring and Agarwala (2006, p. 328) make a similar point. Such asymmetries are especially explicit in what Horowitz (1985, pp. 20–2) terms "ranked" ethnic systems.

largest poor electorate. Specifically, I examine how the Hindu nationalist Bharatiya Janata Party (BJP), traditionally identified as the party of India's privileged upper castes, achieved surprising levels of success with some of the country's least advantaged citizens.

This central puzzle has been produced by the collision of two of the most significant developments within Indian democracy in the past three decades. The first was the mercurial rise of Hindu nationalism during the 1980s and 1990s, which propelled the BJP from political marginality to its current status as one of India's two major national parties.[19] However, this "saffron wave" had a limited social profile and was disproportionately driven by surging upper caste support.[20] Hindu nationalism's top-heavy appeal was not surprising, as it represents an elitist interpretation of Hindu sociocultural traditions, and even included a defense of caste practices.[21] Despite its ambitions to be "a party of all Hindus," the BJP quickly became known as a vehicle of "Brahmin-Bania" (two prominent upper caste communities) interests.

The BJP has consistently exhibited all three major markers of elite parties. As later chapters demonstrate, the party's leadership positions and legislative candidacies have continued to be dominated by upper castes. A similar disproportion was evident among BJP partisans, identified by surveys held during national elections. Among these loyal supporters, upper castes were between two and six times as numerous as Dalit (former untouchable castes) and Adivasi (indigenous tribal communities) voters, despite constituting a much smaller share of the overall electorate.[22] Such elite dominance stood in marked contrast to the BJP's major competitors and consolidated the privileged partisan image of Hindu nationalism.[23] Finally, as Chapter 2 argues, this dominance has also

[19] In 1984, the BJP won only 2 seats in the national parliament. In the very next national election in 1989, it won 85 seats; by 1996, it had won 161 seats, more than any other party that year.

[20] The term *saffron wave* is borrowed from Hansen 1999. Saffron has had a long association with Hinduism, as it is seen as the color of ritual fires. In recent times, the color has specifically become identified with Hindu nationalism, after movement activists systematically incorporated it into their clothing and mobilizing symbols.

[21] For an account of the upper caste bias in the BJP's leadership, see Graham 1990. For an earlier account, see Baxter 1969. Electoral data on the caste profile of BJP partisans is presented in Chapter 2. For an influential critique of Brahminical Hinduism from a subaltern (specifically Dalit) perspective, see Illiah 1996.

[22] Data from India National Election Study 1996, 1999, and 2004. I employ the terms *Dalit* and *Adivasi* because these are the names that these communities have largely self-identified with in India, rather than using the more administrative labels of Scheduled Caste (SC) and Scheduled Tribe (ST). These latter labels referred to these populations being identified not by themselves, but by government lists or schedules of caste communities. This distinction has important ramifications. For example, the Indian Constitution currently does not allow Muslims and Christians to be counted as Scheduled Castes, even though many Dalits belong to these faiths. I also found interviewees from these communities generally preferred Dalit and Adivasi to other options. For a concise, but excellent discussion of the politics of this terminology, see Vishwanath 2012.

[23] The equivalent ratio for the other three largest vote-getting parties in 2004 was less than 1:1. In accordance with the rest of the analysis, I count non-elites as those belonging to Dalit (former

ensured that the party's positions on both economic and cultural issues continue to prioritize upper caste concerns.

Yet, as upper castes flocked to the BJP, a second significant trend began emerging among the country's most marginalized constituencies. Members of these communities began "a silent revolution," increasingly asserting themselves within Indian democracy by forming their own parties, electing co-ethnics to public office, and turning out to vote at rates even higher than those among upper castes.[24] The simultaneity of the saffron wave and the silent revolution was not coincidental; indeed, the two were mutually reinforcing. Elite support for the BJP was reinvigorated by the need to create a political bulwark against growing lower caste political influence. The rapid rise of an upper caste party likewise spurred disadvantaged communities to further self-mobilize.

Indeed, non-elite electorates were widely seen as the force limiting the BJP's rise within Indian democracy. Brass, summarizing this view, argues that the "prideful Hindu identity integral to the upper caste Hindu identification" with the BJP will never be replicated among disadvantaged voters, and that the party "cannot integrate upper and backward castes" into a political coalition.[25] The BJP's elite base and elitist ideology are both seen as especially alienating to Dalits and Adivasis. These two subaltern[26] communities collectively comprise a quarter of the country's population and have been the most marginalized by Hinduism's internal hierarchies.

This increased political polarization among caste groups appeared to set the saffron wave on a crash course with the silent revolution. The 2004 national elections were thought to exemplify just such a clash, as returns indicated angry subaltern voters had repudiated the BJP's ambition to consolidate its position as the governing party of India's Hindu majority. That year, the party had completed its first full term at the head of a broad coalition government in New Delhi, an achievement that had provided the capstone to its rapid rise. Buoyed by positive public opinion polls, the BJP had called early elections, confident of being returned to office. This assurance seemed warranted: the party had presided over a period of rapid macroeconomic growth, and its leader, Atal Behari Vajpayee, was held to be especially popular. Yet, when the final tally

---

untouchable) and Adivasi (tribal) communities. The phrase "partisan image" is borrowed from Green et al. 2002.

[24] In the 2004 elections, turnout among Dalit voters was 60 percent, among Adivasis 61 percent, and among upper castes 56 percent. Differences in turnout rates between these groups narrowed in the 2009 national elections, but even in this instance, subaltern citizens voted at a higher rate (just over 59 percent) than more privileged castes (58 percent). Data from National Election Study 2004, as cited in Kumar 2009, p. 49.

[25] Brass 1993, p. 258.

[26] *Subaltern* was originally a military term used for officers under the rank of captain and was later used to refer specifically to colonial subjects (see Loomba 2005, pp. 48–9). Throughout this book, I use the term *subaltern* as it is commonly used in contemporary studies of South Asia and beyond, to more generally refer to historically marginalized communities with limited access to institutions of power and authority.

of votes was announced, the BJP was forced to concede defeat to a rival coalition headed by the Indian National Congress (Congress).

In attempting to comprehend these unforeseen results, several commentators agreed that poor, lower caste voters were at the root of the BJP's unexpected defeat. This argument made intuitive sense, as subaltern alienation from the upper caste BJP was not only the product of economic inequality but also of generations of social and cultural discrimination.[27] The BJP did not appear to help its cause by choosing a triumphalist 2004 campaign slogan: "India Shining." This platform was built around a celebration of the country's anomalously high economic growth rates and was seen to further put off poorer citizens who had not equally shared in these recent spoils. Drawing on this interpretation, respected observers of Indian elections somewhat extravagantly read the election's tea leaves as "a vote for secular politics"[28] and a "radical shift in the social basis for power,"[29] which offered a chance for a "retrieval of the idea of India" itself.[30]

Yet, these striking headlines misinterpreted the nature of subaltern voting patterns in two fundamental respects. First, in suggesting poor electorates united to oust the BJP from power, popular accounts incorrectly depicted these communities cohering into an electoral bloc. In reality, the 2004 polls saw no such cohesion among Dalits and Adivasis. Although most members of both communities live in conditions of socioeconomic marginality, this shared suffering cannot be assumed to produce a unified national vote bank. Instead, the primary support of these two constituencies went to highly dissimilar parties across

---

[27] I disagree with the view that the BJP has now diluted its communal positions to a point where it no longer qualifies as an ideological party distinct from its secular rivals. Whereas the BJP has certainly modified parts of its program (such as its initial opposition to market reforms), it remained highly distinguishable from more secular formations on issues pertaining to religion. Even in its 2004 campaign, when the BJP was seen to have transitioned to a platform of "good governance" headed by the popular moderate Vajpayee, the party's manifesto retained many distinct positions on key social issues that do not appear in the manifestos of its major national rivals (see Bharatiya Janata Party 2004). In its opening "Highlights" section, the party explicitly states its support for constructing a temple to Ram at the site of a sixteenth-century mosque razed by Hindus in 1992 (pt. 14), its support for banning religious conversions (which targets Christian missionary efforts in India, pt. 17), and an emphasis on returning Kashmiri Hindus to their places of residence (pt. 18). The party's 2004 charter also openly refers to its ties to avowedly Hindu nationalist non-electoral organizations within the movement's Sangh Parivar (organizational family) and refers to Hindu nationalist ideology as a "synonym" for "Indianness." See section labeled "Our Basic Mission and Commitment" in Bharatiya Janata Party 2004. These commitments are not simply words on paper but have remained visible in the symbols, rituals, and language used by the party in its campaign efforts.

[28] Datar 2004.

[29] Yadav 2004a. See also Wallace 2007 and Roy 2007.

[30] Khilnani 2004. In fact, the party's ouster was not due to dramatic swings in its own performance but was largely the result of shifts in coalitional compositions. The BJP lost only 1.5 percent of the vote between its successful campaign in 1999 and its unsuccessful one in 2004, and it was still the second-largest party in 2004 by some margin. Further, only 7 seats separated the Congress (145 seats) and BJP in 2004 (138 seats) out of the 543 seats contested.

different states, ranging from leftist communist parties, to ethnolinguistic regional parties, to the more centrist Congress, to the BJP itself.[31]

Such divergences in subaltern preferences were evident not only across states but also within them, manifesting even between co-ethnic residents of the same village. Yet, these local variations have often been ignored, and even obscured by assumptions of uniformity reflected in popular adages such as "when you cast your vote, you vote your caste." Rather than homogenize disadvantaged groups into vote banks, we need to devote more effort to explaining why members of similarly situated communities make dissimilar electoral choices.[32] Explanations of such divergences are important not only to our knowledge of Indian politics but also for our broader understanding of how disadvantaged voters in developing democracies evaluate and make their political choices.

In addition to understanding variations in subaltern electoral choices, it is imperative to understand why this choice would ever be an elite party such as the BJP. A second misconception with postmortems of the 2004 election was that the BJP was a particular victim of subaltern anger. The idea that the party performed especially poorly with disadvantaged voters was also simply incorrect, as electoral survey data revealed that many non-elite communities supported it at surprisingly high rates. According to a major post-poll survey, more than 30 percent of ballots cast by Dalit and Adivasi voters in 2004 went to the BJP in seven of the country's seventeen largest states (see Figure 1.1). This proportion represents a significant achievement in India's fragmented, multiparty system, in which no party won more than a quarter of all votes cast. Moreover, the gains were recent: just eight years earlier, the BJP had achieved this level of success with Dalit and Adivasi voters in only a single state (Gujarat).

Such recent inroads mark a consequential, yet curiously unnoticed electoral trend within Indian politics: why were so many of Hinduism's most marginalized citizens turning to the party of its most privileged? Such support was even more inexplicable given that the antipathy of non-elite voters toward the BJP was not simply a function of class-based divides. After all, caste hierarchies not only enabled the economic exploitation of subaltern voters but also sought to justify centuries of their intimate social denigration. The close correspondence of caste and class in India, especially at their extremes, meant Dalit and Adivasi communities were separated from the BJP's core across both economic and social divides.[33]

[31] In many states, smaller regional or caste-based parties were the most successful with both communities in the 2004 election. Examples include the Telegu Desam Party (Party for Telugu Land and People, TDP) in Andhra Pradesh or the All India Anna Dravida Munnetra Kazhagam (All India Dravidian Progress Federation, AIADMK) in Tamil Nadu, and the Bahujan Samaj Party (People of the Majority's Party, BSP) in Uttar Pradesh.

[32] Some recent examples of analyses that look to explain poor voter behavior in India beyond the lens of caste include Krishna 2003 and Ahuja and Chhibber 2012.

[33] In the 2004 National Election Study conducted by Lokniti that my research was partially based on, 41 percent of Dalit respondents and 40.02 percent of Adivasi respondents came from

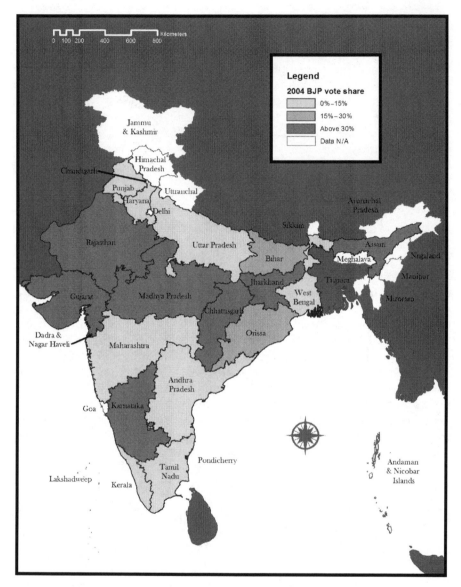

FIGURE 1.1. Map of BJP performance with Dalit and Adivasi voters (2004)
Source: Data from 2004 Lokniti National Election Study; map drawn by Abraham Kaleo Parrish, Yale Map Department, 2012.

households earning less than $1 a day, compared to only 18.12 percent of all other castes. According to a national survey conducted in 2000 by the United Nations Development Programme, Dalits and Adivasis are also less than half as likely as all other castes to live in houses with electricity or to be literate (see UNDP 2000).

This Indian paradox is thus arguably more dramatic and multilayered than its better-known Western analogs and persists whether viewed through the lens of class, caste, or religion. Indeed, it can be simultaneously seen as an instance of poor voters supporting an elite party, of low-ranked ethnic communities backing high-ranked politicians, and of an ideological party winning over voters who are marginalized by its core doctrine. What explains such seemingly inexplicable support? Why was it higher in some Indian states than in others? And what distinguishes those subaltern individuals who decide to vote for the party from their co-ethnics who do not, even within the same state? Does such support indicate a deeper ideological shift to what Brass termed a "prideful Hindu identity,"[34] one that these subjugated communities were never expected to adopt?

THE LIMITS OF CONVENTIONAL ELECTORAL STRATEGIES

The BJP's success is all the more puzzling because it cannot be accounted for by conventional explanations emerging from the literature on political parties. Redistributive programmatic shifts, patronage, and sociocultural appeals – the three major expansionary strategies emphasized by prior scholarship on parties in the global south – all fail to explain why the poor vote for an elite party in the world's biggest democracy.

First, elite parties cannot emulate the programmatic linkages leftist or populist parties forge among the poor. Social democratic parties in Europe for example found success among working classes by advocating policies beneficial to these populations.[35] Within India, the early and continued success of communists with poor voters in the state of Kerala (and to a lesser extent West Bengal) has been argued to derive from popularity of land reforms and other inclusive social policies implemented by leftist parties.[36] For these parties, low-income voters are a core base of support. By contrast, elite parties are constrained from espousing pro-poor redistributive agendas by the powerful constituencies they emerged to represent.[37] Chapter 2 draws on elite interviews, speeches, manifestos, and public spending data to illustrate that to the extent that the BJP displays distinctive policy commitments, it has consistently favored its privileged supporters.

Skeptics will counter that few parties establish programmatic linkages with voters in low-income countries, especially with the poor. Official campaign platforms in these settings often bear little resemblance to how parties actually govern. Instead, voters support those parties they see as most likely to include

---

[34] Brass 1993, p. 258.
[35] Bonoli and Powell 2004, Mair et al. 2004.
[36] Heller 1999, Desai 2007.
[37] On the Egyptian Muslim Brothers, see Masoud 2010, especially pp. 190–201, 218. Chhibber reveals a similar commitment to middle-class preferences in the policies advocated by the Algerian Front Islamique du Salut (FIS). As I show in Chapter 2, the BJP's own campaign platforms and policy records have also prioritized the interests of its upper caste base.

them within circuits of patronage.[38] An earlier generation of scholarship detailed the workings of elite-centered systems of patrimonialism, whereby parties or politicians channeled public sector benefits (patronage) to influential locals in exchange for the support of constituencies under the latter's control.[39] Such hierarchical strategies were identified in cases ranging from Chile in the early twentieth century, to mid-century postcolonial regimes in Southeast Asia, to a number of sub-Saharan African states today.[40] In India too, the early dominance of the Congress Party during the 1950s and 1960s rested primarily on the party channeling patronage to local "big men" who used a mixture of marginal inducements and coercion to deliver the votes of poor citizens under their sway.

However, patrimonial systems in poor countries were primarily associated with incumbent parties that fostered close ties with rural elites presiding over the vote-rich countryside. By contrast, elite parties have depended on the support of urban cultural elites and professional middle classes. Moreover, as urbanization and industrialization began to disrupt these "long chains of patronage," political actors of all stripes had to forge more direct ties with increasingly atomized poor urban migrants.[41] Clientelism, commonly defined as the quid pro quo direct exchange of material benefits in return for political support, emerged as a popular strategy for managing this task.[42] Whereas indirect patrimonialism relied on the social vulnerability of the poor, direct clientelism exploited precarious economic livelihoods that rendered even small payoffs electorally effective. These exchanges can take myriad forms, from the biased distribution of public policies to direct vote buying at election time.[43]

Such discretionary strategies are certainly compatible with policy platforms oriented toward elite supporters. Levitsky shows how the Peronists in Argentina shifted their programmatic orientation to favor middle-class interests, while extending their use of clientelism to retain support among their lower-class base.[44] Yet, he notes that local and national electoral successes were crucial in providing Peronists with the "widespread access to patronage" required to finance their new strategy.[45] Indeed, most successful machines identified by prior scholarship – including that of the PRI in Mexico, Christian Democrats

---

[38] I define patronage to specifically refer to public sector jobs and benefits.

[39] See in particular Scott 1969, 1972. Chubb's (1981, p. 121) analysis of the Christian Democratic machine in Palermo, Italy, also notes the local "boss" was "capable of mobilizing blocks of votes through his personal influence alone…without any exchange of benefits."

[40] On Chile, see Petras and Zeitlin 1968, p. 518; Baland and Robinson 2007. On patron-client relations in Southeast Asia, see Scott 1972, and on Africa, see Van de Walle and Bratton 1994.

[41] Quote from Kohli 2006, p. 261.

[42] See Kitschelt and Wilkinson 2007, Stokes 2007.

[43] See Magaloni 2007, Blaydes 2010. Also see Auyero 2000, and Stokes 2005.

[44] Levitsky 2003. Luna's (2010) work on the conservative UDI in Chile argues that the party uses a similar combination of policies catering to its elite core and vote-buying efforts among poor electorates.

[45] Levitsky 2007, p. 213.

in Italy, or Mubarak's NDP regime in Egypt – are parties that have enjoyed regular incumbent access to state resources.[46]

Elite parties have been prevented from mimicking such an approach by their limited electoral successes. Historically, very few of these actors have consistently won a majority or even a plurality of support across the Middle East, North Africa, and South and Southeast Asia. As I discuss in later chapters, even when these formations do manage occasional electoral breakthroughs – as the BJP has in India – they face pent-up pressures to reward the elite constituencies who stuck with them through their many years of irrelevance. Building pockets of patronage deep enough to move beyond rewarding these core constituencies requires periods of sustained incumbency that most elite parties have simply never enjoyed. To be able to use patronage, elite parties must first find a way to consistently win over poor voters without it.

Of course, even parties in opposition can signal their intentions regarding the distribution of patronage should they come to power. Chandra argues that ethnic parties such as the lower caste–led Bahujan Samaj Party (BSP) in India sent positive signals to poor voters by including candidates from non-elite ethnic backgrounds in their party lists. Yet, the Indian case, with which Chandra's argument was developed, itself illustrates why elite parties cannot mimic their ethnic competitors. When the BJP considered replicating the BSP's approach in the early 1990s, it faced a virulent backlash from the upper caste candidates this strategy would necessarily displace.[47]

Thus, elite parties are circumscribed in their abilities to materially incorporate poor voters through policies or patronage. A third alternative would be to rely on symbolic, nonmaterial appeals to distract the poor from their economic interests. If successful, such an approach could circumvent the need for policy compromises or regular access to public resources. Some analyses have suggested that economically conservative parties in wealthy democracies have indeed won over pious members of poor communities by appealing to their moral preferences.[48] Indeed a version of this claim was Frank's answer to why Republicans enjoy such surprising dominance among poor voters in Kansas.

Within South Asia, one influential version of this distraction argument posits that overcoming extreme divisions between elite and non-elite castes requires equally extreme distractions, namely religious conflict.[49] Hindu nationalism's ideologues have drawn attention to perceived "aggressions" by Muslim and Christian minorities, arguing the latter have lured Hindus into converting to other faiths, demanded preferential government treatment, and even supported

---

[46] For a local test of incumbent advantage in making clientelist appeals, see Watchekon 2003.

[47] Chandra 2004.

[48] See for example Scheve and Stasavage 2006 and De La O and Rodden 2008. Of course, the classic statement on religion as "an opium of the people" comes from Marx 1844. Roemer (1998) provides an elegant formal explanation in a two-party system for how the salience of a non-economic issue can lead to poor voters acting against their "real interests."

[49] Wilkinson 2004. Also see Hansen 1999 and Hansen and Jaffrelot 2001.

anti-state separatist insurgencies. Hindu nationalists have sought to capitalize on the fears they invoked through an array of tactics, including marches that deployed pageantry from Hindu mythology, the organized destruction of mosques and churches, and provocation of communal riots between local Hindu and Muslim communities.[50]

Wilkinson's (2004:165–7) study provides the clearest articulation of the electoral incentives driving such conflict in India.[51] He notes that Hindu nationalists planned preelection violence against Muslims, hoping to polarize electorates along religious lines, thereby uniting Hindu voters across caste divisions. Although not denying the significant repercussions of these polarizing activities, this book argues against viewing Dalit and Adivasi support of the BJP as the product of a manufactured sectarian frenzy. I draw on interviews, voter surveys, and data on ethnic violence to show that these highly theatrical, often violent displays of Hindu chauvinism did not ultimately expand the party's following beyond elite circles. Hindu nationalist leaders themselves confessed that upper caste calls to defend Hinduism held little appeal for lower castes marginalized by the faith's internal divisions.[52] Instead, the next section argues that it was the painstaking implementation of a novel, but far less heralded strategy that broadened the BJP's base.

PRIVATE SERVICES AS AN ELECTORAL STRATEGY

Given the inadequacy of conventional explanations, how can we explain the success of an elite party in India? My main argument is that the *politically motivated, private provision of local public goods* by the BJP's movement affiliates proved central to the party's unexpected success among the poor. These activities – described in detail in Chapter 4 – primarily consist of rudimentary health and educational services, provided via one-teacher schools or village health workers.

Theoretically, I draw on the BJP's experience to conceptualize service as a distinct and important electoral strategy. My analysis emphasizes three key features of such welfare activities. First, these efforts are politically motivated. In the case of Hindu nationalists, such motivations are themselves fairly recent. Whereas the movement has had a long history of charitable work, its initial efforts were not geared toward building mass political support. Accordingly, these prior labors were limited in scope, largely episodic, and not concentrated within subaltern electorates. Yet, I show that the movement's recent expansion of service chapters has been deliberate, targeted toward Dalit and Adivasi communities, and undertaken for political gain. In the wake of several prior

---

[50] I use the term *communal* as it is commonly invoked in a South Asian context to refer to sectarianism along religious lines.

[51] Wilkinson 2004, pp. 165–167.

[52] Author interview with S. N. Jatiya, New Delhi, April 30, 2008.

failures at social expansion, Hindu nationalists hoped local service chapters would provide key channels through which to win subaltern support.

Second, these services are privately provided, in that they are financed by the supporters of the party and movement, and furnished by its activist cadre, without the use of public funds or personnel. Privately financed electoral strategies, outside of some forms of direct vote buying, have received comparatively scant scholarly attention from scholars of the global south. Most studies of distributive politics have instead focused on how parties can manipulate public resources to their political advantage. Yet, for actors who are largely in opposition, including elite parties, strategies that require public resources are not a viable initial option.

Third, even though the basic services I discuss here are privately supplied, they are locally public in terms of how they are accessed. Private welfare offerings are less universally accessible than classic public goods, as they are not available to all citizens within a polity, but only to those residing in proximity to local private providers. At the same time, services are not excludable benefits targeted to specific individuals within these localities, as jobs and contracts (patronage) or handouts of cash and goods (vote buying) can be. Instead, for reasons I shall subsequently explain, private welfare – both in India and elsewhere – is typically provided without discretion, and without explicit demands for electoral reciprocity.[53]

Are services of this type best viewed as "club goods," which are also publicly available to voters within certain constituencies, but entirely unavailable to those residing outside these areas? The key distinction between the two is the manner in which they are financed. Club goods are furnished through biased public policies that provide benefits to specific constituencies funded by involuntary costs imposed on a different, or broader set of voters. Examples of such goods include subsidies for cotton farmers financed by the income taxes of urban voters and special development funds for a particular district that are financed through general tax revenues. Private services of the kind analyzed in this book are also publicly available only to certain constituencies and are usually funded by non-recipients. However, a crucial distinction is that such goods are financed through voluntary, private contributions, not mandatory payments to the public exchequer.

The welfare activities I analyze are therefore best described as privately provided, local public goods, which distinguishes them from most conventional electoral strategies (Table 1.1). These private services are not part of the policies a party promises to enact if elected and therefore do not establish programmatic linkages with voters. Unlike patronage, such welfare is not financed through public resources. Unlike vote buying (which can be privately funded), such services are not distributed under quid pro quo protocols. Given these

---

[53] For a discussion of these differences, see Kitschelt and Wilkinson 2007 and Stokes 2009.

TABLE 1.1. *Service as an electoral strategy*

		Quid Pro Quo?	
		No	Yes
Primary Source of Funding	*Public Resources*	**Programmatic linkages**	**Patronage** (public sector jobs and contracts)
	Party's Resources	**Services** (private provision of local public goods)	**Vote buying** (private handouts of cash and goods)

unconventional characteristics, private welfare has received relatively little attention, particularly as centerpieces of an electoral strategy.

It is possible such neglect stems from the relative improbability of any party providing electorally motivated welfare. Yet, I argue in the next section that this strategy should prove attractive to a number of elite parties beyond the Indian example focused on in this book. However, it is not my intention to use the BJP's experience as a platform for formulating untested generalizations. I cannot and do not argue that all elite parties will follow the BJP's exact manner of deploying welfare as an electoral strategy, or that such efforts will always succeed with poor voters. Instead, I draw on the Indian experience to develop and test logical arguments about *which* kinds of elite parties are most likely to implement this approach, *why* they are attracted to private welfare as an expansionary tactic, *how* such a strategy actually wins votes, and *when* it is likely to succeed or fail. The remainder of this introduction will outline each of these arguments in greater detail.

WHICH PARTIES ARE MOSTLY LIKELY TO USE A SERVICE-BASED STRATEGY?

Which parties are most likely to provide welfare to win over poor voters? To answer this question, it is helpful to focus on two criteria common to most party typologies: the social profile of a party's core constituencies and the depth of its organizational resources (Table 1.2). The first of these influences the demand a party has for a welfare-based approach. Parties with less privileged cores, most obviously leftist, populist, and low-rank ethnic parties, can craft redistributive platforms without the risk of alienating their loyal supporters. These actors are therefore able to directly appeal to the poor and can eschew a painstaking strategy of delivering services privately.

A welfare-based approach thus only holds appeal for parties whose powerful elite cores prevent them from courting disadvantaged communities through direct programmatic appeals. However, not all such actors are equipped to

TABLE 1.2. *Which parties are most likely to divide electoral labor?*

		Organizational Resources (Supply Side)	
		Thin	Thick
Social Profile of Core Constituency (Demand Side)	Elite	**Cadre/Landlord Parties** (Duverger 1954; Baland and Robinson 2007): *ARENA (El Salvador) Conservative Party (mid-twentieth-century, Chile) Ganatanta Parishad (India)* **Middle-Class Reform Parties** (Gibson 1996): *Swatantra Party (India) UCEDE (Argentina) ML (Peru)*	**Religious Elite Parties:** *FIS (Algeria) Muslim Brotherhood (Egypt) Islah (Yemen) PKS (Indonesia) BJP (India)*
	Non-elite	**Electoral Populist Parties** (Roberts 2002): *Fujimori-led parties (Peru) Congress Party (1967– 1984, India) Muslim League – Nawaz (Pakistan)* **Low-Rank Ethnic Parties** (Chandra 2004): *Bahujan Samaj Party (India) Parmehutu (Rwanda)*	**Leftist Parties** (Heller 1999): *Communist Parties of India Worker's Party (Brazil)* **Ethnic/Religious Populist Parties** (Madrid 2012): *UNMO (Malaysia) MAS (Bolivia) Pachutik (Ecuador) Al Nour Party (Egypt)*

bear the supply-side costs of providing basic services. For example, parties that arose as agglomerations of local notables (Duvergerian "cadre" parties) or champions of liberal economic policies (such as UCEDE in Argentina, Movimiento Liberal in Peru, or the erstwhile Swatantra Party in India) often lack the organizational heft to privately provide welfare.

Thus, only those parties that combine an elite social base with thick organizational assets are likely to mimic the BJP's approach. Yet such organizationally thick elite parties may seem like an empirical oddity, especially to conventional typologies based on Western European experience.[54] It is therefore useful to

---

[54] Mair and Mudde 1998 and Gunther and Diamond 2003.

ground this argument with discussions of specific parties. The BJP's own roots point us to an important family of organizationally thick elite parties across Asia and Africa: those emerging out of religious social movements.

Such parties (which populate the top right quadrant of Table 1.2) share three broad characteristics that produce remarkably similar capabilities and constraints. First, they are typically embedded within the "associational nexus" of a broader set of religious social organizations.[55] Indeed, these parties are either the deliberate or unintentional consequence of the efforts of such founding organizations to protect and expand their social influence.[56] The connections elite religious parties maintain with their non-electoral affiliates not only endow them with comparatively rich organizational networks but also produce ideological constraints on their autonomy.

Second, these parties are distinguished by their use of religious appeals and demands to win political support from communities of a particular faith or sect.[57] The tone, centrality, and efficacy of these appeals can vary considerably between religious parties, and within them over time, often reflecting tensions between their electoral ambitions and ideological commitments. Nevertheless, these parties do incorporate faith-based appeals, rituals, and communal demands into their campaigns in a manner that systematically distinguishes them from more secular formations.

Third, these parties are elite, in that they enjoy disproportionate electoral, organizational, and financial support from the upper strata of an electorate. The Muslim Brotherhood in Egypt for example is described as "a movement of the middle classes," whose leadership is concentrated among university-educated professionals, and whose policy platforms represent the interests of relatively privileged voters.[58] The Jordanian Islamic Action Front (IAF), Islamic Salvation Front (FIS) in Algeria, and Islah in Yemen also display elite biases in their internal memberships and enjoy their strongest support from middle-class urban communities.[59] These patterns of support are not particular to the

---

[55] I borrow this phrase from Rosenblum 2003.

[56] Kalyvas (1996) argues that Christian Democratic parties in nineteenth-century Europe were the contingent result of conflicts between the Catholic Church and liberal anti-clerics. However, religious parties in Asia and North Africa were often deliberate creations of communal movements and were launched to defend and advance the latter's political interests.

[57] In identifying parties as religiously oriented, I combine insights from prior definitions that emphasize the importance of religion in influencing either the type of constituency targeted (Rosenblum 2007, pp. 18–19) or the manner in which it targets them (Kalyvas 2000, fn. 1). I also draw on Chandra's (2004) definition of an ethnic party, which provides a similar dual emphasis on strategic methods and targeted constituencies. However, whereas Chandra sees ethnic parties as excluding communities outside their co-ethnic base, I follow Rosenblum and Kalyvas in viewing religious parties as primarily targeting co-religionists but remaining open to the support of members of other faiths.

[58] Masoud 2010, pp. 180, 198. Also see Wickham 2002, pp. 2, 209.

[59] On the IAF, see Azem 1997, pp. 101–103. On the FIS, see Kalyvas 2000, p. 382. On Islah, see Clark 2004, p. 17.

Middle East, as the Islamist PKS in Indonesia has also found its staunchest backers among urban, college-educated citizens.[60] Nor are these patterns exclusively the purview of Islamist parties, as the BJP's own example suggests.

The relatively privileged profiles of these parties reflect the social contexts in which they emerged and expanded. Studies of the Muslim Brotherhood's early growth under founder Hassan al-Banna note that the organization's leadership was composed of culturally elite, literate urbanites.[61] The "most dynamic motors" of the Brotherhood's subsequent growth during the 1970s were the *gama'at* (Islamic student associations), which expanded the party's influence among middle-class student communities.[62] As I discuss in Chapter 7, *tarbiya dakwah* (missionary Islamic education) movements on Indonesian college campuses were similarly crucial to launching and spreading the PKS's network in the post-Suharto democratic period. The elitist philosophy of Hindu nationalism was also initially articulated and disseminated within culturally privileged Brahmin communities in western and northern Indian cities during the early twentieth century.[63]

Across these diverse examples, elite parties with religious roots have proved more limited in their ability to appeal materially to less privileged citizens. Even when such organizations are backed by formally egalitarian philosophies, their practices reveal a reluctance to support progressive public policies at the expense of their elite core supporters. For example, these parties have proven to be stanch defenders of private property, siding with landlords opposing tenant efforts at extensive land reform.[64] They have also sought to defuse lower-class mobilization in favor of class conciliation, promoted an acceptance of inequality rather than its amelioration through redistribution,[65] and focused on issues of morality instead of economic asymmetries.[66] At the same time, these religiously oriented elite parties have rarely won office, precluding their ability to mimic the extensive patronage networks of their dominant incumbent rivals (most often catch-all parties of independence).

An obvious alternative for these parties would be to rely on religious appeals as a mechanism for winning mass support. However, poor voters have largely belied their popular depiction as traditionalists susceptible to communal appeals. Empirical evidence of religion's strength as a political "opiate" has

---

[60] A 2006 Asian Barometer survey in Indonesia has found that among partisan supporters of the PKS, 61 percent came from the top income quintile, whereas only 3 percent came from the bottom quintile. Also see Hamayotsu 2011b.

[61] For a comprehensive history of the Brothers' emergence and early workings, see Mitchell 1969.

[62] Wickham 2002, pp. 2, 115–16.

[63] See Jaffrelot 2007.

[64] For a discussion of such opposition by the Egyptian Muslim Brotherhood, see Springborg 1991 as quoted in Fandy 1994, p. 611.

[65] Tugal 2009, p. 130.

[66] Abu Lughod 1995, p. 54.

been mixed at best, even within advanced, industrial democracies.[67] There are reasons to be even more skeptical of religion's capacity to drive the electoral decisions of poor voters in non-Western settings. A recent round of the World Values Survey (WVS) indicates that although poor respondents from Western countries are systematically more religious than the non-poor, the inverse is true of respondents from Asian and African countries.[68] Second, given the especially harsh poverty of low- and middle-income countries, poor voters within them are even less likely to be able to afford to engage in values voting than their counterparts in wealthier contexts. Thus, even if the poor were largely pious, that piety need not be the basis for their electoral decisions. Take the case of Indonesia, where nearly all voters on the WVS survey identified as religious, yet Islamist parties combined to win only about 15 percent of votes in recent elections (mostly from non-poor constituencies).[69]

Equally importantly, even if poor voters across the global south prioritized their nonmaterial preferences within their electoral decisions, it is unclear this why this would lead them to support religiously oriented elite parties. Masoud quotes Gamal al-Banna, the younger brother of the Egyptian Brotherhood founder, acknowledging a "natural affinity" between the individualism of middle-class sensibilities and his organization's Islamic ideology.[70] By contrast, Clark notes that far from feeling a deep connection with political Islam, "the poor are neglected from the Islamist social and political vision."[71] Perhaps it is not surprising then that a recent survey of citizens of seven countries (Jordan, Palestine, Algeria,

---

[67] Ingelhart's seminal work on "post-material" values voting finds such trends to be most pronounced among middle-class communities, whereas poor communities continue to be motivated by "acquisitive" materialist priorities. Ingelhart 1971, p. 992. More recent analyses also find that even the most salient social issues remain less weighty than economic concerns in driving electoral choices across Europe and North America, particularly among poor voters (see Gelman et al. 2008, esp. pp. 102–6). Bartels (2008) provides compelling evidence against values voting as the central explanation for counterintuitive voting patterns in the United States specifically. Others find the pious poor in Europe vote for conservative parties only when specific institutional conditions provide them with material incentives to support a smaller welfare state, and not because they prioritize their moral preferences (Huber and Stanig 2010).

[68] In the Western Sample, 55 percent of wealthier respondents (those self-reporting as upper or upper-middle class identified themselves as religious, compared to 59 percent of the less privileged sample. Countries included in this sample were Australia, Canada, Finland, France, Germany, Great Britain, Italy, Netherlands, New Zealand, Norway, Spain, Sweden, Switzerland, and the United States. In the sample of Asian and African states, 81 percent of the more privileged sample identified as religious compared to 74 percent of less well-off respondents. Countries included in this sample were Burkino Faso, China, Egypt, Ethiopia, Ghana, India, Indonesia, Iran, Iraq, Jordan, Malaysia, Mali, Morocco, Rwanda, South Africa, Thailand, Vietnam, and Zambia. Data from the fifth wave of the World Values Survey (2005–8).

[69] I discuss the WVS data from Indonesia in greater depth in Chapter 7. However, other studies, including a recent survey experiment (Pepinksy et al. 2012) conducted among voters in the country confirm that support for Islamist parties has very little to do with their ideological platforms.

[70] Masoud 2010, p. 183.

[71] Clark 2004, p. 39.

Morocco, Kuwait, Lebanon, and Yemen) found support for Islamic politics to be higher among college-educated respondents than among those with only primary schooling or less.[72]

These parties share a special affinity with a welfare-based electoral strategy. This affinity is the joint product of two features of these parties: their demand (as elite parties) for an expansionary strategy that protects privileged interests and their supply (as religious formations) of organizational assets. At the same time, the typology presented in Table 1.2 should also clarify that my argument is neither that all elite parties are religious nor vice versa. Certainly, the numerous examples populating the table's top right quadrant suggest a noticeable empirical association between the two characteristics. However, my argument does not imply a necessary conceptual equivalence.

UCEDE in Argentina is an example of an elite party that is not religious. Such parties might also find a welfarist approach highly attractive, especially if they are not in office for long periods of time. However, these formations are limited by their lack of extensive and dedicated cadres. Conversely, the populist Salafist Al Nour Party in Egypt is an example of a religious party whose base is primarily non-elite (specifically the urban poor). Such parties are linked to religious organizations that endow them with the capacity to enact a welfare-based strategy. However, given their non-elite core constituencies, these parties can also deploy populist redistributive appeals without the fear of alienating their base. In this way, they are ironically similar to the leftist parties they abhor, which are also organizationally equipped to provide welfare, but whose redistributive platforms render such a painstaking approach unnecessary.

WHY USE SERVICES AS AN ELECTORAL STRATEGY?

Given the limitations of conventional strategies, the challenge facing elite parties such as the BJP is clear. How can these actors recruit the poor while retaining the rich? This section expands on my argument that elite parties are attracted to service provision because it can help strike this delicate balance. Outsourcing recruitment to grassroots service affiliates provides a material mechanism for appealing to poor voters (contra identity-based appeals), but one that circumvents the need for prior incumbency (contra a patronage-based strategy) and permits the party to maintain economic and cultural policies favored by its elite supporters (contra programmatic shifts).

As the prior section made clear, elite parties emerging from religious movements are uniquely empowered to implement a welfare-based approach because of their considerable organizational resources. The political potential of religious welfare has certainly been widely remarked on, including by party activists themselves. Na'im Qassem, the loquacious second-in-command for

---

[72] Arab Barometer, 2006–2008 wave. More educated voters were found to be 50 percent more likely to support Islamist politics (20 percent overall) than less educated voters (13 percent).

Hizballah in Lebanon, explicitly stated that his party's work in the southern suburbs of Beirut was intended to yield political dividends, arguing that "social work serves to enrich supporters' confidence in the viability for the Party's cause and course."[73] A number of scholars have also commented on the political significance of religious welfare. In her study of religious activism in Egypt, Wickham notes the work of a "parallel Islamic sector" in providing welfare to mobilize support across social classes.[74] Similarly, Tessler argues that a significant portion of Islamist popularity has been built "through the provision of social services and through community assistance projects carried out under the banner of religion."[75]

Yet despite rising interest in such welfare efforts, there have been few systematic efforts to assess their political causes and consequences. Indeed, no study has rigorously examined whether welfare provision does in fact affect electoral outcomes. Prior analyses of religious welfare have been limited to describing the process of service provision, and they cite the aggregate number of service chapters as an indication of welfare's political significance.[76] However, the mere presence of service wings is insufficient evidence of their electoral efficacy and tells us little about the process through which services translate into votes.

The most pressing questions about electorally motivated welfare cannot be answered without systematic micro-level empirical research. Are service networks actually able to garner new support for providers or do they attract only preexisting supporters? Do service activists exclusively influence direct beneficiaries of their efforts or a broader community of voters? Are these activities creating pragmatic material ties or deeper ideological affiliations? And what are the contextual conditions under which this strategy is likely to succeed?

Before addressing such questions, it is necessary to answer a prior one: why would elite parties undertake such painstaking provisioning in the first place? I argue that the primary attraction of private welfare is how it enables a material compromise between wealthy and disadvantaged constituencies. For poor voters, this approach does provide some tangible material benefits and is therefore preferable to strategies based largely on ideological appeals. For elite providers, the fact that this approach relies on private resources is particularly helpful to parties that have wealthy supporters, but limited incumbent access to patronage.

However, a reliance on these private resources requires a service-based strategy to remain appealing to a party's elite financiers. The key to creating such appeal lies in ensuring that welfare chapters affect a large number of poor

---

[73] Qassem 2005, p. 86, as quoted in Williams 2006, p. 42.

[74] Wickham 2002, p. 95.

[75] Tessler 1997, p. 112.

[76] Tessler 1997, Wickham 2002, Clark 2004, Hamayotsu 2011b. Cammett and Issar's (2010) careful study of communal politics in Lebanon attempts to infer political motivations from the spatial distribution of service chapters. However, the challenge of collecting data on voting behavior in Lebanon prevents the authors from assessing these effects at the voter level.

voters for a comparatively low expense, thereby allowing the party to circumvent more costly redistributive strategies for appealing to the vote-rich poor. How can this efficiency be achieved? The BJP's experience shows that making services locally public enables individual providers to establish contact with a relatively large number of poor voters. Meanwhile, the monetary expenses of welfare can be kept relatively low by providing only the most rudimentary of services.

The heavier costs of private welfare provision come in the form of the labors of providers themselves. For traditional elite parties, which were often little more than a collection of local notables, such costs are prohibitive.[77] Yet, elite parties such as the BJP can meet these high labor costs by tapping the motivated cadre of their movement affiliates. These ideologically committed activists are willing to work for low pay, thereby minimizing the costs of providing basic welfare. In India, this technique enabled Hindu nationalists to run one-teacher schools – the centerpiece of their outreach efforts – at close to their advertised "dollar a day" operating costs.

By offering basic local public goods through their non-electoral affiliates, elite parties can reach a large number of poor voters far less expensively than through alternative material strategies, including vote buying. By outsourcing the task of electoral expansion to their movement partners in this manner, these parties are also left free to focus on retaining the affections of their core supporters. Accordingly, they can maintain programmatic positions and personnel profiles that favor their privileged constituencies. For example, I show how private welfare has enabled the BJP to avoid granting Dalits and Adivasis policy-based concessions or greater political representation within the party.

In addition to enabling this material compromise, service offers elite parties several discursive advantages. First, it provides an apolitical channel through which to access poor communities that have been previously non-responsive or even hostile to the provider's ideological vision. At the same time, elite core constituencies are far less threatened by a vision of social justice inspired by their own voluntary charity, rather than the specter of enforced redistribution via policy or personnel shifts. Further, the patronizing terms of "uplift" associated with welfare soothes nervous middle-class communities by reinforcing notions of their superiority and magnanimity. Such rhetoric also helps mobilize the private resources of these citizens with greater ease than less savory tactics (including outright vote buying).[78]

Finally, service provision is particularly helpful to elite parties tied to religious movements because it can easily be portrayed to the movement's ideologues as an electoral tactic in harmony with their goals of social transformation. Whereas the presence of these organizations enhances the capacity of their party affiliates, it also provides them with another constituency to appease. Toward this end, calls to service (such as *da'wa* in Islam or *seva* within Hinduism) are more

---

[77] Duverger (1954, pp. 17–22) famously termed these spare elite-led formations *caucus parties*.

[78] On the distaste of middle-class communities for vote-buying tactics, see Weitz-Shapiro 2012.

effective in energizing grassroots activists than purely electoral campaigns. For example, Hindu nationalist cadres were motivated to provide services to counter similar efforts by (primarily) Christian and Muslim proselytizers among lower caste and tribal communities. Somewhat ironically, Hindu nationalism's successes came from mimicking the strategies of its hated proselytizing rivals on a far larger scale.

HOW SERVICES WIN VOTES

In addition to examining why elite parties such as the BJP are compelled to use private welfare, this book is also concerned with how such a strategy wins over poor voters. The ties created by private welfare do not neatly fit within existing classificatory schemes. As these linkages are not based on official party platforms, they are clearly not programmatic in nature. Nor can they be conceptualized as a clientelist exchange of goods for votes, for reasons that I will subsequently outline.

Instead, this book draws on micro-level qualitative and quantitative data to argue that the support won through this strategy is largely based on voluntary goodwill. This goodwill is earned by activists through their provision of valued material benefits and through their everyday interactions with ordinary voters. I specify three distinct types of political connections welfare providers forge among the poor:

1. *Binding, contingent relationships* with a small cadre of non-elite *members* recruited into formal and informal positions within the service network.
2. *Strong, non-binding material connections* to a larger pool of *beneficiaries* of this provisioning.
3. *Relatively weak social ties* to many *non-beneficiaries* with whom welfare activists interact while dispensing services.

These linkages are arranged in increasing order of their breadth and decreasing order of their depth of impact. The strongest, but narrowest of these connections are the binding relationships created among a small minority of poor citizens who find employment opportunities within service networks, as teachers, informal health workers, or part-time helpers. These positions within service chapters are offered to poor recruits to protect more valued positions within the party for elite supporters.[79] Recruits become members of the provider's organizational network, attend meetings, plan events, and even fundraise for future activities. Some of these members are subsequently funneled into the political party itself as campaign workers, and in some exceptional cases as electoral candidates.

---

[79] My argument here is similar to Panebianco's (1988, p. 29) discussion of collateral roles, which help party organizations widen their influence without depreciating the value of existing internal positions.

This non-elite cadre receives a mixture of material benefits (salary) and status (heightened local social profile and connections) from their inclusion within service organizations. At the same time, these organizations require continued and vocal commitments from employees, not simply at the polls but in public life. Recruits in India not meeting these standards were criticized by their superiors and occasionally replaced. The ties created with this cadre of members thus most closely approximate the individualized contingent transactions that typify clientelist exchange. Yet, although crucial to a service strategy's efficacy, these relationships are far too few in number to be the basis of broad electoral shifts.

In areas with dense service networks, a far greater number of poor voters access sectarian welfare without formally affiliating with the movement or party itself. Like members, these beneficiaries receive material benefits from local activists. However, as I have already mentioned, the activists I observed do not prevent any residents from accessing their offerings. Unlike with their subaltern employees, service chapters also do not withdraw benefits from anyone who does not meet some standard of political reciprocity. Further, service workers continue to provide benefits in areas where they had not garnered many votes and do not expect to do so in the near future. Finally, my extended fieldwork with providers and recipients confirmed that service chapters do not even engage in the subtle techniques of blackmail described in Auyero's masterful account of the Peronist machine in Argentina.[80]

Such sustained, inclusive provisioning constitutes a clear violation of quid pro quo protocols. Thus, electorally motivated private welfare is not best conceptualized as a contingent exchange of goods for votes, or "bricks and mortar clientelism."[81] Indeed, my study more broadly suggests the pitfalls of making automatic assumptions that distributive strategies among poor voters in the global south are necessarily clientelist.[82] The absence of punishment I observed among Hindu nationalists is also not idiosyncratic to the subcontinent, as numerous accounts of service provision in the Middle East have also noted that these actors "do not demand any quid pro quo of political support from beneficiaries."[83]

---

[80] Auyero's (2000, p. 123) ethnography reveals that party brokers wield political leverage over residents by portraying themselves as "the guarantors of social assistance" rather than explicitly demanding votes from beneficiaries. Yet, he notes that the strategy's efficacy hinges on brokers establishing a threat of citizens losing their flow of benefits if these activists were to lose their position within government.

[81] Cammett and Issar 2010.

[82] See Min and Golden 2012.

[83] Richards and Waterbury 2008, p. 369. See also Norton 2007, pp. 110–11. Another example is from Masoud (2010, p. 192), who interviews an activist with the Egyptian Muslim Brothers who "was anxious to tell me that the Brotherhood makes no effort to try to mobilize those who receive its [welfare] support." Clark (2004) also argues that service organizations create bonds more through solidarity than sanction.

However, an absence of sanctioning does not mean that service activities do not yield electoral payoffs. Instead, Hindu nationalist welfare efforts won support by creating goodwill rather than by enforcing compliance. Skeptics might rightly wonder how much goodwill can plausibly be generated through services I have described as exceedingly modest. Indeed, such modesty was crucial in keeping the redistributive costs of this strategy within acceptable limits for elite supporters. Yet, I find the political and social effects of such humble activities can still be profound and are so because benefits are unconditionally, inclusively, and reliably provided for sustained periods. Such patient efforts among largely neglected populations earn service providers gratitude that far exceeds the tangible physical value of their efforts.

Such material appreciation does not however tell the full story of welfare's local impact. I also find that service activists are able to influence the decisions of voters not directly benefiting from their efforts. The key to this broader appeal lies in the daily interactions service provision requires, which embed providers more deeply within recipient communities than episodic transactions around elections. By portraying themselves as politically neutral service providers during these interactions, activists earn an invaluable apolitical moral standing among the wider local community. Providers can use these neutral reputations to engage in strategies of political persuasion that even skilled party brokers can find difficult to enact.

Additionally, welfare providers in India developed networks of friends and associates, which in combination with their own non-partisan credentials, allowed them to effectively combat Hindu nationalism's elitist image, disseminate positive reports about their preferred political candidates, and even spread rumors against rival contestants. As one might expect, such delicate mechanisms proved to be less powerful and predictable than material linkages to direct beneficiaries. Yet, they do serve as testament to the ability of service activists to provide Hindu nationalism with a more inclusive face, and in doing so make the BJP more palatable to a broad swathe of poor voters. These ties were thus crucial in extending the electoral influence of service activists well beyond their circle of beneficiaries.

My argument here resonates with other accounts of the importance of local standing in enabling political influence. Studies of confessional politics in the United States describe how the everyday activities of Protestant church networks ensure their political messages "receive a respectful hearing," "enjoy substantial credibility," and are even able to "alter opinions" among their flock.[84] Within a lower-income setting, Tsai found the ability of Chinese public officials to elicit citizen compliance to also be contingent on their local moral standing.[85] My research extends these observations to countries that are both poor and

---

[84] Wald et al. (1988, p. 533) as quoted in Wittenberg 2006, p. 52.
[85] Tsai 2007, esp. p. 356.

democratic, revealing how local standing earned via apolitical activism can shift the electoral choices of poor voters in these settings.

More broadly, illustrating the impact of such nonmaterial mechanisms demonstrates the value of studying the everyday relations between political parties and poor voters. One consequence of the dominant focus on clientelism in studies of the global south has been that the linkages between parties and voters are increasingly described as episodic and individualized transactions. Accordingly, a great deal of attention is devoted to how budgets are biased, policies are targeted, conditional cash transfers are dispensed, and cash and other handouts are distributed, particularly around elections. Within this framework, the role of social ties has been reduced to one of monitoring voter compliance within clientelist pacts.[86] However, threat-based mechanisms of supervision are just one way through which quotidian interactions can influence electoral behavior. The BJP's experience reveals a wealth of alternative mechanisms – based on goodwill, friendship, suggestion, and rumor – that are all equally worthy of our attention.

Finally, I argue that the electoral victories of service activists cannot be read as evidence of deeper ideological shifts among the poor. Service activists may have somewhat diminished Hindu nationalism's elitist image, but they failed to increase support for Hindu nationalism's core doctrine among poor communities. Quantitative and qualitative evidence suggests that recipients of religious welfare were neither preexisting supporters of the provider's ideology nor radicalized by their experiences as beneficiaries. Thus, welfare activities appear to have provided poor voters with a blend of material and social reasons to vote for the BJP, but they have not succeeded in creating deep and stable preferences for Hindu nationalism.[87]

WHEN SERVICE SUCCEEDS

Services can foster a fragile success for elite parties equipped to provide them. However, even these limited victories are not always achieved where services are provided. This lack of sufficiency prompts a final question for my analysis: under what contextual conditions does a service-based electoral approach succeed or fail?

A comparative evaluation of service networks across Indian states reveals the electoral impact of welfare to be heavily contingent on the strategies it competes against. I examine how effective Hindu nationalist services were when pitted against three competitors. Each of these rivals represents a larger class of political party common to countries of the global south, and each pursued a distinct approach among poor voters. Specifically, I examine how the BJP fared against a leftist class-based party, a (caste-based) ethnic party, and a catch-all

---

[86] See Medina and Stokes 2002.
[87] I draw here on a distinction made by Wood (2003, p.231, fn. 4).

party of independence. Through these local comparisons, I isolate two features of rival tactics that prove especially important in affecting the electoral efficacy of service.

First, if rival parties rely on *pro-poor programmatic linkages* to win the support of disadvantaged communities, services are unlikely to succeed in winning poor voters' support. Parties dependent on such linkages with the poor are more likely to implement progressive social policies, thereby ensuring relatively robust public services (this scenario is marked as "A" in Figure 1.2). The availability of cheap and reliable state services in turn attenuates the demand for private alternatives.[88] I substantiate this claim with a range of data from the Indian state of Kerala, which is home to both impressive social policies and an extensive Hindu nationalist service network. In Kerala, the BJP had to compete against a leftist party that won programmatic support from subaltern voters through its strong pro-poor policy record, including some of the country's best basic health and educational services. I find poor voters in the state consistently prefer the reliable services provided by a government they voted for to those furnished by an upper caste movement with an elitist cultural agenda. When such dependable public options are available, service activists are blocked from the outset, unable to garner the goodwill so crucial for their subsequent political efforts.

The logic of this argument extends beyond the subcontinent. For example, Hamayotsu finds the Malaysian government's extensive basic service infrastructure "largely explains why PAS [the Malay Islamist party] is unique...in its unwillingness and inability to provide social and welfare services to expand their constituencies."[89] Such programmatic linkages among the poor are a relative rarity, both in India and other developing democracies. It is far more common for parties to pursue non-programmatic strategies that do not require them to ensure that basic public services are adequate or accessible to poor voters. Private providers, including those tied to religious organizations, have found a grateful audience for their efforts in these areas.[90]

Hindu nationalist service activists have indeed found many takers for their offerings in regions where they competed against non-programmatic rivals. Yet, my research cautions against assuming that an acceptance of welfare

[88] The crux of this argument resonates with accounts, dating back to Durkheim (1912), of how the functional role of religious networks can be reduced by an expanding, modernizing welfare state.
[89] Hamayotsu 2010, p. 171. Although the PAS's decision not to develop service wings precludes an analysis comparable to the one I conduct in Kerala, it provides strong evidence that effective public services attenuate the electoral efficacy of religious welfare. In a prior comparative analysis (Thachil 2009), I examine how greater government commitment to primary education in Malaysia has enabled the ruling United Malays National Organisation regime to keep its Islamist opposition at bay. I contrast this case with both India and Pakistan, where inadequate expenditures on basic health and education during the 1990s provided openings for sectarian providers to gain a foothold with poor communities.
[90] For example, Cammett and MacClean (2011, p. 15) have found that sectarian non-state service providers in Lebanon "profit from the weak status quo of public service development."

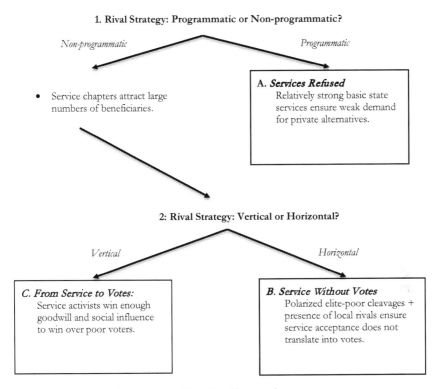

FIGURE I.2. How rival strategies affect the efficacy of service

automatically translates into votes for parties providing them. The electoral impact of services in these situations was further contingent on a second factor: whether poor voters were "horizontally" self-mobilized as a political constituency or "vertically" incorporated through historically privileged intermediaries.

In the former scenario ("B" in Figure 1.2), private welfare providers struggle to convert their own popularity into electoral support for their party arm. This failure is due to the increased difficulty of bridging elite-poor cleavages that become highly politicized when the latter self-mobilize. Such mobilizations need not only occur along class lines, especially in contexts where economic asymmetries overlap with ascriptive differences. Take for instance the recent rise of indigenous parties in Latin America, such as Pachakutik in Ecuador and the Movimiento al Socialismo (MAS) in Bolivia. Both of these parties seek to unite various indigenous communities through ethnopopulist demands that blend economic and cultural critiques of more privileged, non-indigenous populations.[91] In India too, poor communities have often politically mobilized along

---

[91] The MAS has sought to unite previously divided indigenous subgroups, principally Quechuas and Aymaras, while also appealing to *mestizos* with ties to indigenous communities (Madrid 2005, 2008).

ethnic or regional lines. I examine the case of Uttar Pradesh, where an ethnic party led by lower castes has directly sought the support of subaltern communities through ethnically targeted patronage and symbolic politics.

These non-programmatic tactics do not produce the broad-based gains for poor voters that more programmatic approaches do, particularly in the realm of social policy. In Uttar Pradesh, basic health and educational services remain highly inadequate, despite the considerable electoral successes of a lower caste party. However, these horizontal strategies do sharply politicize subaltern communities in opposition to the core constituencies of elite parties. Such polarization widens the gap service activists must bridge and renders their efforts insufficient for shifting political allegiances. Additionally, rival parties that seek direct ties with the poor are compelled to develop their own networks of mobilizing agents within these communities. Hindu nationalist providers in Uttar Pradesh found such local rivals to be a constant thorn in their side. These operatives publicly questioned the political motivations of service activists and closely monitored their activities. Consequently, Hindu nationalists were hemmed into the narrow role of welfare providers and were unable to perform the acts of political persuasion they do in less hostile environs.

Consequently, service activists prove most electorally successful in contexts where rival parties have appealed to the poor through vertical, non-programmatic strategies via traditional elites (scenario "C" in Figure 1.2). These tactics most commonly involve parties disbursing patronage to local notables who in turn deliver the support of poor voters within their spheres of influence. Such approaches remain pervasive across a number of countries in the global south, including in Yemen, which I discuss in more detail in Chapter 7. In my study, this strategy was most clearly illustrated by the efforts of the Congress Party in the central Indian state of Chhattisgarh. As the party of national independence, the Congress is neither a leftist nor an ethnic party, but a catchall incumbent that has historically drawn support across the spectrum of Indian voters. In Chhattisgarh specifically, the Congress has maintained its success through an elite-centered patronage network that indirectly mobilized subaltern communities.

Such vertical strategies typically do little to improve the quality of basic public service infrastructure and to reduce poor voters into recipients of occasional largesse from their local benefactors. Not surprisingly, private service providers are able to find many takers for their offerings in these areas. Unlike in scenario B, the vertical, dyadic dependencies poor voters are locked into prevent them from horizontally mobilizing as a political constituency. Additionally, such elite-centered strategies do not require parties to maintain a direct presence among the poor. Thus, disadvantaged communities are neither organized against the core constituencies of elite parties nor monitored by the latter's partisan rivals. When

Pachakutik in Ecuador has similarly sought to unite previously multiple fragmented communities, chiefly highland Quechuas and lowland Amazonian groups (see Van Cott 2005, Yashar 2005).

placed in this facilitative situation, service activists in India are able to use welfare to access poor voters and convert this access into electoral shifts.

The two features of rival strategies emphasized in this section help explain variations in the efficacy of service within a common institutional setting. Indeed, one of the advantages of my subnational design was its ability to control for important institutional variables (such as electoral rules or levels of fiscal decentralization) while analyzing variations in elite party performance. However, it is worth noting that India's institutional context does highlight some important broader scope conditions for my argument. Most fundamental were the demand-side incentives provided by democratic competition and the civic freedoms the BJP's affiliates enjoyed. Absent these conditions, elite parties are more likely to remain focused on organizational survival (and hence on core voter retention), instead of on electoral expansion. Second, India's first-past-the-post system compelled the BJP to expand beyond its elite base, as upper castes do not constitute a plurality in practically any Indian constituency. Finally, India's populous constituencies raised the monitoring costs of individualized clientelist pacts, thereby incentivizing Hindu nationalists to focus on providing local public goods. Chapter 7 discusses in greater detail how these scope conditions affect the broader applicability of my argument outside South Asia.

EMPIRICAL STRATEGY AND PLAN FOR THIS BOOK

Why should this book focus on the Indian experience? There are both theoretical and empirical reasons for why the subcontinent is a productive setting in which to address the questions motivating this book. First, as discussed, poor voter support for the BJP has always been regarded as especially unlikely and is puzzling from multiple perspectives. Accordingly, India constitutes a "least likely" case for disadvantaged voters backing an elite party. An analysis of how support was won within this unlikely scenario is helpful: if an electoral strategy worked for the BJP in India, it certainly has the potential to do so elsewhere.[92]

Second, a study of Hindu nationalism brings a much-needed comparative perspective to the study of other elite parties with religious roots, notably Islamist parties. The latter have dominated scholarly attention on faith-based politics in non-Western settings, but they have been largely analyzed as a distinct class of political actors. Similarly, Hindu nationalism has been primarily studied in isolation, as yet another South Asian political peculiarity. However, in being sensitive to the particularities of these religious political forces, we have obscured the potential of productively comparing them. Chapter 7 illustrates such potential by examining how arguments derived from the BJP's experience might help further our understanding of similar parties outside South Asia. With the consolidation of a competitive democracy within Indonesia, elections in Tunisia,

---

[92] On case study research, see Eckstein 1975, George and Bennett 2005, Gerring 2007.

and other potentially democratizing shifts across the Middle East, a number of religious parties simultaneously experience fewer restrictions on their actions and face heightened electoral imperatives to expand their support.[93] Given these wider contextual shifts, the strategic efforts of Hindu nationalists operating within India's more mature democratic setting might prove particularly instructive.

Finally, an explanation of the BJP's success advances our understanding of how developing democracies can survive mediocre records of providing for their poor. The sharply unequal distribution of incomes in India – exacerbated by the top-heavy gains accruing from recent economic growth – means that most voters earn less than the average national income. Consequently, standard political economy models would expect a majority of citizens to strongly push for economic redistribution.[94] Scholars anticipate that if such demands are not met, "democratic consolidation itself is threatened" by mass mobilizations or elite repression.[95] Yet despite India's woeful track record in addressing poverty and arresting rising inequality, its democratic institutions have not been overthrown by popular discontent and have largely consolidated over time. An understanding of why many poor voters respond to their own neglect by turning to an elite party, in lieu of more radical responses, is central to any explanation of such exceptional democratic resilience.[96]

In addition to these theoretical motivations, India provides several methodological opportunities for social science research. The country's size, internal diversity, and permissive research environment afford well-known advantages for comparative research, especially on sensitive topics such as the electoral effects of religious welfare.[97] Comparisons within a common national institutional setting are especially helpful for my analysis, as they control for the considerable impact of electoral institutions on voting patterns, including on popular support for elite parties.[98] At the same time, Indian states are both large and dissimilar enough to provide the meaningful variations needed for effective comparative analysis.[99] Scholars have already demonstrated the fertile terrain

---

[93] Of course, the promise of such shifts was significantly reduced in July 2013, when the elected Egyptian government headed by the Muslim Brotherhood–affiliated Freedom and Justice Party was deposed by the military, a development that was followed by widespread violent crackdowns against Brotherhood supporters.

[94] Meltzer and Richard 1981.

[95] Quote from Heller 2000, p. 491. Also see Linz and Stepan 1996, pp. 12–13, Acemoglu and Robinson 2006.

[96] On the "puzzles" India presents to theories of democracy, see Weiner 1989, esp. pp. 21–37; Kohli 2001. For a critique of the premise of the puzzle itself, see Jalal 1995.

[97] For an overview of the advantages of subnational research designs, see Snyder, 2001.

[98] For example, Iverson and Soskice (2006) argue that non-elite voters in plurality systems are more likely to support conservative parties than their counterparts in proportional representation systems.

[99] Data from 2011 Indian National Census. The seventeen major states analyzed here are home to 1.14 billion people, and the three chosen for case studies each have populations of at least 27 million (roughly the size of Malaysia).

the country offers for subnational comparative research, on topics ranging from economic development to ethnic conflict.[100]

Building on this rich tradition, I utilized a variety of research strategies over twenty months of fieldwork, conducted in three stints between 2007 and 2010. My empirical findings are organized into chapters that follow the logic of the argument they present. Chapter 2 draws on a combination of archival research, content analysis, and elite interviews to examine the past failures of the BJP to expand beyond its elite base. The documents consulted included party manifestos and campaign speeches, press clippings on Hindu nationalism available through the Indian Parliamentary Library, each issue of the *Organizer* (the movement's English-language weekly newsletter) between 1980 and 2007, and the rich scholarly literature on Hindu nationalism. Based on these materials, I developed interview questionnaires to flesh out details about each strategy from people who were influential in its implementation. Through these focused interviews, as well as the internal documents given to me by interviewees, I outlined the trajectory of Hindu nationalism's prior disappointments among the poor.

Chapters 3 to 6 present my main arguments and evidence regarding electorally motivated private welfare. One of the biggest empirical challenges for this analysis was the need to simultaneously examine micro-level processes and macro-level patterns.

Understanding how local service networks influence political behavior requires earning the confidence of ordinary villagers and Hindu nationalist activists. Both of these populations often live in fairly inaccessible areas and are understandably reticent about speaking to outsiders about their personal and political lives. Gaining the trust of both activists and voters required an immersion into their lives through intensive fieldwork in specific locales. However, solely basing this study on such research would have prevented me from systematically analyzing whether the local processes I uncovered were isolated to a few individuals or villages or were driving broader patterns of electoral behavior.

To meet the dual requirements of depth and breadth, I adopted a multipronged research strategy that combines extensive qualitative fieldwork with quantitative analyses of national and local survey data (Figure 1.3). First, I examine the voter-level determinants of BJP support among elites and nonelites using the broadest available sample of both constituencies, drawn from an electoral survey conducted in 2004 with 3,263 upper caste and 5,460 subaltern respondents. I use this data to eliminate alternative explanations of subaltern support for the BJP and to provide evidence of the broad division of labor between party and movement anticipated by my argument. I show that upper caste supporters of the BJP were distinguished by their support of the party's

---

[100] Influential examples include Kohli 1987, Varshney 2002, Chandra 2004, and Wilkinson 2004.

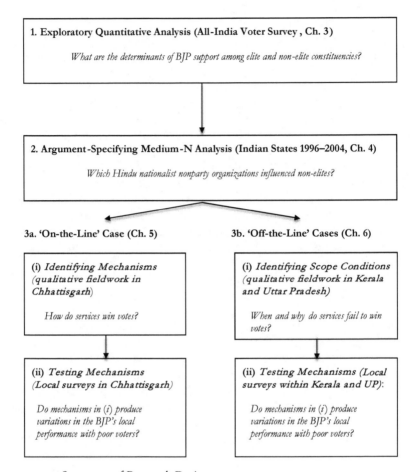

FIGURE 1.3. Summary of Research Design

electoral platform, whereas non-elite voters were marked by their contact with its non-electoral affiliates.

Chapter 4 builds on these findings by specifying which of Hindu nationalism's many non-electoral associations spearheaded outreach efforts among the poor. Using information from elite interviews and the movement's internal records, I document the massive proliferation of welfare networks during the 1990s, and the motivations for this expansion. Drawing on an original panel dataset of major Indian states between 1996 and 2004, I examine why service chapters were concentrated in particular Indian states. I also make sure that the strong observed relationship between the density of service networks and subaltern support for the BJP is not a product of welfare chapters being built where the BJP was already successful.

These all-India analyses combine to establish the strong correlation between service organizations and the BJP's unanticipated electoral successes, but they fall short of establishing a causal relationship. Toward this end, Chapter 5 presents a case study of the central Indian state of Chhattisgarh, which the prior national analysis revealed to be an "on-the-line" case: a place with dense service organizations and strong BJP performance among subaltern voters. To probe this correlation more deeply, I conducted extensive fieldwork in the state in three separate visits between 2007 and 2010, totaling six months. Both Hindu nationalist organizations and local subaltern villagers in central India were understandably reticent about sharing their thoughts and experiences with a stranger, and so I spent the first several weeks establishing myself with village communities in a single district. I then moved on to actually observing Hindu nationalist service chapters and conducting extensive and repeated interviews with welfare providers, local BJP leaders, and rival politicians in that area. I also conducted semi-structured interviews with more than one hundred poor families who were regularly exposed to religious welfare, and with whom I had gained personal familiarity.

This fieldwork, conducted over four months, gradually revealed the myriad mechanisms through which service activists create and utilize political influence within local subaltern communities. Having explored the local causal mechanisms linking service to voting, I carried out an original survey of subaltern voters to test whether the mechanisms actually aggregated into broader electoral shifts. To ensure that the survey protocol was reliably implemented within remote villages, and with a population not used to being surveyed, I personally interviewed each of the 360 respondents with the help of a single research assistant over seven weeks. The survey results revealed the considerable impact of service on the political choices of direct beneficiaries, as well as on the broader communities in which activists worked.

Chapter 6 examines why services failed to win votes in the southern state of Kerala and the northern state of Uttar Pradesh. The national analysis in Chapter 4 revealed these states to be prominent "off-the-line" outliers: places where a service strategy was actively attempted, but non-elite support for the BJP remained marginal. I used a similar blend of extensive qualitative fieldwork and original surveys in each state, over a combined four months of fieldwork, to help specify the conditions under which a service-based strategy succeeds or fails.[101] Chapter 7 places the arguments of this book in broader perspective by comparing the BJP's experiences with those of Islamist parties in Egypt, Yemen, and Indonesia. Chapter 8 concludes by summarizing some of the broader implications of my study, with particular attention to the numerous challenges to sustaining electoral gains won through private service provision.

[101] Lieberman 2005.

2

The Anatomy of a Puzzle: Dissecting the BJP's Struggles with Poor Voters

> The obvious candidate for national confessional politics is the "Hindu majority." But this majority...is an artifact of categorization...15 percent (105 million) are members of the scheduled castes or ex-untouchables. Their categorization as Hindus is as much a result of census enumeration as of their own choosing. Most are not susceptible to political appeals based on a Hindu identity or Hindu interests. Similarly, it is questionable whether the forty-two million of fifty-two million tribals classified as Hindus in the 1981 census share a Hindu identity. They too are not available for appeals to Hindu nationalism and interests.
>
> – Rudolph and Rudolph, *In Pursuit of Lakshmi*, 1987.

This book argues that the expansion of private welfare played a key role in explaining the unlikely success of an elite party within the world's biggest democracy. This chapter seeks to set this argument in historical context by addressing two prior questions. First, why is poor voter support for an elite party in India unexpected in the first place? How did a party purporting to represent all Hindus become so strongly identified with upper castes and viewed as so unlikely to attract lower caste and tribal support (as the epigraph suggests)? Second, why are elite parties such as the BJP constrained from using more conventional strategies – based on policies, patronage, or ideological appeals – to win mass support?

The chapter's initial section focuses on tracing the origins of the Indian paradox examined in this book. I show how the philosophical origins of Hindu nationalism and the social profile of the movement's initial membership imparted it with a clearly elite partisan image.[1] I also discuss how Hindu nationalism's rise within upper caste communities took place during a period of increasing subaltern self-mobilization. These simultaneous developments are

---

[1] See Green et al. 2002 for an account of how partisan images of a party are rooted in the social identities of its core supporters.

key to understanding why lower castes were widely regarded as the Hindu nationalist movement's least likely supporters. As caste-based cleavages became increasingly politicized through subaltern mobilization, nervous upper castes began congregating behind Hindu nationalism's conservative defense of Hindu social traditions. Thus, the BJP consolidated its position as an elite party by representing upper caste interests in the face of lower caste assertiveness, and in doing so increasingly alienated the latter.

This discussion highlights how the Indian poor voter paradox resonates with, but does not neatly replicate, the class-based examples of Western democracies. Subaltern alienation from the BJP is premised on the complex interplay of economic inequalities, social stigmatization, and ritual hierarchy produced by caste. However, rather than diminish the salience of India's poor voter paradox, these complexities reveal it to be perhaps even more dramatic than its better-known Western analogue. Indeed, non-elite support for the BJP can be seen as puzzling from multiple perspectives. From a class-based perspective, we can ask why poor voters would support an advocate of urban, middle-class interests. From a caste-based perspective, we can ask why lower caste communities would back a party stocked with upper caste personnel. Finally, viewing this puzzle through the lens of religion, we can ask how a Hindu nationalist party won over voters alienated by its core doctrine.

Each of the perspectives also suggests a possible explanation for this puzzle. A class-based perspective suggests that the BJP may have increased its appeal among poor voters through redistributive programmatic shifts in its electoral platform. An emphasis on ethnicity indicates the party may have won over lower castes by increasing the latter's representation within its ranks. A faith-based perspective suggests Hindu nationalists may have used communal appeals to distract poor Hindus from their material concerns. The chapter's second half draws on a range of data, including original interviews, a content analysis of primary documents, and data from major Indian states, to document how none of these alternatives adequately explains the BJP's success. While attentive to the specific difficulties each strategy encountered, I also argue that these approaches shared a fundamental inability to reconcile the tensions between recruiting mass support and serving elite interests. Some strategies proved insufficiently appealing to subaltern communities; others entailed levels of compromise unpalatable to entrenched elite interests within the BJP.

Although I outline each of the strategies separately for conceptual clarity, my account is not meant to imply a neat chronological order. Some of the strategies were deployed as a result of the perceived failure of earlier options, but there were also temporal overlaps in the implementation of several of these approaches. However, none of these efforts produced the electoral expansion Hindu nationalists sought. It was this collective failure that informed the emergence of a service-based electoral strategy. The latter approach was therefore not a move of prescient genius, but the outcome of a painful process of trial and error.

THE ELITE ORIGINS OF HINDU NATIONALISM

Why did a party meant for all Hindus become pigeonholed as the vehicle for upper caste interests? In this section, I outline the upper caste sociocultural origins of Hindu nationalism and discuss how its ideological doctrine reflected these origins. To do so, I first briefly sketch the contours of Hindu nationalist ideology, especially as it relates to caste practice. I describe the movement's philosophical critique of Hinduism, especially the faith's lack of firm doctrine and non-proselytizing nature. To address these "weaknesses," Hindu nationalists sought to present a codified, even racialized theory of Hinduism that would facilitate the creation of a cohesive religious community. However, this unifying message was betrayed by the movement's continued support for many aspects of caste praxis. This elitist philosophical orientation translated into an upper caste bias within both the membership of Hindu nationalist organizations and the support base of the movement's electoral arm.

Although Hindu nationalist doctrine offered its own distinct interpretation of Hindu sociocultural practice, it also clearly emerged out of a set of concerns shared by a wider array of late-nineteenth-century religious revivalist movements. One key concern was that Hinduism's lack of internal unity prevented the faith's followers from withstanding foreign cultural incursions. Such interventions were increasingly explicit, in both the expanding purview of British colonial administration and the growing organizational efforts of rival non-Hindu faiths. A specific fear of many Hindu elites was that the more aggressive proselytizing efforts of followers of Islam and Christianity (the latter seen to be especially aided by colonial governments) would attenuate Hinduism's flock. Upper caste Hindus worried that lower caste and tribal communities, seeking to escape their marginalized places within Hinduism, would prove especially susceptible to such overtures.[2]

In response to these concerns, turn-of-the-century reformist associations, such as the Arya Samaj in Punjab and Brahmo Samaj in Bengal, emphasized the need to remove the worst of caste inequalities, which provided rival faith-based organizations with opportunities to poach Hinduism's oppressed.[3] Hindu reform movements began to adapt traditional ritual practices to directly counter such perceived threats. For example, the custom of *Shuddhi* (purification), originally performed to purify higher castes "polluted" by unwanted contact with lower castes, was transformed into a ritual for lower castes themselves. By participating in this adapted ceremony, lower castes were supposedly purified of their polluted status.[4]

---

[2] See Malaviya 1923 in Jaffrelot 2007, p. 69.

[3] On early religious revivalist movements in India, see Jones 1989.

[4] Swami Shraddhananda, a social activist affiliated with the Arya Samaj, reinvented this tradition and also performed this ritual with lower caste Hindus who had converted to other religions to integrate them back into Hindu society (see Jaffrelot 2007, pp. 79–85). The impact of this heritage on current Hindu nationalist attempts at recruiting lower castes is evident in the obvious parallels

The upper caste leaders of these reform movements also campaigned against iniquitous practices such as untouchability, calling them modern perversions of an essentially egalitarian and tolerant religion. Importantly, these movements looked to integrate lower castes within Hindu traditions, not dismantle those traditions altogether. Indeed, reforms targeted the worst excesses of caste discrimination, precisely to defend the caste system as an organic division of labor, rather than an iniquitous hierarchy.

Hindu nationalism was clearly informed by the reformist impulses and strategic decisions of these prior movements, but it also offered a distinct articulation of Hindu identity. Vinayak Damodar Savarkar, a Brahmin from the state of Maharashtra, is credited as the original architect of the ideology, which he labeled "Hindutva." In his influential 1920 tract *Hindutva: Who Is a Hindu?* Savarkar laid out a logic linking the cultural traditions of Hinduism with the political form of the nation-state.[5] Specifically, Savarkar advocated that the territory of India be marked as a "Hindu Rashtra" (Hindu state), based on a specific conceptualization of Indian nationalism.

Savarkar believed nationalism depended on three prerequisites: geographical unity, a common racial heritage, and a common culture, which in India were only provided for within his interpretation of Hinduism. He argued that all Hindus descended from the Aryans who were the original inhabitants of India. Thus, Savarkar believed every Hindu naturally looked upon India as his "fatherland," unlike Indian Muslims and Christians whose spiritual centers were located outside the subcontinent.[6] He also believed that all Hindus possessed a common racial heritage and a shared set of cultural practices that collectively defined what it meant to be not just Hindu, but Indian.

Savarkar's doctrine specified a necessary equivalence between being Hindu and being Indian. Later ideologues, such as Madhav Sadashiv Golwalkar, expanded upon these efforts by articulating even more explicitly racialized versions of Hindutva. Golwalkar argued that "race is by far the most important ingredient of a Nation" and that "people of a foreign origin" (which according to Savarkar's conceptualization encompassed all non-Hindus) needed to "inextricably" be fused into "the mother race" of Hinduism.[7] Those failing to do so,

---

between *Shuddhi* and the Sangh's recent *ghar vapasi* (returning home) campaign to induct tribal converts to Christianity back into the Hindu fold.

[5] Savarkar 1923.

[6] Savarkar believed that Muslims formed a tight-knit community that was bound by pan-Islamic sympathies generated by the concept of *umma* (a wider transnational community of Muslims). He saw the location of Muslim holy sites outside of India as indicative of their supporting Islam rather than a nationalist support for the Indian state and therefore believed Islam to be inherently anti-nationalist. This belief was only strengthened in Savarkar's eyes by the support of many Indian Muslims for transnational agitations following the fall of the Ottoman Empire (termed the Khilafat or Caliphate movement).

[7] As quoted in Jaffrelot 2007, p. 102.

in Golwalkar's opinion, "may be considered at best members of a common state, but they can never form part and parcel of the National body."[8]

One of the purposes of this focus on territory and race was to provide a standardized definition of Hindu identity. Such definitions were required to unite Hinduism's followers across India, despite their extremely differentiated practices.[9] At the same time, Savarkar and other Hindutva ideologues sought to reform this heterodoxy of praxis itself, which they viewed as the source of Hinduism's inability to thwart the predatory threats of more centralized, monotheistic religions. The *Organizer*, the Hindu nationalist English-language weekly newsletter succinctly summed up this position:

Another challenge to the Hindu civilization arises from an internal factor, namely the weakness of unifying forces within the Hindu society. Even at the best of times, Hindu society was only a loosely knit body, more federal than unitary in nature...A reorganized Hindu society rallying round her eternal principles, re-embodied in new institutional forms, had to emerge.[10]

Yet, spreading an organized, institutionalized Hinduism based on common "eternal principles" would require a network of dedicated volunteers throughout the country.[11]

Building this network was the core mandate of the Rashtriya Swayamsevak Sangh (National Organization of Volunteers, RSS), the main organizational arm of the Sangh Parivar – the "family" of Hindu nationalist organizations. The RSS was founded in 1925 by yet another Brahmin, K. B. Hegdewar, and developed a vast network of local *shakhas* (centers), where local volunteers repeated an identical set of rituals, from prayer to play. Such simultaneous repetition created an "imagined community" of young male recruits across India, with each *shakha* striving to symbolize a "Hindu Rashtra [state] in miniature."[12]

The gravest internal threat to Hinduism's unifying forces came from the centrifugal potential of caste distinctions. Hindutva philosophers hoped their creation of a discourse of shared bloodlines and standardization of daily ritual praxis would overcome these debilitating fissures. Yet, Hindutva's doctrine revealed clear elite biases that alienated the very communities it hoped to incorporate. The movement's Brahminical orientation was most evident in its efforts to defend caste as an organic system for dividing society into harmonious components. Hindu nationalists sought to defend the ethical basis of caste-based social distinctions, even as they argued these did not produce unequal relations between Hindus.

Of particular importance were the views of Savarkar and other Brahmin leaders on the controversial *Laws of Manu*, a second-century tract by an

---

[8] As quoted in ibid.
[9] Jaffrelot 1993, p. 27.
[10] "RSS," 1980, p. 8.
[11] Perhaps the preeminent early work on the RSS is Anderson and Damle 1987.
[12] The quotations are from Jaffrelot (1993, p. 64), who borrows from Anderson's (1983, p. 39) famous formulation of nations as "imagined communities."

influential Brahmin philosopher that included a moral defense of the denigration of lower castes. According to Manu:

One occupation only the lord prescribed to Shudras [non-elite castes] to serve meekly these other three [higher] castes. A Shudra, who insults a high caste man with gross invective, shall have his tongue cut out for he is of low origin...No collection of wealth must be made by a Shudra...for a Shudra who has acquired wealth gives pain to Brahmanas [Brahmins].[13]

The fact that Hindu nationalist ideologues defended these "laws" immediately positioned Hindutva as an elitist defense of casteism – literally a *manuvadi* (of Manu) ideology. Savarkar defended the division of Hindu society into four caste groups (the *chaturvarna* of Brahmins, Kshatriyas, Vaishyas, and Shudras) as necessary to "regulate [Hinduism's] noble blood on lines believed – and on the whole rightly believed."[14] Golwalkar echoed this defense, famously supporting the myth of Hindu castes as parts of a *Virat Purusha* (Divine Man/also the first incarnation of the Hindu god Brahma) in which "the Brahmin is the head... and Shudras the feet."[15] A third prominent Hindutva ideologue, K. R. Malkani, noted that Golwalkar in fact "saw no reason why Hindu law should break its links with *Manusmriti* [the laws of Manu]."[16]

Unsurprisingly, the elite origins and elitist philosophy of Hindutva translated into an organizational bias within the movement. Early ideologues for the movement came from predominantly upper caste backgrounds, and their initial recruiting efforts largely took place within their own caste communities. In addition, the customs RSS organizations advocated, from vegetarianism, to abstention from drinking alcohol, to speaking a formal Sanskritized Hindi, were clearly identifiable as Brahminical. Even the supposedly egalitarian practices of the RSS's *shakhas*, such as common intercaste seating for meals, included measures that were "carefully designed to preclude the accidental 'pollution' of upper castes by crucial forms of contact – such as having everyone wash the plates and glasses they eat from."[17] Some lower castes were still drawn to movement out of a hope that mimicking Brahmin practices would enable their own upward mobility (a process dubbed "Sanskritization").[18] However, such enrollees were few and far between. The elite bias within RSS *shakhas* was so pronounced that the organization's leaders often referred to their initial recruits simply as "Brahmin youths."[19]

---

[13] From Mueller 1886, as quoted in Islam 2005, pp. 25–26.
[14] Savarkar 1923, p. 85, as quoted in Islam 2005, p. 31.
[15] Golwalkar 1939, p. 36.
[16] Malkani 1980, p.73, as quoted in Gatade 2011.
[17] Mathur 2008, p. 96.
[18] See Anderson and Damle 1987, p. 45. The term *Sanskritization* was coined by Srinivas 1952; 1956.
[19] Bacchetta 2005, p. 140, fn 7.

The narrow social profile of Hindu nationalism did not shift following the movement's decision to found a political party in 1951. This move itself was significant, given the initial reluctance of movement leaders to involve their organizations in electoral politics. Activists worried that such involvement would create electoral incentives to dilute the movement's fundamental goal of societal transformation. However, Sangh leaders also realized that their ability to effect such a transformation themselves was severely compromised without a political advocate within elected bodies.[20] To counter the powerful opposition they faced, most significantly from Prime Minister Jawaharlal Nehru and the dominant Indian National Congress government, RSS leaders joined forces with pro-Hindu politicians to found a party in 1951 committed to Hindutva's cause.[21]

This party, the Jana Sangh, was the precursor to the BJP and depended greatly on its movement affiliates. The party's internal structure mirrored that of its RSS parent organization and was tightly controlled by the latter.[22] The RSS's dominance heavily influenced the Jana Sangh's style of politics, which remained closely wedded to a Hindutva platform and followed a cadre-based model of expansion.[23] Available evidence suggests the limitations of these strategies. A 1967 survey provides the only evidence of caste-wise voting for this era, and it indicates that Hindu elites were extremely overrepresented among backers of the Jana Sangh. Upper castes constituted exactly half of the party's supporters, a far higher proportion than within any other major party.[24]

However, the upper caste image of Hindu nationalism need not necessarily preclude subaltern support for the Jana Sangh, and later the BJP. Indeed the focus of the reform movements discussed in this section was precisely to integrate lower castes into the Hindu fold without subverting fundamental Hindu traditions. If the view of caste as an ethical division of labor rooted in religious

[20] See Frankel 2005, p. 703. Indeed, the decision of the Sangh to enter politics was closely tied to the assassination of Mahatma Gandhi at the hands of RSS activist Nathuram Godse. The RSS was banned as an organization in 1948–1949, when the government arrested Golwalkar along with 20,000 of his *swayamsevaks* (volunteers).

[21] The key political figure here was Shyam Prasad Mukherjee, formerly a cabinet member under Nehru. Mukherjee, following pressure from Nehru to sever his ties with the conservative Hindu Mahasabha, approached Golwalkar about founding an independent Hindu nationalist party.

[22] The lowest-level bodies within the Jana Sangh from local working committees to their national bodies were based on equivalent units within the RSS. Golwalkar, the head of the RSS, also loaned several of his full timers (*pracharaks*) to the Jana Sangh to act as an informal secretariat for the party, the *sangathan mantris* or organizational secretaries. See Graham 2005, p. 246.

[23] Thomas Hansen (1999, p. 128) notes that the Jana Sangh's early election campaigns centered on Hindutva favorites, including the campaign for Hindi as the national language (1958–1965), and the anti-cow-slaughter campaign (1950s onward).

[24] Further, the survey reported that urban voters were also overrepresented among the Jana Sangha's supporters (35 percent compared to 22 percent for the Congress), from 1967 National Election Survey data cited in Sheth 1971.

tradition had been broadly accepted by lower castes, then caste-based distinctions could have remained compatible with cross-caste political coalitions. Why was such lower caste acceptance not forthcoming?

EMERGING NON-ELITE CHALLENGES TO THE CASTE ORDER

As Hindu nationalism emerged, drawing and differentiating itself from a range of Hindu revivalist movements, it did so within a context of growing subaltern self-mobilization. From the mid-nineteenth century onward, non-Brahmin communities began to increasingly challenge the depictions of caste as a consensual religious ordering of people put forward by upper caste reformers. It is beyond the scope of this book to provide a detailed account of these wide-ranging efforts.[25] Instead, I focus on how they affected the political trajectory of Hindu nationalism. Specifically, I outline how lower caste communities increasingly challenged the depiction of caste as an ethical religious order or a benign division of labor. Instead, caste was reconceptualized as a form of social and economic inequality predicated on coercion and conquest. It was this politicization of caste differences that underpinned subaltern antipathy to upper caste Hindu nationalism.

One of the earliest influential non-Brahmin critiques of caste came from Jyotirao Phule (1827–1890), an activist in the western state of Maharashtra. Phule forcefully argued that the major cleavage within Indian society was between Brahmins and non-Brahmins. He viewed all non-Brahmin castes as part of a "Bahujan Samaj" (literally, majority community), which had collectively resisted Aryan-Brahmin invaders from the north centuries earlier. According to Phule, victorious Brahmin leaders subsequently imposed the caste system, partly as punishment, and partly to fragment solidarities among the conquered. To rekindle such solidarities, Phule undertook a range of initiatives, which included the founding of an association in 1873 (the Satyashodak Samaj) devoted to organizing lower caste political communities.

Phule's work had a significant impact on subsequent activism among non-Brahmin communities elsewhere. In the state of Tamil Nadu, E. V. Ramaswamy (also known as Periyar) quit his post in the Indian National Congress in 1925 in protest that the party served only Brahmin elites, and devoted himself to organizational work among lower caste communities. Periyar directed a "self-respect movement" that attempted to unite a broad swathe of non-elite groups under the encompassing label of "Adi Dravidians" or original inhabitants of the south. Following Phule, this ethno-regional identity was also defined in opposition to upper castes, the latter again depicted as descendants of Aryan outsiders hailing from the Hindi-speaking north.

---

[25] Some excellent works on this subject include Jaffrelot 1993, Prasad 2000, Gooptu 2005, Zelliot 2005, and Rao 2009.

Among communities labeled "untouchable," the most influential critique of caste hierarchies came from B. R. Ambedkar, India's preeminent Dalit political figure. A lawyer by training, Ambedkar served as the country's first law minister, and the chairman of the committee tasked with drafting its constitution. Over the course of several decades of writing and activism, he also provided the most comprehensive critiques of caste articulated from a Dalit perspective.

In his writings, Ambedkar referred to the caste system as an unequal division of *laborers*, rather than an ethical division of labor.[26] This phrasing was a direct challenge to upper caste social reformers, especially Gandhi. Gandhi described caste as a societal division of labor based on sacrifice and service.[27] Within this division, the greatest sacrifice had been made by untouchables, whom Gandhi dubbed "Harijans," or people of god. Gandhi argued all other castes owed Harijans a great spiritual debt, which would be repaid not by eliminating caste altogether, but by recognizing and respecting lower caste sacrifice. In other words, Gandhi opposed the differential values placed on the occupations of particular caste communities, not the legitimacy of the occupational division itself. Gandhi's interpretation thus offered possibilities of convergence with Hindu nationalism's view of caste as an organic division of labor.[28]

Against the grain of Gandhi's voluntarist, consensual interpretation, Ambedkar conceptualized caste as a system of "graded inequality."[29] This system incentivized each caste community to aspire to the status of the group immediately above it and hold those below them in contempt. Ambedkar's reframing acknowledged the close correspondence of caste and class, but also their non-equivalence. He noted that caste aligned with class in that Dalits suffered systematic material deprivation. However, class was inadequate in capturing the social stigmatization Dalits also suffered under the caste system, the intimate ways in which marginality was inscribed on their bodies.

Ambedkar believed the finely graded distinctions of caste prevented lower castes from uniting to fight for their common interests within the political arena. To combat such divisiveness, he led a multipronged effort to consolidate a Dalit political community capable of advancing its own political interests. First, he led demands for particular political privileges for lower caste communities, head-lined by a call for separate electorates for Dalit voters.[30] This effort famously brought Ambedkar into direct conflict with Gandhi, who undertook a fast unto death in protest of the colonial government's awarding of separate electorates to

---

[26] Ambedkar 1937.

[27] Gandhi 1964.

[28] However, acknowledging that upper castes owed Dalits a special spiritual debt was anathema to Sangh leaders who were also far less strident than Gandhi in mobilizing against practices of untouchability.

[29] Nagaraj (2010) incisively argues that both Gandhi and Ambedkar came to be heavily influenced by the other's thinking through their intense disagreements on the issue of caste.

[30] Under such a system, in addition to a general vote, Dalits would be exclusively allowed to vote for their representatives in areas in which they lived in large numbers.

lower castes in 1932. Gandhi's fast forced a compromise solution that remains in effect today, whereby certain Indian constituencies are reserved for lower caste candidates, but for whom all citizens within the constituency are eligible to vote.

Partly in response to this setback, Ambedkar looked to organize lower caste communities within India's party system. Toward this end, he founded the Independent Labour Party (later the Scheduled Caste Federation), India's first political party with the primary mandate to work for lower caste interests. Although this party was not particularly successful, its example inspired more electorally effective lower caste formations, including the Bahujan Samaj Party (discussed in Chapter 6).

Finally, Ambedkar developed the use of religious conversion out of Hinduism as a strategy for asserting Dalit political autonomy. He prepared the ground for this strategy by outlining a new genealogy of Dalits as Buddhist nomadic tribesmen defeated in battle by Hindu Brahmins and then forced into subjugated lower caste roles. This narrative facilitated Ambedkar's conversion "back" to Buddhism, along with several hundred of his followers, in 1956. This high-profile ceremony, which took place shortly before Ambedkar's death, stoked long-standing upper caste fears about the threat religious conversions could pose to the Hindu social order. As I discuss later in this book, such fears wielded an important influence on Hindu nationalist strategic choices.

The challenges articulated by Phule, Periyar, and Ambedkar were echoed in the efforts of many other lower caste activists and thinkers, too numerous to list here. Collectively, these activists organized petitions, demonstrations, and marches demanding access to a range of public services, including schools, water sources, and temples. These wide-ranging efforts were enabled by emerging educational opportunities for disadvantaged citizens (including those within Christian missions), discursive and legal opportunities within colonial bureaucratic orders, and organizational opportunities afforded by increasing subaltern migration to Indian cities.[31]

What effect did such subaltern mobilizations have on the political ambitions of Hindu nationalists? The most crucial cumulative effect of these efforts was to reframe caste relations in terms of imposed inequality, rather than consensual religious tradition.[32] However, it is important to bear in mind that the goal of subaltern activists was to abolish the hierarchical ordering of caste identities, not the identities themselves. These movements sought to draw attention to the exploitative history of the caste system, without losing the contemporary mobilizing potential of lower caste identities. In short, subaltern mobilizations transformed caste from a marker of place in a vertical hierarchy into a tool for fostering horizontal cohesion within lower caste communities. In

[31] See discussion in Rao 2009, p. 13.
[32] Both Phule and Ambedkar drew polemical comparisons between caste and Atlantic slavery to reframe caste relations in idioms of exploitation and inequality rather than religious order (see Rao 2009, pp. 13, 129).

horizontally mobilizing subaltern communities and politicizing them against the upper castes, these efforts dealt a significant body blow to the expansionary ambitions of Hindu nationalists.

THE NEED FOR EXPANSION

As caste-based inequities became the source of political contestation, Hindutva's Brahminical underpinnings ensured that its social message held little resonance for non-elite communities. Hindu nationalists failed to adequately grapple with the severity of the tension between their elite orientation and their desire for social expansion. For most of the first three decades following Indian independence, the emphasis within both movement and party organizations remained on targeting all of Hindu society with a message of unity. Little thought was given to the possibility that many Dalit and Adivasi citizens would explicitly reject being counted as members of the Hindu flock.[33]

It took the confluence of two developments to shake the Sangh Parivar into seriously considering such problems. The first was the dissolution of the Jana Sangh and the launching of a successor party, the Bharatiya Janata Party in 1980.[34] This shift in name, from Jana Sangh, or "People's Organization," to Bharatiya Janata Party, or "Indian People's Party," was not merely symbolic; it reflected a broader shift in the party's political outlook. The BJP's leadership demonstrated a deeper commitment to electoral pragmatism than its more ideologically rigid precursor had ever displayed. In one of the BJP's first National Executive meetings, party president Atal Behari Vajpayee emphasized the need to adopt new techniques to widen the party's base beyond upper castes. He suggested that an emphasis on slow, deliberate recruitment through organizational building had failed to gain widespread popularity.[35] Another National Executive Report explicitly noted this failure, arguing that "this cadre party by itself will not enable us to reach our goal" and advocating that the party work to "promote specific issues and programmes that can interest and attract major sections of the society."[36]

A greater emphasis on vote maximization focused attention on the need to expand the party's following among subaltern constituencies. A second development, barely a year after the BJP's creation, sharpened this focus even further. In 1981, Hindu nationalists were shaken by the mass conversion of one

[33] Some early voices did caution that a neglect of the specific case of lower castes could prove debilitating for upper castes themselves. See Shervani 1980.

[34] This change came shortly after the Jana Sangh's first taste of political success as part of a diverse coalition of parties that came together to oust the dominant Indian National Congress from power in 1977. The 1977 elections were the first held following the state of emergency declared by Indira Gandhi from 1975 to 1977 in a bid to maintain power in the face of growing opposition to her tenure.

[35] Vajpayee 1985, in BJP 2005, p. 213.

[36] "National Executive Resolution, 1985," in BJP 2005, p. 36.

thousand Dalits to Islam in the village of Meenakshipuram in the southern state of Tamil Nadu. A quarter century after Ambedkar's conversion to Buddhism, the Meenakshipuram episode was seen as a dire reminder of Hindutva's limited appeal among subaltern communities. The conversions ignited a vigorous discussion within the BJP and the wider movement on the need for more concerted efforts to prevent such episodes from recurring.[37]

Thus, the 1980s marked a period of growing Hindu nationalist awareness of the need for more targeted efforts among disadvantaged communities. What strategies did the BJP attempt to address this need? The remaining sections of this chapter outline why three major strategies considered by the party – programmatic shifts, religious appeals, and ethnic representation – failed to win over its least likely supporters.

THE PROGRAMMATIC CONSTRAINTS OF AN ELITE CORE

Examining the puzzle of Dalit and Adivasi support for the BJP through the lens of class prompts the question of why poor, rural voters would support a party that emerged to represent the interests of relatively privileged middle-class constituencies. Viewed from this perspective, one possible explanation is that the elite party won mass support through pro-poor programmatic shifts: by diluting its emphasis on Brahminical Hindutva while strengthening its commitment to addressing problems of economic equality and social justice.

Scholars of Indian politics largely agree that the country's partisan terrain cannot be organized according to the standard left-right spectrum of advanced industrial democracies. However, a lack of conformity with Western convention is too often taken to imply a completely haphazard policy arena, one in which a particular party's programmatic orientation is impossible to discern. Against this view, I argue that the dimensions of political contestation in India do provide windows of opportunity for examining the BJP's commitments toward poor members of the lower castes. My analysis found no evidence of sustained shifts in the BJP's redistributive commitments capable of overcoming its traditional elite social image. Indeed, to the extent that the party exhibited distinctive policy commitments, its positions consistently reflected a concern with representing the interests of its upper caste core constituencies.

---

[37] This conversion was widely understood as orchestrated by the Muslim League and was viewed by the RSS as exemplifying the ways in which proselytizing religions could prey on Hinduism's downtrodden. The BJP sent a team led by Vajpayee down to Meenakshipuram shortly after the conversions to investigate the reasons behind them. Vajpayee delivered a speech denouncing the practice of untouchability, which he said was not part of Vedic-era Hinduism and should be abolished immediately. "Press Statement by Shri A. B. Vajpayee, President Bharatiya Janata Party, at Madras on 17/7/1981," Nehru Memorial Library Clippings Collection.

Content Analysis of Manifestos and Speeches

Empirically, I first performed a content analysis of key party documents from 1984 to 2004, the years in which the party rose to national prominence. These documents included the BJP's election manifestos for national parliamentary elections held during this period, which provide the most comprehensive available outline of the party's program. However, Indian party manifestos are documents that are rarely, if ever, read by actual voters. To the extent that we care about how citizens perceive the BJP's programmatic orientation, it is necessary to examine how the party publicly presents itself to voters. Consequently, I also examined the content of important party speeches, specifically the major annual address delivered by the BJP president, outlining the key components of the party's platform at its national convention.

I began the analysis by reading through these documents and making a list of words and phrases used to discuss key issues relating to three major programmatic areas: cultural nationalism (specifically the core issue of a Hindu nationalist agenda), ameliorating poverty and economic inequality, and advancing social justice (specifically for Dalit and Adivasi communities).[38] I followed this procedure so that the subsequent content analysis would be structured via the terms used by the party itself in articulating its position on a given issue. The three issue areas are by no means exhaustive and were selected to fit my specific analytic purpose. Principally, I wanted to determine whether the BJP is indeed devoting less attention to its core Hindutva agenda, and also whether it is increasing its verbal commitment to improving both the economic disadvantage and social stigmatization faced by Dalits and Adivasis. Next, I analyzed the percentage of each document that was composed of words and phrases within a given issue area.[39] Finally, I examined how the weighting of the three major issue areas varied over time.

Figure 2.1 summarizes the results of this analysis. The vertical axis measures the weight of a particular issue in percentage points (in this case from 0 percent to 1 percent of all words). For reference, the most used term across the documents (*party* and its synonyms) accounts for 1.21 percent of all words. The figure shows little evidence of a dramatic programmatic shift by the BJP to cater to non-elite communities. Instead, the weight of each issue within the party's election manifestos appears to be relatively constant across the panel.

Trends within presidential speeches are more volatile but still do not paint a picture of programmatic reinvention. First, there is no evidence of a sustained effort to deemphasize Hindutva within the BJP's program to expand the party's appeal among those alienated by this doctrine. Instead, the significance of

---

[38] A list of the individual words and phrases used in the analysis is included in Appendix B.

[39] Every occurrence of a relevant word or phrase was then individually checked for two purposes: to make sure the specific instance was being correctly included within a given issue area, and (when necessary) to determine support or opposition for a particular measure.

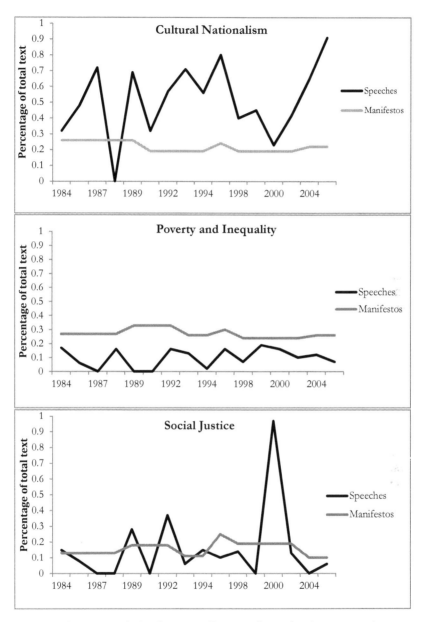

FIGURE 2.1: Content analysis of BJP manifestos and speeches (1984–2004)

cultural nationalism appears to wax and wane, rising until 1996, declining for a few years, and then rebounding again after 2000. Additionally, the discursive weight of cultural nationalism remains systematically higher than issues of inequality or social justice. In fact, the latter seldom received mention in the speeches of BJP presidents across the duration of the panel. The sole exception to this pattern is a speech made in August 2000 that explicitly attempted to discursively "harmonize" the messages of Ambedkar with Hindutva, which is discussed later in this chapter.

In short, the content analysis of BJP party documents provides little support for the idea that a dramatic programmatic shift underpinned the BJP's ability to expand its support among Dalits and Adivasis. Whereas this analysis is helpful for assessing general patterns, it is unable to provide in-depth details about the party's programmatic agenda. I therefore also examined the BJP's positions on caste-based affirmative action and liberalizing market reforms. The first has indisputably been the most prominent social policy issue in India regarding lower castes, whereas the second is arguably the preeminent economic policy issue of the past three decades. Across these important issue areas, a close reading finds evidence of the party's commitments to its upper caste core, rather than an increasing concern with representing non-elite interests.

Positions on Key Issues

The BJP's elite orientation was perhaps most apparent in the party's stance on the highly divisive issue of mandatory quotas for non-elite caste communities within India's public sector. In 1990, a coalition government in Delhi said it would implement the recommendations of the independent Mandal Commission, which had suggested that 27 percent of posts in government administrations and corporations be reserved for members of the Other Backward Classes (OBCs). OBCs are a sprawling and highly differentiated agglomeration of caste communities that are placed one rung above Dalits and Adivasis in traditional caste hierarchies. However, even though the latter communities had been accorded quotas since independence, OBCs had not received such benefits.

The Mandal issue forced the BJP, which was in opposition at the time, to choose between its twin goals of core voter retention and social expansion. Upper castes were virulently opposed to extending reservations (the term used for quotas in India) to OBCs, which would necessarily shrink the pool of positions for which they were eligible. Further, the party's movement allies were quick to openly criticize expansions of caste-based affirmative action. Such policies posed a significant threat to the Sangh's desire to frame caste as an organic and harmonious division of labor, not an iniquitous system in need of redress.

As the reservations being debated under Mandal did not apply to Dalits and Adivasis, but to backward castes, it is reasonable to assume that these former communities did not have systematic preferences in favor of reservations. However, survey data revealed overwhelming Dalit and Adivasi solidarity with the OBC cause.[40] Hindu nationalists helped stoke this solidarity when the

---

[40] According to the first major National Election Study conducted in 1996, 84 percent of Dalits and 80 percent of Adivasis supported the extensions of reservations to backward castes.

head of the RSS (the Sangh's parent body) argued in 1994 for a reduction in caste-based quotas, not only for OBCs but also for Dalits and Adivasis.[41]

As a political party, the BJP was in a tricky position. Strongly supporting the extension of quotas risked alienating the party's movement partners and upper caste electoral base. Opposing Mandal risked running afoul of a massive swathe of backward-caste voters. To solve this dilemma, the party eschewed articulating a clear position on affirmative action. Instead, it chose to intensify its pro-Hindu communal agitations as a counter to Mandal (discussed in the next section). At the same time, individual leaders within the BJP did voice concerns with the reservation policy. For example, the party's 1991 manifesto argued for considering reservations on the basis of class rather than caste, thereby opening the door for poor members of upper castes to receive benefits. Four years later, at a meeting of major Indian parties, the BJP was the only party that went against long-term extensions of reservations for Dalits and Adivasis, and also opposed raising the threshold of all quotas beyond 50 percent.[42]

The outright rejection of Mandal by the BJP's movement partners, and the party's own hesitance, received widespread attention in the Indian press and was seen to have "brought [the party] further support from the upper castes," while ensuring that low castes "remained indifferent or hostile to its propaganda."[43] The party's waffling on the question of caste-based quotas also distinguished it from most other parties and was easily portrayed by its rivals as another instance of Hindu nationalists prioritizing the preferences of their elite core. Consequently, when the BJP finally decided to voice qualified support for reservations for OBCs, it was simply too little, and too late, to help it shed its Brahmin-Bania reputation.

The Mandal episode thus clearly illustrated the interconnected nature of growing lower caste assertiveness and upper caste support for Hindu nationalism. The constraints placed on the BJP by its core supporters were also visible in its positioning on other important policy issues, most notably its dramatic shift on market reforms. Historically, Hindu nationalists had strongly opposed economic liberalization of any kind. Sangh ideologues saw efforts to integrate India into a global marketplace as directly opposed to Hindutva's core mandate to construct a strong national culture capable of repelling exploitative foreign interventions.

Instead, the party embraced the doctrine of *Swadeshi* or self-reliance. Lal Krishna Advani, former BJP president, made this position clear in 1987, arguing that the cure to India's economic problems "does not lie in credits or technology from abroad, but in giving a boost to domestic production and exports based on total mobilization of national resources."[44] During the next

---

[41] Jaffrelot 2010.
[42] Ibid., p. 508.
[43] Quote from Jaffrelot 1993, p. 412. Also see discussion in Chhibber 1997, p. 150.
[44] Lal Krishna Advani, Speech to BJP National Council, Vijaywada, January 2–4, 1987, reproduced in BJP 2005, vol. 2, p. 159.

couple of years, the party emphasized this position in its economic resolutions, expressing "alarm at the growing scale of the invasion of our national economy by multinationals,"[45] calling for "encouraging import substitution in every possible sphere," and even arguing that "the liberalization of sectors where the country is on the verge of self-sufficiency or where the stocks are mounting is unpatriotic and motivated to obtain kickbacks."[46]

Although the BJP's economic nationalism stemmed from its ideological doctrine, the party could have opportunistically leveraged this position to win support from some poor voters. During the early 1990s, the leaders of the rival Congress Party had embraced a number of reforms aimed at dismantling the import-substituting institutions their own predecessors had installed. The fiscal austerity that accompanied such structural adjustments provided an opening for the BJP to portray itself as the populist defender of the *aam aadmi* (common man), for whom such belt tightening was an unwelcome development.

However, this potential was rendered moot by the BJP's shift from its oppositional stance, driven entirely by the party's desire to maintain its connections with relatively privileged voters. Chhibber notes that the urban, middle-class communities that had been left out of the Congress's patronage machine supported a reduced role of the state in managing the economy.[47] These citizens tended to be well educated, urban, and employed in the private sector; thus, they were best positioned to take advantage of the economic opportunities liberalizing reforms would unleash.[48] As these unincorporated elites also comprised the BJP's core constituency, the party had to choose between pleasing its electoral base and supporting its nationalist movement partners.

The BJP tried to manage this conflict by reconceptualizing *Swadeshi* to be more accommodative of liberalizing reforms. In 1992, the BJP leadership issued a resolution clarifying that the party advocated "not the Swadeshi of an inward-looking nation afraid to face an increasingly complex and aggressive world outside, but the Swadeshi of a self-confident, modern nation that can deal with the world."[49] Within a space of five years, the party had shifted from denouncing market reforms as unpatriotic to linking national confidence with export competitiveness within a liberalized trade regime. To maintain its reputation as a defender of Indic traditions, the BJP vocally opposed the liberalization of a small handful of sectors. These included junk food imports and beef exports, which could easily be linked to undesirable Western and Islamic agendas, thereby providing considerable ethno-nationalist bang for the buck.[50]

---

[45] National Economic Resolution, February 4, 1987.
[46] National Economic Resolution, July 24, 1987.
[47] Pradeep Chhibber 1997. Also see Frankel 2005, pp. 693–788.
[48] Teltumbde 2005, p. 52.
[49] National Economic Resolution, April 13, 1992.
[50] An Economic Resolution passed on March 4, 1995, denounced investment in "junk food which does not add value to our assets," a position that informed the party's slogan of "computer chips

By 1993, just three years after the Congress government imposed the first set of reforms, Advani made the break with his party's earlier opposition to liberalization complete, announcing as BJP president that "the concept of *swadeshi* as enunciated by the RSS ... was unacceptable to the party" and that "the idea of boycotting foreign goods was no longer as relevant as it was before independence."[51]

Having rapidly pivoted on reforms, the BJP now sought to present itself as the original champion of liberalization, noting "it has been asking for [the reforms] long before the Congress realized that [the inward-looking] Nehru model was a failure."[52] During the party's lone full term at the helm of the national economy between 1999 and 2004, it continued the trajectory of reforms initiated by the Congress, lifting quantitative restrictions on consumer imports, opening up the insurance sector to foreign capital, and promoting the increase of foreign direct investment.[53] The BJP also strongly supported privatizing public sector enterprises, calling such steps "essential" for improving productivity.[54]

Such policy maneuvers were clearly taken with the party's elite core in mind, as opinion polls showed that a large proportion of Dalit and Adivasi voters remained wary of key aspects of market reforms. For example, the 1996 National Election Study found that only 18.3 percent of these voters supported the privatization of public sector utilities, whereas only 31 percent agreed that foreign companies should be allowed free trade in India (compared to 52 percent of Brahmin upper castes).[55] Recent data from the 2008 World Values Survey reveals similar discrepancies.[56]

Yet, considerations of subaltern voter interests remained strikingly absent in the BJP's internal debates on liberalization, despite the party's awareness of its prior failures among the poor. Instead, these discussions focused on how to negotiate divisions within its elite core, principally between its ideologically committed movement radicals and the wider swathe of upper

---

not potato chips." The same resolution also complained about how the "promotion of meat exports and unchecked smuggling of cattle to Bangladesh have played havoc with our cattle wealth and our agriculture." Such calls aligned well with traditional Hindu nationalist demands to ban the slaughter of cows.

[51] L.K. Advani as quoted in Sonwalkar 1993.

[52] National Economic Resolution, November 15, 1996.

[53] Lakha 2007, pp. 110–11. This decision strained relations between the BJP and its movement partners. In 1992, the RSS launched a *Swadeshi Jagran Abhiyan* (Awareness-Raising Movement for Self-Reliance) that openly campaigned against economic reforms, thereby forcing the BJP to take an explicit stand on liberalization.

[54] National Economic Resolution, April 15, 2000.

[55] A two-tailed difference of means test revealed this difference was statistically significant at the 99.99 percent confidence level (data is from the National Election 1996).

[56] The World Values Survey did not collect data on the caste profile of respondents. However, the survey found that among university-educated respondents (among whom upper castes dominate), 29 percent strongly supported increased private ownership of business and industry, compared to just 19.21 percent among the least-educated subsample (in which lower castes are disproportionately represented). By contrast, 38 percent of less-educated voters strongly supported increased government ownership, compared to just 27 percent of highly educated respondents.

caste constituencies who favored reforms. This core-centric shift on market reforms is not unique to the BJP. For example, Tugal notes a similar shift among Islamists in Turkey, who were also initially opposed to economic liberalization. However, liberalizing reforms implemented by secular government in the 1980s enriched urban merchants and tradespeople.[57] These actors were also the primary supporters of Islamist politics. Accordingly, Tugal notes that "as a response to this shift, the new economic program of the [Islamist] RP (Welfare Party) emphasized private enterprise and an export orientation more than 'heavy industrialization.'"[58] The AKP party – the RP's successor has only strengthened these commitments during its decade at the helm of Turkish government.

Analysis of Public Spending

The prior two sections report little evidence of a systematic pro-poor programmatic shift within the BJP's publicly articulated positions. However, a party's actions do not always conform to its official proclamations. I therefore supplement the preceding discussion with an analysis of how the BJP's electoral performance correlates with the proportion of budgets devoted to basic public goods particularly valued by poor communities. Acemoglu and Robinson, summarizing a vast literature, note that a standard result of political economy models is that "the rich prefer too few public goods while the poor prefer too many."[59] Accordingly, if the BJP really was concerned with representing the programmatic preferences of upper castes, the party's performance should be associated with a reduced commitment to spending on public services disproportionately consumed by non-elite communities.

Empirically, I analyzed patterns of public spending from 1967 to 2007 in fifteen major Indian states, which together comprise approximately 95 percent of India's population.[60] I focused on spending by state governments, because they have the most control over the budgets for those services that most immediately impact local communities. Within state government budgets, I tracked the proportion of funds devoted to social services, a budgetary category that included education, health and family welfare, water supply, and housing. On average, expenditures on education alone comprised more than three-fifths of such spending. Prior studies of Indian political economy have noted that

[57] Tugal 2009, p. 124
[58] Ibid., p. 50.
[59] Acemoglu and Robinson 2006, p. 107.
[60] The states included were Andhra Pradesh, Assam, Bihar, Gujarat, Haryana, Karnataka, Kerala, Madhya Pradesh, Maharashtra, Orissa, Punjab, Rajasthan, Tamil Nadu, Uttar Pradesh, and West Bengal. The sample is fifteen and not seventeen (which is the number analyzed in Chapters 3 and 4) because two states, Chhattisgarh and Jharkhand, were only created in 2000 and so did not exist for most of the panel's duration.

spending on social services is both more inclusive of poor voter material interests and less likely to be narrowly co-opted by privileged elites than expenditures on other major budgetary categories.[61]

To test the relationship between BJP performance and social spending, I regress the percentage of a state's budget spent on social services on the percentage of seats won by the BJP in state assemblies. The models include fixed effects for states, which help ensure that the impact of the BJP's perform-ance does not reflect unobserved differences between the states themselves. Instead, the results measure the effect of the BJP's political performance on patterns of spending within a given state. I also include fixed year effects, which control for economic or institutional shocks common to all states in a given year, and a time trend to account for the effect of expanding state budgets during this period. Additionally, I control for important economic factors that impact the fiscal resources available to state governments, such as levels of economic development (measured by per capita state domestic product), the rate of economic growth in the state, and the dependence of a state on grants from the Indian central government.

The models tested in Table 2.1 also include political variables that have been argued to influence public spending patterns in India. For example, party system fragmentation within a state (indicated by the "effective number of parties" measure) has been understood to dampen the incentives for inclusive public spending.[62] Previous studies have also hypothesized that public spending is systematically different in the run up to elections, so I include a dummy variable identifying all election years.[63] I further control for the competitiveness of elections, measured as the difference in vote share between the top two parties in a state. I also include a binary variable indicating if a government was formed by a multiparty coalition. This measure controls for a prior argument that the political uncertainty under which coalition governments function compels them to increase spending on public goods.[64] Finally, I include measures of the performance of prominent parties other than the BJP that emerged to challenge the longtime hegemony of the Indian National Congress over the duration of the panel. I group these other challengers into two categories: those that mobilize along a broad regional ethnic identity (such as the Dravida Munnetra Kazhagam in Tamil Nadu or Telegu Desam Party in Andhra Pradesh)

---

[61] Although clearly not immune from instrumental co-option, education, health, and social welfare programs have found the greatest consensus as public goods in prior studies. This view seems justified when comparing social services with the other major categories within Indian state budgets: economic services (which include expenditures on crop and animal husbandry, irriga-tion, energy, industry and minerals, and programs falling under the nebulous headings of "rural development" and "special area programs") and nondevelopment services. See Chhibber and Nooruddin 2004; Saez and Sinha 2009; Thachil and Teitelbaum n.d.

[62] Chhibber and Nooruddin 2004.

[63] Khemani 2004.

[64] A version of this argument within an Indian context is made by Saez and Sinha 2009, p. 112.

TABLE 2.1. *BJP performance and social service spending*

	Percentage of State Budget Spent on Social Services	
	1967–2007	1988–2007
BJP Performance	−0.00245	−0.0370*
	(0.0223)	(0.0153)
Political Factors		
Party Fragmentation	0.00379	−0.000893
	(0.00277)	(0.00567)
Winning Margin	−0.000459	−0.000634
	(0.000427)	(0.000424)
Election Year	−0.00202	0.00159
	(0.00306)	(0.00332)
Encompassing Ethnic Party Performance	0.0442**	0.0302*
	(0.0147)	(0.0127)
Narrow Ethnic Party Performance	−0.0360	0.00856
	(0.0452)	(0.0427)
Coalition Government	−0.00515	−0.0194**
	(0.00738)	(0.00697)
Economic Factors		
Central Grants	0.223***	0.274**
	(0.0748)	(0.123)
Per Capita Domestic Product	−0.0597	−0.0549
	(0.0385)	(0.0424)
Growth	0.000141	0.000204
	(0.000174)	(0.000313)
Time	−0.000352	−0.00186
	(0.00141)	(0.00206)
Constant	1.311	4.304
	(2.648)	(3.969)
Observations	463	208
R-squared	0.692	0.741

***p<.001 **p<0.01, *p<0.5.
Note: Models included fixed state and year effects not reported here. Robust standard errors clustered by state are reported in parentheses. Political variables coded from Election Commission of India reports (various issues). Economic variables from Reserve Bank of India *Annual Bulletin* (various issues).

and those that mobilize through narrower caste-based ethnic networks (such as the Bahujan Samaj Party in Uttar Pradesh or Rashtriya Janata Dal in Bihar).[65]

---

[65] This distinction draws on a prior collaborative analysis of public spending across the Indian states (for a disaggregation of the parties within each of these categories, see and Thachil and Teitelbaum n.d.)

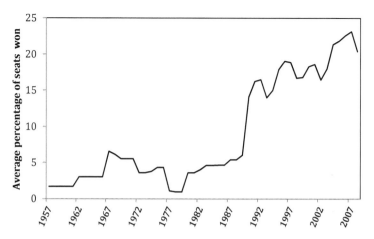

FIGURE 2.2: Average BJP seat share (unweighted) within major state assemblies (1957–2008)

The results in Table 2.1 indicate that the BJP's performance is negatively correlated with inclusive patterns of public spending across both periods. Moreover, this result is statistically significant if we restrict the panel to the two decades when the BJP became a significant player within Indian state assemblies (Figure 2.2).[66] Within this latter panel, the substantive impact of BJP performance is also significant: a 10 percent improvement in the party's seat share within a state resulted in an average shift of approximately $13 million from spending on social services toward less inclusive budgetary categories.[67] Interestingly, the BJP's influence on spending stands in contrast to that of broad-based regional parties whose performance is positively correlated with spending on basic services.[68] These differences are in line with what we might anticipate given the distinct social profile of these parties: whereas the BJP has traditionally been supported by upper castes, regional parties typically sought to mobilize broad coalitions of non-elite castes under an encompassing regional identity.

It is interesting to relate these broad empirical patterns back to the BJP's officially declared positions. During its tenure at the helm of the national governing coalition, the party argued that it would oversee a shift in the Indian state's role "from directly providing goods and services in the coming decades [to a] focus on enabling the private and cooperative sectors of society to provide

[66] In state elections before 1988, the BJP on average won less than 5 percent of seats, whereas after this date, the party has won on average 17.5 percent.
[67] In line with the results of prior analyses, the performance of regional parties was positively correlated with more inclusive patterns of spending, as was dependence on grants from New Delhi.
[68] This result regarding the salutary impact of encompassing ethnic party performance is consistent with a similar result in Thachil and Teitelbaum (n.d.).

them."[69] The party also argued that "the privatisation programme is a key to improving resource allocation, *especially to the social sector...* Hence, it should be aggressively pursued."[70] At the same time, the BJP vocally criticized the redistributive populist agendas of many regional parties.[71]

The BJP's positions appear to align with the views of its core supporters. According to data from the World Values Survey (conducted in 2006 in India), only 34 percent of BJP supporters strongly agree with the need to make incomes more equal. This is significantly lower than equivalent figures for its major rivals, from the Congress (42 percent) to the Communists (54 percent), to the Dalit-led Bahujan Samaj Party (55 percent).[72]

In sum, there is little in the BJP's programmatic orientation – whether measured through patterns in manifestos, speeches, or public spending – to suggest that a programmatic shift was responsible for its changing fortunes among marginalized voters.[73] Such a strategy was particularly difficult for an elite party such as the BJP to follow for two reasons. First, unlike its competitors, Hindu nationalists would have had to make especially distinctive and sustained progressive policy shifts to overcome their historically established upper caste partisan image. Second, the BJP's elite core and ideologically rigid movement partners constrained it from pursuing any such dramatic shifts. Even the most generous assessment would be hard pressed to find evidence of a programmatic reinvention. If anything, the evidence in this section suggests that the BJP's policy commitments remained closely wedded to the interests of its elite core, helping to solidify its image as the party with which "the middle classes could find almost everything they dreamt of."[74]

THE LIMITS OF RELIGIOUS AGITATION

Viewing the puzzle of Dalit and Adivasi support through the prism of religion instead of class suggests an alternative explanation for the BJP's success: the distracting potential of faith-based appeals. Scholars of Western democracies have often remarked upon the potential of religion to distract poor voters from

[69] National Economic Resolution, August 27, 2000.
[70] National Economic Resolution, April 12, 2002, emphasis added.
[71] The party complained that "the real challenge to the effective implementation of the second-generation [market] reform is the state of economy of the State governments. Unfortunately, some of the state Governments indulge in populist measures at the cost of their own economic health." National Economic Resolution, April 15, 2000.
[72] Data from Q. 116 on the 2006 World Values Survey.
[73] The party's 2004 campaign manifesto was also headlined by agenda items that clearly speak to the interests of urban elites, rather than poor lower castes. These included putting India at the center of the "knowledge economy" (via improving opportunities for business process outsourcing and strengthening the accreditation of Indian universities), converting Indian metros into "cities of global standing" (including via implementing a national policy on slums), and the building of world-class highways and telecom structures.
[74] Palshikar 2003, p. 172.

their material interests. These explanations presume an intrinsic resonance of such appeals among the poor. However, as I have discussed, the Brahminical orientation of Hindu nationalism only further alienated Dalits and Adivasis marginalized by the faith's internal hierarchies. In fact, examining the Indian paradox from a religious perspective raises a further question: how can an ideological party succeed among voters who are not attracted to its core doctrine?

Within South Asia, the most significant distraction arguments have focused on the role of religious agitation and violence. A great deal of scholarly attention has been paid to Hindu nationalism's diverse array of agitational activities, which range from small local protests to the instigation and organization of large-scale acts of communal violence. By polarizing relations between Hindus and non-Hindus, could such mobilizations deemphasize intra-faith caste distinctions?

The Sangh has a long history of involvement in sectarian agitation, but the political potential of such efforts was more closely considered in the wake of the movement's failure to expand. Seven years after the aforementioned Meenakshipuram conversions of Dalits to Islam in Tamil Nadu, an editorial in the Sangh's weekly *Organizer* warned that the gap between upper caste Hindus and subaltern groups was still pressing.[75] Around the same time, movement leaders began actively discussing the potential of protest politics as a tool for drumming up political support from communities beyond the organizational reach of the Sangh's network of local chapters (*shakhas*). Internal BJP reports recommended "a national-level agitation once or twice a year" organized with sufficient notice for "leaders at various levels to build up the right climate" to ensure the agitation was a broad success.[76]

The increasing emphasis on communal agitations, and not simply on patient organization building, was ironically facilitated by a gradual shift within the rival Congress Party during the 1970s and 1980s. The Congress's leadership had begun to transition away from Nehru's vociferous critiques of Hindutva as a "narrow-minded attitude" that, if successful, would "most certainly ruin India."[77] Indira Gandhi, Nehru's daughter, began slowly appropriating soft communal appeals during her tenure as the party's premier.[78] She hoped such direct overtures would help compensate for the Congress's waning popularity and further her own personal brand as she sought to centralize control of the party.[79]

---

[75] "Hindu-Dalit," 1988, p. 5. Also see Anand 1987.

[76] National Executive Resolution, 1985, in BJP Press 2005, p. 38.

[77] Speech at a gathering of the workers of the Congress Party in the prime minister's house, New Delhi, May 25, 1953. From *Sahi Rasta* (published by Friends of New Kashmir Committee), Mahakoshal PCC Papers, NMML, Original in Hindi.

[78] Vanaik 1990, p. 18.

[79] Kochanek 2002.

By deploying pro-Hindu rhetoric, the Congress under Gandhi helped fertilize India's political terrain for the Sangh Parivar's agitational efforts. Sensing these increased opportunities, the Parivar moved quickly to create new militant wings, the Bajrang Dal (Army of Hanuman) and Durga Vahini (Army of Durga), to mobilize young men and women respectively into forces capable of protecting Hindu culture.[80] Through an increasingly diverse organizational front, Hindu nationalists began to deploy a wide array of protest tactics to draw attention to their cause. The centerpiece of such efforts was an aggressive symbolic strategy that adapted *yatras* (pilgrimages) to significant Hindu sites of worship into agitational processions designed to polarize religious communities. Placing idols on *raths* or chariots, the Sangh managed to mobilize massive processions of Hindus across great swathes of India.

The most famous of these agitations was the *Rath Yatra* (chariot pilgrimage), in which BJP leader Lal Krishna Advani traveled several thousand miles to the fabled birthplace of the god Ram. Advani was transported in a Toyota Jeep, rigged to resemble a chariot from Hindu mythology, to the site of the Babri *masjid*, a mosque in the northern town of Ayodhya. Hindu nationalists alleged that the mosque had replaced a Hindu temple marking the exact place of Ram's birth. They claimed this temple been demolished by the Mughal emperor Babur, a Muslim, in the sixteenth century. In 1985, a group of activists demanded that Hindus be allowed to worship inside the mosque. The Sangh Parivar took this demand a step further, calling for the mosque to be replaced by a temple. Hindu nationalists worked hard to publicize the issue, even organizing a domestic and international collection of bricks with which to build such a temple. These bricks, termed *Ram Shilas*, were collected in large, often frenetic religious ceremonies, in which the stones were blessed before being sent on to Ayodhya.

The Ram *Janmabhoomi* (birthplace of Ram) movement kept gathering steam during the latter half of the 1980s. The selection of the hawkish Advani to replace the relatively moderate Vajpayee as BJP president also resulted in the party's official discourse becoming far more vitriolic.[81] Advani argued that minority communities were "becoming increasingly aggressive and ominously reminiscent of the pre-1947 years [the period leading up to the partition of India

---

[80] Hanuman refers to the monkey god who plays a significant role in the Hindu epic, the *Ramayana*, in which the god Ram is helped by an army of monkeys to defeat the demon-king Ravana who has kidnapped Ram's wife Sita. Durga meanwhile is revered as the militant avatar of the wife of the Hindu god Shiva, and is famous for defeating the demon Mahishasur.

[81] The party's manifesto in 1991 was perhaps its most aggressive until that point, evidenced by its provocative title "Toward Ram *Rajya* [rule]: Midterm Poll to Lok Sabha: Our Commitments." It was also at this time that Hindu nationalist leaders developed the concept of "positive secularism," a counter to the Indian state's version of secularism, which the BJP believed was better understood as a policy of minority appeasement (or what Advani famously dubbed "pseudosecularism"). Positive secularism was defined in contrast as "justice for all but appeasement of none." Lal Krishna Advani, Presidential Address to National Council Meeting, Bombay, September 25, 1989, in BJP Press 2005, p. 113.

and creation of Pakistan]."[82] He warned that "these threats have to be met head on and squarely spiked."[83]

The Ram temple mobilizations were accelerated in the wake of the Mandal Commission's aforementioned recommendation to extend caste-based quotas to backward castes. The agitation became Hindu nationalism's response to the divisive threat of caste politics that Mandal threatened to unleash. Tensions over Ayodhya kept mounting and eventually culminated with the destruction of the Babri *masjid* on December 6, 1992. Large crowds led by Sangh Parivar foot soldiers razed the mosque under the encouraging eye of many senior BJP leaders. In many respects, the demolition marked the crest of Hindu nationalism's saffron wave.[84]

A full account of the destruction and its aftermath, which included waves of communal riots across India, is beyond the scope of this chapter and is available elsewhere.[85] More pertinent for this analysis is that the BJP was able to use this aggressive brand of nationalistic politics, both before and after the mosque's demolition, to make political inroads into the Indian electorate. The party quickly rose from garnering a grand total of 2 seats with 7.74 percent of the vote in the 1984 national parliamentary elections to 85 seats from 11.36 percent of the vote in 1989. By 1991, the year before the mosque fell, this share had gone up to 120 seats from 20.08 percent of the vote.

Upon closer analysis, however, this mercurial rise appears to have been disproportionately fueled by surging upper caste support. Hansen argues that election results from 1991 "suggested that the large constituency won by the BJP was generally fairly young, predominantly male, urban, and upper caste," and noted that the party was able "to make itself a 'respectable' choice in the fast-growing middle class in many provincial cities."[86] A prominent national poll conducted a couple of years after the mosque's destruction estimated that the BJP had overtaken the Congress Party among upper castes nationally, an impressive achievement considering that the party had begun the 1980s as a virtual non-factor with every electoral group.[87] In Uttar Pradesh – the heart of the Ayodhya agitation – the BJP won an estimated 60 percent of upper caste votes by 1991.[88]

---

[82] Advani in BJP 2005, p. 112. Advani is referring to the period of increasing demands by Indian Muslims for social and political autonomy, which contributed to the pressures for the creation of separate states of East and West Pakistan, in addition to special considerations for Muslim communities remaining in India.

[83] Ibid., p. 112.

[84] Hansen 1999.

[85] See Jaffrelot 1993; Hansen 1999.

[86] Hansen 1999, p. 167

[87] The poll reported 33 percent of upper castes voted for the BJP as opposed to the Congress's 29 percent. "MARG" 1996, p. 27.

[88] This estimate is based on a recall question in a survey conducted in 1996 by the Lokniti Institute. Figure reported in Yadav and Kumar 2007c.

Among upper castes, the BJP's communal tactics had helped popularize the party beyond the few dedicated cadres enrolled within the Sangh Parivar's local chapters. Yet, these belligerent displays of Hindu unity were less successful in their efforts to attract lower castes. As Wilkinson expertly argues, Hindu nationalists fanned communal flames in the hope of polarizing local voters along religious lines, thereby overwhelming intra-Hindu caste divisions.[89] However, anti-Muslim mobilizations proved relatively ineffective in accomplishing this goal, especially among Dalits and Adivasis. Historical patterns of Hindu-Muslim violence in the post-independence era appear to have little bearing on the BJP's subsequent popularity within these communities. Using data collected by Varshney and Wilkinson, I find the number of Hindu-Muslim riots in a state between 1950 and 1995 does positively correlate with the BJP's vote share among Dalits and Adivasis in 1996, but this is entirely due to one outlier, the western state of Gujarat.[90]

I discuss Gujarat in more detail in Chapter 8. For now, it bears mentioning that the scholarly focus on this riot-prone state should not distract from its exceptionality. First, the BJP did not enjoy especially high levels of support from Dalits and Adivasis in Uttar Pradesh and Maharashtra, the other two states with high historical levels of Hindu-Muslim conflict. In these cases, the party won subaltern votes at a similar rate as in far less riot-prone states (such as Haryana, Assam, or Rajasthan). Second, once we exclude Gujarat from the sample, the bivariate relationship between conflict and BJP support among these groups is no longer statistically significant. This lack of correlation persists if we restrict the sample to include only riots occurring between 1990 and 1995, the years immediately preceding the 1996 election, and a period that encompasses the apex of the signature Ayodhya mobilizations (see the top panel of Figure 2.3).

It is also important to examine trends during the period when the BJP most rapidly expanded its following with subaltern groups. As of 1996, the party had won more than 30 percent of the combined Dalit and Adivasi vote share only in Gujarat. By 2004, it had crossed this threshold in an additional six states. Did this pattern of recent gains correspond to contemporary trends in communal violence? The bottom panel of Figure 2.3 maps the relationship between the change in the BJP's subaltern vote share between 1996 and 2004, and the average number of communal incidents during this same period.[91] The figure

---

[89] See Wilkinson 2004, pp. 165–7.

[90] Riot data from Varshney, Ashutosh; Wilkinson, Steven, 2006-02-17, "Varshney-Wilkinson Dataset on Hindu-Muslim Violence in India, 1950–1995, Version 2," hdl:1902.2/4342 Inter-university Consortium for Political and Social Research [Distributor].

[91] Unfortunately I was not able to use riot data from the Varshney-Wilkinson dataset for the contemporary analysis, as its panel ends in 1995. Therefore, I utilized data on "communal incidents" kept by India's Home Ministry. Wilkinson (2004, pp. 243–244) himself notes that these statistics "provide an accurate picture of overall trends in Hindu-Muslim violence at the state level." Indeed, the chief deficiencies he notes about this data – that it does not extend to the pre-independence period and is not disaggregated at the town level – do not interfere with my goal of comparing state-level variations in contemporary electoral trends.

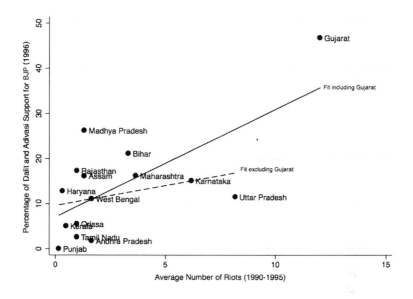

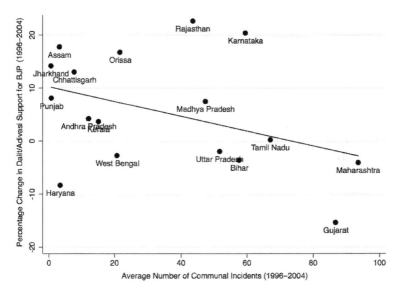

FIGURE 2.3: BJP performance and Hindu-Muslim riots
Source: Election data from National Election Survey, 1996, 2004. Historical riot data from Varshney-Wilkinson dataset on Hindu-Muslim violence. Contemporary communal incident data from Indian Home Ministry (data collected from Rajya Sabha Starred Question No. 52, dated 6/27/2000 and Lok Sabha starred question no. 294, dated 12/21/2004, collected by Indiastat online database).

shows the overall relationship to be negative and statistically insignificant. Four of the six states in which the BJP increased its vote share by double digits (Assam, Chhattisgarh, Jharkhand, and Orissa) experienced some of the lowest rates of communal conflict across the sample. At the other end of the spectrum, the BJP actually lost ground among subaltern electorates in five of the six states most wracked by such conflict.

Thus, for the overwhelming majority of Indian states, communal mobilizations do not appear to have underpinned the BJP's success with non-elite electorates. In a speech made several decades before the Ayodhya movement, Ambedkar, the aforementioned Dalit political icon, offered a prescient explanation of this failure:

There are many lower orders in the Hindu society whose economic, political and social needs are the same as those of the majority of Muslims and they would be far more ready to make a common cause with the Muslims for achieving common ends than they would with the high caste Hindus who have denied and deprived them of ordinary human rights for centuries.[92]

Whereas many upper castes were understandably moved to rally against perceived threats to a faith that had historically privileged them, Dalits and Adivasis exhibited no such inclination.

Even the explicit attempts in the Ayodhya movement to recruit lower castes focused on symbolic gestures of inclusion, rather than more fundamental efforts to reform Hindutva to accommodate subaltern perspectives. For example, the *shila* (brick)-gathering initiative for the Ram temple in Ayodhya asked for individual donations of a very small amount (Re. 1.25 or $.03), to be accessible to even the poorest contributor.[93] Other moves included choosing a Dalit citizen to lay down the foundation stone for the temple and the Sangh-backed appointment of a Dalit priest at a temple to the god Hanuman in the town of Patna, the capital of Bihar state.[94] However, even these gestures often exposed the casteist nature of the movement's leadership. For example, a Brahmin Sangh activist controversially balked at handing over the *shilas* to a lower caste colleague who had been tasked to serve as the caretaker of the blessed bricks.[95]

The limitations of its signature communal campaign were brought home to the BJP most forcefully during a series of state assembly elections in 1993. The

---

[92] Ambedkar, as quoted in Ahir 2007, p. 359, as quoted in Gatade (2011).
[93] One example was the organization of a camp by the Vishva Hindu Parishad in July 1982 in Andhra Pradesh, where 100 Dalits were trained as priests for performing religious rites and leading prayers at temples, tasks that were traditionally reserved for upper caste [*savarna*] groups ("Lakhs" 1982, p. 4). Another example was the student union Akhil Bharatiya Vidyarthi Parishad's decision to observe the death anniversary of Dalit leader Babasaheb Ambedkar as Social Equality Day ("ABVP" 1980, p. 15).
[94] The wing responsible for both decisions was the Vishva Hindu Parishad (VHP). See Sinha 1994.
[95] See Udit Raj (chairperson of the All India Confederation of SC/ST Organisations) 2002; Arun 2002.

party entered these elections confident that it could ride the Ayodhya mobilizations to convincing victories in the north and central Indian states where the movement had been strongest. Instead, the BJP suffered defeats so unexpected that members of the party's national executive confessed that "we were so confident of victory that we did not bother to chalk out a strategy for defeat. And now we are totally unable to cope with the reverses."[96] The failure of the Sangh's much-publicized sectarian agitations seemed to confirm Brass's conclusion that lower castes could never be incorporated within the BJP.[97] The saffron wave had not yet managed to reach Dalit and Adivasi vote banks. Hindu nationalists would need to manufacture a new tide to reach those distant electoral shores.

RIDING TWO HORSES: THE FAILURE OF ETHNIC ENGINEERING

Dalit and Adivasi support for the BJP is surprising when viewed through the lens of either class or religion. But for close observers of Indian democracy, it is perhaps most surprising when viewed through the prism of caste. After all, India has come to be characterized as a democracy in which caste-based ethnic ties are the primary determinant of electoral behavior, leading to the popular adage "when you cast your vote, you vote your caste." If this is the case, how could the BJP – a party stocked with upper caste personnel – attract lower caste and tribal voters?

In the wake of the Ayodhya mobilizations, the BJP's success with subaltern electorates remained woefully behind that of its rivals. A prominent BJP ideologue confessed that the party was left "desperately needing a mechanism through which to appeal to lower caste populations."[98] Grasping for straws, Hindu nationalists looked to their competitors for inspiration. The BJP began contemplating a new strategy that was informed by the rising success of ethnic parties led by lower castes. The most prominent of these latter rivals was the Dalit-led Bahujan Samaj Party (BSP) in the state of Uttar Pradesh, which had burst onto the Indian electoral scene during the late 1980s and early 1990s. The BSP had risen to prominence through rhetorical attacks on upper caste political dominance and by promising subaltern voters access to the channels of patronage they had historically been excluded from.[99] The party signaled its intentions by granting subaltern candidates a far higher degree of internal representation than mainstream national parties had previously offered.

---

[96] "No BJP strategy" 1993.

[97] Brass 1993, p. 258.

[98] Interview with K. N. Govindacharya, New Delhi, May 15, 2008. One example of the party's failure was its continued lackluster performance in constituencies reserved for Dalits (SCs) and Adivasis (STs). In 1989, the party won a combined 18 SC and ST constituencies out of the 117 that were reserved for these populations. By 1991, this number had only increased to 22. Data from Electoral Commission of India, www.eci.gov.in. Accessed September 20, 2007.

[99] Chandra 2004.

The BJP clearly could not engage in discursive attacks on its upper caste support base. However, the party did consider accommodating a greater number of lower castes as a signal that it was more willing to share patronage with subaltern constituencies if elected to office. A push to adopt this new approach, termed *social engineering*, came after the aforementioned state-level losses in the wake of the Babri mosque's demolition. Such an approach promised to help the BJP "free itself from the confines of its traditional identification with upper caste Hindus, sink roots among the lower castes, and further an ideological-political vision."[100]

A major architect of this strategy was K. N. Govindacharya, who at the time held the position of general secretary within the party.[101] Govindacharya's mercurial rise within the BJP was the result largely of his skillful organization of the previously described *rath yatras* in connection with the Ayodhya mobilizations. Yet, Govindacharya himself realized the failure of communal agitation and the need for a new expansionary strategy:

We needed a mechanism which took into account lower caste populations. So in 1991 I mentioned during the Ram [Ayodhya] movement, that their participation in the movement was largely ceremonial. And ultimately in 1993 the results [of the State Assembly elections in five states] were so loud that no one could ignore it. We had the slogan *"aaj panch pradesh, kal sara desh"* [today five states, tomorrow the whole country] and then were wiped out in the Assembly elections. So I used to say a kind of social engineering is needed within the party – *chal, charitra, chehera* [the walk, character, and face] must change. In the functioning of the party itself there has to be a radical change so that those sections not represented should be able to feel at home and look towards this party with a feeling of belonging.[102]

Govindacharya convinced the party to promote candidates from backward (OBC), Dalit, and Adivasi backgrounds to positions of power and was instrumental in fostering the rise of non-elite BJP leaders, including Kalyan Singh, Vinay Katiyar, Uma Bharati, and Bangaru Laxman.[103]

The BJP's mimicry of its lower-caste rivals sparked significant controversy within the Sangh Parivar. The adoption of a social engineering strategy became another massive point of contention between the party and its movement affiliates. The RSS opposed any efforts to explicitly strategize on the basis of caste – doing so broke with their efforts to unify Hindu society.[104] Other wings within the Sangh believed that the movement should continue to limit outreach efforts

---

[100] Bidwai 2005.

[101] Jaffrelot (2001, p.31) calls Govindacharya "the main advocate of the inclusion of an increasing number of low-caste members at all the levels of the party apparatus"; several accounts in the Indian press also identify him as "social engineering's chief ideologue" (Bidwai 2005; Times of India 2005).

[102] Interview with K. N. Govindacharya, New Delhi, May 15, 2008.

[103] Many of these leaders, Singh and Bharati in particular, managed to win elections for their party in the key states of Uttar Pradesh and Madhya Pradesh, respectively.

[104] "BJP runs," 1999.

to symbolic gestures of inclusion, rather than the active political promotion of lower castes.[105]

Even certain leaders within the BJP were openly disdainful of Govindacharya's program. Former BJP president Murli Manohar Joshi argued that "if the party has to change its character, thinking, etc., it means that the party is not worth it."[106] Joshi went on to say that to the extent that social engineering "means disturbing something or throwing up something based on purely caste considerations, then it has its own implications...that are not good for the party."[107] Indeed, a number of upper castes within the party tried to counter Govindacharya's influence by outlining how the BJP's primary message should always be one of Hindu unity over caste-based politicking, that lower castes should be looked on as family rather than as vote banks.[108]

These arguments against social engineering were mostly framed as critiques of its disruption of Hindu unity, but such rhetoric masked growing concern among upper castes of the costs of subaltern empowerment. Reports surfaced indicating that "Brahmins are feeling stifled with the BJP because of the 'social engineering theory'"[109] Ironically, social engineering stars such as Uma Bharati and Kalyan Singh, who delivered electoral successes for the BJP, were the biggest sources of concern for its upper caste leaders. Party elites were perpetually anxious that these leaders, tasting success, would break ranks with the BJP's Hindutva platform to begin campaigning on caste lines as independent candidates.[110] These fears only accelerated when non-elite candidates began demanding even higher levels of representation for their caste communities within the party.

[105] For example, in 1994, much was made of several VHP leaders paying a visit to Sandip Rai Chawdhury, the Dom Raa of Varanasi (or head of the Doms, who are considered at the bottom of the caste hierarchy because of their traditional profession of cremating the dead) and breaking bread with him. Mukhopadhyay 1994.

[106] Interview (not conducted by author) with Murli Manohar Joshi, Sunday, January 26, 1997. Transcript available at http://inhome.rediff.com/news/feb/04joshi.htm

[107] Ibid. Also see Ghimire and Singh 1992.

[108] In his 1991 presidential address, Joshi noted, "The BJP has always advocated special concessions for the backward and oppressed classes. But we do not look on them as a vote bank. We look on them as a part of a big family." Murli Manohan Joshi, Address to National Council, Jaipur, February 1, 1991, in BJP Press 2005, p. 43. Other prominent upper caste critics of social engineering included Bhanu Pratap Shukla (the editor of the RSS Hindi weekly *Panchajanya*), Brahma Dutt Dwivedi, Kalraj Mishra, and Lalji Tandon.

[109] Mukhopadhyay 1994.

[110] Interview with Vidya Subraminium, political editor, *Hindu*, New Delhi, February 3, 2008. Ms. Subraminium was basing her comments on an interview with Uma Bharati, a star of the social engineering approach. Indeed, as a consequence of Bharati's vociferous campaigning for OBC reservations, the BJP first removed Bharati from her position as chief minister of Madhya Pradesh in 2003, shunting her into an organizational post before eventually removing her from their party ranks, with several upper caste leaders calling her "a loose cannon" and "unfit for public life" (Vyas 2005).

Under pressure from its own elite lobbies, the BJP leadership felt "forced to rework its strategy to first consolidate its traditional support base before attempting to reach out to others."[111] Accordingly, the party began replacing the very leaders it had earlier elevated. Influential examples included Kalyan Singh (an OBC former chief minister of Uttar Pradesh) and Suraj Bhan (the Dalit governor of the same state), who were both replaced by upper castes in 1996. These removals followed statements by each politician seeking larger allocations of internal party posts for lower castes, with Singh demanding no less than 75 percent of the BJP's candidates in Uttar Pradesh be from non-upper caste backgrounds.[112] The existing upper caste leadership was obviously reluctant to sign off on its own displacement, which such radical prescriptions would require.[113]

Subaltern politicians within the BJP meanwhile began to complain that they were expected to remain subservient to upper caste power brokers within the party. As Nand Kumar Sai, the first Adivasi to become a state-level president for the BJP noted:

It was a real struggle to be an Adivasi in the party – I won't lie to you. I wanted to run for the Vidhan Sabha [State Assembly] a few elections ago, but I wasn't given a ticket. Then another time when I was state president they wanted me to step down, and thought maybe they [the BJP leadership] should put someone who would just be a rubber stamp for them. They thought to make someone more junior the Chief Minister, and they were afraid that I would buck their interests. Therefore they wanted to bring someone who would run their program.[114]

The problem for the BJP was that it had adopted a strategy that it was structurally unsuited to implement. New lower caste parties such as the BSP did not have to accommodate existing upper caste elites when providing lower caste personnel with a large share of candidacies. These subaltern candidates could therefore construct their own patronage networks relatively unfettered by previously entrenched elites. However, within the BJP, lower caste candidates selected for advancement were told not to disturb prior upper caste–dominated networks. Instead, these newly promoted candidates were expected to serve as largely ceremonial leaders willing to run the programs of their elite colleagues.

Sai's assertion that Adivasis within the BJP were punished for displaying independence was not simply a personal gripe but reflected a concern voiced by other non-elite personnel I interviewed.[115] Another subaltern BJP leader

---

[111] Vyas 2000.

[112] Jaffrelot, Brotel, and Chaturvedi 2003, pp. 159–61.

[113] Raman 1996.

[114] Interview with Nand Kumar Sai, New Delhi, March 17, 2008.

[115] Another problematic instance brought to my attention by Adivasis within the BJP occurred when the party leadership bypassed Karia Munda, a senior Adivasi politician, for the position of chief minister of the newly formed state of Jharkhand in 2000. The BJP did nominate another Adivasi, Babulal Marandi, to the post. However Marandi, who was far less experienced than Munda, was

noted that separate wings set up explicitly for Dalits and Adivasis within the BJP were never intended to fulfill their stated purpose as "aggressive organizations" set up to foster leaders who were "self-guided." Such autonomy, he complained, proved "too difficult to digest" for upper castes.[116]

Instead, the top BJP brass looked to advance precisely any subaltern leader who "will never assert his own rights, has no initiative, and will not challenge for power."[117] One such quiescent leader did not deny upper caste dominance within his party but instead offered a curious defense of this elite control:

See socially, educationally, and economically, they [lower caste personnel] are backward, and so the people who come out are not going to be *chamakdar* [impressive/charismatic] at first. As a result, they will necessarily not be great, and *will need help in learning how to govern*. But what is the problem with this? We need to learn how to look at this positively – this is developing the SC/ST community, so that the next generation of leaders will be better.[118]

The interviewee's language defines the terms under which the incorporation of subaltern candidates was palatable to upper castes. Non-elite inductees had to be willing to be guided by the paternalistic hand of party elites who would help develop them into more impressive leaders, presumably with an appreciation of the correct policies to support.

In short, subaltern leaders needed to (at least outwardly) support such condescending views of their own capabilities to be considered acceptable to existing elites. However, in demanding such docility, the BJP undermined the ability of a social engineering strategy to fulfill its original expansionary purpose. Unsurprisingly, subaltern leaders chosen for being acceptable to upper castes were often not popular among their own co-ethnics. Indeed, after interviewing some of these non-elite personnel, Jaffrelot concludes that they "revealed a certain reluctance to present themselves as low caste leaders" and often "attract[ed] little support from voters of the same social milieu."[119]

To add insult to injury, the BJP's primarily upper caste cadres often thoroughly disrespected their own party's lower caste candidates, preventing the latter from running effective campaigns. As Govindacharya himself recalled:

I came from seeing a campaign in Madhya Pradesh, and the campaigners were there in a jeep, and after they got down, and I was introduced to all the workers, I found the persons sitting in the jeep were forward castes who were workers, and the candidate who was Scheduled Caste [Dalit] was made to sit in the back. Therefore this [social engineering]

seen to be selected because of his roots within the RSS, which made him less threatening and "more acceptable to non-tribals who in fact call the shots in the party" (Ahmed, 2000; see also Chaudhuri 2000). As it happens, Marandi was himself unable to consolidate his position and was subsequently replaced in 2003.

[116] Interview, member of BJP SC Morcha (wing), name withheld on request, New Delhi, June 20, 2010.
[117] Interview with K. N. Govindacharya, New Delhi, May 15, 2008.
[118] Interview with Satya Narayan Jatiya, April 30, 2008, emphasis added.
[119] Jaffrelot 1993, p. 509.

strategy could not take hold with SCs and STs [Adivasis] because how can effective leaders emerge from those communities in such conditions of tension?[120]

The material interests of upper castes thus combined with their feelings of cultural superiority to effectively thwart social engineering from its outset.

Recent electoral data confirms that the BJP's success with Dalits and Adivasis is not a product of the latter's increased representation within the party. The BJP is required to field Dalit and Adivasi candidates for certain seats due to mandatory legislative quotas. However the proportion of these seats has remained relatively stable since independence, and *all* parties are required to field candidates from these communities for these posts. Candidate profiles in reserved constituencies are therefore unlikely to serve as the basis for shifts in non-elite support toward the BJP specifically.

However, it is possible that the proportion of Dalit and Adivasi candidates voluntarily nominated by the party to non-reserved seats informed its pattern of success with voters from these populations. Data from the Election Commission, which began reporting the caste profile of legislative candidates in national and state elections in 2004, does not support such an argument.[121] In the 2004 national election, the BJP fielded eighty-nine Dalit or Adivasi candidates across India's seventeen largest states (home to 95 percent of the country's population). Only six of these candidates stood in elections outside of constituencies reserved for them by electoral law. In sharp contrast, the lower caste–led BSP nominated forty-nine Dalit or Adivasi candidates to non-reserved general seats.

Data from state assembly elections held between 2004 and 2009 further confirm this difference (Table 2.2). Dalits and Adivasis constituted only 3 percent of BJP candidates within non-reserved constituencies across the same sample of states, compared to more than 30 percent of BSP nominees. Further, variations in the BJP's success with subaltern voters do not correspond with the latter's representation within the party. In the seven states in which the BJP has won more than 30 percent of Dalit and Adivasi votes, only 2.3 percent of candidates in non-reserved seats came from these two communities. In fact, this constitutes a slightly lower proportion than in the ten states where it has continued to struggle with these voters (3.6 percent). In general, the low number of tickets voluntarily allotted by the BJP to lower caste and tribal candidates confirms the inability of Hindu nationalists to mimic the BSP's approach. By contrast, upper castes remain highly overrepresented among the BJP's elected officials, and even more so within the party's executive bodies.[122]

---

[120] Interview with K. N. Govindacharya, New Delhi, May 15, 2008.

[121] From 2004, Election Commission of India reports indicate whether a candidate came from a Dalit or Adivasi community even in non-reserved constituencies.

[122] According to data collected by Jaffrelot (2003, pp. 469–70), the percentage of the BJP's national executive leadership coming from an upper caste background ranged from roughly 60 percent to 75 percent during the 1990s. By contrast, the share of OBCs, Dalits, and Adivasis combined was

TABLE 2.2. *Non-elite candidates in the BJP and BSP*

Percentage of Dalit or Adivasi Candidates in Non-reserved Seats
(2004–2009 Assembly Elections)

State	BJP	BSP
Andhra Pradesh	4.54	58.46
Assam	3.12	N/A
Bihar	0	15.73
Chhattisgarh	4.34	10.88
Gujarat	0.7	10.1
Haryana	0	21.21
Jharkhand	3.13	15.00
Karnataka	1.76	13.17
Kerala	0.82	69.47
Madhya Pradesh	0.67	6.8
Maharashtra	6.45	63.12
Orissa	3.13	27.78
Punjab	0	34.91
Rajasthan	2.23	10.00
Tamil Nadu	3.39	51.91
Uttar Pradesh	0.75	1.50
West Bengal	16.67	74.19
National Average	3.04	30.26

Note: States in bold indicate those in which the BJP won more than
30 percent of Dalit and Adivasi votes in 2004 national elections.
Source: Election Commission of India Election Reports.

In short, the social engineering strategy was inconsistently deployed and rapidly discontinued. The few genuinely successful subaltern figures empowered by this approach were reigned in or cut loose by nervous upper castes. To protect elite interests, the party moved away from selecting genuinely charismatic lower caste leaders to promoting quiescent politicians who were often unpopular among their own co-ethnic communities. Further, many of these docile candidates found themselves marginalized by their upper caste campaign staffs. The party's elite base thus undermined the core principle of social engineering, which was to recruit effective lower caste leaders. Once again, the party proved unable to "ride two horses," to preserve elite dominance while gaining non-elite support.[123]

less than 16 percent, despite these communities constituting a far larger share of the Indian population. Similarly the proportion of upper castes among BJP members of Parliament within the northern Hindu belt states remained between 45 percent and 55 percent from 1989 to 1999, always equaling or exceeding the combined share coming from OBC, SC, and ST backgrounds.
[123] Vyas 2000.

OTHER FAILURES

Following a string of failed outreach strategies, Hindu nationalists were left struggling to find ways to broaden their following. Both the Sangh and BJP have implemented other, more localized strategies, such as forming strategic electoral alliances or targeting specific subcastes within Dalit and Adivasi communities. The movement has also made piecemeal attempts to adapt Hindutva into a more inclusive ideological message that is less alienating to lower castes. However, none of these strategies, which I briefly review here, have been able to reverse the party's dismal performance among subaltern voters.

Electoral Outsourcing

As India's party system became increasingly diversified, the BJP considered reaching out to disadvantaged voters through the channels afforded by coalition politics. Specifically, the party looked to form pacts with rivals that enjoyed higher levels of lower caste or tribal support to make up for its own deficiencies.[124] The BJP found occasional success through this outsourcing of electoral work, which enabled it to be part of ruling governments in several states where its lack of subaltern support had previously prevented it from taking office.[125]

However, alliances suffer from some major limitations as the centerpiece of an expansionary strategy. First, this approach made the BJP increasingly vulnerable to the vagaries of coalition politics, which can be particularly explosive in the Indian context. Several of the party's national and state-level alliances collapsed before their full term, following highly publicized disagreements between the coalition partners.[126] These public rifts with parties that were popular among non-elite voters caused the outsourcing strategy to backfire

---

[124] The party made alliances with a variety of partners, ranging from the Trinamool Congress (Congress of the Downtrodden, TMC) in West Bengal, the All India Anna Dravida Munnetra Kazagham (All India Dravidian Progress Federation, AIADMK) in Tamil Nadu, the Samata Party (Equality Party, SMT) in Bihar, the Jananta Dal (S) (People's Front, JD [S]) in Karnataka, the Haryana Vikas Party (Haryana Progress Party, HVP) in Haryana, and the Biju Janata Dal (Biju People's Front, BJD) in Orissa.

[125] In the 1996 national elections, the party's alliance with the HVP, which was far stronger with lower caste voters, helped the BJP come to power in the state. The HVP won 34.4 percent of the OBC vote (compared to the BJP's 18.8 percent). National Election Study, 1996, Center for the Study of Developing Society, New Delhi. The party's performance in Bihar, in which it had a seat-sharing alliance with the Samata Party, and later with the Janata Dal (U), was similarly improved. Here the BJP-SMT combined won a staggering 73.7 percent of the vote of two large subgroups (*jatis*) within the state's OBC population, the Kurmis and Koeris, enabling it to compete with the opposition Rashtriya Janata Dal's popularity with the largest OBC subgroup (the Yadavs). Subsequent alliances with the Janata Dal (U) in the state have enabled the BJP to remain an electoral presence in Bihar despite only having a strong backing from upper castes in the state.

[126] In its 1999 national coalition to form the central government, the BJP lost a key ally in the AIADMK in Tamil Nadu, when its leader Jayalalitha withdrew suddenly following her annoyance at the BJP's refusal to use its power at the center to dismiss the Tamil Nadu government

badly and often reduced the BJP's own popularity among subaltern constituencies to below its pre-alliance level.

Second, whereas the BJP viewed alliances as channels for expanding their influence, its rivals-turned-partners often had the same motives. These partners often turned the tables on Hindu nationalists by using coalitions to strengthen their own political position at the BJP's expense. For example, the party found itself repeatedly outmaneuvered by the Dalit-led BSP in a series of high-profile alliances during the 1990s in Uttar Pradesh. As I detail in Chapter 6, the BJP hoped these alliances would signal its heightened commitment to social inclusion, thereby helping it recruit a portion of the BSP's Dalit base. Instead, lower caste support for the BSP remained entrenched, and the latter used these alliances to improve public perceptions of its ability to win elections. The BSP even poached some of the BJP's upper caste supporters en route to winning a majority of seats in the state's 2007 state assembly elections.

A third problem with alliances was that, in addition to their unpredictable electoral effects, they remained highly unpopular with the BJP's movement partners. For the Sangh Parivar, the project of winning lower caste votes is just one step in the conscription of poor Hindus into Hindutva's ideological camp. Coalition politics fundamentally compromised this mandate, as several electoral partners required the BJP to moderate its Hindutva rhetoric as a precondition of any alliance. As this tactic appeared to yield few gains in the BJP's own subaltern following, many movement leaders complained that it required an undesirable amount of ideological compromise for an uncertain electoral gain.

Divide and Conquer?

The previous discussion is not meant to imply that the BJP does not still actively participate in coalition politics, as it is impossible to be a viable national party in India without doing so. However, as the limitations of alliances became more apparent, and as non-elite parties grew in political clout, the BJP felt itself increasingly painted into a corner. Under pressure to respond, the party began considering ways to politically capitalize on fissures within Dalit and Adivasi electorates. For example, the BJP considered emphasizing its appeals to Dalit voters outside the Chamar *jati* [endogamous subcaste], which is the largest Dalit *jati* in many states and is also at the core of the Dalit-led BSP's electoral base.[127]

---

headed by her rival, the Dravida Munnetra Kazagham. More recently, the BJP entered an alliance with the Janata Dal (S) in Karanataka in 2005, whereby the chief ministership was meant to rotate between the two. However, after the JD(S)'s candidate completed his tenure, the party was reluctant to relinquish control to the BJP and ultimately withdrew from the coalition.

[127] See Deshpande 2005. For example, Rajnath Singh, the party's president in Uttar Pradesh in 2007, began systematically organizing its party lists to note *jati* distinctions to ensure they would specifically choose non-Chamar candidates in constituencies reserved for Dalits. Interview with Bangaru Laxman, New Delhi, July 10, 2008.

Unlike past efforts at social engineering, this approach was only intended for those areas where participation in electoral contests was restricted to Dalit candidates, thereby avoiding any displacement of upper castes from the party. This strategy culminated with the BJP appointing its first Dalit national party president, Bangaru Laxman – a member of the Madiga subcaste – in 2000.[128] However, the party's local rivals once again thwarted these efforts. In response to the Laxman's promotion, BSP leader Mayawati gave a statement proclaiming that the new BJP president was not a Chamar or even a Madiga, but a member of a much smaller and less influential Dalit subcaste (the Valmikis).[129] In a personal interview, Laxman himself admitted that his Dalit rival had made the label stick, thereby reducing perceptions of his ability to unite non-Chamar communities.[130]

The BJP further aided its opponents by exposing its elitism even when supposedly working toward the empowerment of its own lower caste personnel. For example, Laxman became quickly regarded as little more than a token party president, as he was given few organizational powers and was noticeably absent from important functions during his own tenure as the head of the party.[131] Further, the BJP's rivals excoriated the party over its handling of an incident in which Laxman was heard on tape accepting bribes during a sting operation by an investigative news journal in 2001. Whereas the BJP made its Dalit president resign from his post, an upper caste BJP leader exposed by the same operation was allowed to continue in his.[132] This differential treatment is still cited by senior Dalits within the BJP today as a source of their disillusionment regarding their future within the party.[133]

Reformulating Hindutva as an Inclusive Ideology

The specific case of the BJP's first Dalit president just described provides a prominent illustration of a more general problem for Hindu nationalists. The fact that the BJP's rivals can successfully raise doubts about its subaltern personnel indicates that the credibility of such figures is compromised by their very involvement with a party widely viewed as elitist. BJP and Sangh leaders have been forced to consider how this disadvantage stems directly from Hindutva's image as a casteist ideology. Faced with the persistent gap

[128] The Madiga subcaste traditionally hails from the southern Indian state of Andhra Pradesh and is one of the two main Dalit communities in that state.

[129] Interview with Bangaru Laxman, New Delhi, July 10, 2008. This accusation was confirmed in a recent media report (Parashar 2011).

[130] Interview with Bangaru Laxman, New Delhi, July 10, 2008

[131] Kumar 2000.

[132] Menon 2001. Also see "Tehelka" 2001, and "Flunking" 2001.

[133] For example, P. M. Velayuthan, the leader of the Kerala branch of the BJP's Dalit organizational wing, confessed that even a decade later, he remained "very disappointed by the party's decision to remove Laxman," interview, Ernakulam, August 8, 2008.

between their self-perception as a pan-Hindu movement and the BJP's narrow base of electoral support, Hindu nationalists have gone through a painstaking re-thinking of their rhetorical treatment of subaltern communities, especially of prominent lower caste political figures.

Initially, the Sangh largely criticized these subaltern leaders for spreading divisive rhetoric through a misplaced focus on caste. Hindu nationalists were particularly critical of the highly publicized mass Dalit conversions to Buddhism organized by Ambedkar. However, as the BJP repeatedly failed to win over lower caste voters, there were increasing efforts to find commonality between Ambedkar and leading Sangh ideologues.[134]

The former president of the BJP's Dalit organizational wing (SC Morcha) articulated this attempted co-optation. He noted that his organization looked to blend Hindutva with Dalit rights under a banner of "social equality with national integration." This blend was achieved by "mixing the message of equality of Dr. Ambedkar, with the message of Dr. Hegdewar [the founder of the RSS], which is to remove differences within society."[135] The Sangh thus sought to transform Ambedkar's specific, scathing demand for the annihilation of caste into more abstract, less polarizing demands for social equality from a Hindu reformer.[136] The Sangh also revised its prior opposition to Ambedkar's conversion to Buddhism and began celebrating it as an indication of his negative view of Islam and Christianity.

By incorporating a Dalit political icon into the pantheon of its revered leaders, the Sangh hoped to convince lower castes that their demands could be met within Hindutva's ideological framework. The Sangh has worked hard to educate its young recruits in this new interpretation of Ambedkar's politics.[137] One former supreme leader (*sarsanghchalak*) of the RSS went so far as to declare that Ambedkar had been personally impressed with the Sangh activities, a claim for which I could find no historical evidence.[138] The RSS has also launched a wing specifically to attract Dalits, which it founded on Ambedkar's birthday. Fortuitously for the RSS, this date coincided with the birthday of Hegdewar, its

---

[134] These efforts were exemplified by Bangaru Laxman in his presidential address to the BJP party convention in 2000, where he argued that "while Gandhiji, Ambedkar, and [Sangh founder] Hegdewar may outwardly seem to belong to three conflicting ideologies...we believe that not only is there no contradiction and conflict between their respective beliefs and actions, but there is indeed a deeper convergence of their ideals...Nationalism was the fire that burnt in all these three hearts (speech reproduced in BJP Press 2005). On a similar point, see Gatade 2011.

[135] Interview with Satya Narayan Jatiya, New Delhi, April 30, 2008.

[136] See Ambedkar 1937.

[137] "RSS to educate," 2003.; "RSS chief" 2006.

[138] See, "Wipe out" 2005. This statement seems to be an extension of an oft-quoted claim the RSS has often made about Mahatma Gandhi's visit to an RSS *shakha*. Another more recent example came during the 2009 national election campaigning, when BJP prime ministerial candidate L. K. Advani accused the Congress Party of "not doing justice" to Ambedkar within the party ranks. See "Congress" 2009.

own founder, which provided another opportunity to advertise the intellectual symbiosis between the two figures.[139]

Whether such efforts have succeeded in spawning new subaltern attachments to Hindutva is a matter for empirical investigation that is taken up in subsequent chapters. However, the inability of Sangh leaders to maintain a consistently progressive line on caste sheds doubt on the efficacy of this effort to recast Hindutva. Even as upper caste leaders were paying lip service to Dalit leaders, they continued to offer defenses of the underlying principles of caste.

A senior leader of the cultural affairs wing of the Sangh Parivar exemplified this rhetorical ambivalence during the course of an interview. At first, he outlined how caste hierarchies were a non-Hindu invention:

We tell Dalits and Adivasi that you were never an Adivasi, or a Scheduled Caste [Dalit] – this was a creation of the medieval period. This was created by Muslims and Christians – a myth – see it's like this – those people who were defeated by Muslim invaders – they were turned into lower castes.[140]

However, immediately after this proclamation, when asked if caste should be abolished – as Ambedkar suggested – he immediately backtracked:

No. This [abolishment] is not a good idea. After all it [caste] is such a good thing – that is why it has been alive all this time. See today you make a club and invite members – that is all *jati* [endogamous subcaste] is, a club, a network, and that is very useful. If I want to go to a new city and find a place to stay, then I will stay with people of my own caste, it is natural.[141]

Such contradictions were equally evident in the speeches of RSS top leaders, one of whom called for the "wiping out of caste barriers,"[142] in 2005, yet less than a month later offered a standard Brahminical defense of caste practice:

That earlier caste system was "non-discriminatory" and every caste was given "job reservation" under it. "The caste system used to be like a fence around the farm. Those who violated its rules were ostracized. It was not discriminatory. Rather, it provided for job reservation. Every caste was given reservation in a particular job. A mason could not do a carpenter's job and a carpenter could not do a sweeper's job," he said.[143]

Such tensions are also apparent in the Sangh's local activities. For example, one Sangh activist related to me his efforts to combat casteism in the central Indian town of Bilaspur. He mentioned that during the nine-day celebrations of the Hindu festival of Dussehra in a neighborhood with a sizeable Dalit population, lower castes were not allowed to sing on the platform with higher castes. Finding such discrimination unfair, the activist advocated for educated

---

[139] This new wing was called the Samajik Samrasata Manch (Social Assimilation Platform). See Shah 1994.
[140] Interview with Acharya Giriraj Kishore, New Delhi, May 28, 2008.
[141] Ibid.
[142] "Wipe out" 2005.
[143] "Old caste system" 2006.

lower castes to be allowed on the platform with higher castes (the latters' educational credentials were not checked).[144]

Such internal contradictions have prevented the Sangh from formulating a clear message capable of dispelling its image as the defender of caste hierarchies. The BJP's waffling on caste also made it an easy target for increasingly assertive non-elite rivals. A solution for the caste problem based on an extensive reformulation of Hindutva ideology therefore continues to remain unlikely.

CONCLUSION

This chapter has outlined how the mercurial rise of Hindu nationalism during the 1980s and 1990s did not encompass all the social groups the movement sought to unify. I have briefly described how the philosophical orientation and organizational origins of the movement informed its elite bias and detailed the BJP's struggles to expand this limited social profile. In the policy arena, the party maintained positions that were oriented toward the preferences of its powerful and privileged base in terms of public spending, market reforms, and caste-based reservations. Communal mobilizations in defense of Hinduism failed to distract subaltern voters historically denigrated by Hindu traditions. Strategies of ethnic representation threatened upper castes entrenched within the party and were abandoned.

Collectively, these failures ensured that the BJP's reputation as an upper caste party endured well into the 1990s. This persistence is best illustrated by data from a 1996 National Election Study, which asked voters to identify a party that was representative of the interests of their caste community (Figure 2.4).[145] Among respondents identifying the BJP, upper castes outnumbered Dalits and Adivasis (SC/ST) combined by a ratio of six to one. Further, in all of the national electoral surveys conducted between 1996 and 2004, upper castes outnumbered Dalits and Adivasis by at least a two to one ratio, despite constituting a far smaller proportion of the electorate. By comparison, the ratio among those identifying the Congress Party was nearly exactly one to one and was lower than one for the leftist CPM and the Dalit-led BSP. Despite the efforts outlined in this chapter, the BJP remained branded as an elite party in a poor democracy.

Even if we accept this chapter's argument that upper caste support for the BJP was conditional, the party's continuing prioritization of this constituency to the exclusion of other electorates runs counter to the expectation of majoritarian models of politics. These models anticipate that parties will follow strategies that maximize votes to win office. By implication, elite parties such as the BJP should

---

[144] Interview with AH (name withheld to protect anonymity), Bilaspur, July 27, 2010.

[145] The exact wording of the question (Q17 and 17a) is: "Some political parties specially care for the interest of particular caste group or community, while others don't/ How about your caste group/ community? Is there any political party that looks after the interests of your caste group/ community?"

Congress Partisans

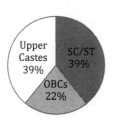

CPM Partisans

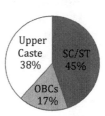

BJP Partisans

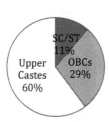

BSP Partisans

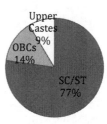

FIGURE 2.4: Social profile of voters identifying a political party as representing the interests of their caste community
Note: SC/ST refers to Dalits and Adivasis respectively. OBCs refer to intermediate castes known as Other Backward Classes.

shift to targeting the pivotal median voter of an electorate.[146] Consequently, the party should be more willing to sacrifice some of its core upper caste support to appeal to India's vote-rich poor communities. How can we explain its seemingly irrational loyalty to upper castes?

The first point to note is that the BJP is far from unique. A number of studies have documented the fact that politicians across the globe "regularly depart from the median despite the clear electoral benefit for having moderate positions."[147] Scholars have therefore questioned the validity of assuming that political elites choose policies solely to maximize votes and win office. Instead, critics argue these elites are often motivated by their own policy agendas and the preferences of their partisan constituencies, instead of those of the supposedly crucial median voter.[148]

---

[146] This literature has been reviewed in Chapter 1, but the seminal accounts here are Downs 1957; Meltzer and Richards 1981.

[147] Gelman 2008, p. 148.

[148] Scholars have argued that parties may particularly hold autonomous objectives when there is uncertainty in the outcome of elections (Wittman 1983) or when parties cannot credibly commit to arbitrary policy platforms (Alesina 1988).

The argument that parties hold their own political commitments is particularly applicable to the BJP, as the party emerged out of a broad ideological movement, rather than from the electoral ambitions of a set of office seekers.[149] The BJP was in this respect distinct from several Indian parties that have been established by elites defecting from an established party (usually the Congress) following an internal power struggle.[150] Accordingly, Hindu nationalists have had a long history of eschewing purely vote-maximizing positions in favor of policy objectives in line with their founding ideology. As this book itself argues, these ideological commitments do not mean that the BJP is uninterested in winning over new voters. Indeed, the party may seek to moderate specific policy positions in search of electoral majorities, as winning also enables it to better serve its core. Yet unlike purely Downsian vote-maximizing parties, the BJP has shown a reluctance to enact sustained policy shifts that fundamentally compromise elite interests, even at the cost of winning office.

A second observation of prior studies is that parties are not equally responsive to voters from all sections of an income distribution. Instead, they are often more sensitive to the preferences of wealthy voters, because political influence increases with income.[151] Wealthier voters have the financial and organizational resources to articulate their demands and consistently apply pressure to ensure they are met. At the other end of the spectrum, Bartels argues that elected officials in America "are utterly unresponsive to the policy preferences of millions of low-income citizens."[152] Given these asymmetries, critics have argued that democratic systems are better conceptualized using a "one dollar, one vote" framework than the traditional "one person, one vote" assumptions of majoritarian explanations.[153]

These arguments are particularly appropriate for understanding elite parties such as the BJP. Upper castes founded the movement from which the BJP emerged and continue to disproportionately populate the party's candidate lists and staff positions. These constituencies also provide their co-ethnics within the party with most of their financial resources, support that is particularly important given the weakness of mass fund-raising institutions in the

---

[149] In India, most such defections came from established political parties such as the Congress and Janata Dal, so this difference is broadly analogous to Shefter's (1977, p. 415) influential distinction between "externally mobilized" parties established by regime outsiders and "internally mobilized" parties "founded by elites who occupy positions within the prevailing regime and who undertake to mobilize a popular following behind themselves in an effort either to gain government or to secure their hold over it."

[150] Examples of parties formed via elite defections in India include the Indian National Congress (Organization), Trinamool Congress in Bengal, Biju Janata Dal in Orissa, Samajwadi Party in Uttar Pradesh, and Rashtriya Janata Dal in Bihar.

[151] For example, Gilens (2005) finds that U.S. government policy is far more closely related to the preferences of individuals in the 90th percentile of the income distribution than either median-income or poor voters. Also see Becker 1983; Grossman and Helpman 1996.

[152] Bartels 2008, p. 2.

[153] Karabarbounis 2011.

subcontinent. The interests of BJP party personnel thus cannot be separated from the elite constituencies from which they emerged, and within which they remain embedded.

Citing Gibson's discussion of core constituencies, the influence of upper castes within the BJP "lies not necessarily in the number of votes they represent, but in their influence on the party's agenda and capacities for political action."[154] Thus, elite parties such as the BJP remain fundamentally committed to their core constituencies, even when looking toward expanding their vote share.[155] However, contra Gibson, my goal in this chapter has been to show that party efforts with core and non-core constituencies must be studied as inherently interactive, and not as "analytically distinct processes."[156] The strategies the BJP could pursue with subaltern voters cannot be understood without an appreciation of the constraints placed on it by its elite core.

In conclusion, the failures documented in this chapter illustrate the depths of the BJP's electoral dilemma. The evidence presented here confirmed the BJP's enduring status as an elite party in terms of its internal composition, programmatic orientation, and partisan profile (the three traits highlighted in my conceptualization of such parties). Yet, electoral survey data shows that by 2004, the BJP had succeeded in winning votes from Dalit and Adivasi in several Indian states. Given the inefficacy of the tactics outlined here, what strategy was responsible for this turnaround? What strategy was able to reconcile elite interests with non-elite recruitment?

[154] Gibson 1996, p. 7.
[155] Ibid., pp. 9–10.
[156] Ibid., p. 14.

3

Why Rich and Poor Voters Support an Elite Party in India

Constrained by their powerful core constituencies, how can elite parties manage the dual tasks of recruiting the poor while retaining the rich? Even as Hindu nationalists rose from obscurity to prominence within India, the BJP remained pigeonholed as an urban, upper caste party. As the prevous chapter outlined, a number of electoral strategies failed to reverse the party's traditional struggles among non-elite voters. Yet, more recent data suggests the BJP has managed to make significant gains among its least likely supporters in several states. Across the seventeen largest Indian states, home to more than 95 percent of India's population, the BJP won just 15.01 percent of Dalit and Adivasi votes in 1996 (the first year for which caste-wise national electoral data is available). Yet by 2004, the party had won 22.41 percent of subaltern votes across these same territories, a 50 percent increase that represents a significant achievement within India's fragmented, multiparty arena.[1]

In Chapter 1, I argued that elite parties with thick organizational assets can draw on them to recruit the poor, while remaining programmatically oriented toward their elite core. Was such an organizational division of labor behind the BJP's unlikely success? To provide an initial attempt at addressing this question, I examine separately patterns of elite and non-elite support for the BJP at the broadest level possible. I use data from a national electoral survey to provide the first (to my knowledge) statistical assessment of how the determinants of an Indian party's support vary among different caste communities.[2]

---

[1] These figures are calculated as the proportion of combined Dalit and Adivasi respondents casting their votes for the BJP (excluding non-responses). In 1996, the BJP won 321 out of the 2,139 active Dalit and Adivasi votes recorded in the survey. In 2004, it won the support of 1,032 out of 4,606 respondents across this same sample (which now included the new states of Chhattisgarh and Jharkhand, which were created in 2000 out of portions of Madhya Pradesh and Bihar, two states within the original sample).

[2] Prior analyses have largely focused on examining which castes are more likely to support particular parties, but not how the reasons for supporting the same party may vary systematically by caste group.

This socially segmented analysis finds that among upper castes, backers of the BJP are distinguished by their affinity to the party's *electoral* platform. However, these factors do not identify Dalit or Adivasi backers of the party. Instead, subaltern supporters of the BJP are distinguished by their contact with *non-electoral* associations. These divergent results are indicative of a broad division of labor between Hindu nationalism's movement and party arms. The data used in this section cannot however further specify the contours of such a division. Subsequent chapters will therefore provide more fine-grained evaluations of which nonparty organizations were at the helm of subaltern voter recruitment, and how they forged ties with poor voters.

A QUICK WORD ON DATA

The data used in this chapter is drawn from the 2004 National Election Study (NES) conducted by the Center for the Study of Developing Society (CSDS) in New Delhi. CSDS conducts the most systematic and widely utilized electoral surveys available in India, which are particularly invaluable for this project as they contain information on both the electoral choices and social profile of a large, representative sample of voters. These surveys have been regularly conducted since 1996, both for Lok Sabha (National Parliament) and Vidhan Sabha (State Assembly) elections. I decided to use the NES 2004 data because it was the largest and most recently conducted survey available at the time of my research. I was granted access to this data during my time as a visiting researcher at CSDS from September 2007 to March 2008. For my analysis, I worked with a sample of 5,460 Dalit and Adivasi voters and 3,263 upper caste Hindus across seventeen major states. This large dataset provides invaluable empirical opportunities to examine how the BJP's appeal varied across different constituencies at the broadest possible level.

As the survey team was particularly interested in understanding state-level politics even within national elections, it used a stratified random sampling technique to ensure representative samples within each state.[3] To achieve this, the sample included at least 1,000 respondents in each state, accounting for the large total sample size of the full survey (N=25,433). Importantly for this analysis,

---

[3] The NES used a multistage weighted sampling design, similar to the protocol used on other large surveys in developing countries (such as Afrobarometer). Within each state, the NES selected a random number of parliamentary constituencies (adjusted for the size of the state's electorate). In total, the survey sampled 420 out of 543 parliamentary constituencies. Within each parliamentary constituency, the NES selected a random number of state assembly constituencies (the units relevant for state-level politics, total N=932). Within each assembly constituency, the local sampling unit was individual polling station areas (typically villages or urban wards), which were again randomly selected (N=2380). From each polling station, 15 people were selected randomly from the electoral register. For reference, this is nearly double the number of people interviewed at each principal local sampling unit for the Afrobarometer surveys. The response rate for the 2004 survey (AAPOR Response Rate 1) was 65.18 percent.

Dalits and Adivasis, two traditionally under-sampled populations, were actually overrepresented within the overall NES sample. There was only one instance in which either community was under-sampled within the seventeen states used in my analysis (Adivasis in the eastern state of Orissa). The NES has also done an exemplary job of recruiting enumerators from Dalit and Adivasi backgrounds and of trying to match enumerator and respondent caste backgrounds as much as possible.[4]

In the words of its executors, the 2004 NES is not an exit poll, but a post-poll survey whose primary purpose is not "predicting the number of seats that a...coalition is likely to get. Rather, it is a survey that takes the results as given, and then tries to understand the reasons why voters chose the parties they did."[5] The survey was conducted after the votes had been cast in each constituency, but before the results were officially declared, to assess political opinions uninfluenced by knowledge of the election's outcome. To obtain responses on questions dealing with electoral choices, the survey questionnaire used secret mock ballots.[6]

Using a national election dataset instead of a compilation of state assembly election data was a major decision that requires brief explanation. There would have been obvious advantages to using Vidhan Sabha data for this study. Under the Indian federal system, state governments possess a great deal of autonomy over a variety of public policies, and for this reason state elections are often more politically meaningful for local populations than Lok Sabha elections. Further, given that I am specifically looking at disadvantaged populations for whom the most important public services are those controlled by state administrations, there is a strong rationale for examining their political behavior when voting in assembly elections.

Having said this, there were stronger reasons for employing national parliamentary data that ultimately led to the decision to use the 2004 Lok Sabha survey. The biggest concern was the lack of comparability among separate state assembly surveys, as the questions on each differed greatly. This variance made it impossible to aggregate responses across the state-level surveys for more than a small handful of questions. Responses to questions crucial for this analysis were

---

[4] The 2009 NES published data on the caste profile of its enumerators (who were selected in a highly comparable manner for the 2004 survey used here). This data showed that 21 percent of enumerators came from a Dalit background, and 11 percent came from Adivasi backgrounds (Kumar 2009b). In each case, this was actually higher than their respective proportions within the national electorate. Further, the survey teams were designed to match the caste profile of enumerators with those of the majority of interviewees. This strategy does have limits however, given the caste heterogeneity of Indian voters even at the local level. For additional details on the NES and its suitability for this analysis, see Thachil 2014 (online appendix, Section 8).

[5] For a more detailed report of the methodology of the survey, see Lokniti Team 2004.

[6] I was given access to the responses for Dalit, Adivasi, and upper caste Hindu voters in seventeen major states: Andhra Pradesh, Assam, Bihar, Chhattisgarh, Gujarat, Haryana, Jharkhand, Karnataka, Kerala, Madhya Pradesh, Maharashtra, Orissa, Punjab, Rajasthan, Tamil Nadu, Uttar Pradesh, and West Bengal.

thus either unavailable or unevenly measured across states. Further, as state assembly elections happen by rotation across the country, the responses were not collected synchronously, compounding problems of comparability. Finally, the methodologies used on the various surveys differed somewhat in their sampling techniques, including their methods for replacing missing respondents. Given these concerns, the national election data appeared to offer the best opportunities for systematically examining support patterns for the BJP across India.

POTENTIAL DETERMINANTS OF BJP SUPPORT

The aim of this chapter's analysis is to separately consider the determinants of *individual*-level support for the BJP among elite and non-elite constituencies. My theoretical argument anticipates contact with the BJP's movement affiliates (specifically those providing welfare) to be a primary determinant of subaltern support for the party. By contrast, I expect upper caste supporters to be distinguished by their support for the BJP's cultural and economic platform. To test these arguments, I separately tested several logistic regression models among upper and lower caste samples. The dependent variable for these analyses was coded 1 if a voter supported the BJP in the 2004 national elections, and 0 otherwise. As I am interested in direct support for the party, I did not code votes for its coalition partners as positive outcomes in these specifications.

I regressed this outcome variable on six explanatory factors, each of which was carefully chosen and is theoretically justified in the next section. The first three test my key arguments about the varying reasons for which elite and non-elite citizens vote for the BJP. The second three were included for two reasons. First, all three are important potential determinants of BJP support in their own right. Second, they are also important potential confounders of my central contention that Hindu nationalist movement organizations played a major role in recruiting Dalit and Adivasi votes for the BJP.[7] Consequently, each of these three variables must be included in any test of my core argument.

Key Explanatory Variables

1. Associational Membership
As a party embedded within a broader social movement, the BJP has long been argued to hold a comparative organizational advantage over its rivals, with the possible exception of leftist parties in some states. However, whereas the latter are seen to have well-developed formal party organizations, the BJP's particular advantage has stemmed from its access to movement networks that remain formally outside the party arena. Is there evidence that these non-electoral networks helped the BJP at the polls? To answer this question, I examine responses

[7] Ray 2003; Achen 2005.

to a question on the survey asking voters if they were members of "non-party associations." This encompassing term included the sub-categories of "religious associations" and "welfare organizations" that Hindu nationalist movement organizations fall under.[8] I constructed a binary indicator, *Membership*, coded 1 for voters answering yes, and 0 otherwise.

Unfortunately, the survey instrument prevented me from identifying voter contact with specific associations, which remains a task for subsequent portions of the analysis. However, this measure remains extremely useful in assessing the plausibility of my argument across a national sample of voters. If Hindu nationalist organizations delivered the BJP a comparative organizational advantage over its rivals at the polls, then the party should fare better with associational members than with nonmembers. Further, this advantage should specifically manifest among the subaltern voters these non-electoral affiliates are tasked with recruiting. Conversely, I do not anticipate *Membership* to significantly predict elite support for the BJP, as I argue that upper castes are primarily drawn to the party's cultural and economic platform.

2. Communalism

Citizens who view Hindu nationalism more favorably might reasonably be expected to support the BJP at higher rates than their less sympathetic co-ethnics.[9] To evaluate this possibility, I include a variable, *Communalism*, which measured support for the signature ideological demand of Hindu nationalism across a four-point scale. Specifically, it measured agreement with the controversial call for a temple dedicated to the god Ram to exclusively replace the mosque demolished by Hindu protestors in the northern town of Ayodhya in 1992. Again, I expect support for this agenda to be a key predictor of elite support for the BJP, but not of subaltern support. It is worth noting that the results presented in the next section are robust to using alternative indicators of communal beliefs provided by the survey instrument. For example, the results don't change if we substitute a measure of voter agreement with the need to ban religious conversions, which has also come to occupy an important place within the Hindutva platform.[10]

3. Economic Liberalization

The symbiotic relations between the BJP and its non-electoral partners emphasized by my argument should not obscure their real disagreements. One

---

[8] Membership was based on responses to Question 18 and Question 19 on the 2004 NES. The first question asked if a respondent was a member of a religious/caste organization, and the second if a respondent belonged to cooperatives, farmer's associations, trade unions, welfare organizations, or cultural and sports organizations.

[9] See Jaffrelot 1993; Hansen 1999; Rajagopal 2001.

[10] Results for this test are in this book's online supplement (Table A.8). As I discuss at greater length in Chapters 4 and 5, this preoccupation with conversion is rooted in fears of the proselytizing efforts of minority religions, especially among Dalit and Adivasi communities.

point on which the BJP and some of its movement affiliates have openly differed is support for measures of economic liberalization. For its part, the movement's non-electoral wings remain largely wedded to economic nationalism (termed *swadeshi*) and oppose deregulating measures that have been incrementally implemented since the 1990s. However, as discussed in Chapter 2, the BJP broke dramatically with its movement partners on this issue once it became clear that many upper caste voters, particularly those outside the Congress's patronage network, supported market reforms. Past studies have noted that "the advocacy of less state intervention by the BJP gives the party an identity on economic matters different from that of other political parties."[11]

If this is the case, then it is possible that both elite and non-elite respondents who favor liberalization are more likely to support the BJP than those opposing such measures. However, my own argument anticipates such economic policy preferences will only distinguish upper caste supporters of the BJP. I operationalize these preferences through a variable, *Liberalization*, which is a twelve-point index measuring agreement with four broad reforms aimed at reducing the size of the public sector and providing a larger role for the private sector in the national economy.[12]

Control Variables

1. *Religiosity*

It is important to distinguish between a commitment to a religious political ideology and spiritual devotion: to be a devout Muslim or Hindu is not equivalent to being an Islamist or Hindu nationalist. It is possible the BJP will do better among pious voters irrespective of the level of their support for Hindu nationalism specifically. Pious upper castes might be especially drawn to the BJP's pro-Hindu rhetoric.

Among more disadvantaged Hindus, higher levels of piety might shift the determinants of electoral choice away from material concerns and toward social issues on which they hold positions closer to those of the BJP.[13] Yet, higher levels of religiosity might also plausibly make these poor citizens more likely to join the BJP's welfare affiliates. As religiosity might therefore confound the key relationship of interest among Dalits and Adivasis, accounting for it is especially important.

Empirically, I follow Chhibber in utilizing a composite measure of voter piety based on several survey questions pertaining to religious life.[14] Specifically, I use principal component analysis to construct an index variable, *Religiosity*, out of

[11] Chhibber 1997, p. 633.
[12] The statements are taken from Q30b, c, d, and e on the NES 2004 questionnaire. The measure is constructed using principal component analysis.
[13] Manza and Brooks 1997; Norris 2004.
[14] Chhibber 1999.

responses to questions asking how often voters pray, how many times they go to temple, how frequently they keep religious fasts, and how frequently they attend religious services.[15]

2. Income

One potential explanation of the BJP's growing success with Dalits and Adivasis is that the party has primarily recruited the economically elite strata within these lower caste categories. Partly as a result of the history of mandated quotas for members of these communities in legislative and public administrative institutions, there has been some financial differentiation even within lower caste and tribal populations.[16] As individuals from within these communities ascend the class hierarchy, they might be more inclined to support an elite party than their less financially fortunate co-ethnics for a number of reasons.[17] First, as their incomes swell, these voters might also genuinely find more in common with the economic demands of upper castes. Second, some scholars have argued that as these subaltern elites enjoy improvements in material conditions, they also begin striving for higher social status: "Despite coming from similar social origin, one does find a perceptible difference between the experiences, grievances and aspirations of the Dalit masses and that of the Dalit middle classes. These middle class Dalits have a desire to assimilate with the upper caste middle class ... [to] imitate them in their thinking and behavior."[18] The new elite identity these primary beneficiaries of sustained reservations (popularly termed the *creamy layer* within India) seek to acquire might make them more susceptible to the Hindutva's cultural ethos.[19] Such a process – dubbed "sanskritization" by Indian sociologists – might not only entail supporting the BJP but also joining Hindu nationalist organizations historically associated with elitist traditions of cultural practice.[20]

Thus, income serves as another important confounding factor to account for among subaltern respondents. Among upper castes, the BJP's elitist cultural and economic platform might also hold greater appeal for financially well-off voters than for their less fortunate co-ethnics. I therefore include a categorical variable

---

[15] Q34a and b, and Q34aa, ac from the NES 2004. The principal component analysis was conducted separately within elite and non-elite subsamples, and so the exact weights within the index vary across the two groups. I am mindful of the distinction made by some scholars between measures of religious "participation" and "belief" (Huber 2005). However, separate indices based purely on attendance have a nearly identical impact as those based on belief, and so I present results using the original composite index here.

[16] Chaudhury 2004.

[17] Shah 1994, p. 60.

[18] Quotes from Pendse 2005 in Gatade 2009.

[19] Subramanian 2006. However, it also bears noting that despite the growth of this creamy layer, the correlation between caste and class remains very strong in India, for a variety of reasons ranging from lack of access to public resources to discrimination on the part of employers (see Newman and Thorat 2007).

[20] See Srinivas 1956.

Income, which measures the household monthly income of the respondent, in my analysis of both constituencies.[21]

3. Ethnic (Caste) Leader Influence

How might the salience of nonreligious ethnic identities, specifically those of caste, affect support for the BJP? As a party that has been traditionally associated with both the cultural and material interests of upper castes, it is plausible to assume that the party might do particularly well with elite voters for whom caste identities hold significant political salience. However, beyond this privileged base, the BJP has hoped to downplay caste distinctions to overcome the electoral liabilities of its Brahmin-Bania image. Given this elite image, the party might be less likely to attract non-elite voters who are politically motivated by their caste identities. At the same time, poor voters strongly politicized along caste lines will plausibly be less likely to join Hindu nationalist organizations, which often preach the importance of subsuming intra-faith caste distinctions to their flock. Strongly politicized caste identities thus constitute a third important potential confounder to account for among non-elite respondents.

One useful measure of the political salience of caste identities is whether individuals look to co-ethnic leaders when making decisions at the polls. My analysis includes a binary variable (*Caste Influence*) coded 1 for those voters who cited their caste community leaders as the most important political influence on their electoral choices and 0 otherwise. I expect the BJP to fare better among upper castes heavily influenced by their co-ethnic leaders. However, I expect the reverse to be true among Dalits and Adivasis. This latter expectation seems plausible, as lower caste ethnic leaders often find their own positions to be threatened by the encompassing language of Hindu nationalism. As we see in Chapter 6, such threats prompt many subaltern leaders to vigorously oppose the activities of both the BJP and its non-electoral affiliates.

Before proceeding to the results of my analysis, it is useful to briefly review how I anticipate each factor listed here will affect the likelihood of BJP support. My theory proposes two primary implications for empirical assessment. First, I have argued that elite supporters of the BJP are drawn to its economic and cultural platform, whereas poor voters are not. Thus, communal values and support for economic liberalization should identify BJP supporters within the former sample, but not the latter. Second, I anticipate contact with non-electoral associations to distinguish subaltern supporters of the BJP, but not its elite backers. In addition to these key implications, I have outlined why increasing levels of piety and income might plausibly increase the likelihood of a voter from any caste constituency backing the party. However, although I expect the

---

[21] The scale of this variable ran from 1 to 7, with the lowest category (1) indicating a monthly income below Rs. 1000 (roughly $25) and the highest (7) indicating a monthly income of more than Rs. 20,000 (roughly $500). The results do not change if we substitute a broader measure of asset ownership using principal component analysis.

salience of caste identities to increase the likelihood of elites voting for the BJP, I anticipate it will reduce the likelihood of non-elites doing so.

TESTING THE DETERMINANTS OF BJP SUPPORT

The general specification of the models tested in this section can be written as

$$logit(\pi) = \alpha + \beta 1 Membership + \beta 2 Liberalization + \beta 3 Communalism$$
$$+ \beta 4 Religiosity + \beta 5 Income + \beta 6 Caste\ Influence + \varepsilon,$$

where $logit(\pi)$ is the logit function of probabilityϵ that a voter supports the BJP. Before testing the models, the data was checked and cleaned of any individual observations that exerted high levels of influence on parameter estimates, and independent variables were inspected for potential issues of collinearity within both elite and non-elite samples.[22] The models are estimated with heteroskedasticity – robust standard errors clustered by state. As the analysis is interested in assessing the determinants of individual voter choices, all four models also include state fixed effects to account for unobserved state-level differences that influence patterns of BJP support. The coefficients for each explanatory variable in the analysis should therefore be interpreted as indicating its impact on distinguishing supporters of the BJP from non-supporters within the same state.[23]

Comparing Elite and Non-elite Constituencies

The analysis was conducted separately on the elite and non-elite samples of the 2004 NES. The first two columns of Table 3.1 report the results for upper castes. Model 1 regresses BJP support on the six explanatory variables discussed earlier, along with standard demographic controls measuring a respondent's age, gender, and level of education. Model 2 used a dependent variable specified to identify core upper caste supporters of the BJP, defined as those who voted for the BJP in both the 1999 and 2004 national elections.

The results show that contact with nonparty associations did little to distinguish upper caste supporters of the BJP, which was insignificant across all four specifications. Instead, elite supporters were consistently distinguished by their support for economic liberalization and Hindu nationalist ideology. Moving from strongly opposing to strongly supporting market reforms increased the predicted probability of supporting the BJP from 35 to 49 percentage points

---

[22] Collinearity between the independent variables was not found to be an issue (the variance inflation factor of each of the variables was barely more than 1). High influence was defined as three times the mean value of the Pregibon's delta-beta statistic within each sample. The results are unchanged if using a standard of twice the mean value instead.

[23] The results are robust to specifications excluding these fixed effects or using parliamentary constituency-level fixed effects instead.

TABLE 3.1. *Determinants of support for the BJP*

	Upper Castes		Dalits and Adivasis	
	Voted for BJP	Core BJP Supporter	Voted for BJP	Switched to BJP (1999–2004)
	(1)	(2)	(3)	(4)
Membership	.271	.234	.466**	.331*
	(.177)	(.196)	(.176)	(.140)
Liberalization	.045**	.064***	.051	.039
	(.018)	(.164)	(.029)	(.031)
Communalism	.135*	.147*	.032	.061
Control Variables	(.067)	(.076)	(.047)	(.049)
Income	.052*	.057	.059*	.036
	(.024)	(.030)	(026)	(.034)
Caste Influence	−.477**	−.288	−.408**	−.471
	(.176)	(.164)	(.151)	(.319)
Religiosity	.048***	.040**	.060**	.050*
	(.015)	(.015)	(.023)	(.026)
Age	.005	.005	−.002	−.008*
	(.004)	(.004)	(.002)	(.003)
Male	.022	−.010	.150*	.076
	(.053)	(.046)	(.075)	(.115)
Education	.088***	.088**	.021	.011
	(.029)	(.030)	(.025)	(.046)
Constant	−4.056***	−3.841***	−4.081***	−4.287***
	(.238)	(.275)	(.398)	(.564)
States	17	17	17	17
N	2637	2637	5177	4454
Percentage predicted correctly	72.81	74.94	81.11	88.95
Log Likelihood	−1435.38	−1442.351	−2244.95	−1375.259

***p<.001 **p<.01 *p<.05

Note: The specifications shown are logistic regression models with robust standard errors that have been corrected for clustering by state. State-level fixed effects included but not reported here.

across the models tested. Put differently, an upper caste voter who supports liberalization was roughly 40 percent more likely to support the BJP than a co-ethnic within the same state who opposed such policies. Support for Hindu nationalist ideology also emerged as a comparably significant predictor of BJP support, increasing the likelihood of voting for the party by 10 percentage points (from 35 to 45 percentage points, or 30 percent) on average. Further, the results of Model 2 indicate that cultural and economic preferences also distinguish upper castes who voted for the party in the 1999 and 2004 national elections. Thus, these programmatic preferences specifically identify the party's loyal elite supporters.

As expected, the BJP also did better among wealthier, more educated, and pious upper castes. Whereas scholars have anticipated that the BJP particularly appeals to upwardly mobile non-elites, this analysis suggests the party in fact enjoys the support of a privileged creamy layer of upper caste Hindus. However, against expectations, the party appears to fare worse among elites who are heavily influenced by their caste community leaders. Thus, Hindu nationalists appear adversely affected by the increasing salience of caste identities even within their traditional support base. One potential explanation for this finding could be that caste leaders and the organizations they run, even within upper caste circles, are threatened by the subsuming pan-Hindu aspirations of the Sangh Parivar.

How did these results compare with those among non-elite voters? Were subaltern supporters of the BJP distinguished along the same dimensions as the party's upper caste backers? If so, the puzzle of poor voter support for the BJP could simply be a product of the growing appeal of the party's economic and cultural platform among a wider swathe of Indians. Or did the party's success among non-elites stem from a different source than its popularity among upper castes, as my theory suggests?

Model 3 in Table 3.1 replicates Model 1's specification among the sample of Dalit and Adivasi voters. The results reveal some similarities between the two samples: wealthier and more pious subaltern voters were also more likely to support the BJP, whereas those citing their co-ethnic community leaders as important electoral influences were less likely to do so. However, this latter result was expected among non-elite respondents, as politically salient caste identities were anticipated to reduce the likelihood of lower caste support for an upper caste party.

However, the analysis also reveals some striking dissimilarities between the party's elite and non-elite supporters. First, whereas *Membership* was an insignificant determinant of elite support, it emerges as the most consistent and influential predictor of BJP support among non-elite voters. Indeed, contact with non-electoral associations doubles the probability of subaltern support for the BJP (from 14 to 30 percentage points).[24] This impact was the largest of any of the explanatory factors by some margin, with no other variable registering more than a 10 percentage point effect.[25]

Equally strikingly, the results indicate that the BJP's support with lower caste and tribal voters is not being forged through programmatic linkages. In stark contrast to the results within the upper caste sample, non-elite supporters of the

---

[24] Predicted values were obtained using 1,000 simulations for each predicted value estimate, holding other variables constant at their mean values.

[25] For a list of all the substantive effects, see Appendix B, Table B.2.

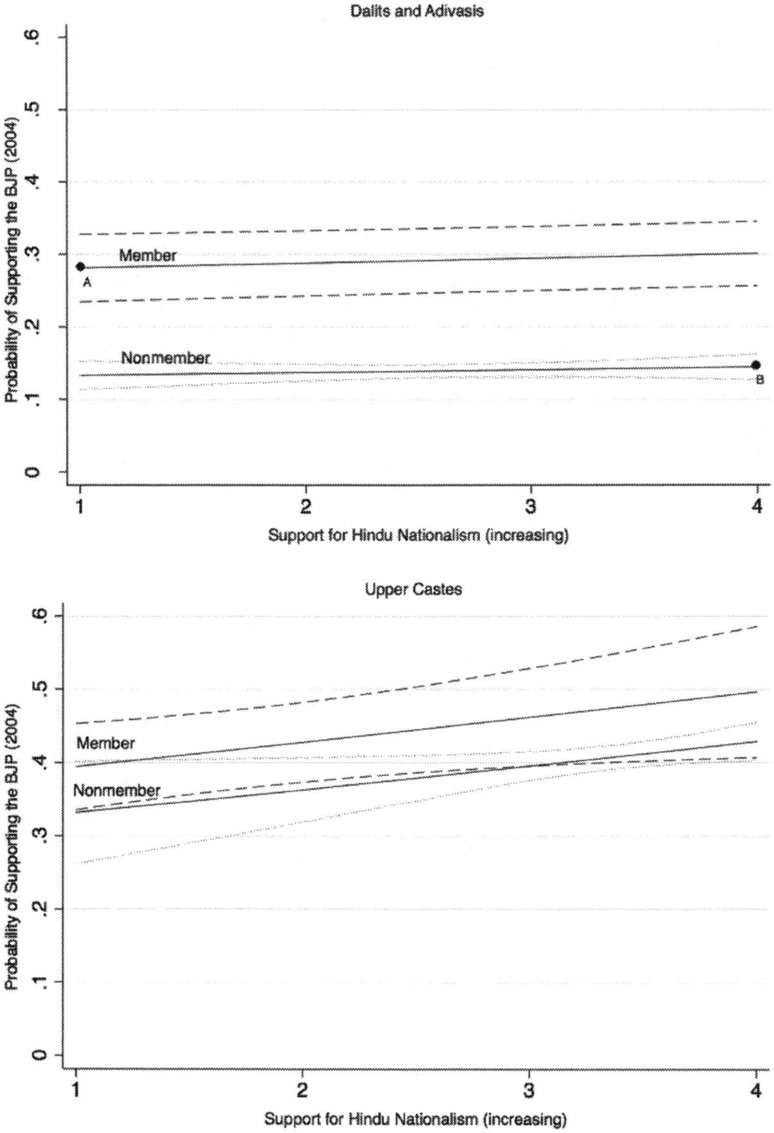

FIGURE 3.1. Impact of associational membership vs. support for Hindutva
Note: Dashed lines indicate 95 percent confidence intervals for members; dotted lines indicate 95 percent confidence intervals for nonmembers.

BJP were not distinguished by their support for economic liberalization or Hindu nationalist agendas. The consistent insignificance of *Communalism* might particularly surprise observers who view the BJP's support as centrally driven by ideological affiliation. Yet, the top panel of Figure 3.1 shows that the impact of associational membership far outstripped that of Hindutva among Dalit and Adivasi respondents. Even a *strongly secular* subaltern member (indicated by point "A") was twice as likely to support the BJP (28 percent) as a *strongly Hindu nationalist* nonmember (14.5 percent, indicated by point "B").

The comparison of organizational and ideological effects is not only striking within the Dalit and Adivasi sample but also between elite and non-elite constituencies. The two panels of Figure 3.1 compare the substantive influences of associational incorporation and communal values across upper and lower castes. For Dalits and Adivasis, membership increased the likelihood of BJP support by roughly 15 percentage points regardless of a respondent's communal values (the gap between the two solid lines in the top panel). Meanwhile, shifts in Hindu nationalist beliefs (the slope of these lines) produced a shift of less than 3 percentage points for both members and nonmembers. In contrast, among upper castes the weight of these influences was completely reversed (see the bottom panel of Figure 3.1). Highly communal upper castes were 10 percentage points more likely to support the BJP than more secular co-ethnics, more than double the impact of membership within this sample.

The comparative analysis in Figure 3.1 is not intended to minimize the importance of ideological factors within the workings of Hindu nationalism. Indeed, my analysis demonstrates that affiliation to Hindutva is an influential determinant of the BJP's appeal within its traditional upper caste base. Further, I will later demonstrate how ideological commitments were also central in motivating movement activists to expand the party's appeal among Dalits and Adivasis. However, my findings do strongly challenge the popular assumption that communal attitudes necessarily underpin all electoral support for the BJP. Poor voter support for the party need not necessarily signal intrinsic support for Hindutva, or an ideological false consciousness engineered by manipulative party elites.[26] Instead, my analysis suggests the need for developing more nuanced understandings of the complex role ideology plays within the success of faith-based elite parties.

Figure 3.2 provides a similar comparison of the substantive effects of membership (which was statistically significant for only the Dalit and Adivasi sample) and support for economic liberalization (significant for only the upper caste sample). Once again, nonparty membership had a far larger substantive influence than policy preferences among lower caste and tribal electorates, and these influences were reversed among the upper caste sample.

The arresting divergences illustrated in Figures 3.1 and 3.2 are consistent with a theory of elite parties indirectly recruiting poor voters through non-electoral organizations while maintaining direct programmatic linkages with rich voters. At the same time, evidence from India also suggests hard limits to this strategy. Replicating the tests used in columns 3 and 4 of Table 3.1 on the NES survey's sample of poor Muslims and Christians finds that nonparty membership does

---

[26] See Teltumbde 2005.

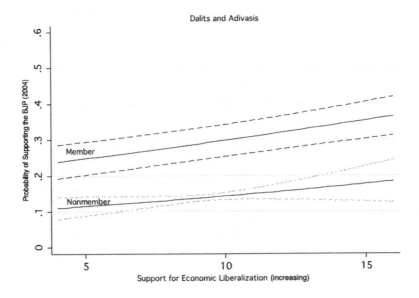

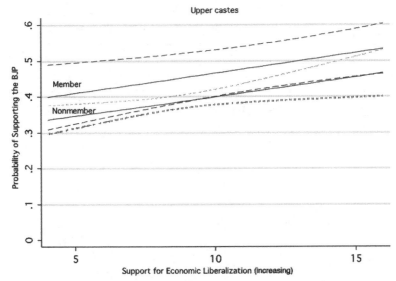

FIGURE 3.2. Impact of associational membership vs. economic preferences
Note: Dashed lines indicate 95 percent confidence intervals for members; dotted lines indicate 95 percent confidence intervals for nonmembers.

not exert the same positive effect on support for the BJP among poor respondents of either faith.[27] Further, the survey found relatively few poor Muslims or Christians to be incorporated within nonparty associations in the first place. The NES data cannot however discern whether these low numbers stem from Hindu nationalist aversion to incorporating religious minorities (supply side) or from the latter remaining wary of affiliating with a movement whose ideological mandate they distrust (demand side). Adjudicating between these two options remains an important question for further inquiry.

CHECKING THE RESULTS

The key finding of the prior section was the striking impact of non-electoral organizations on Dalit and Adivasi support for the BJP. Before proceeding, it is worth pausing to consider several concerns regarding the robustness of this central result.[28] First, a skeptical reader might well wonder if the impact of associational networks was restricted to only a small fraction of BJP supporters. Such a possibility is anticipated by prior accounts of Indian politics that have argued that the penetration of civil society associations within Indian society remains weak.[29] Such concerns prove somewhat unfounded, as these associations encompassed a nontrivial number of Dalit and Adivasi respondents (18 percent). More importantly, there was considerable heterogeneity in the partisan profile of associational members, who constituted three out of every ten subaltern BJP supporters (28 percent). This rate was double the average of all other parties (16 percent). It was also significantly higher than the corresponding figures for the BJP's two biggest national rivals (according to vote share) among lower caste and tribal voters: the Indian National Congress (15 percent), and the Dalit-led Bahujan Samaj Party (10 percent).[30]

A second set of concerns focuses on the importance of voter ties to political parties themselves. My argument emphasizes the importance of the BJP's non-electoral affiliates in recruiting poor voters. Toward that end, I showed that the party enjoys an advantage among poor voters incorporated within nonparty associations. But what if the BJP enjoyed a similar advantage among poor voters who were members of party organizations? Such a finding would suggest the BJP benefits from its general organizational strength, rather than the specific work of its movement affiliates.

---

[27] "Poor" religious minorities were defined as those within the bottom two income categories on the survey, which was roughly half of each sample. The full results of the regressions are available in the online web supplement.

[28] Unless otherwise noted, the detailed results from tests referenced but not presented in this section are available in this book's online supplement.

[29] Chhibber 1999.

[30] According to the 2004 NES, these three parties combined to win 70 percent of the votes cast by members of these two communities.

To check this possibility, I substitute a measure of individual membership within political parties for the nonparty membership variable in my analysis. I find that among non-elite voters, party membership had a slightly negative and statistically insignificant impact on support for the BJP.[31] Among upper castes however, this variable positively and significantly distinguishes BJP supporters, with party members emerging as 36 percentage points more likely than non-members to support the BJP. Rather than trouble my argument, these divergent findings reconfirm the contours of the division of labor I specify.

A related issue is whether the impact of membership is really underpinned by a voter's preferences for the BJP itself. Given their conceptual proximity to vote choice, such partisan preferences are notoriously tricky to include as explanatory variables within analyses of electoral decisions. Yet, if the impact of membership remains robust even after including such a strong predictor, our confidence in the autonomous impact of nonparty associations will be significantly improved. I therefore retested Model 3 from Table 3.1 with several measures of respondent satisfaction with the BJP. These tests found membership's impact to be statistically (p<.001) and substantively (15 percentage points) robust to controlling for such satisfaction with the BJP.[32]

A third potential problem is that associational incorporation may have followed rather than preceded a voter's decision to support the BJP. Such a possibility is obviously difficult to preclude with cross-sectional data. However, the survey instrument did provide some empirical leverage for addressing this issue. Although the NES does not provide panel data across multiple elections, respondents to the 2004 survey were asked whom they voted for in the previous national election held in 1999. This information can help ascertain whether nonparty organizations are winning new votes for the BJP or simply attracting the party's prior supporters.

If organizational inclusion preceded a change in electoral preferences, we would expect members to be more likely than nonmembers to shift to supporting the BJP in 2004. To examine if this was in fact the case, Model 4 of Table 3.1 repeats the analysis on a sample that excluded voters who supported the BJP in 1999. In effect, this meant that the dependent variable now measures if a voter shifted to supporting the BJP between 1999 and 2004. The results indicate a continued significant influence of membership, this time in distinguishing new supporters of the BJP. This continued effect suggests that rather than exclusively

---

[31] This insignificance persists if we run the analysis with party and nonparty membership measures simultaneously, and the inclusion of party membership does not confound the robust effect of nonparty organizations. Full results are in online appendix Table A.4.

[32] The key measure of satisfaction draws on a five-point response to the question: "What is your opinion of the NDA [central government coalition headed by the BJP] performance during the past five years?" (Q12 on NES 2004). The impact of nonparty associations is also robust to controlling for a respondent's explicit preference for the BJP over the Congress on a range of issues (corruption, governance, employment, and terrorism) and for "liking" the BJP. Results in Tables A.5 and A.6 in online appendix.

attracting previous supporters of the BJP, contact with nonparty associations corresponds to an increased likelihood of respondents turning toward the party. The *Membership* variable also continued to have a strong substantive impact in this specification, making a voter 9.27 percentage points more likely to have shifted to supporting the BJP between these two national elections.[33]

Of course, this specification doesn't preclude a voter from deciding to switch over to the BJP at some point between 1999 and 2004, and only then joining a nonparty association. However, associational inclusion also increases the likelihood of BJP support among respondents who reported making their 2004 voting decision within a few days of the election. Further, membership increases the likelihood of such late deciders switching to vote for the BJP. In this last specification, membership necessarily precedes the decision to begin supporting Hindu nationalists, unless the respondent decided to join a nonparty association on election day or just before. Although not irrefutable, these tests provide substantial evidence that poor voters shifted toward the BJP after their organizational incorporation, and not before.[34]

A fourth potential concern is that the analysis remains dependent on observational data, where the "treatment" of nonparty membership was not randomly assigned. The problem with nonrandom assignments of treatment is well known: it is impossible to assume that the treatment is independent of observed and non-observed baseline variables.[35] Thus, it might be that members systematically differ from nonmembers in some additional manner that compromises our ability to isolate the autonomous influence of membership itself. As randomization of this treatment via experimental techniques raises practical and ethical concerns, the analysis instead needs to work toward fulfilling what Sekhon has termed a "strong ignorability of assignment," if not actual independence of the treatment selection.[36]

To do this, I first examine whether Dalit and Adivasi members systematically vary from nonmembers within the NES sample. Table 3.2a indicates there were in fact statistically significant differences between these two groups across the other major explanatory variables included within the analysis (although these differences are substantively quite small). Given these differences, it would be helpful to prune the sample of voters in a way that minimizes these differentials between members and nonmembers, in order to better isolate the impact of membership itself.

---

[33] This increase was from 15.1 percentage points (for a nonmember) to 24.3 percentage points (for a member), a jump of roughly 60 percent.

[34] Alternatively, people may have joined associations before 1999, voted for a party other than the BJP, and then changed their minds in 2004. However, this sequencing is less problematic for my argument, which emphasizes that organizational incorporation precedes vote choice, not necessarily that these shifts must be immediate.

[35] Sekhon 2008, p. 3.

[36] Ibid., p. 7.

An increasingly popular way to produce such overlap is through matching analysis, which trims the data sample to retain only those individuals within each group who are as similar as possible with respect to a given set of characteristics.[37] There are several ways to specify the contours of the match, with the overall goal of minimizing the distance between the treatment and control groups. One common matching protocol is nearest-neighbor propensity score matching, which first assesses each observation's likelihood or propensity to have been treated, based on observed covariates (in this case, the five listed variables plus age, education, and gender).[38] Each treated case is then matched to one control case with the closest propensity score (its nearest neighbor). As the far right column of Table 3.2a shows, this matching procedure does improve the balance between members and nonmembers, eliminating significant differences between these two groups across the five key potential confounding variables.[39] Is the impact of associational membership robust to this matching? Table 3.2b reveals that it is: members remained 10.5 percentage points more likely to support the BJP than their nearest neighbor nonmembers, a 60 percent increase that was statistically significant.

Matching on observed covariates is of course no panacea. One crucial concern is that the results cannot account for the possibility of unobserved or omitted variables that might increase the ex ante likelihood of members supporting the BJP, relative to nonmembers. Whereas estimating the magnitude of this potential bias with observational data is impossible, we can use the protocol developed by Rosenbaum to estimate how strong such a confounding effect would have to be to undermine the results of the matching analysis.[40] This sensitivity analysis (reported in Table 3.2c) finds that an omitted variable would have to make members 70 percent more likely to support the BJP than matched nonmembers to confound the impact of membership.[41] It is difficult to think of an omitted variable that would make individual members so much more likely to support the BJP than their nearest neighbor nonmembers who are otherwise so similar to them on so many important potential dimensions.[42]

---

[37] Ho et al. 2007, pp. 210–11.

[38] More specifically, such propensity scores generally refer to the predicted probability of receiving the treatment based on certain observed predictors or covariates, which are generally obtained from logistic regression analysis.

[39] More than 97 percent of matched pairs had a propensity score difference of .001 on a 0–1 scale, and none were greater than .01; 85 percent of control units were used only once.

[40] Rosenbaum (2002). For propensity score matching, I use the *psmatch2* package developed by Lueven and Sianesi (2003), and for post-match sensitivity analyses, I use the *mhbounds* package developed by Becker and Caliendo (2007).

[41] This result uses the standard $p<.05$ threshold of statistical significance.

[42] These results were also robust to other techniques such as exact matching, which matches each member exactly to each nonmember across all five potential confounding variables (results are available in the online supplement).

TABLE 3.2. *Propensity matching and sensitivity analysis*

a: *Balance statistics of potential confounders (pre- and post-match)*

Variable Name (scale in parentheses)	Mean Score (Members)	Mean Score (Nonmembers)	Means Difference (unmatched sample)	Means Difference (matched sample)
Liberalization(4–16)	9.77	9.39	.38***	.09
Ethnic Influence(0–1)	.08	.11	−.03***	.015
Income(1–8)	2.38	2.12	.26***	.05
Communalism(1–4)	2.70	2.77	−.07**	.00
Religiosity(5–20)	12.84	12.52	.32***	.09

b: *Average treatment effect of membership*

	Probability of Supporting BJP		
	Members	Nonmembers	Average Treatment Effect
Unmatched	.301	.136	.165***
Matched	.280	.174	.105***

c: *Sensitivity analysis*

Odds of Differential Assignment	Significance of Assumption (p-values)	
	Overestimation of Treatment Effect	Underestimation of Treatment Effect
10%	.000	.000
20%	.000	.000
30%	.000	.000
40%	.001	.000
50%	.005	.000
60%	.025	.000
70%	.077	.000
80%	.180	.000

Note: *p<.05 **p<.01 ***p<.001

Although we cannot definitively preclude this possibility, the sensitivity analysis, along with the numerous checks presented in this section, help broadly confirm the important positive effect of nonparty networks in generating subaltern voter support for the BJP.

A fifth and final potential concern with this chapter's analysis is whether the impact of membership is a function of nonparty organizations that are not run by Hindu nationalists. This important concern stems directly from the broad wording of the survey question used to construct the membership measure. As the NES itself gives us limited leverage on this matter, I rely on additional data to address this issue in Chapters 4 and 5.

COMPARING DETERMINANTS OF LOWER CASTE VOTER SUPPORT

The results thus far emphasize the importance of non-electoral organizations in winning and shifting non-elite support toward the BJP. Does this reliance on external networks distinguish the BJP from its primary challengers? To assess this question, I compared the determinants of Dalit and Adivasi support for the four formations that received the largest number of votes from these two constituencies in the 2004 election: the Congress, the BJP, the Dalit-led Bahujan Samaj Party (BSP), and a leftist coalition of India's two major Communist parties.[43] I estimated a multinomial logit model that used the Congress as a base category, a decision informed by the party's centrist positioning and its longtime electoral dominance among Dalits and Adivasis. The coefficients of the model reported in Table 3.3 can therefore be interpreted as the impact of a given variable on the likelihood of a voter supporting the BJP, BSP, or Communists, relative to the likelihood of their supporting the Congress.

The results help shed light on the different sources of appeal these major parties hold for Dalit and Adivasi voters. The first column reiterates the importance of nonparty networks to the BJP's success. The positive influence of membership is even stronger in the specification used in Table 3.3, where the party is directly compared with the Congress. This enhanced impact makes sense given the latter party's organizational trajectory. Whereas the Congress did have relatively robust extra-party networks while it was at the helm of India's nationalist movement, these resources eroded considerably during its postcolonial incumbency. As it shifted to increasingly rely on elite-dominated patronage networks to capture lower caste vote banks, the Congress's incentives to directly mobilize poor constituencies concomitantly decreased.[44] Further damages to its organizational resources were self-inflicted by factional disputes and national leaders looking to centralize authority.[45] Given this deterioration, it is not

---

[43] I collapsed the vote share of the two major Communist formations, the Communist Party of India and the Communist Party of India (Marxist) into one party category, which is defensible as these parties are closely allied and contest elections collaboratively.

[44] Nehru himself foresaw this change in a letter to Gandhi in which he worried that with sustained incumbency, the party's personnel would descend to "the level of ordinary politicians" (Herring 1988, p. 405).

[45] Kolhi 1990; Kochanek in Hasan 2002.

TABLE 3.3. *Comparing determinants of support for major parties (multinomial logit model, Congress base party)*

	Party Voted For in 2004		
	Elite Party (BJP)	Ethnic Party (BSP)	Leftist Party (CPI/M)
Membership	.714***	.239	.504
	(.176)	(.324)	(.318)
Liberalization	.002	−.190***	−.100*
	(.027)	(.050)	(.043)
Communalism	.038	−.125	.028
	(.044)	(.066)	(.080)
Ethnic Influence	−.297	.836***	.045
	(.200)	(.237)	(.390)
Income	.049	−.136	.037
	(.039)	(.052)	(.086)
Religiosity	.056*	−.083	.024
	(.023)	(.060)	(.020)
Age	−.003	.005	−.002
	(.002)	(.005)	(.005)
Male	.135	.009	−.135
	(.083)	(.134)	(.147)
Education	.013	.037	.002
	(.034)	(.057)	(.050)
Constant	−2.968***	−1.166	−1.284*
	(.367)	(.709)	(.516)
Number of States	17	% predicted correctly	81.53%
		Log	−2609.171
N	3262	Likelihood	

***=p<.001 **=p<.01 *=p<.05

Note: State-level fixed effects included. Robust standard errors have been corrected for clustering by state.

surprising that the BJP's reliance on non-electoral organizations is even more starkly apparent when directly compared with India's onetime hegemonic party.

By contrast, the results in the middle column of Table 3.3 indicate that the strongest determinant of support for the Dalit-led BSP was the influence of co-ethnic caste leaders. The revealed importance of these leaders resonates with Chandra's emphasis on the importance of visible co-ethnics (albeit not specified in the survey instrument to be political candidates – the protagonists of her account) in attracting Dalit support for the BSP. The analysis cannot however provide leverage for assessing Chandra's argument as to why subaltern voters are attracted to parties with higher proportions of their co-ethnics. According to her study, this attraction is based on an expectation that subaltern leaders will funnel resources toward their co-ethnics and away from established upper caste circuits of patronage. Others have argued that these linkages also stem from the psychological and social benefits subaltern voters receive from seeing members of their community in powerful positions.[46] Irrespective of the exact mechanism at work, these results confirm the importance of local ethnic intermediaries as key channels through which the BSP links to its lower caste base.

Finally, the far right column of Table 3.3 reports lower caste backers of leftist parties to be distinguished from Congress voters only along an economic policy dimension. The communists, the most vocal and consistent critics of market reform in India, enjoy support from subaltern voters who are distinguished by their opposition to liberalization. This result largely conforms to conventional understandings of the party's relatively high dependence on policy-based programmatic linkages with poor voters in its regional strongholds.

Overall, the major national parties in India exhibit some clear differences in how they appear to appeal to poor voters. Whereas the left relies on economic policy positions, and the BSP on caste-based linkages, the BJP's dependence on nonparty networks for building a subaltern support base is confirmed by this comparative analysis. More broadly, the considerable heterogeneity in why subaltern voters support these major parties suggests the inadequacy of viewing any single factor, including caste identities or patronage politics, as centrally driving all poor voter behavior in India. Such monocausal explanations of political behavior, although theoretically parsimonious, are empirically unconvincing and obscure significant variations in the electoral decisions of similarly situated voters. Recognizing and analyzing such variation, as I have attempted to do here, is essential for our ability to more accurately explain the political choices of poor people in poor democracies.

CONCLUSION

The key dilemma laid out in this book is how elite parties can craft strategies that simultaneously appeal to the poor while retaining the affections of their elite base. To begin understanding how the BJP achieved some success in this endeavor, this chapter explored the determinants of the party's success among upper- and lower caste constituencies. Do elite and non-elite supporters of the BJP vote for the party for different reasons? Are such divergences consistent with the division of labor my theory emphasizes? Or does subaltern support for Hindu nationalism simply reflect the expanding appeal of the BJP's economic and cultural platform?

---

[46] See Lerche 1999; Pai 2004.

The large samples of the NES afforded the broadest possible investigation of these important questions. The results presented in this chapter reveal the widely varying sources of the BJP's appeal across different social constituencies. Among upper castes, the traditional base of Hindu nationalism, supporters of the BJP were marked by economic and ideological preferences matching the party's own positions. However, equivalent analyses of Dalit and Adivasi voters found no evidence of such programmatic linkages to the BJP. Instead, survey evidence reveals the importance of nonparty organizations in winning and shifting lower caste and tribal support toward the BJP.

Statistical tests revealed that the influence of these non-electoral networks was not confounded by income, ideological support for Hindu nationalism, membership within the BJP party, or even preexisting support for the party in prior elections. Matching analyses further confirmed that this result was not driven by systematic underlying differences between associational members and nonmembers. Finally, the BJP's reliance on these external affiliates was found to distinguish it from its primary challengers for subaltern votes.

In short, this segmented analysis provides initial evidence of a novel solution to the conundrum facing elite parties: an organizational division of labor between the party and its nonparty affiliates. Yet, even as the evidence in this chapter was well poised to suggest this striking strategy, it remains insufficient for confirming it. Most importantly, the survey data was unable to specify which nonparty organizations took the lead in mobilizing disadvantaged voters. Is there evidence that these organizations were specifically run by Hindu nationalists? If so, which of the movement's many organizational wings spearheaded non-elite recruitment? Building on the foundation laid by this chapter, the next chapter begins to address these more specific questions about how India's elite party forged an unlikely coalition of extremes.

4

Why an Elite Party Turned to Services

The BJP's experience suggests a novel solution to the dilemma facing elite parties. By outsourcing poor voter recruitment to their non-electoral affiliates, these parties can preserve their core-friendly programmatic orientation. Of course, this strategy is only available to those elite parties who have such affiliates to call upon in the first place. The introductory chapter outlined why such organizationally thick elite parties, both in India and elsewhere in the global south, are most likely to emerge out of religious social movements. These founding movements provide their party affiliates with access to dense organizational networks that can be deployed toward recruiting the poor. Yet, even organizationally thick elite parties must figure out which specific wings can successfully recruit poor communities. This challenge is particularly tricky if, as in India, subaltern citizens have traditionally kept their distance from the elite party and its movement affiliates. Given such difficulties, which organizations are best poised to spearhead poor voter recruitment?

In this chapter, I argue that within the broader panoply of the Hindu nationalist movement, it was the deliberate expansion of wings devoted to the provision of basic services that proved crucial in improving the BJP's fortunes with subaltern voters. I address three sets of questions prompted by this central claim. First, when and why did Hindu nationalists turn to welfare as a mobilizing strategy? Second, what was the nature of the services provided? Finally, is there any empirical evidence that subnational variation in Hindu nationalist service efforts corresponds to those in the BJP's electoral performance with Dalits and Adivasis?

Briefly, I argue that although welfare activities have always been a part of the Hindu nationalist agenda, the broad proliferation of service chapters for political purposes is a contemporary phenomenon. In the wake of their past failures at social expansion, the Sangh Parivar began developing its service network in the early 1990s. Service provision emerged as a popular option because it was uniquely able to appeal to poor voters and elite core supporters. Basic services provided clear and non-polarizing benefits with which to appeal to subaltern communities that had shied away from prior, more ideologically charged efforts. At the same time, private provision was attractive to elite supporters of the BJP, as it circumvented the need for the more painful concessions entailed by the strategic alternatives discussed in Chapter 2. Movement activists were meanwhile attracted by the potential of service activism to transform subaltern communities into loyal Hindu nationalists, and to undercut the appeal of Christian missionary welfare efforts. These dedicated cadres were thereby motivated to provide rudimentary services in difficult circumstances for a low wage. By minimizing the costs of poor voter outreach, these cadres enabled the BJP to continue to directly serve the programmatic interests of its upper caste core base.

The second part of this chapter then shifts to test some observable implications of my argument. First, I explain why service chapters were built in states with large subaltern populations and in states with higher proportions of religious minorities (particularly Christians). Next, I establish that the concentration of the Sangh's welfare chapters, but not its non-service networks, correlates strongly with the BJP's aggregate performance with lower caste and tribal voters. I also demonstrate that this observed association is not a product of the demographic criteria used to select where service chapters were built in the first place or of other features of a state's political and social arena.

A TURN TO SERVICE

Whereas the failure of Hindu nationalists to broaden their appeal through ethnic representation and communal agitations has received considerable commentary, other developments within the movement have received comparatively scant attention. Chief among these has been the marked expansion of Sangh chapters oriented to providing basic social services to Dalit and Adivasi communities. Service activities are certainly not a contemporary innovation within the Sangh's rich history of organizational activism. As the moniker Sangh Parivar (literally "family of organizations") itself makes clear, Hindu nationalists had long given priority to a "sanghathanist" (organizational) approach to growing their social presence and political clout. In accordance with this prioritization, the focus of Hindu nationalists for the first several decades following Indian independence remained on building a vast network of *shakhas* (community-level branches), each of which would mold its members to align with Hindutva's core doctrine.

Even in its early years, the Sangh's leaders contemplated the potential of service work to expand the movement's following even further. More than forty years ago, M. S. Golwalkar, a former Sangh Parivar *sarsanghchalak* (the highest leadership position within the movement), outlined how social work might enable Hindu nationalism to become a mass phenomenon that would reach even the poorest Hindus. Golwalkar notes in one of Hindu nationalism's foundational texts:

It is now up to us to go to those neglected brethren of our society and strive our utmost to better their living conditions. We will have to work out plans by which their primary physical needs and comforts could be satisfied. We will have to open schools, hostels and training courses to equip them to benefit from these schemes. Alongside this physical amelioration, love and pride in Hindu *Dharma* [traditions] and the spirit of identity with the rest of Hindus have to be rekindled in their minds.[1]

Balasaheb Deshpande, the founder of one of the Sangh's major service wings, also believed "service not agitation" would prove crucial to the movement's future success.[2]

Accordingly, the RSS, the central organization of the Sangh Parivar, has maintained a strong tradition of social work, especially in the provision of emergency relief. The organization garnered significant attention for its work with Hindu communities migrating from present-day Pakistan during the partition of the subcontinent in 1946–1947. The RSS also made a name for itself as a provider of effective relief during natural disasters, including the 1955 Punjab floods, the 1955 Tamil Nadu cyclone, and the 1977 cyclone in Andhra Pradesh.[3] Sangh leaders even tried to promote their own service credentials by suggesting the RSS acronym stood for "Ready for Selfless Service."[4] However, social work during this earlier period tended to be focused on events such as Partition, which could be easily linked to the overall goal of the movement to preserve Hindu society.[5] This initial focus on high-profile incidents meant that service efforts tended to be episodic, and not specifically targeted toward lower caste communities.

More quotidian efforts by Sangh organizations were also circumscribed in their ability to expand the movement's appeal, primarily because of their geographic and programmatic orientation. Everyday activities were concentrated within *shakhas*, local branches that primarily served the upper caste communities from which most Hindu nationalist *swayamsevaks* (volunteers) came. These chapters expanded considerably during the 1970s and 1980s but did not offer concrete social services such as health care or education to attendees. Instead, activities in the *shakha* focused on cultural and militaristic "recreational" activities designed to popularize Hindu nationalist doctrine. Not surprisingly, non-service wings that were ideologically explicit and located within elite neighborhoods primarily attracted upper caste sympathizers of the movement. Consequently, the BJP's comparative organizational advantage over

---

[1] Golwalkar 1966, p. 361.
[2] As quoted in *Seva Sadhana* (2008), p. 11 of the report.
[3] Malkani (1980) in his insider's portrait of the RSS, notes that during Partition, the RSS set up a Hindu *Sahayata Samiti* (Hindu Aid Society) and even issued a questionnaire to refugees, inquiring about their background and training, in its efforts to help rehabilitate them. The Sangh also organized similar relief efforts, although on a smaller scale, with refugees from East Pakistan in the 1950s. During the 1977 Andhra cyclone, Malkani says, "the name 'RSS' became so popular that at one stage the local government named its camp 'RSS' to attract villagers seeking relief."
[4] See "RSS means Ready for Selfless Service," 1980, p. 10.
[5] Malkani 1980, p. 153.

other parties, especially the rival Indian National Congress, did not necessarily translate into a denser presence among non-elite communities.[6]

In addition to their lack of a systematic organizational presence among the poor, the Sangh had to face the harsh reality that even its most successful communal mobilizations had failed to attract significant non-elite support. The Ram *Janmabhoomi* (birthplace of Ram) agitations outlined in Chapter 2 had palpably failed to develop a following among lower caste constituencies. Even as they pondered these disappointments, Hindu nationalists observed a surge in caste-based politics following the Mandal Commission's decision to extend quotas to a wider swathe of the electorate in 1990 (also discussed in Chapter 2). The confluence of their own failures and the rise of alternative caste-based political rivals dealt a double blow to the BJP's aspirations to rally a cross-caste Hindu coalition and intensified the need to find a more successful mobilizing strategy.

It was only against the backdrop of these rising political pressures that the movement's leadership began viewing the provision of everyday services as a strategy for mass recruitment. In 1989, on the birth centenary of its founder, K. B. Hegdewar, the Sangh launched a new *seva vibhag* or "service division." In many ways, this marked a transition of service from a means to maintaining Hindu solidarity to a technique for actively integrating poor Hindus. "The Sangh knew that our presence was mostly with *savarnas* [upper castes]," a service activist admitted to me in an interview, "so we decided to make a separate *seva vibhag* to help us work among our backward brothers."[7] Other activists corroborated this increasing emphasis on service work since the 1990s:

Sangh Activist: I came to Seva Bharati in 1990. See the Sangh was always into service – but it was in 1990 that the Sangh really decided to enter society in a full way using service. The Sangh did not always do this *constant* [emphasis added] service work – they did disaster relief, etc., things that occurred only periodically, but they did not do this everyday kind of service work. So Deorasji [the RSS *sarsanghchalak* from 1973–1994] gave us the directive to go into society more completely. He said that the *saman samaj* [ordinary people] cannot always afford to come into Sangh *shakhas*.

TT: Why could they not afford to come to *shakhas*?

Sangh Activist: Well, because they had to work, but also because they see them as Hindu institutions and sometimes that can be a problem – you know what I am talking about…Initially we were working individually, but by 1993, our work became even more systematic. From 1993 onwards our projects grew very rapidly – not just education and health, but vocational training such as sewing centers, especially among SC/STs [Dalits and Adivasis].[8]

This conversation provides several clues as to how Hindu nationalists viewed the potential of expanding service provision. First, the proliferation of

---

[6] For the best analysis of the Jana Sangh's political history, see Graham 1990.

[7] Interview with Sewa Bharati activist BB, Agra, January 6, 2010.

[8] Interview, with Seva Bharati activist AB, Bilaspur, Chhattisgarh, July 27, 2010.

TABLE 4.1. *Main organizations of the Sangh Parivar*

Name of Organization	Function within the Sangh
Rashtriya Swayamsevak Sangh (RSS)	Parent organization, grassroots mobilization
Bharatiya Janata Party (BJP)	Political party arm
Vishva Hindu Parishad (VHP)	Cultural affairs and international activities
Bharatiya Kisan Sangh	Farmer union
Bharatiya Mazdoor Sangh	Workers union
Sewa Bharati	Social service
Vanvasi Kalyan Ashram (VKA)	Social service (Adivasis)
Akhil Bharatiya Vidyarthi Parishad (ABVP)	Student union
Bajrang Dal/Durga Vahini	Male/female youth wing

service chapters in the 1990s was clearly the result of a deliberate and politically motivated decision.[9] Second, this interviewee notes that the Sangh had realized the need for organizational differentiation to widen its network beyond upper caste constituencies. The centerpiece of Hindu nationalist organization, the *shakhas*, had reached their saturation point in expanding the movement's appeal. *Shakhas* provided few incentives for poor families with long working hours and limited means, especially given their reputations as ideologically polarizing Hindu institutions. To grow their presence among the "ordinary people" for whom Hindutva held little intrinsic appeal, the Sangh needed a new form of outreach.

As the activist notes service wings were chosen as the centerpiece of this outreach. The two major wings within the Sangh network (Table 4.1) devoted to service provision were the Seva Bharati (Service to India) and the Vanvasi[10] Kalyan Ashram (Association for the Welfare of Tribals, VKA). The former undertakes a range of services falling under four categories: education, health, social organization, and self-reliance projects. Education and health projects range from schools (including one-teacher schools in remote areas) to blood banks and medical dispensaries. Social organization and self-reliance projects include vocational training centers, typing centers for providing services such as writing letters or claims, and centers for manufacturing local handicrafts. The second organization, VKA, was founded during the 1950s, with the specific mandate to work

---

[9] Indeed, when viewed through the prism of this tactical shift, the stagnation of everyday *shakhas*, widely interpreted in the press as a sign of the Sangh's "shrinking footprint," are better viewed as a reallocation of organizational resources. See for example Pathak 2010.

[10] The use of the term *Vanvasi* instead of Adivasi is itself an ideological move by Hindu nationalists. *Adivasi* translates as "original/native inhabitant." This term troubles Hindu nationalists who believe the original inhabitants of India are of Aryan descent, not of tribal lineage. Instead, *Vanvasi* translates as "forest dweller," and in addition to denying nativity, also has a patronizing connotation used by Hindu nationalists to justify their work to uplift these communities. See Sundar 2006.

among Adivasi populations, and it also conducts a range of activities including schooling, hospice care, and small infrastructure development projects.

Data from the internal records of Hindu nationalists reveals that although the number of non-service *shakhas* has stagnated in recent years, both service organizations grew at unprecedented rates during the past two decades. Figures 4.1a and 4.1b clearly demonstrate that the vast majority of the VKA's

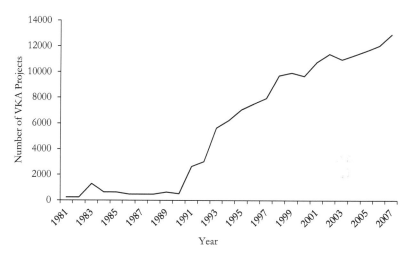

FIGURE 4.1A. Growth in Vanvasi Kalyan Ashram projects, 1981–2007
Source: Data collected by author from VKA annual records, Jashpur, Chhattisgarh.

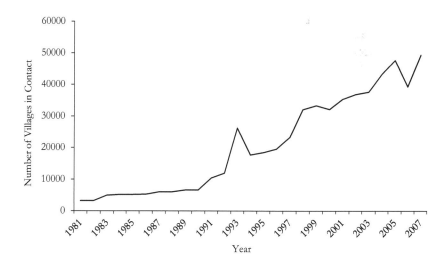

FIGURE 4.1B. Growth in Vanvasi Kalyan Ashram villages contacted, 1981–2007
Source: Data collected by author from VKA annual records, Jashpur, Chhattisgarh.

chapters were built after 1990; Figures 4.2a and 4.2b show a similar pattern of development for Seva Bharati, which saw a fourfold increase in the number of its chapters over the same time span.[11] Why did service provision emerge as a

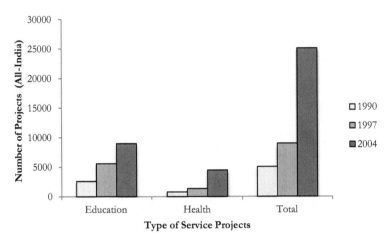

FIGURE 4.2A. Growth in Seva Bharati projects across India (1990–2004)
Source: Rashtriya Seva Bharati, New Delhi.

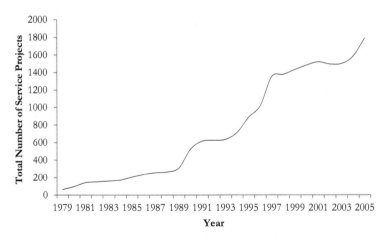

FIGURE 4.2B. Growth in Seva Bharati projects (Delhi Wing, 1979–2005)
Source: Collected by author from Seva Bharati office, gol market, New Delhi (July 2010).

[11] Both journalistic reports and ethnographic studies corroborate this story of recent growth. See Mathur 2008, p. 30, and "Service projects" 2006.

popular strategic choice for the movement to deploy among the poor? And why did these efforts focus on Dalits and Adivasis specifically?

First, service provided substantive inducements to disadvantaged citizens and thus provided a material basis for winning their support. However, to keep costs to a minimum, the services provided by Hindu nationalists (described in more detail in the next section) were necessarily basic. Such frugal offerings were only going to be attractive to the poorest of India's citizens, and of the communities the BJP regarded as Hindu, Dalits and Adivasis were by far the most uniformly impoverished.[12] Consequently, the Sangh nationalists believed a welfare-based approach would be more likely to succeed among these communities than other non-elite caste groups, notably the Other Backward Classes (OBCs).

Dalits and Adivasis were also far less consistently self-mobilized as a political community than OBCs. Of course, there are important variations in the degree to which lower castes and tribals themselves are mobilized across Indian states. Indeed, the argument laid out in Chapter 1 acknowledges the importance of these subnational variations in structuring the electoral efficacy of welfare. However, there are also significant differences in levels of political mobilization between major caste groupings. In this regard, OBCs are far more mobilized than Dalits and Adivasis across most Indian states. This asymmetry is perhaps most evident in the differentials in the number of prominent political parties these respective communities lead.[13] Greater self-mobilization among OBCs makes these caste groups far less prone to vertical incorporation by an upper caste party. As one BJP leader explained, the reason the party had to focus on mobilizing Dalits and Adivasis, and not on backward castes, was because the latter "already have groups for themselves to do this."[14]

Given the relative prosperity and visible mobilization among OBC communities, they appeared a far harder portion of the electorate to appeal to via private welfare. At the same time, Dalits and Adivasis were nearly as numerous as OBCs in several major Indian states, at least according to the most reliable data available on caste-wise demographics.[15] Table 4.2 shows that in six of India's

---

[12] Government data from 2009 to 2010 on poverty (Government of India 2011b) shows the rural poverty rate among Dalits (42.3 percent) and Adivasis (47.4 percent) is far higher than for OBCs (31.9 percent). There are similar discrepancies in the urban poverty rates (34.1 percent for Dalits, 30.4 percent for Adivasis, and 24.3 percent for OBCs).

[13] The only electorally significant Dalit-led party is the Bahujan Samaj Party, which is discussed in Chapter 6. The most prominent political party in which Adivasis play a major role is the Jharkhand Mukti Morcha, which is a relatively small regional party with a presence in only a single state. By contrast, OBCs lead a number of prominent political parties across all of India, including the Samajwadi Party in Uttar Pradesh, the Rashtriya Janata Dal and Janata Dal (United) in Bihar, and the Janata Dal (Secular) in Karnataka.

[14] Interview with O. Rajagopal, Thiruvananthapuram, August 4, 2008.

[15] Data on the size of Scheduled Caste and Schedule Tribe populations has been consistently collected by the decennial Indian census. However, data on the size of India's OBC population is more controversial, because the census did not collect information on OBC households between

TABLE 4.2. *Caste-wise demographic makeup of major Indian states*

	Percentage Dalit	Percentage Adivasi	Percentage Dalit and Adivasi	Percentage OBC	OBC-Dalit/ Adivasi
Andhra Pradesh	16.19	6.59	22.78	43.5	20.72
Assam	6.85	12.41	19.26	12.5	−6.76
Bihar	15.72	0.9	16.62	49.9	33.28
Chhattisgarh	11.61	31.75	43.36	49.67*	6.31*
Gujarat	7.09	14.76	21.85	23.6	1.75
Haryana	19.34	0	19.34	21.4	2.06
Jharkhand	11.83	26.3	38.13	37.99*	−0.14*
Karnataka	16.2	6.55	22.75	40.3	17.55
Kerala	9.81	1.14	10.95	40.5	40.5
Madhya Pradesh	15.17	20.27	35.44	39.8	4.36
Maharashtra	10.2	8.85	19.05	22.6	3.55
Orissa	16.53	22.13	38.66	29.6	−9.06
Punjab	28.85	0	28.85	16.8	−12.05
Rajasthan	17.15	12.56	29.71	23.2	−6.51
Tamil Nadu	19	1.04	20.04	73.4	53.36
Uttar Pradesh	21.14	0.01	21.15	26.2	5.05
West Bengal	23.02	5.5	28.52	4.5	−24.02

Source: Data on Dalits, Adivasis, and Christians from 2001 Indian Census. Data on OBCs from National Family Health Survey-2, conducted in 1998–1999.
* Data on OBCs for Chhattisgarh and Jharkhand from 2004 NES Sample, as the NFHS-2 was conducted before these states were formed in 2000.

seventeen major states, the proportion of Dalits and Adivasis was greater than that of OBCs and was within 5 percentage points in another five cases. Thus, Dalits and Adivasis both constituted a sizeable electorate and were regarded by Hindu nationalists as more likely to prove responsive to a service-based approach.

Even if welfare was regarded as an attractive strategy for outreach efforts among subaltern voters, why was it palatable to the BJP's elite core? We saw in Chapter 2 how upper castes stymied various efforts at social expansion seen to threaten their interests. Why was service any different?

1931 and 2011, and because estimates are required to inform the scale of affirmative action programs for OBCs. Many analyses just use data projections from the 1931 census, and the Mandal Commission used this data to place India's OBC population at 52 percent. However, this is obviously problematic given potential differences in population growth rates over a period of several decades. Therefore, I use data from the National Family Health Survey (NFHS), which was based on a sample of more than 91,000 households interviewed in 1998. The NFHS found 32.4 percent of the population to be OBC, which was in line with a later survey by the National Survey Sample in 1999–2000, which put the figure at 31.1 percent.

Crucially, furnishing low-cost services eschewed the more fundamental redistributive compromises entailed by strategic alternatives. Private service provision necessitated neither the implementation of pro-poor policies nor the greater representation of lower castes in candidate lists. Even the possibility of such compromises had drawn the ire of the party's internal elites and upper caste supporters, both of whom feared a loss of power, resources, and status within "their" party. Finally, service provision's reliance on private organizational networks also circumvented the need for a sustained incumbent access to state resources that the BJP had not yet enjoyed.

In addition to balancing the material concerns of rich and poor, service proved remarkably rhetorically malleable. This flexibility enabled Hindu nationalists to simultaneously sell the strategy to three sets of actors: skeptical lower caste communities, fretful upper caste supporters, and an ideologically committed activist core.[16] Among disadvantaged voters, service provided a depoliticized discourse through which upper caste activists could repeatedly access voters hostile toward the Brahminical orientation of Hindu nationalist ideology. As I later detail, the ability of these activists to portray themselves as service providers instead of upper caste Hindu nationalists proved crucial to their acceptance within these initially wary communities.

At the same time, a welfare-based approach had to appeal to the upper caste Sangh ideologues who would be required to furnish services. Yet committed movement activists had been critical of many of the BJP's past expansionary tactics detailed in Chapter 2, on largely ideological grounds. For example, both a social engineering strategy based on elevating non-elite candidates and the formation of electoral alliances with lower caste parties explicitly acknowledged caste identities as a sociopolitical reality. Sangh activists believed that such acknowledgment undermined the larger project of constructing a unified Hindu nation across such subdivisions and thus diluted Hindutva's core doctrine.

By contrast, service work did not engage the fracturing language of caste and simultaneously energized activists by offering a means to counter similar efforts made by predatory activists of foreign faiths. Hindu nationalists feared these religious rivals were using welfare to induce conversions among subaltern recipients, a concern the following call to Sangh activists highlights:

Today throughout the nation, some Dalit, Muslim, Christian and communist organizations are collecting crores [tens of millions] of rupees abroad and using this wealth to mislead some of our brothers among the Harijans [Dalits], the poor, the vanavasis

---

[16] The foundational account of the different ways in which "frame alignment" can be pursued by social movement organizations is provided in Snow et al. 1996. For more general discussion of framing processes, see Snow and Benford 2000; Johnston 2002.

[Adivasis], and other backward groups to fulfill their scheme to separate them from Hindu society...We have to save the nation at all costs and to free our brothers of the backward sections of society from the clutches of these treacherous forces. It is only when the different sections of Hindu society get involved with such social work that we will be able to join the Hindu brothers.[17]

Thus, a strategic approach based on service provision for the poor elided the fundamental friction between the electoral interests of a party seeking office and the ideological commitments of a movement seeking deeper social change.[18]

Finally, the patronizing language of "upliftment" used to promote service activities reassured upper castes fearing a loss of priority within the party, thereby encouraging them to actively finance provisioning efforts. I found that service workers would repeatedly frame their activities to potential donors using language that invoked the uniting terminology of a fraternity while also acknowledging upper caste superiority. An illustrative example came from one fund-raising effort in Agra, where a Seva Bharati activist noted:

We don't do this work for publicity – does a man seek newspaper praise if he feeds his children? See the way this will work is that our brothers have to put their hands up, and we have to reach down and pull them up. Only then will there be unity – but it is for us to act first.[19]

To understand why this framing is attractive to upper castes, it is important to consider the distinction between upliftment and empowerment. Private welfare was most certainly not a project of subaltern empowerment. It did not hope to help Dalits and Adivasis develop their own political autonomy or articulate and advance their own interests. Instead, it was a project of upliftment, which for Hindu nationalists meant providing basic benefits to help convert subaltern recipients into obedient Hindus.

Accordingly, Hindu nationalists hoped that progress for subaltern communities would become identified with mimicking elite practice (the ethos of Sanskritization discussed in Chapter 2). Dalits and Adivasis would pin their hopes on earning upper caste parental approval (note the equation of lower castes with children in the previous quote). Such approval did not of course connote the actual equality of even the most dutiful lower caste mimics with upper castes, but rather their improved acceptability to the latter. And of course, the ability to grant such approval would only cement the social

---

[17] Internal VHP circular as quoted in Shubh Mathur 2008, p. 125.
[18] Such symbiosis may not always manifest. For example, Van Cott (2005, p. 128) notes that a "dual strategy" dividing electoral labor between the Ecuadorian indigenous movement and its party arm (Pachakutik) proved to be "a double-edged sword," as it led to "confusion and even open conflict" between the two over the relative prioritization of electoral and social goals.
[19] Interview with Seva Bharati activist BC, Agra, January 6, 2011.

power of Hindu elites, rather than actually serve as a channel for subaltern social mobility. A widespread acceptance of this Sanskritized ethos could thus manage the central tension between Hindu nationalism's need to forge cross-caste solidarity and desire to maintain caste-based distinctions. Toward this end, welfare chapters held the potential for creating channels of social influence through which to disseminate Sanskritization's vision of acquiescence in place of caste antagonism. The degree to which such potential was realized is discussed in later chapters.

In sum, the mass expansion of service provision for political purposes did draw on a long history of Hindu nationalist organizational activism, but it also clearly constituted a new shift in the movement's approach among lower caste communities.[20] But what did these organizations actually do among the poor?

The next two sections provide an overview of the grassroots activities of each of the Sangh's two major service wings, Seva Bharati and Vanvasi Kalyan Ashram, drawing on fieldwork conducted with both organizations. These accounts describe the broad array of undertakings of each organization and the ways through which service activists embed themselves within local communities. These descriptions also introduce certain challenges that service chapters face in both urban and rural settings. Accounts of the VKA draw from fieldwork in remote Adivasi villages in the central Indian state of Chhattisgarh; those of Seva Bharati focus on the organization's efforts with Dalits in the northern Indian state of Uttar Pradesh. These descriptions do not intend to imply a simple geographical division of labor between the two wings. Although the VKA does primarily work in rural areas where Adivasis reside, Seva Bharati has a significant presence among both urban and rural communities. Instead, the following two sections are meant to provide some descriptive context for the subsequent analysis of the impact of service chapters on non-elite voting patterns.

SERVICE ORGANIZATIONS IN THE COUNTRYSIDE: THE VKA
IN CENTRAL INDIA

The VKA is the Sangh organization devoted to working among India's Adivasi populations. It was founded in 1952 in the district of Jashpur, located within the central Indian state of Chhattisgarh, and its origins are intertwined with the long

---

[20] Similarly the ABVP, the Sangh's student wing, shifted from simply organizing students within the university toward social outreach programs with tribals, for example by bringing scores of tribal students from the northeast to Bombay and other cities and putting them up with local families.

history of Christian missionary activity in the state. Sundar notes that after the establishment of a Jesuit mission in Jashpur in the late nineteenth century, missionaries used an array of tactics to recruit converts, including monetary incentives for conversion, running cooperative banks, and even organizing boycotts against non-Christians.[21] She argues that missionary activities came to the attention of the RSS when Hindu nationalists began suspecting Christian organizations in the area of coordinating a regional movement for a new (subnational) state of Jharkhand, which the Sangh viewed as a separatist affront to Indian unity, akin to the Muslim "demand for Pakistan."[22] To confront this "menace," the Sangh began considering with renewed urgency how to quell the growing influence of missionary networks among local Adivasis.

Ironically, decisions by the rival Congress Party helped Hindu nationalists in their endeavors. A Congress chief minister appointed Balasaheb Deshpande, a Sangh *pracharak* (full-time activist), to the post of regional director of tribal welfare, partly in response to mounting complaints by Hindu nationalists about the activities of Christian missionaries in the region.[23] Deshpande, the cousin of the third *sarsanghchalak* of the RSS came to Jashpur and discovered the extent to which missionaries had established a social presence, particularly in the field of education. He eventually quit his government position in 1952 to work full time on countering this influence. Deshpande's efforts centered on establishing an organization whose explicit mandate would be to run its own schools to compete against those run by missions and to emphasize the teaching of Hindutva in its curriculum. He set up the VKA to be this organization, and within five years his efforts drew recognition from Sangh leaders who began to dispatch senior *pracharaks* to help expand Deshpande's efforts.[24]

In 1956, just as the VKA was getting off the ground, the Congress-ruled state government of Madhya Pradesh commissioned a report on missionary activities in the region, headed by Shankar Niyogi, a former high court justice. The report was based on interviews with more than 11,000 villagers spread across fourteen districts of Madhya Pradesh and concluded that "conversions are mostly brought about by undue influence, misrepresentation, etc., or in other words

---

[21] Sundar 2006, p. 362.

[22] Ibid., p. 364. Jharkhand was created in November 2000, along with two other new states – Chhattisgarh and Uttarakhand. Jharkhand shares its southern border with the northern border of Chhattisgarh.

[23] This chief minister was Ravi Shankar Shukla, the father of V. C. Shukla, who was a prominent politician in the state until his death in 2013. This apparent irony is readily explained by the fact that Shukla came into the Congress from the Hindu Mahasabha (the Hindu traditionalist wing of the party).

[24] The first activist to arrive was Moreshwar Ketkad, who was later joined by K. Bhaskar Rao, the latter a *pracharak* working in Kerala, who went on to became the first organizing secretary of the VKA.

not by conviction but by various inducements offered for proselytization in various forms."[25] The report suggested thousands of tribals had been converted across the districts under study, and that in the area of Jashpur alone, 546 tribals had been converted to Christianity in the decade following independence.[26] The committee recommended that "those Missionaries whose primary object is proselytization should be asked to withdraw" and that "the large influx of foreign Missionaries is undesirable and should be checked."[27]

Not surprisingly, the Niyogi Committee's conclusions were extremely controversial. Critics argued that the commission deliberately selected respondents with known ties to Hindu revivalist groups such as the Arya Samaj, biasing the report's findings. Many aspects of the report did support Hindu nationalist complaints of the predatory behavior of non-Hindu faiths and thereby increased the legitimacy and influence of the VKA in the region. However, it is important to remember that despite its symbolic importance, the VKA housed a limited network for the first four decades of its existence. A narrow mandate of countering missionary activities actually served to circumscribe its presence to only those few locations where Christian organizations were active. In contrast, since the 1990s, when the VKA was given the much broader task of enhancing the Sangh's appeal among all Adivasi communities, the organization expanded at unprecedented rates across the country. Figures 4.1a and 4.1b showed that in the first four decades (from 1952 to 1990), the VKA built a presence in less than 10,000 villages nationwide. After 1990, this figure increased fivefold (to more than 50,000 in 2007) in less than two decades. The organization's eventual goal is to have a presence in each of the roughly 153,000 villages across India it has designated as "Vanvasi" or tribal dominated.[28]

The first generation of VKA activists in any area is overwhelmingly composed of upper castes, many of who hail from outside the state in which they work. These activists were most often deputed to their posts by superiors within the Sangh but are instructed to find local recruits as quickly as possible to expand the organization in a sustainable manner. The VKA's own records indicate that it

[25] Government of Madhya Pradesh, Niyogi Committee Report, Volume 1, Part 4, point 3 (1956). The report cited a "general complaint from the non-Christian side that the schools and hospitals were being used as means of securing converts" and to other "illegitimate methods alleged to be adopted by the Missionaries for this purpose," which even included "the kidnapping of minor children and abduction of women and recruitment of labour for plantations in Assam or Andaman as a means of propagating the Christian faith among the ignorant and illiterate people" (Niyogi Committee Report, Volume 1, Part 1,,Introduction, point 6). The "villager testimonies" included in the report for the Sarguja district, for example, include promises of easy credit and low or no interest, free clothes and medicine, and help with obtaining land (Niyogi Committee Report, Volume 2, Part A, "Explanatory Tour Notes for Sarguja").
[26] Niyogi Committee Report, Volume 2, Part A, "Replies to Questionnaire concerning the area covered by Jashpur, Khuria, and Udaipur of the Raigarh district."
[27] Niyogi Committee Report, Volume 1, Part 4, point 72.
[28] Figures from Vanvasi Kalyan Ashram 2007.

was largely successful in this endeavor; by 1998, more than half of the organization's workers came from Adivasi communities.[29] This ability to quickly embed within and recruit from Adivasi communities is of considerable political significance and is discussed in greater detail in the next chapter.

The services these activists provide are broadly divided into three spheres: education, medical services, and economic development, of which the first two are by far the most significant.[30] In the field of education, which covers about 70 percent of the organization's activities, the VKA offers three main types of services. The majority of education projects are *ekal vidyalayas* (one-teacher schools), which operate at the village level. These schools are meant to provide basic primary education in reading and mathematics, and the teachers in these schools typically have between a tenth- and twelfth-grade education, with a small minority possessing a college degree.

In some villages, the VKA runs *bal kendras* (child centers) that are held after regular school hours, typically between about 4 p.m. and 7 p.m. Students attending these centers are helped with their homework, are sometimes given additional assignments to strengthen their reading or arithmetic, and are also given a chance to play some organized games. There are clear ideological overtones to many of these exercises, especially those that have been adapted from games played in upper caste, non-service *shakhas*. However, as is detailed in the next chapter, the VKA does not advertise these leanings when recruiting students from families in the village. Instead, the organization predominantly markets itself as a service organization and consistently downplays its ideological proclivities during initial interactions with villagers.

In a few villages, the VKA operates a *chatravaas* (residential hostel) where students are given free room and board throughout the school year. In some cases, the VKA also runs a full-time school adjoining its hostel, where boarders are enrolled. In other instances, students reside in the VKA hostel but attend the closest government school during the day.

Each of these programs serves local communities somewhat differently. The one-teacher schools are seen as substitutes for local government (or more rarely, private) options and run concurrently with public school hours. In contrast, the after-school *kendras* provide two main benefits. First, enrolled students get extra assistance with their schoolwork that their (often illiterate) parents are not able to provide. At the same time, busy parents benefit from the free supervision of their children for a few hours each day. The *chatravaas* provides even more obvious material benefits, namely free meals, lodging, and even clothing for its students, as well as twenty-four-hour supervision. Further, these residential hostels enable parents to send their children to school outside of their own

---

[29] Figure from "Vanvasi Kalyan Ashram" section in Seva Bharati, *Seva Disha* 1997 report, p. 45.

[30] Economic development projects, which can range from the digging of wells to small vocational centers for adult women, are by far the smallest of these categories, comprising less than 10 percent of the VKA's total activities across India.

village, which is crucially important if local facilities are either inadequate (e.g., because of high teacher absenteeism) or simply unavailable (especially common for those seeking schooling beyond the primary level in remote villages).

As in education, the VKA's interventions in the field of health take several forms. The backbone of the organization's health initiatives across India is its village health worker program. These local activists offer only the most basic care, working with about fifteen to twenty basic medicines for colds, coughs, nausea, dysentery, flu, malaria, and other common illnesses.[31] Most of these "doctors" have no more than a secondary school education and almost never have any prior medical training. The VKA takes these local recruits to the organization's state headquarters, where certified medical doctors (who are also VKA activists) provide some basic training. The training sessions are usually offered about once a month and typically last for about three days, during which time health workers are given basic information on symptoms of common illnesses and the appropriate medicines to give in each case.[32]

The VKA does not consider the local health workers to be full-time employees equivalent to the village-level teachers who make up the bulk of its activist cadre.[33] Instead, the workers are expected to make themselves available to patients for short periods in the mornings and evenings. Most of the time there are no formal clinic hours. Given the size of most village communities, it is easy enough for a patient to make an appointment directly with the worker. In contrast, teacher-activists running either one-teacher schools or after-school centers are expected to be regularly available for large portions of each day. Consequently, the VKA does not offer its health activists a wage; instead, it provides them with free medicines and lets them keep any money patients may give them for treatment (usually about Rs. 5, although no fee is required). For this system to work, the VKA sees it as absolutely imperative that future generations of health workers be drawn from a village's own residents:

---

[31] Interview with VKA doctor AF, Jashpur, July 24, 2010.

[32] When asked about the potential hazards of such a system, the VKA claims that the organization only gives its village workers those medicines that "would do no harm even if incorrectly given to a patient." The assumption that medicines can be thus administered without harm or that such a system does "more good than harm" is clearly tenuous at best. Privately, VKA leaders admit their concern over the possibility of mistreatment but argue that the organization safeguards against such a possibility by training their workers to immediately help patients get to the nearest government primary health care center if their condition deteriorates after treatment (based on interviews with VKA doctors AF, Jashpur, July 24, 2010, and AD, Jashpur, April 2, 2008).

[33] The VKA tries to set up village committees (*samitis*), which are responsible for the non-service-related organizational work in a village. This work includes keeping track of visits to the village by other VKA activists and organizing cultural celebrations. The *samiti* ranges in size from about three to ten people and gets chosen for the year. The VKA usually sends out a call at the beginning of each year for volunteers for the *samiti*, which meets about once a month. The *samiti* is also in charge of running festival celebrations such as *sthapana divas* (the VKA's founders day) and *guru purnima* [a Hindu festival celebrating the contribution of teachers].

We have also now really tried hard to make sure the person is from the village itself. Otherwise we have a hard time retaining them. If they are from the village this becomes like a bonus job, with extra income for them. They can work on the farm, or do household chores during the day, and still have time to administer medicines in the morning and evening.[34]

Teachers however are paid a monthly stipend, ranging from Rs. 800 to Rs. 1500 ($15 to $30, with some long-term employees making slightly more), and therefore the imperative to find a local from the village itself is not as pressing when filling these positions.

In addition to keeping permanent workers in villages, the VKA also maintains more professional medical staffs, which primarily work in larger, more central-ized facilities at the district or regional level. These health centers (*chikitsa kendras*) usually offer some basic medical procedures, in addition to consulta-tions with trained doctors and a wider array of medications than village activists can provide. These headquarters also serve as the centralized dispensary from which medicines are distributed to all VKA operations in the state. Depending on the density of the VKA's local network, supplies will either be sent directly to villages or to smaller, local dispensaries (*chikitsa upkendras* or medical subcenters) operating in large villages or small towns in the district, which disburse supplies to local activists. These local subcenters also usually have a slightly more educated activist who keeps regular dispensary hours from 9 a.m. to 6 p.m., is paid a salary, and has a better stock of basic medical supplies.[35]

Another feature of the VKA's services is its weekly *bazaar* (market) days, which have been held in Chhattisgarh since 1991. The organization sends a certified doctor and two compounders (pharmacists) to a local market to see patients for free for several hours. An activist working in the bazaar in Lokhandi village of Jashpur observed that this particular technique generated a lot of bang for the VKA's organizational buck. People from the surrounding thirty to forty villages come to any one market day and can combine other tasks with seeking medical assistance. He noted, "that is a major convenience for people – they can do both jobs at once. If someone is sick at home, they can bring some medicine for them, but they can also buy some vegetables for the house."[36]

These comments appeared to be accurate, as I personally observed long lines of patients for the full four hours of operation on several of these market days. On average, the teams I observed saw between eighty and ninety patients per

---

[34] Interview with AF, Jashpur, July 24, 2010.

[35] However, these activists are also limited in what services they can offer. An operator of one of these subcenters, Activist AI, said the biggest difficulty he faced in his work was "when very sick people come here and want us to be able to treat them – when we are not able to do that, and tell them to go to the government hospital, they often demand some medicine from us anyway. They believe going to the doctor means getting medicine, and it is difficult to explain when we cannot do that" (interview, Sitanagar [assigned name], - July 23, 2010).

[36] Interview with AK, Kutki village, July 24, 2010.

day, which tallied with the numbers marked in the official registers I inspected.[37] The activists told me that they have become so well known over the past few years that they don't even feel the need to hang up the organization's banner because "everyone knows who we are here."[38] Indeed, in my conversations with people visiting the market from nearby villages, it was clear that the Ashram needed little introduction.

The final component of the VKA's health program is an initiative through which a team of one doctor and a couple of aides drive out in a "mobile dispensary" (a jeep painted in ambulance colors, stocked with medical supplies) for local visits to villages across a district by rotation. The teams usually aim to visit two villages (usually adjoining each other) each day, spending between five and seven hours at each location. In these *svasthya shivirs* (health camps), villagers have a chance to get more complete care than their local VKA activists are equipped to provide, and on average the team attends to about fifty patients per village, and about ten villages a month.[39] The activists often spend the night in the second village they visit in a day, giving them a chance to consult with local VKA workers, as well as eat and talk with local villagers.

SERVICE ORGANIZATIONS IN THE CITY: SEVA BHARATI IN AGRA

The second major Sangh service organization, Seva Bharati, was founded in 1979, nearly three decades after the VKA. Yet, it too remained a fairly marginal presence until the 1990s, after which it has also rapidly expanded, quickly surpassing its service partner and establishing itself as one of the largest civil society organizations of any kind in the country. A national apex body centrally coordinates Seva Bharati's operations, but local level units primarily determine the contours of their grassroots activities. The information from this section draws largely from fieldwork with one such chapter, located in Agra, a city in the northern state of Uttar Pradesh. However, this unit functioned similarly to wings I spent time observing in southern and central India and thus provides a fairly representative glimpse of the organization's activities across the country.

The city of Agra, roughly 130 miles from Delhi, is best known as the home of India's most globally iconic monument, the Taj Mahal. Yet, in the shadow of the city's numerous luxury tourist hotels lies a vast network of urban slums, home to Agra's large lower caste population. There are 252 officially registered slum areas in Agra, although independent reports have documented close to 400 such

---

[37] These observations are based on several personal visits to these market days across Chhattisgarh during multiple trips in 2007, 2008, and 2010, as well as personal access to the attendance records kept by the VKA medical staff in Jashpur and Bastar.

[38] Interview with AL, Kutki village, July 24, 2010.

[39] According to the log of the activists whom I shadowed on several trips, the team visited 124 villages during the 2009 calendar year, attending to 5,622 patients.

settlements, where most of the city's quarter million Dalits live. Although Dalits are only one-fifth of the city's residents, they comprise half of its slum population. During the 1990s, Seva Bharati in Agra (SBA) has rapidly expanded its service network within this sizeable constituency and has emerged as a significant organizational presence in the city.[40]

The depolarizing potential of service work was evident in the term s*eva bastis* (settlements for service work), used by upper caste SBA activists to mark the places they worked in. This generic term helped avoid the caste-based monikers (Balmiki *basti*, Harijan *basti*, etc.) often used to identify slum settlements in urban India. By 2010, the SBA had 106 activists running projects in 155 *seva bastis* in the city, including 44 one-teacher schools.[41] These schools function similarly to those of the VKA, with a teacher typically holding class within either a home or public space in the *basti*, for roughly three to four hours a day. Additionally, the SBA runs numerous health-related programs in the city, the best known are its mobile dispensaries, whereby a doctor and two assistants travel to individual slums to render basic medical care (again similar to the VKA model). The SBA has also developed a network of doctors within the city whom it recruits to provide these services via a rotating system. The organization also maintains its own blood donor lists and runs periodic immunization drives.

A number of SBA services specifically target women in the city's slums. Most prominent among these are twenty *silai kendras* or sewing centers, which offer short training courses in stitching popular clothing items such as shirts, pants, and sari blouses. The aim of these programs is to help trainees find opportunities for paid sewing work, often obtained through the SBA's considerable middle-class network in the city. Sewing centers are especially valued by Hindu nationalists for being able to provide tangible material benefits to enrollees, while also encouraging women to remain within more domestic roles. In addition, SBA workers manage nineteen self-help microcredit groups for young women in the city.[42] These groups primarily collect money to lend in rotation to members at low or no interest but also function as a support group for women to discuss broader personal difficulties they might be facing. These groups are somewhat variable in size, with most ranging between twenty and forty women.

Like their VKA counterparts in Chhattisgarh, the SBA offers a diverse array of services to lower caste communities in Agra. Most of the funds for running the services come from private donations from local upper castes, with as much as 60 percent coming from the city's vibrant network of merchant castes with

[40] I am grateful to Christophe Jaffrelot for bringing my attention to this point.
[41] The Sangh employs its own geographical units for organization. Regions are composed of *prants*, with each *prant* further subdivided at the local level. Agra is part of Braj *prant* (one of six comprising Uttar Pradesh) and is further subdivided by the Sangh into eighteen divisions known as *nagars* (towns).
[42] Figures from Seva Bharati Agra Mahanagar, *Annual Report*, published by Saraswati Shishu Mandir, Subhash Park, Agra.

whom the Sangh maintains strong ties.[43] The SBA also sells advertising space in its monthly newsletter *Seva Prasoon*, most of which is bought at inflated (by the SBA's own reckoning) rates by upper caste supporters of the organization.[44] The group even occasionally engages in door-to-door fund-raising among the city's middle-class neighborhoods during important Hindu festivals.

The vast majority of the SBA's operating budget is raised locally, although all chapters receive some financial assistance from the national headquarters, which is also set up to receive international donations.[45] The sums required are not inconsequential in absolute terms but are strikingly modest given the scale of social outreach efforts they finance. The SBA requires Rs. 1.4 million or roughly $30,000 annually to maintain its current level of service provision.[46] Within this limited budget, Hindu nationalists hope to appeal to thousands of lower castes within the city. Relative to the scope of these ambitions, the financial requirements of service provision appear far more palatable than costly shifts in policy or patronage.

Although united by a common set of aims, service provision in the city and countryside presents distinct challenges for the Sangh. Nowhere are these differences more apparent than in the recruitment of activists. The VKA's expansion requires volunteers to relocate to remote tribal areas for years at a time to grow the organization's base in a specific region. As service provision within cities clearly does not necessitate such challenging displacement, the activist profile of the SBA is quite different from that of the VKA. Whereas the latter is composed mostly of young bachelors, the former mostly recruits a somewhat unlikely cadre of recent male retirees and young, unmarried women.

Sewa Bharati's leadership tends to come from these male retirees who often have long-standing links with the Sangh's parent organization, the RSS. These men usually oversee the finances, fund-raising, and planning of project expansion. They are experienced, have considerable free time, and are willing to work for little or no pay, as they are often retired from public sector employment with adequate pensions. SBA leaders keep track of who within their local Sangh membership is on the verge of retiring and actively recruit them to join in service efforts as soon as possible. This strategy maximizes the period for which older recruits will be able to serve as physically active volunteers.[47]

[43] See Jaffrelot 2005, p. 173.
[44] The total revenues from each issue roughly total Rs. 30,000 ($600), which yields about $7,000 annually.
[45] See Sabrang Communications and SACW, "The Foreign Exchange of Hate," online at http://www.proxsa.org/newsflash/index.html. This comprehensive report outlines the nature of international donations, especially from the Indian diaspora in the United States and United Kingdom, to Sangh affiliates in India. See especially Appendices D (on Seva Bharati), F (Vanvasi Kalyan Ashram), and H (on money flows to these groups) of the report.
[46] This estimate of expenses is based on the organization's own estimates for different types of chapters and the number of such chapters it currently runs in the city (e.g., Rs. 15,000 for its medical centers and Rs. 6,000 for each of its one-teacher schools). Estimates were collected from SBA treasurer (informant BB) by author, January 10, 2011.
[47] Discussion with Seva Bharati workers, Madhav Bhavan, Agra, January 5, 2011.

However, many of the projects are actually run by young, unmarried women, often also from Sangh-affiliated, upper caste households. SBA organizers believe that targeting this demographic is most practical in terms of finding young volunteers with sufficient free time and energy to run welfare chapters. The assumptions informing this recruitment strategy again reflect the Sangh's own conservative views on pre-matrimonial female availability compared to the rigidities of post-matrimonial domesticity.[48]

Whereas the primary obstacle for the VKA has been recruiting activists to move to isolated areas, the main challenge for the SBA has ironically been exacerbated by the proximity of service work to the volunteer's home community. SBA workers admitted that they often face great difficulty in training upper caste volunteers to overcome prejudices against the enforced intimacy of service work. Many activists feared a loss of status in the eyes of other Hindu elites as a result of their daily contact with residents of untouchable communities. Training manuals given to SBA workers reflect the organization's efforts to grapple with such prejudice: the first instruction given to activists when entering a new locality is to ask for water and ensure it comes from someone's house and not from a public hand pump.[49] Organization leaders confessed that despite their best efforts, getting activists to rid themselves of ideas of *choot-achoot* (casteist prejudice concerning who is touchable and who is untouchable) was at best a difficult and slow process.[50] Such anxieties are actually heightened in urban contexts where service providers work in greater proximity to upper caste communities. For example, many families express concern over hurting the matrimonial prospects of their daughters by allowing them to work for the SBA.[51] By contrast, the relative isolation of tribal village communities offers VKA activists a degree of protection from the monitoring eyes of their co-ethnic critics.

These introductory overviews of service work in places such as Jashpur and Agra briefly reveal the array of efforts Hindu nationalists have been making with Dalit and Adivasi constituencies since the early 1990s. However, it is not immediately apparent how the expansion of formally nonpolitical groups yields an electoral payoff. As a first step, we may ask whether the BJP fares any better with these target constituencies in states where service chapters are more active. If so, are these service wings located in places where lower caste and tribal voters might already be more susceptible to supporting the BJP for other reasons? The next section of this chapter turns its attention to these questions, looking at

---

[48] See Sarkar 2005a, 2005b. The Sangh has oscillated in its attitude toward female employment but in general has promoted what Sarkar (2005b, p. 181) terms "restrictive strictures on domesticity" that have often been advanced by housebound female members of the Sangh themselves. She observes that these views have possibly contributed to declining affiliation among upper caste, middle-class young women.

[49] Pamphlet (Hindi): *Seva Karya: Udaysha Aur Karyavidhi, Shikshak aur Nirakshak ke liye* (Service Work: Purpose and Process, for teachers and inspectors), p. 14.

[50] Interview with SBA Madhav Bhavan worker BD, Agra, January 14, 2011.

[51] Interview with BC, Agra, January 9, 2011.

subnational patterns of service provision across seventeen major Indian states from 1996 to 2004.

SERVICE NETWORKS AND ELECTORAL PERFORMANCE ACROSS INDIAN STATES

As previously mentioned, the BJP increased its vote share with Dalit and Adivasi voters from 15.01 percent in 1996 to 22.41 percent by 2004 across India's major states. However, these overall gains were highly concentrated in seven states (Table 4.3), across which the BJP won more than a third of the subaltern vote on average. Yet in the remaining ten states in the sample, the party won only about one in ten votes from subaltern communities in 2004 and actually lost ground with these voters between 1996 and 2004. This divergence in the BJP's performance was recent, as the party experienced broadly similar levels of success with subaltern voters across both groupings of states in 1996. Why was the party able to expand its profile in some states but unable to do so in others? Did the density of service wings correlate with this uneven pattern of success?

As a first cut, it is useful to look at whether any broad association exists between service provision and the BJP's performance at the state level. To do so, I constructed an index of the density of Sangh social service wings. I first collected data on the number of projects undertaken by both Sewa Bharati and Vanvasi Kalyan Ashram across India from the records kept by both organizations. I then divided this figure by each state's total Dalit and Adivasi population to arrive at a per capita measure of service density (individual state totals are

TABLE 4.3. *BJP gains with Dalits and Adivasis (1996–2004)*

State	BJP Vote Share		
	1996	2004	Change
Assam	16.67	33.79	17.12
Chhattisgarh*	23.14	39.16	15.96
Jharkhand*	12.50	35.23	22.73
Karnataka	15.49	35.42	19.93
MP	26.25	33.63	7.38
Orissa	5.48	22.10	16.62
Rajasthan	17.24	39.86	22.62
Weighted Average (N=7)	17.75	34.33	16.58
Remaining states (N=10)	13.46	11.20	−2.26

* *Note:* Percentages for Chhattisgarh and Jharkhand were calculated by aggregating data from the parliamentary constituencies that would become part of the new states in 2000. These figures were calculated from the 1999 NES, because the sample size for this truncated sample in 1996 was too small to afford a reliable estimate.

Source: National Election Study 1996, 2004.

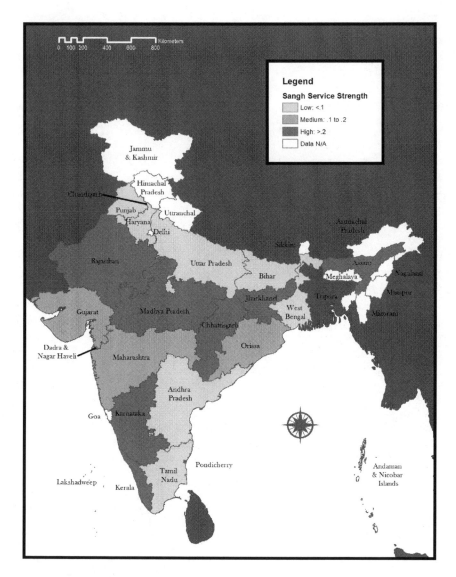

FIGURE 4.3. Density of Sangh service networks across India (2004)

reported in Appendix A). Figure 4.3 shows the distribution of these service chapters across major Indian states.

If the BJP does indeed benefit electorally from the work of its service wings, it stands to reason that its aggregate performance with disadvantaged constituencies should be stronger where these affiliates have a more significant presence. Figure 4.4 shows the relationship between the logged service index and the

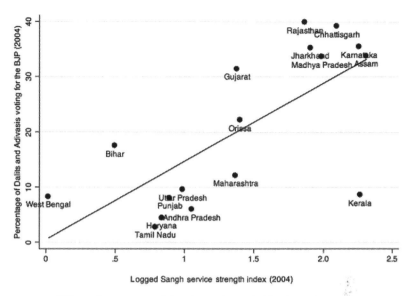

FIGURE 4.4. BJP performance and Sangh service activities (2004)
Note: Logged index has been rescaled for readability.

percentage of total Dalit and Adivasi voters in a state supporting the BJP during the 2004 national election, which conforms quite strongly to the hypothesized pattern.

A correlation, however striking, is hardly sufficient evidence of the primacy of service organizations in determining the BJP's electoral fortunes. First, if service chapters were systematically built where non-service wings had a robust presence, it is possible that the general presence of Hindu nationalist organizations, rather than the activities of service chapters specifically, undergird the BJP's pattern of success. My argument therefore implies that there should be no particular correlation between the BJP's performance and the aggregate presence of non-service chapters (principally the *shakhas* discussed previously). Figure 4.5 confirms this implication, as an identical index using the number of local *shakhas* instead of service projects does not appear to correspond with the BJP's performance with Dalit and Adivasi voters.[52]

A second issue raised by Figure 4.4 is the critical question of temporal sequencing: were service networks being built in states where the BJP was already doing well among marginalized electorates? If so, the argument presented here would be reversed: service chapters are built where the preexisting popularity of the BJP is facilitative for such endeavors. To evaluate this possibility, I looked at data on voting patterns from the first major National Election

---

[52] Figure 4.5 replicates the formula used to compute the service index exactly and so uses the state's combined Dalit/Adivasi population in the denominator. However, adjusting for the state's entire population does not make a difference, and a significant correlation is still not observed.

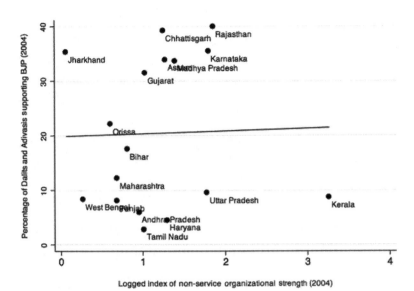

FIGURE 4.5. BJP performance and Sangh non-service activities (2004)
Source: Data from RSS *shakhas* from Rashtriya Swayamsevak Sangh, Jhandewalan office, New Delhi, 2007.

Study conducted during the 1996 national elections.[53] Had service work followed strong prior electoral performance with Dalits and Adivasis, then we would expect denser networks in 2004 to be located in states where the BJP was already performing relatively well with these communities in 1996.

However, no such relationship was apparent in the data. Indeed, the BJP's 1996 average vote share among subaltern electorates in states in the top half of service index scores (16.1 percent) was barely distinguishable from its performance in those in the bottom half (14.8 percent). Had prior BJP success determined where service organizations were built, we would have expected a broadly similar welfare effort to be have been made in Haryana (where the BJP won 12.82 percent of Dalit and Adivasi votes in 1996), Karnataka (15.49 percent), Maharashtra (16.35 percent), and Assam (16.67 percent). Yet, although service networks expanded rapidly in Karnataka and Assam, they remained marginal in Haryana and Maharashtra.

In other words, prior BJP support among lower caste and tribal voters did not appear to drive service network expansion during this period. Instead, by 2004, the BJP had experienced significant gains with Dalit and Adivasi voters in those states where it built its service network in preceding decade. Figure 4.6 shows that

[53] CSDS did conduct a voter survey in 1967, but this survey was one-off, much smaller in size, and not broadly comparable with the more contemporary surveys conducted regularly since 1996.

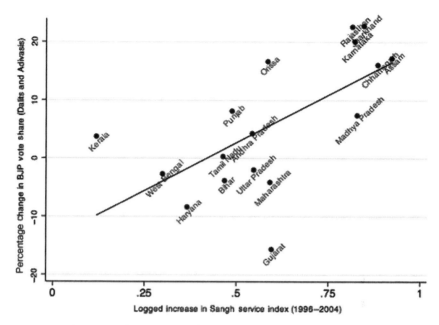

FIGURE 4.6. Service and BJP gains and losses, 1996–2004
Sources: Election data from national election study 1996, 2004; Seva Bharati service data from Seva Disha reports 1997, 2004; VKA data from VKA headquarters, Jashpur, Chhattisgarh.

the electoral inroads made by the party with non-elite voters between 1996 and 2004 were sharpest where service networks had most rapidly expanded during this period. The BJP saw gains of more than 15 percent in five of the six states in which service networks grew the most quickly, and of more than 7 percent in the sixth case (Madhya Pradesh). By contrast, in six of the remaining ten states, the BJP lost vote share with Dalit and Adivasi electorates and made no gains in a seventh over the same time span. Thus, states in which service networks were built did not have strong pools of preexisting lower caste support for the BJP, but instead they stand out as sites of improved performance for the party.

Where Are Service Chapters Built?

Of course, the descriptive data presented thus far cannot determine the direction of causal influence between the growth of service chapters and increases in BJP vote share. Making more robust causal inferences will require more disaggregated quantitative and qualitative analyses to tease out, which will be the central focus of subsequent chapters. Before proceeding to such fine-grained evaluations, additional evidence at the state level can help address two related concerns. First, where do Hindu nationalists choose to build service chapters?

Second, even if welfare networks are not located in states that were preexisting sites of BJP success, were they concentrated in states that are conducive to the party's future expansion for some other reason? Could such selection effects be powerful enough to confound any observed correlation between welfare and Dalit and Adivasi support for the party?

In the remainder of this chapter, I draw on a panel dataset of seventeen major Indian states from 1996 to 2004 to address these questions. I first analyze the state-level determinants of Sangh service efforts and then examine whether these determinants confound the association between service and voting. In Chapters 5 and 6, I use district- and village-level data to address the issue of selections effects at a more local level.

The first key variable for this state-level comparative analysis is the per capita index of Hindu nationalist service provision used throughout this chapter (labeled *Religious Welfare*), which was calculated from internal reviews conducted by these organizations in 1995, 1997, and 2004. This variable is first examined as an outcome to be explained, and then as the key independent variable in models where the outcome is state-level support for the BJP. This latter measure is gauged by the party's vote share among a state's combined Dalit and Adivasi electorate in the 1996, 1999, and 2004 elections, calculated from the relevant National Election Studies.

Each additional explanatory variable in the analysis was chosen because it could plausibly influence the location of welfare chapters and the electoral prospects of the BJP. This theoretically motivated selection process served two purposes. First, it let me examine the effects of each variable on the location of welfare networks. Next, it allowed me to control for this factor's potentially confounding effect on welfare's impact on BJP performance. I isolated seven such variables for inclusion within the analysis.

First, I included a measure of party fragmentation (the effective number of parties or *ENPV*) within a state.[54] States with higher numbers of political formations, such as Kerala or Bihar, can also make for much more crowded and fractious organizational arenas. Consequently, the Sangh may have chosen to focus its service efforts in states such as Andhra Pradesh or Madhya Pradesh, which have far less crowded party systems. Yet, the BJP also stands to independently perform better with Dalits and Adivasis in states where it faces fewer electoral competitors for the support of these communities.

[54] The effective number of parties is a widely employed measure, thought to reflect the number of salient political parties competing in a given election, as it is weighted to reflect parties that actually have some measure of success in elections. The measure is $= 1/\Sigma x_i^2$ where x_i refers to the percentage of votes captured by the ith party. See Clark and Golder 2006. In calculating ENPV, I count independents who won more than 2 percent of the state-level vote and include them as separate parties when computing the measure, as suggested by Chhibber and Kollman 1998, espically the discussion of ENPV measure in the article's appendix. The data was taken from Election Commission Reports for the 1996, 1999, and 2004 Lok Sabha elections.

Second, prior data in this chapter has suggested that the BJP did not enjoy stronger ex ante electoral support among Dalits and Adivasis in states where service networks expanded most rapidly. Perhaps welfare organizations were instead built in states such as Gujarat and Rajasthan, where the BJP enjoyed a greater following among upper castes. As elites often fund and support service networks, areas where they traditionally support the BJP at high levels might also house denser networks of its affiliates. Yet, subaltern voters in these states might already be more inclined to support the party simply because they see it as more likely to win office than in states such as Punjab and Tamil Nadu, where the BJP struggles even among upper castes.[55] To account for variations in the party's perceived "winnability," I included a measure of elite-caste support for the party (*Elite Support*), also drawn from the 1996, 1999, and 2004 National Election Studies.

Third, the Sangh might have chosen to concentrate its efforts where caste-based political divisions are less sharp. In arenas highly polarized along ethnic lines, upper caste service activists may have a more difficult time embedding themselves within subaltern communities. At the same time, the BJP's elite partisan image may be especially alienating in states where caste communities systematically vote for other parties. To account for this possibility, I adapted an index of ethnic voting developed by Huber (*Ethnic Voting*) to Indian states, again using NES data.[56] Higher values of the index, such as those recorded in Uttar Pradesh and West Bengal, indicate that ethnic partisan preferences are more sharply differentiated. Lower values, such as those recorded in Haryana and Karnataka, indicate more homogeneous political preferences across these communities. The groups included in calculating the index were Hindu upper castes, Hindu OBCs, Dalits, Adivasis, and the three largest religious minorities within a state (typically Muslims, Christians, and one other non-Hindu faith).

Fourth, demographic factors might also jointly influence provision of services and BJP performance. Past scholarship has argued that the BJP is more effective in polarizing communities for electoral gain in areas with larger proportions of religious minorities. Equally, the threats posed to Hinduism by non-Hindu faiths (specifically Christianity or Islam) might also be higher in these regions, prompting Sangh service activists to concentrate their efforts in these areas. I have already discussed how the welfare activities of Christian missionaries provided particular inspiration to the Sangh's activist cadre. I therefore include measures

[55] For a discussion of such a politics of consent, see Stokes 1995, esp. ch. 1.

[56] The index is developed in Huber 2011. The formula for Ethnic Voting (EV) is given by $\left(EV = \frac{1}{\sqrt{\frac{G-1}{2G}}} \sum_{g=1}^{G} EVg * sg \right)$ where G is the total number of groups in the country and *sg* is the proportion of group *g* in the country's voting population. The individual component of ethnic voting for each group EV_g is given by the formula $\sqrt{1/2 \sum_{j=1}^{P} (Vg - Vj)^2}$, where V_g is the proportion of individuals in group *g* who support party *j*, *Vj* is the proportion of individuals in society that support *j*, and *P* is the number of parties.

of a state's Muslim (*Muslim Population*) and Christian population (*Christian Population*) in the analysis.[57]

I also separately examined the influence of the proportion of Dalits (or SCs) and Adivasis (or STs) in a state's population (*Non-elite Population*). My theoretical expectation was that the Sangh might expand service networks where these populations were more substantial. However, according to certain theories of ethnic politics, the BJP might actually fare worse in states with large non-elite communities. In areas where marginalized communities are closer to a winning plurality, they may have stronger incentives to self-mobilize politically and therefore be less likely to be incorporated into an upper caste party.[58] Given these hypothesized inverse effects of group size on the outcome and key independent variable, not accounting for this factor might actually dampen any existing correlation between service chapters and BJP performance.

Finally, I included a measure of economic development (*Development*), measured as per capita state domestic product.[59] I anticipated this factor to also have inverse effects on the density of welfare chapters and subaltern support for the BJP. Service activists may well have concentrated their efforts in relatively underdeveloped states where the poor will especially value their offerings. However, some prior studies have found class-based voting is stronger in poorer regions, in which case subaltern voters might be less likely to support the BJP in the very areas the Sangh targets.[60]

Table 4.4 reports how these various factors affected the BJP's performance across seventeen Indian states from 1996 to 2004. The models used for this analysis were generalized least squares panel regressions with robust standard errors corrected for clustering within states.[61] Model 1 first assesses where Hindu nationalist service networks were built by regressing the service index on the various explanatory factors described in this section.[62] The results indicate that service networks were not systematically expanded in states with higher degrees of caste-based political polarization or party fragmentation. Thus, Hindu nationalists did not appear to concentrate their efforts in potentially more favorable political arenas – such as those where they faced fewer

---

[57] Population statistics were taken from the 1991 and 2001 Indian census.

[58] Posner 2006.

[59] Net state domestic product data was from the Reserve Bank of India's *Bulletin* (various issues).

[60] See Inglehart 1971; Gelman et al. 2008; Huber and Stanig 2009.

[61] I used a random-effects specification in Models 1 and 2, as Hausman tests failed to reject the null hypothesis that the state-specific random effects are uncorrelated with the regressors. However, the results are checked with state fixed effects in Model 3. Given the short duration of the panel, I preferred using robust clustered errors to panel-corrected standard errors (Beck and Katz 1995). The use of clustered standard errors is justifiable because observations within a state over time are likely to be highly correlated. However, the relatively small number of clusters in the sample (seventeen) is a cause for concern, and so the results were checked using naïve standard errors. The effect of *Religious Welfare* remains robust in these latter specifications (at the .01 level).

[62] Although the models do not include a time trend, a trend variable was found to be insignificant and did not change any of the results reported here.

TABLE 4.4. *Determinants of state-level BJP support (1996–2004)*

	Q1. Where Are Welfare Chapters Built?	Q2. Does Prior Welfare Correlate with Subsequent BJP Support?				Q3. Does Prior BJP Support Correlate with Subsequent Welfare?
	DV: Service Index (logged)	DV: Non-elite Support for BJP			DV: Upper caste support for BJP	DV: Subsequent Religious Welfare
		Baseline Model	w/fixed effects	w/lagged DV		
	(1)	(2)	(3)	(4)	(5)	(6)
Religious Welfare (log)		.455** (.178)	.276* (.124)	.568* (.290)	.330 (.243)	.050 (.312)
Prior BJP Support (log)				.263 (.167)		1.008 (.591)
Party Fragmentation (log)	−.236 (.273)	.184 (.761)	1.241 (.612)	.279 (.494)	.031 (.890)	−.046 (.260)
Elite Support (log)	.209 (.123)	.485** (.191)	.315 (.240)	.608*** (.200)		.095 (.358)
Ethnic Voting (log)	−.334 (.241)	−.101 (.618)	−.218 (.444)	−.461 (.425)	−.593 (.590)	
Development (log)	.216 (.214)	−.055 (.268)	−.044 (.289)	.032 (.315)	−.201 (.391)	.355 (.323)
Non-elite Population	.026* (.012)	.040 (.023)	−.067 (.056)	.048 (.025)	.011 (.030)	.020 (.038)

(continued)

TABLE 4.4. (continued)

	Q1. Where Are Welfare Chapters Built?	Q2. Does Prior Welfare Correlate with Subsequent BJP Support?				Q3. Does Prior BJP Support Correlate with Subsequent Welfare?
	DV: Service Index (logged)	DV: Non-elite Support for BJP			DV: Upper caste support for BJP	DV: Subsequent Religious Welfare
		Baseline Model	w/fixed effects	w/lagged DV		
	(1)	(2)	(3)	(4)	(5)	(6)
Christian Population	.096***	.061*	.474	-.056	-.083	.020
	(.019)	(.027)	(.503)	(.041)	(.041)	(.029)
Muslim Population	-.004	-.040	-.315	.049*	.031	-.004
	(.022)	(.025)	(.249)	(.024)	(.035)	(.021)
Constant	-5.934***	1.614	4.219	.402	3.468	-5.640
	(1.514)	(3.194)	(4.513)	(2.706)	(4.315)	(3.057)
State Fixed Effects?	No	No	Yes	No	No	No
N*T	47	47	47	32	47	30
R^2	.64	.64	.72	.63	.33	.19

Note: *p<.05 **p<.01 ***p<.001. All models include year fixed effects. The panel is slightly imbalanced (47 instead of 51) because of missing data on some explanatory variables for Chhattisgarh and Jharkhand for 1996 and 1999, as these states were formed in 2000.

competitors or where social relations between their core and target constituencies were more amicable. As Chapter 6 argues, the BJP's electoral rivals appear to influence how successful a welfare-based strategy would subsequently prove, rather than where it was initially attempted.

Model 1 also suggests that welfare chapters were not specifically built in areas with higher concentrations of Muslims, or even higher levels of upper caste support for the BJP.[63] This latter result is particularly interesting and indicates that any revealed effect of welfare on subaltern support for the party is unlikely to be a function of coattail effects driven by strong upper caste support. The only factors that did significantly impact the location of welfare chapters were the percentages of Christians and of Dalits and Adivasis in a state. Both of these variables positively correlated with service network density.

What do these results tell us about the strategic decisions underpinning Hindu nationalist welfare expansion? Most importantly, they suggest that the targeting of service was a joint product of the electoral interests of the BJP party and the ideological interests of its Hindu nationalist movement partners. States with large Dalit and Adivasi target populations clearly served the BJP's strategic calculus. It was in such states that welfare had the best chance of helping an upper caste party capture a winning plurality. At the same time, the BJP's movement affiliates were not motivated only by electoral incentives. As discussed in this chapter, providers – particularly those working within the Vanvasi Kalyan Ashram – also saw welfare as a counter to proselytizing efforts of rival faiths, particularly Christian missionaries.[64] Accordingly, it makes sense that Hindu nationalists would also concentrate their efforts specifically where local Christian populations are larger.

Probing these results in some more detail using simple descriptive statistics is instructive. Building on the findings from Model 1, Figure 4.7 plots the correlation between the Sangh service index and the state-level percentage of Dalits and Adivasis. The five cases with above-average Christian populations are additionally marked with a box reporting the percentage of Christians within the state.

---

[63] Diagnostics for all models reported in Table 4.4 revealed no issues of multicollinearity between the explanatory variables and no first-order autocorrelation within the panel.

[64] Following this thread, I did examine whether welfare chapters were correlated with the historical presence of missionaries. In a separate analysis using data collected by Woodberry, I found no correlation between Hindu nationalist welfare and the number of protestant missionaries in the state as of 1923. However, this analysis is limited by several factors, including that the data is not for current missions and does not account for missions started by Indians themselves. Given the recent timing of Hindu nationalist service expansion, these more contemporary efforts of Christian missions are likely to prove more influential in shaping the former's activities. Collecting comprehensive contemporary data is quite difficult, given the fragmented nature of missionary activity in India, and was beyond my capabilities for this project. However, exploring the relationship between missionary and Hindu nationalist presence remains a promising area for further research. Missionary data from Woodberry et al. 2010. I am grateful to Robert Woodberry for making this data available to me.

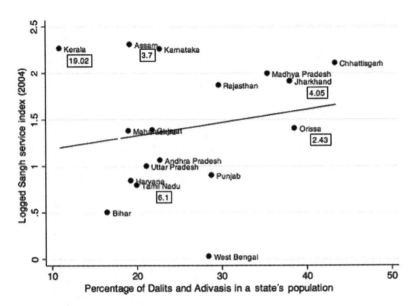

FIGURE 4.7. Subaltern population size and service network density
Note: Boxed figures indicate percentage of state's population that is Christian.

The figure reveals a few interesting facts. First, welfare chapters have a sizeable footprint in all five states with the largest combined Dalit and Adivasi populations. Further, four of the seven states in which welfare is concentrated most heavily (Madhya Pradesh, Chhattisgarh, Jharkhand, and Rajasthan) have sizeable Dalit and Adivasi populations that match the state's OBC population (see Table 4.2 for reference). In these cases, there are clear electoral incentives for providing welfare to subaltern voters. The three obvious outliers from Figure 4.7 in terms of service effort are Kerala, Assam, and Karnataka. Yet two of these three cases – Assam, and especially Kerala – have above-average Christian populations and are seen by Hindu nationalists as sites of extensive Christian missionary activity.

Thus, the two demographic factors that emerge as important in Model 1 do help us understand the selection of the majority of cases where service networks were expanded. Of course, this analysis also suggests we would expect greater service efforts to have been made in a few states, most obviously Orissa and Tamil Nadu, which both have sizeable subaltern populations and a relatively high proportion of Christians. It will therefore be worth tracking whether service networks do expand in these states over the next few years, and some preliminary evidence (discussed in Chapter 8) suggests that they have.

Based on this discussion of state-level factors that are likely to influence where service networks are built, Chapter 5 examines those factors that influence Hindu nationalist decisions about which villages to place service activists in. Before proceeding to that analysis, we still need to evaluate whether the observed correlation between welfare and BJP support holds up to more rigorous testing. Toward that end, Model 2 in Table 4.4 shifts to regressing BJP performance with Dalits and Adivasis on the service index and other state-level explanatory variables. The results reveal that the density of welfare chapters retains a strongly significant and positive effect on the BJP's performance, even when accounting for these important potential confounders. Especially as the key predictor and outcome variables are both log transformed, the results indicate that holding other variables constant at their means, a 10 percent increase in the service index results in an average increase of about 4.5 percent in the BJP's vote share.[65]

The results also show that the BJP did not fare better with Dalits and Adivasis in states where it faced fewer salient rivals, which indicates that the party had to actively court subaltern voters and could not count on simply becoming a default option when voters faced limited alternatives. Surprisingly, the insignificance of the ethnic voting index suggests that the BJP is also not automatically more successful where caste communities are less electorally polarized. Indeed, only the BJP's vote share among upper castes exerted a significant, positive impact on its performance among subaltern groups, although patterns of elite support did not confound the autonomous impact of service networks. Finally, the proportion of Christians in a state was revealed to have a negative effect on subaltern support for the BJP, the inverse of its impact on the density of welfare chapters. Given these opposite effects, this variable cannot be driving the positive association between service and voting, even as it does inform where welfare chapters are built.

Models 3 and 4 further test the robustness of the association between Sangh welfare networks and BJP performance through alternative specifications. As Model 2 accounts only for the impact of observable confounders, Model 3 additionally controls for state fixed effects.[66] The continued significance of service in this model shows that an expansion of service wings is correlated with improved BJP performance within the same state over time. The electoral impact of service is therefore not simply attributable to unobserved, stable differences between states in the sample.

Model 4 tests the impact of the service index when including a lagged measure of subaltern support for the BJP.[67] Systematic caste-wise electoral data is not available prior to 1996, so this specification attenuates the sample to thirty-two

---

[65] Interpretation of the coefficients is tricky because they include both the within-entity and between-entity effects. In the case of TSCS data, the coefficient represents the average effect of X over Y when X changes across time and between countries by one unit.

[66] A separate test failed to reject the null hypothesis that all year coefficients are jointly equal to zero in the fixed effects specification, and therefore year fixed effects were not technically necessary in this specification.

[67] For a clear discussion of why a lagged dependent variable cannot be combined with state and year fixed effects, see Angrist and Pischke 2009, pp. 243–6. Note that this specification does attenuate the sample, as data on the outcome variable was not available prior to 1996.

observations. However, including this gauge of past performance helps control more directly for the distinctive trajectory of Hindu nationalism with non-elite voters in each state. Importantly, the results show that the impact of service networks remains robust to controlling for the BJP's prior performance with Dalits and Adivasis.[68] Overall, the consistently robust impact of service on BJP performance across these different specifications helps increase confidence that the results are not the artifact of a particular modeling strategy.

Finally, Models 5 and 6 present placebo tests for which my central theory predicts no effect. Finding an effect in either instance would therefore cast doubt on the support this analysis provides for my argument. First, I anticipated welfare network density to have no impact on upper caste support for the BJP, as service chapters are explicitly not meant to treat these populations. Model 5 regresses upper caste support for the party on religious welfare and indeed finds no impact. Model 6 tests whether prior BJP performance (measured in 1996 and 1999) correlates with subsequent levels of Hindu nationalist service provision (measured in 1997 and 2004). A significant coefficient on the welfare index in this specification would indicate a violation of the causal logic implied by my argument. However, the model suggests that prior BJP support does not correlate with where welfare chapters were subsequently concentrated.

We can also combine the state-level data examined here with the NES survey data from Chapter 3 to address aforementioned concerns of measurement validity with the *Membership* variable used in the voter-level analysis in the previous chapter. The NES survey question used to construct the membership measure in Chapter 3 measured participation in a range of associations. The analysis was therefore unable to preclude the possibility that participation in non-Hindu nationalist organizations drove membership's observed impact on BJP support. To address this concern, we can leverage the reasonable assumption that membership is more likely to reflect participation in Hindu nationalist welfare associations where these organizations have more local chapters for voters to join. Consequently, my argument anticipates membership to correlate with BJP vote choice more strongly in states with dense aggregate welfare networks. Conversely, my theory would be troubled if we find membership's effect to be stronger in states with weak service networks (where it is far less likely to reflect inclusion in Hindu nationalist networks).

To test the intuition that the density of welfare wings in the state conditions membership's impact, I interacted the welfare index value for the state in which

---

[68] The results were also robust to using a generalized estimating equation (GEE) model, a different technique for dealing with observations that are correlated within clusters using population averages (Liang and Zeger 1986). The results for *Religious Welfare* were robust to using GEE models that were specified to assume an exchangeable correlation structure among observations within the same state. Again, this result is an added check but should also be interpreted with caution, given the small number of clusters available.

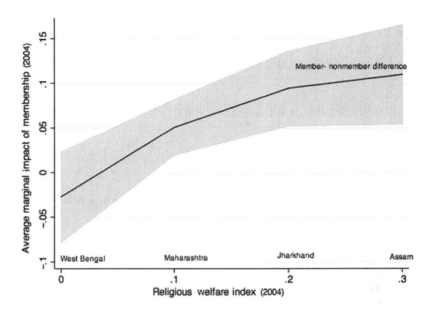

FIGURE 4.8. Average marginal impact of membership increases where Sangh service networks are denser
Note: Shaded area indicates 95 percent confidence intervals.

respondents reside with their individual membership status (*Service*Member*).[69] I follow Long in using simulated probabilities to interpret the interaction effect within a nonlinear framework.[70] Figure 4.8 charts the average marginal impact of membership on BJP support across a range of welfare index values. This effect is actually negative (and statistically insignificant) for low values of the religious welfare index, but it steadily increases for higher index values. The impact becomes positive for values greater than .05, and statistically significant for values greater than 0.1 (roughly the index value for the state of Maharashtra).[71]

Thus, in line with my argument, the marginal impact of membership on BJP support becomes more pronounced where Hindu nationalist welfare networks are denser. Of course, these tests must be read with caution, as the interaction term still does not uniquely identify members of Hindu nationalist associations. However, additional analyses also found subaltern associational members to

---

[69] I am grateful to Ana De La O for a helpful discussion on this point. See this book's web supplement for the full results of these tests (Table A.10).

[70] Long 2009.

[71] The results are similar if we calculate the individual interaction effect for each observation separately, using the protocol suggested in Norton et al. 2004. The average interaction effect is positive (.488) and significant (p<.01), and practically each individual interaction effect is positive. See online supplement for detailed results (Figures A.1 and A.2).

display traits more consistent with participation in Hindu nationalist associations than in more secular associations, such as those based around labor or caste.[72] Triangulating the numerous layers of evidence provided in these past two chapters thus strengthens confidence in the general validity of the *Membership* measure.

CONCLUSION

Let us consider the conceptual implications of the combined empirical analyses presented thus far. Chapter 3 revealed that among Dalits and Adivasis, nonparty organizations played a crucial role in the BJP's success. This chapter more precisely defined the contours of poor voter recruitment. Within Hindu nationalism's vast organizational penumbra, I isolated the importance of wings specifically devoted to basic service provision. Collectively, these all-India analyses reveal how Hindu nationalists used their movement affiliates to provide basic services to poor voters, enabling the BJP to continue to programmatically appeal to elite constituencies.

In detailing this strategic mixture, this analysis contributes to the broader literature on electoral linkages in several respects. First, it departs from prior studies of party politics, particularly in non-Western settings, that have identified a particular party with a single linkage strategy. In part, this tendency has been the product of our view of many electoral strategies as mutually exclusive. For example, the programmatic logic of policy-based appeals has conventionally been understood as incompatible with the discretionary nature of clientelism.[73] Yet, a single linkage strategy is often simply unable to forge support across constituencies with widely divergent interests. It is difficult to imagine public policies that appeal to the preferences of voters on opposite ends of the socioeconomic spectrum: big landowners and landless laborers, business owners and their workers, and so on. Similarly, increasing the share of patronage or pork to members of certain communities necessarily entails cutting the share of other groups. Given these trade-offs, parties often seek to deploy separate tactics with specific social constituencies; yet studies of such strategic mixtures remain rare.[74]

---

[72] Additional logistic regression tests examined whether *Membership* is likely to be capturing participation in secular associations, specifically labor unions and caste associations. This analysis found that members are not more likely to come from more heavily unionized occupation categories or to oppose measures to reduce the size of the public sector (where most formal unionized employment in India is located). I also found members are also not more likely to vote with their caste community or to oppose intercaste marriages (both attitudes expected of members of caste associations). Instead, members are marked by higher levels of participation in religious life, consistent with expectations of those who join Hindu nationalist organizations of the kind described here. The results of these tests are available in the online supplement (Tables A.11a, b, and c).

[73] For example, Kitschelt (2000) notes that beyond a certain point, the universalist logic of policy-based programmatic politics is incompatible with the exclusivist logic of clientelism. Also see Kitschelt and Wilkinson 2007, pp. 1–49.

[74] For exceptions, see Levitsky 2003; Luna 2010.

Second, in outlining how the BJP used a novel blend of tactics to appeal to the poor while retaining the rich, my analysis shifts from the debate on whether parties minimize risk by targeting loyal supporters or maximize vote share by focusing on new recruits.[75] The binary nature of this debate has diminished attention to the reality that most parties face, namely that they must reward prior supporters and recruit voters outside this base to remain electorally competitive. This task is especially pressing for elite parties in poor democracies. In India, the BJP's growing appeal with upper castes was sufficient to bolster a rise from obscurity to prominence, but it was insufficient to consistently deliver electoral victories. Yet, the BJP also could not presume upon continued elite support as it pursued poor electorates, evidenced by the rapid backlashes the party faced when it considered expansionary strategies that compromised upper caste interests.

There have been few studies that explicitly examine how parties can balance core and non-core strategies, and most of these have been based on the experiences of longtime incumbent parties with sustained access to government resources. Accordingly, scholars have primarily illustrated how balancing can be achieved through the strategic division of public monies.[76] Opposition parties, or less assured incumbents in competitive democratic settings such as India's, must develop other tactical portfolios. My study illustrates one such approach relying on differentiated private organizational assets to jointly implement tactics of recruitment and retention.

Finally, this chapter has specified why an elite party particularly favored service provision within its organizational approach. Descriptions of the range of activities undertaken by Sangh service wings illustrated their potential to directly appeal to the needs of poor families, as well as to provide a non-polarizing frame for upper caste activists to access distrustful lower caste voters. At the same time, the BJP's elite supporters were appeased by the low costs of service provision, which circumvented the need for more fundamental concessions. Finally, upper caste movement activists were energized by service's potential to effect social transformation, while countering the predatory conversion efforts of minority religious actors.

In addressing some important questions, the past two chapters have inevitably raised others. Specifically, the national-level evidence is unable to provide finer grained evaluations of how service organizations win electoral support, and when this approach is likely to succeed or fail. These remaining questions compel a more detailed, grassroots examination of the political effects of service networks, to which I now turn.

---

[75] Cox and D. McCubbins 1986; Calvo and Murillo 2004; Dixit and Londregan 1996; Stokes 2005; Nichter 2008.

[76] For example, Diaz-Cayeros, Estevez, and Magaloni (2010) show how the PRI used a government program in Mexico primarily to reward its loyal constituencies but increased short-term transfers to voters outside its traditional base during the run-up to elections. Other examples of balancing include Levitsky 2003 and Luna 2011.

5

How Services Win Votes

How does the private provision of local public goods win votes? Why would the work of actors formally outside the electoral arena yield electoral dividends? The comparative analysis of Indian states in the prior chapter demonstrated that the regional density of private welfare corresponded with the electoral success of an elite party among the country's poor. But is this aggregate pattern reflective of micro-level realities? Are individual beneficiaries of private welfare subsequently more likely to vote for an elite party? Further, is the electoral influence of service networks circumscribed to these direct beneficiaries, or does it also affect a broader community of voters? And what are the mechanisms through which service provision affects electoral choices?

Answering these important questions requires a worm's-eye view of how a service-based electoral strategy is implemented and received. To develop a more fine-grained understanding of the politics of provisioning, this chapter presents a detailed micro-level study of Hindu nationalist efforts in the state of Chhattisgarh in central India, based on fieldwork conducted in three stints between 2007 and 2010. Chhattisgarh was selected as an "on-the-line" case from the prior state-level comparative analysis in Chapter 4. As home to both dense networks of service organizations and high levels of political support for the BJP, the state provides fertile terrain for examining the mechanisms linking service to votes.

This chapter iterates quantitative and qualitative analyses to scrutinize my argument at several levels. First, I carried out extensive qualitative fieldwork to examine how service work influenced voting decisions. Personal interviews with ordinary voters helped uncover their reasons for accepting Sangh services, as well as their perceptions of the providers. Extensive conversations with, and observation of, Hindu nationalist service workers revealed the ways in which they tap the multifaceted potential of service. These activists first use the discursive opportunities welfare provides to gain access to distrustful communities, and then the material appeal of services to forge bonds with many villagers. Such bonds enable activists to recruit valuable cadres of subaltern candidates and party workers for the BJP. Additionally, embedded activists prove to be incredibly effective political mobilizing agents, using their officially non-partisan positions to affect electoral decisions, including those of many who do not directly benefit from their efforts.

Qualitative fieldwork revealed an interactive array of material, discursive, and organizational mechanisms through which service provision influences political life. Next, I carried out an additional layer of quantitative tests designed to scrutinize the mechanisms revealed by my fieldwork. First, I used data on more than 700 villages to examine why welfare chapters are placed in particular villages and not others, and to examine if village-level selection effects confound the electoral impact of welfare. This analysis builds on Chapter 4's discussion of state-level selection effects to provide a multi-level understanding of why service chapters are located where they are. Second, I analyzed data from a survey I conducted across four districts within Chhattisgarh, selected to take advantage of the considerable intrastate variation in the density of Sangh service networks. This internal comparison of otherwise extremely similar districts allows for a highly controlled assessment of the electoral impact of service work. This local survey also affords more precise tests of the impact of Hindu nationalist service wings on individual subaltern political choices than the all-India datasets.

The structure of the chapter follows this research design. After briefly describing the context in which this study took place, I move on to detailing the mechanisms uncovered via close observation of service work and then the results of the quantitative analyses at the village and voter level.

SETTING THE CONTEXT

Chhattisgarh is a relatively recent entry into India's list of states. Previously, the state's territory was considered part of Madhya Pradesh, India's largest and sixth most populous state. However, on November 1, 2000, sixteen administrative districts of Madhya Pradesh were formally declared to now constitute the new state of Chhattisgarh. It was to be the first of three new Indian states, along with Jharkhand (carved out of the state of Bihar) and Uttarakhand (carved out of Uttar Pradesh), all formed by central government decree in the space of two weeks. Chhattisgarh literally translates as "36 forts," a reference to the number of princely forts whose prior administrative areas are encompassed by the new state. By Indian standards, the state has a relatively small population of 21 million people, but it is topographically varied, with fertile central plains flanked to the north and south by densely forested hilly regions.[1]

Although there were demands for regional recognition of present-day Chhattisgarh in the early twentieth century, a robust and sustained push for independent statehood never materialized either during British colonial rule or India's post-independence era. The first organized pressures for separate

---

[1] See Berthet 2008. Data from Indian National Census, available at www.censusindia.net.

statehood came from the *Chhattisgarh Bhratra Sangathan* (Chhattisgarh Brotherhood Organization, CBS), which was formed in the late 1960s. The CBS tried to mobilize local and official support for regional autonomy, as well as greater government attention toward ameliorating Chhattisgarh's relative economic underdevelopment. During the 1970s, the *Chhattisgarh Mukti Morcha* (Movement to Free Chhattisgarh, CMM), a trade union movement that enjoyed considerable success, also framed many of its demands in regional terms as part of a broader discursive strategy.

However, the CMM's primary focus was not on the need for separate statehood, but on effectively organizing the state's large Adivasi population to fight for a wide range of basic rights, from land security to fair wages.[2] The organization was subsequently crippled by a number of coercive retaliations by local industrialists whose interests were threatened by such agitations. The CMM was particularly devastated by the murder of its leader, Shankar Guha Niyogi, shot by unidentified gunmen in what is widely viewed as the culmination of these retaliatory efforts.[3] The organization thus never developed into the spearhead of a broad movement advocating independent statehood, nor did it produce an effective political party arm in the manner of the similarly named *Jharkhand Mukti Morcha* (JMM), which is currently part of the ruling coalition in the neighboring state of Jharkhand.

In contrast with Jharkhand and Uttarakhand, its fledgling peers, Chhattisgarh's creation was thus marked by a noticeable absence of any popular mobilization.[4] In all three regions, political leaders clearly sought to leverage demands for autonomy to create political opportunities to their own advantage. However, in Jharkhand especially, in the words of one observer, "the idea of statehood had deep popular resonance" as well.[5] By contrast, in Chhattisgarh, the process was driven entirely by regional elites who felt marginalized by their more influential counterparts from "mainland" Madhya Pradesh. Whereas these elites often framed the demand for Chhattisgarh in terms of reclaiming a space for Adivasis, tribals were not integrally involved in the process of the state's creation.

Instead, local elites sensed an opportunity to expand their influence and even revive their flagging political careers through regionalist appeals.[6] At the same

---

[2] See Chandhoke 2003.

[3] See Bakshi 1992.

[4] Mawdsley (2002, p. 7) notes that "although the struggle in Jharkhand was often violent, and the demand for statehood in Uttaranchal was intense, the decision to make the Chhattisgarh region into a state was certainly not the act of a reluctant government succumbing to overwhelming popular protest and pressure."

[5] Tillen 2011, p. 78. I certainly do not intend to deterministically imply that the creation of Jharkhand was purely the result of sustained grassroots agitation. Indeed, the JMM itself was not initially concerned with demanding statehood. Yet Tillen (2011, p. 74) does note the call for Jharkhand did come to be integrated into "a broader repertoire on which the JMM could and did draw."

[6] For example, Berthet (2008, p. 329) notes that V. C. Shukla, a prominent Congress politician, joined the demand for a separate state in a move "better understood as a late attempt to revive his political career."

time, the demands of India's rapidly growing national economy increased incentives for local politicians to seek greater control over Chhattisgarh's rich natural resource base. Growing pressures for autonomy thus came from local factions within the party system, forcing the national leadership of both the BJP and the Congress (the two major parties in the region) to consider supporting the demand or risk the defection of key personnel. Several prominent leaders from both parties duly began voicing support for a Chhattisgarhi state during the mid-1990s. As one newspaper account noted "nothing except electoral arithmetic" prompted either party to side with the demand for statehood.[7] By the late 1990s, the election manifestos of both major parties included the demand for the new state of Chhattisgarh. By 2000, a state purportedly for "Adivasis in the hills" was created by upper castes in the plains with little tribal involvement.

CATCHING THE CONGRESS

Party politics in Chhattisgarh has been relatively understudied, but the state is a particularly promising one in which to study the BJP's attempts at social expansion. Adivasis comprise 31.8 percent of the Chhattisgarhi population, one of the highest concentrations in the country, which along with the state's 11.6 percent Dalit population gives these two marginalized communities a substantial electoral presence.[8] As a result, there have been obvious demographic imperatives for the BJP to court subaltern voters, as well as to seriously cull these populations for suitable leaders to contest the forty-four (out of ninety-one) state assembly seats reserved for Dalit and Adivasi candidates.[9]

To the puzzlement of several keen observers of Indian politics, the BJP performed extremely well with marginalized voters in state and national elections in Chhattisgarh. The party won 36 percent of the Adivasi vote in the 2003 assembly elections, matching the Congress, which had long enjoyed massive majorities among these electorates. An analysis of the 2003 elections by Yadav and Kumar notes that "the greatest surprise was the [equal] division of the Adivasi vote."[10] The authors argue that it was the significant reversal of the Congress's fortunes in constituencies reserved for Adivasis, where the BJP won twenty-four of thirty-four seats, which proved to be the former's "Waterloo." By catching the Congress while still maintaining its traditional edge with upper castes, the BJP crafted a winning position in Chhattisgarh.

In following elections, the BJP consolidated and even expanded this support. The party followed its impressive 2003 performance in the state assembly by winning 37 percent of the Adivasi vote in the 2004 national election, helping it to

---

[7] *Deccan Herald*, September 10, 1998, as quoted in Mawdsley (2002, p. 10).
[8] All population figures are from the 2001 Indian national census.
[9] This figure was valid for the period that fieldwork for this project was carried out. Of the forty-four seats, thirty-four were reserved for Scheduled Tribes and ten for Scheduled Castes in 2007–2008.
[10] Yadav and Kumar 2003.

secure nine of Chhattisgarh's eleven parliamentary seats, including all four reserved for Adivasis. In the 2008 state assembly elections, the party retained incumbency, again winning a sizeable majority of the constituencies reserved for Adivasis (twenty-three of twenty-nine seats).[11] Even in the 2009 parliamentary elections, where much was made of the reversals the BJP suffered nationally, the party won an unprecedented 40 percent of the combined Dalit and Adivasi vote in Chhattisgarh.[12] Indeed, in this instance, the party actually outstripped the Congress with the state's marginalized voters, a previously unthinkable feat. The BJP's sustained popularity, including in constituencies dominated by tribals, signaled that the saffron wave had arrived in the forests of Chhattisgarh.[13]

What made this success particularly puzzling was the speed with which an elite party overturned a long-standing pattern of incumbent dominance with non-elite voters. The Congress's prior success had been forged through its prototypical mobilizing strategy: constructing an effective patronage network through arrangements with local leaders.[14] This tactic was particularly effective in Chhattisgarh, where large swathes of territory fell under princely rule during the colonial period. As a result of the continuing influence of such notables following independence, the Congress focused on successfully incorporating them into its fold. The party was in turn rewarded with large majorities from the constituencies controlled by these leaders.[15] Through sustained incumbency, several Congress politicians from the Chhattisgarhi area developed a considerable regional following, with some even going on to acquire a national profile.[16]

The state unit of the Congress was thus a powerful adversary, an ideal blend of prominent leadership and effective patronage politics. Even as the BJP began its political rise in north India, its success in Chhattisgarh was therefore circumscribed to upper caste urban areas within the region's central flatlands. By contrast, one of the BJP's longtime leaders within Chhattisgarh noted of the

---

[11] As a result of a new delimitation of constituencies by the Electoral Commission in 2008–2009, Chhattisgarh now has twenty-nine seats reserved for Adivasis (the number for Dalits remained constant). Electoral data is from the Election Commission of India.

[12] Data based on 2009 Lokniti National Election Study.

[13] Hansen 1999.

[14] Kothari 1964 is the classic statement on this system.

[15] These relationships were certainly not always harmonious. Berthet (2008, p. 15) notes the "tumultuous relationships between Pravir Singh Deo, descendant of the princely family of Bastar, and the Congress are indicative of these difficulties to integrate sustainably the tribal areas into the party's fold."

[16] The Brahmin Shukla family for example became a local dynasty. Ravi Shankar Shukla, a longtime Congress activist who helped build the party unit out of Raipur, was the chief minister from 1947 until 1956. His son Shyam Charan Shukla has also been elected chief minister for Madhya Pradesh on three occasions, and his second son Vidya Charan Shukla also built a considerable following under the aegis of the state Congress before defecting to the Nationalist Congress Party (NCP) in 2003. He then moved from the NCP to the BJP in 2004, and this move caused a lot of internal controversy within the BJP. See "Editorial: Shukla" 2004; also see "Editorial: Chhattisgarh" 2004.

area's tribal regions: "This whole area belonged to them [the Congress] it was their *garh* [stronghold]. All the tribals were under the thumb of the *bare log* [big people] of the Congress. When I would talk to villagers they would just tell me, 'for generations my family is with Congress, so I have to vote for Congress.'"[17] The Adivasi inhabitants of the area's hilly flanks thus remained squarely under the thumb of Congress notables.

Adding to the BJP's woes was that the party's upper caste core restricted the tactical options available for challenging the Congress's established dominance. For example, the BJP's elite base prevented an increase in lower caste authority within the party's internal apparatus. Even after the BJP rode a tide of tribal support to power in the Chhattisgarh assembly in 2003, the social profile of the party's state cabinet remained disproportionately elitist. Although 58 percent of the BJP's legislators came from a Dalit or Adivasi background (because of the high proportion of seats that had to be reserved for these communities in the state), only 21.3 percent of its executive cabinet members were from these communities.[18] Further the main candidates discussed in 2003 for the top position of chief minister in the state were all upper castes, despite the frustrations voiced by Adivasi hopefuls within the party.[19] In 2008, the state wing of the party nominated only one Dalit and one Adivasi candidate in the forty-six "general" constituencies where it was not compelled to do so by mandatory quotas.[20] The BJP's difficulties were compounded by the fact that it could not rely on its ideological appeal to win non-elite support in Chhattisgarh. As I detail later in this chapter, Sangh activists themselves confessed that their more communal efforts were met with suspicion and hostility by subaltern communities in the state.

Does the expansion of service provision then help account for the unexpected turnaround in the party's electoral fortunes? I have already detailed the rapid growth of Hindu nationalist service wings across India, as well as their impressive array of local activities in states such as Chhattisgarh. This speedy proliferation, particularly of the Vanvasi Kalyan Ashram (VKA) – the primary service wing in Chhattisgarh – has not gone entirely unnoticed by scholars of the region. Froerer's ethnographic analysis of the Sangh notes that her fieldsite village, a longtime Congress stronghold in Chhattisgarh, returned a favorable result for the BJP some years after the Sangh had installed a local health activist there.[21] Similarly, Berthet has observed that the strong VKA network in the state may have played a key role in helping the BJP win all four seats reserved for Adivasis (Bastar, Kanker, Sarguja and Raigarh parliamentary constituencies) in both the

---

[17] Interview with Dilip Singh Judeo, former union minister and member of Parliament (Bilaspur) and party leader in the state, Jashpur, July 22, 2010.

[18] Data collected and coded by Jaffrelot and Berthet (reported in Berthet 2008).

[19] The primary contenders evaluated by the party were Raman Singh (the eventual winner), Lakhiram Agarwal, and Dilip Singh Judeo. Interview with Nand Kumar Sai, New Delhi, April 28, 2008.

[20] Author calculations using data from Election Commission of India 2008.

[21] Froerer 2006. See also Pandey 2008.

1999 and 2004 national elections.[22] Yadav also argues that the decline in the Congress's fortunes since 1991 (when it swept Chhattisgarh by a double-digit margin) was in part the result of the BJP "reaping the political dividends" of the work of its organizational affiliates.[23]

These observations regarding the potential electoral impact of service work have not been confined to Chhattisgarh. For example, Corbridge notes that the RSS continues to be "very active" in the neighboring state of Jharkhand, where "it enjoys a formidable reputation for providing high quality educational and health-care facilities [that] helped to lay the foundations of the rise to power of the Bharatiya Janata Party in the region in the 1990s."[24] However, these claims about the political influence of service work have been largely speculative. To rigorously examine whether and how services win votes in central India, I relied on a blend of qualitative and quantitative analyses, to which I now turn.

HOW SERVICE PROVISION WINS VOTES

The research for this section draws on fieldwork that was primarily carried out in the *tehsil* (sub-district) of Jashpur, located within the district of the same name (see Figure 5.1), in three stints between 2007 and 2010.[25] I draw on this fieldwork to detail several specific ways in which the VKA translated its welfare activism into political influence. First, a service-based strategy held tremendous discursive potential, allowing upper caste activists to access distrustful subaltern communities through the apolitical channel of service work. Once established, these activists won gratitude from local Adivasis and distinguished the VKA from public alternatives through its reliable delivery of basic services. The VKA then worked to translate this goodwill into electoral support for the BJP through a variety of mechanisms. Although these strategies were understandably most effective with direct beneficiaries of the VKA's programs, the social influence of activists appeared to spill over to sway a broader community of voters. Thus, a grassroots examination revealed a complex, interactive set of material and social mechanisms through which service work influenced electoral politics.

Gaining Acceptance: The Discursive Value of Service Provision

It would be a mistake to assume that disadvantaged communities embraced VKA activists simply because of their acute need for basic services. For such services to be accepted, providers must be trusted. Yet, many of the Sangh activists I interviewed discussed their difficulties in gaining acceptance from

---

[22] Berthet 2008, p. 6.
[23] Yadav 2004b.
[24] Corbridge 2000, p. 68, fn 8.
[25] All names in the figure of fieldsite villages, local Sangh activists, and ordinary respondents have been changed to protect their identities.

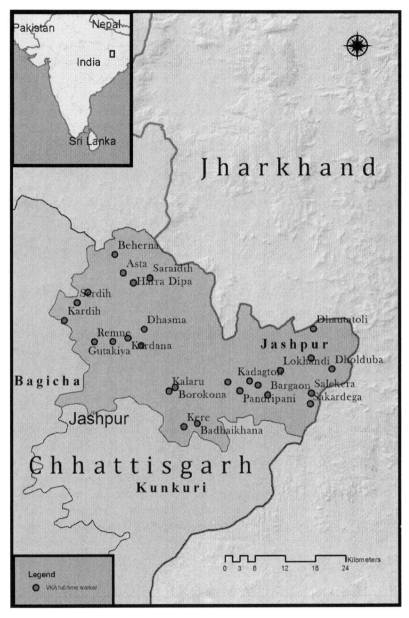

FIGURE 5.1. Location of VKA activists in fieldwork site (Jashpur Sub-district, Jashpur District, Chhattisgarh)
Source: Information given to author by VKA Office, Jashpurnagar, July 20, 2010.

subaltern voters, particularly in villages where their predecessors had alienated locals through ideologically explicit mobilizing efforts. Ethnographic studies of the region have documented the long history of tribal resistance to "civilizing" campaigns, including the prior efforts of Hindu nationalists in the region. Such oppositions ran so deep that many local Adivasis had openly reappropriated the term *jangli* (of the jungle), despite its traditionally derogatory connotations, to more clearly demarcate their differences with urban upper caste social practices.[26]

Far from having a ready-made constituency for their services, VKA workers had to work hard to even be allowed to live within subaltern communities. Most Adivasi villagers were convinced that Sangh activists were primarily concerned with reshaping daily cultural life to conform to Brahminical notions of Hindu tradition. As one Sangh activist explains: "Yes, there was a reaction among villagers when we first started visiting, that these people must have come with a political agenda. Many would even tell us to leave their neighborhood. They saw our work as part of the work of 'Hindu institutions' and that can be a problem here."[27] Similar issues arose all over the state. Another activist admitted that he had trouble when starting a one-teacher school, because villagers didn't understand that the "main directive" of his organization was service, not enacting a cultural agenda. For the first month, he had to go door-to-door every day pleading with families to send their children to him.[28]

A senior VKA doctor who worked for many years in villages primarily populated by the Pahari Korva tribe (with whom the VKA has been particularly effective) concurred with this view: "In the beginning... people are suspicious as to what the motive is... they have heard that we don't approve of practices like the drinking of liquor or the worshipping of trees. There is distrust at first and will continue until you actually go to them and work amongst them."[29] This admission reflects the depth of the challenge that Hindu nationalists faced to be accepted as providers within a village. More fundamentally, it questions the common assumption of a neat teleology between inadequate public service provision and the popularity of alternatives offered by religious providers. Abysmal government infrastructure, as was the norm in these parts of Chhattisgarh, did not automatically lead Adivasis into the VKA's waiting arms. How then did service providers win acceptance within these communities?

My fieldwork revealed that winning over distrustful villagers required discursive as well as physical efforts. What emerged as particularly crucial in initial interactions was for activists to deemphasize the VKA's cultural project and stress their role as ideologically neutral service providers.[30] As one VKA activist explained:

---

[26] Froerer 2007, p. 32.

[27] Interview with respondent AB, Bilaspur, July 27, 2010.

[28] Interview with AC, Anola village July 21, 2010.

[29] Interview with AD, Jashpur, April 2, 2008.

[30] Menon (2010, p. 111) also notes seva wings attempt to portray a "benevolent side of the movement" in her study of Seva Bharati in Delhi.

We don't tell them not to drink liquor and eat meat at first anymore – if we do we will be denied entry. Once they have gotten to know us a bit as service workers, then we start talking about how drinking alcohol can hurt their economic situation. Only later will we try to say it is also not according to Hindu tradition.[31]

I witnessed this discursive sequencing during one of my trips with a VKA worker, Ramesh, to several villages where the organization had not yet established a chapter. Ramesh and a couple of VKA workers rounded up people in each village and held an informal meeting. He began by speaking about how the VKA sought to establish a one-teacher school in the village and asked for potential volunteers to help him do so. He spoke at length about the value of literacy, and the help the VKA could provide students. However, he did not mention *dharma jagran* (spiritual awakening), which the organization privately notes as its central goal.

Ramesh later told me that the lukewarm reception he seemed to get at the village was normal during early interactions in a given locale. In fact, the rotating overnight visits of the VKA's medical team (described in the previous chapter) are often preferred as a method of first contact. Administering medicines was found to be the easiest activity to frame apolitically, and these short visits introduced the organization to the community while arousing minimal local suspicion.[32] The VKA's teacher-activists also engage in a gradual approach during their early days in a village. Teachers often reach out to children or families in the village, recruiting students individually until they have the numbers required for a full class:

At first we teach little things – what are the letters, what are the birds in your neighborhoods, what games you can play in school. With these little pieces of information we gain their trust, and through them, their families' trust, to the point that when we come by parents will tell their children "go run – see what *chacha* [uncle] wants."[33]

Teacher-activists covet the status of *chacha*, and they take great pains to acquire it by cloaking the ideological currents running through their curricula in politically neutral terms. For example, VKA teachers would explain the *samskars* (traditions) – a term with clear religious connotations – that they sought to impart as "teaching children to be well-mannered."[34]

[31] Interview with AE, Anola village, March 20, 2008.

[32] As one health activist noted: "See conversation can happen even as you are giving medicines. When we go for medical camps, we will stay in one of the villages overnight so that we can talk with villagers, see how they are faring, and get to know them better. And we always make sure to tell them we are here as health workers, our only job is to look after your health and to help you if you are feeling poorly" (interview with AF Jashpur, July 24, 2010).

[33] Interview with AB, Bilaspur, July 27, 2010.

[34] As one service activist noted to me proudly, "You can tell if a house has one of our students in it, because all the shoes will be arranged in a neat line outside." Interview with AG, Raipur, July 20, 2010.

Service activists would emphasize the secular aspects of these good manners, telling parents that they would ensure that pupils respected their elders, kept clean personal habits, and performed household chores without complaint. Take the case of Laxmi, who runs a VKA after-school program for about thirty children in a small village in Jashpur district (home to roughly eighty families) and doubles as a health worker in the village. She remembers that during her initial efforts, she "would go door-to-door saying, 'look in my *kendra* [center] your children will learn to study better, will learn better behavior, and will get the chance to sing and play games also,'" to convince residents to come to her school, while making no mention of the VKA's commitment to Hindutva.[35] Now that she has established herself in the village, she says, most of her students come from families who send their children unasked.

Although clearly ideologically motivated, upper caste VKA workers found these more neutral self-descriptions greatly enabled their efforts to embed themselves within wary Adivasis communities. A senior doctor in the VKA organization explained this depoliticizing value of service in some detail:

They [Christian missionaries in the area] worked out a great medium to gain new followers: through service. See education and health care are the first thing a person needs for their life to be lived. If anyone is sick, and if someone treats them and makes them better, then they will forever have their ear. If someone is illiterate, and someone teaches them to read, then again they will always listen to their teacher and have their sympathy. That is why we work in health and education. See I told you about the dispensary [in Jashpur] and the medical vans [which go around villages to dispense basic medical care]. Then we have hostels and schools in the village. Through these mediums, you can go to anyone at anytime. After we establish ourselves, then we can begin work with *dharma jagran* [spiritual awakening] and get people to come sit with us, to learn *bhajans* [prayers/religious chants] to come to *mandir* [temple], etc.[36]

In addition to confirming the importance of missionary activity in motivating Hindu nationalist service activists, this explanation hints at how the VKA utilizes the discursive potential of service to first obtain the permissive space required for its daily operations. The next section examines how the VKA converted this acceptance by subaltern communities into active goodwill.

Forging Goodwill: The Material Appeal of Services

Even if Hindu nationalists were allowed into subaltern spaces, why would these residents choose to avail themselves of the VKA's services? To assess the motivations of these villagers, I personally conducted semi-structured interviews with eighty households across five villages within the district of Jashpur. As I was especially interested in ascertaining when villagers might choose Hindu nationalist services over public alternatives, the five villages were deliberately selected

[35] Interview with Laxmi, Ber village, July 24, 2010.
[36] Interview with AF, Jashpur, April 1, 2008.

to have functioning VKA chapters, as well as a government primary school. Sixteen respondent households within each village were selected at random and asked a mixture of closed- and open-ended questions regarding their choices about where to obtain different services, as well as their opinions of providers. The interviews were conducted in villages where I had made multiple prior visits and had also previously held open focus group discussions to ensure a higher degree of comfort and responsiveness on the part of households interviewed.

The distribution of responses suggests that the VKA schools rate quite favorably among villagers. Among those interviewed, 47.5 percent (N=38) of respondents said they sent their children to a VKA-run school, compared to 37.5 percent (N=30) who sent their children to government school, and 11.25 percent (N=9) who sent them to schools run by Christian missionaries. What factors informed the VKA's popularity?

The interviews confirmed that the primary attraction of VKA services was not their infrastructural superiority over public alternatives. As described earlier, the vast majority of projects run by the VKA are of a rudimentary variety, operating on an extremely tight budget. For example, even the residential hostels, which provide meals and board, function on about Rs. 20 (about 50 cents) per student per day. The *ekal vidyalaya* (single-teacher day schools) run on even less and advertise as operating on a "dollar-a-day" budget in fund-raising efforts among the Indian diaspora in the United States.[37] Costs are kept low by employing teacher-activists who work for low pay (usually between $15 and $30 a month), and by using a single home or a public space in the village to hold classes.

Further, even though the VKA does not charge its day scholars tuition, and often waives its minimal fees for its residential programs, it does not enjoy a comparative advantage in terms of its affordability. The reason is that the VKA's limited budget cannot furnish the wide range of incentives, including mid-day meals, that government schools offer their students. Sangh activists admitted this inability put them at a disadvantage in attracting local attention.[38] Indeed, just less than four in five households saw government schools as the "most affordable option" for their children, because they helped reduce the general household bill through the various extra incentives offered to students.

Nor did the VKA's appeal stem from the cultural preferences of particular subaltern families. The national survey analysis had suggested that explicit affiliation to Hindutva played a minimal role in the political decisions of lower castes. Interview evidence similarly suggests that the desire for a particular type of cultural curriculum did not prominently figure in household decisions about schooling; 46 percent of interviewees said the primary reason they educated

---

[37] See "Ekal Vidyalaya Chicago holds fundraising concert," *NRI Today*, (http://www.nritoday.net/national-affairs/453-ekal-vidyalaya-foundation-chicago-holds-fundraising-concert). Similar descriptions were found in advertisements for a fund-raising marathon to be held in Silicon Valley in October 2011 (http://www.ekalmarathon.org/programdetails.html).

[38] Interview with AC, Anola village, July 21, 2010.

their children was to enable them to get a salaried job. The desire to find such non-agrarian employment stemmed from Malthusian concerns, as successive generations within a family were forced to squeeze livelihoods from smaller and smaller divisions of their ancestral holdings.[39] Another 46 percent of respondents said they thought education might help their children learn and protect their rights, the most common example of which was obtaining the requisite documentation for obtaining government benefits for Adivasis or for below poverty line (BPL) families.[40] In contrast to these fairly material motivations, only 3 percent of interviewees identified "learning cultural values" as the primary impetus for sending their children to school.

If infrastructure, cost, or ideological orientation did not favorably distinguish VKA schools from government alternatives, what was the source of the former's appeal? Interviewees did perceive the VKA as providing a better quality of education than public options. Indeed, the number of respondents rating the VKA as providing the best schooling was more than twice the number who chose government schools (Figure 5.2). The fact that private, fee-charging institutions (the second most favorably rated option) were not seen as financially viable for most villagers only served to enhance the VKA's comparative advantage.[41]

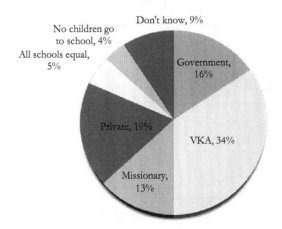

FIGURE 5.2. Which school provides the best quality of education?
Source: Author interviews (2010).

---

[39] Household interview respondent, Kikar village, August 1, 2010.
[40] The biggest example villagers gave was getting a BPL (below poverty line) card, which is needed for schemes such as receiving subsidized rice.
[41] Interestingly, some villagers in Bael village who rated private schools as providing the best quality of schooling also confessed they had no personal experience with these alternatives. Instead, they based their opinion on the assumption that private school facilities would be better because that is where *amir log* (rich people) sent their children (July 18, 2010).

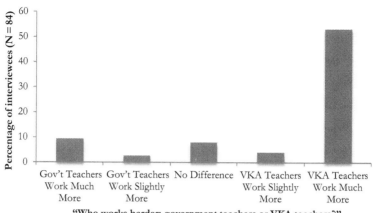

FIGURE 5.3. Comparing VKA and government schoolteachers
Source: Author interviews (2010).

More specifically, in open-ended questions about disaggregating schooling quality, villagers identified *regularity* and *availability* as the chief attractions of services offered by the VKA.[42] These features of VKA education were in turn the product of the perceived dedication of the activists themselves. As Figure 5.3 highlights, an overwhelming number of villagers agreed that VKA teachers outworked their government counterparts.

This view seems largely warranted. In a majority of the government schools I visited across more than forty villages in Jashpur, there was either no teacher present or even more commonly the teacher was not engaged in actual teaching at the time of my unannounced arrival.[43] High teacher absenteeism in Adivasi areas is driven by the fact that most applicants who met the educational requirements for public schoolteachers came from non-Adivasi families in urban areas; once allotted a remote rural posting, they frequently do not show up for the full quota of workdays. This local pattern is in line with the results of broader studies of public social infrastructure in India.[44] In a study of health care provision in Rajasthan, Banerjee and Duflo find that high rates of doctor absenteeism in local health centers was made worse by the unpredictability of that absenteeism. Such compounded uncertainties led patients to opt for non-government alternatives,

---

[42] Focus group discussion, Kulthi village, Jashpur district, March 13, 2008.
[43] I have written elsewhere (Thachil 2009) about the potential boost given to the demand for religious schools as a result of inadequate educational infrastructure in South Asia.
[44] One study (Kremer et al. 2005) ranked Chhattisgarh in the bottom quarter of Indian states in terms of teacher attendance, with almost a third of public schoolteachers missing school every day, and fewer than half actually doing any teaching in class.

even though the latter were usually staffed by less well-qualified personnel than their public sector counterparts (especially outside major cities).[45]

In contrast, Sangh teachers are committed to residing in the locations in which they work, maintaining constant contact with their pupils and ensuring high rates of attendance:

There is a big difference between our schools and the government schools. Because see, our service is for twenty-four hours a day, theirs is just for a couple of hours. We never leave this area, and even outside of school we work to keep our students disciplined. So students know if they arrive late for school, we will get to know and punish them. . .see I know all the people in the area, and I tell them, if you see one of my kids going to bathe in the pond or something like that during school hours, let me know.[46]

The local VKA leadership was acutely aware that developing rapport with Adivasi communities hinged on making their centers more desirable than public alternatives. Given their low operating budgets, VKA service chapters identified reliability of provision as a way to positively differentiate themselves from government options, a view reflected in the previous quote. The VKA has even taken institutional steps to ensure high teacher attendance. For example, the organization employs *nirakshaks* (inspectors) who periodically assess village projects to verify enrollment figures and monitor teacher absenteeism.[47]

These efforts have paid off. A telling example of the high local regard for VKA services came from the village of Kikar. I interviewed the village's government schoolteacher, who confessed he viewed the VKA school as superior to his own and had therefore enrolled his son in it.[48] Another striking illustration came from the village of Anola, where a Christian interviewee who openly opposed the BJP and Sangh Parivar still enrolled his son in the VKA school because he believed it offered a better education.[49] A second resident of the same village said that most of his neighbors rated the VKA chapter higher than the government school. He further worried that these favorable ratings would make it difficult for his son to secure a spot in the school for the upcoming year, especially if the teacher decided he had to cap enrollments.

Other interviewees said that they enrolled their children in VKA chapters because they needed to count on a few hours of reliable child care within the day. Two residents of Bael village, both relatively poor members of the Oraon Scheduled Tribe, said they especially valued the VKA's after-school programs.[50] Without this service, their only alternative would be to leave their children unsupervised, and they invariably found ways to get in trouble. Further, they complained that government schools could not be counted on for providing

[45] Banerjee and Duflo 2009.
[46] Interview with AH, Seva Bharati activist, Bilaspur, July 27, 2010.
[47] Field notes from Jashpur headquarters, March 28, 2008.
[48] Interview with WA, Kikar village, July 20, 2010.
[49] Interview with WB, Anola village, July 18, 2010.
[50] Interview with WD and WE, Bael village, July 16, 2010.

regular supervision, even during normal school hours, given the teacher's irregular presence. The reliability of the VKA's rudimentary health efforts won similar praise from villagers. Many villagers preferred to seek the VKA's help for the everyday illnesses the organization was equipped to handle, because "they will always see you, whereas with the government center we never know whether we will even see a doctor that day."[51]

Bhaskar, who runs a residential hostel for the VKA in the state, said that Adivasi parents could not send their children to for-profit private schools, but that local government education was not of a quality to "make a difference in the lives of these children."[52] The reason for this, Bhaskar continued, was not simply public teacher absenteeism, but that "the government gives their teachers so many different tasks to do even outside of education, that they cannot do their main job well." These tasks include the time-consuming preparation of electoral rolls, monitoring poll booths during elections, maintaining records of public welfare schemes, and helping with government survey work. The consequence of this work is that even dedicated government teachers are often unable to fulfill their primary role as educators. For example, a resident of Anola village noted that she had originally sent her daughter to the government school, but that the teacher (who she actually described as an honest worker) had too many other things on his plate to devote adequate attention to his students.[53]

Of course, some interviewees did voice concerns about the VKA's presence within their villages. For example, a resident of Ber complained that even though the VKA health activist was always available, his abilities were limited, and his treatments often had little positive effect on her ailments.[54] Non-Adivasi villagers also complained that the VKA prioritized tribal residents in their efforts. Although this focus is hardly surprising, given the organization's mandate to work among Adivasi communities, it does sometimes lead to local tensions. For instance, one interviewee from the Lohar *jati*, who falls within the OBC caste grouping, said he was trying to get his family reclassified as Scheduled Tribe.[55] If successful, he planned to reattempt gaining his son admission to the local VKA school, which was currently oversubscribed and therefore only taking new students from Scheduled Tribe households. A different concern came from a Christian resident of Lokhandi village, who feared that the VKA would not treat residents of all faiths equally, although she did also admit that they did not turn away non-Hindu Adivasis from their schools.

---

[51] Interview with WC, Anola village, July 18, 2010.
[52] Interview with Bhaskar, Sanna, July 23, 2010.
[53] Interview, Anola village, July 15, 2010. Absenteeism was also noted as a problem with local public health facilities. A respondent in Bael village (interview, July 18, 2010) noted that the VKA village activist always saw her family members, whereas several trips to the local primary health center (PHC) proved fruitless with no medical staff available to treat them.
[54] Interview with WF in Ber village, July 19, 2010.
[55] Interview with WG, Anola village, July 15, 2010.

From Service to Votes: The Electoral Repertoire of the VKA

The last two sections have attempted to describe the interactions between VKA activists and Adivasi communities in the sequence in which they unfolded. Service provision enabled the VKA to present a qualitatively different vision of the Sangh Parivar to disadvantaged populations. Activists attempted to replace images of a movement fixated on preserving upper caste traditions or engineering violence against minorities with that of an organization primarily invested in the basic *bhala* (welfare) of the poor. Having gained acceptance within village communities, activists were able to display their dedication by reliably providing services, thereby capitalizing on the opening afforded by erratic public provisioning.

However, this goodwill for the VKA did not automatically result in political support for the BJP. To translate services into votes, VKA activists took on a range of mobilizing activities through their embedded positions within Adivasi communities. Three features of this embedded mobilization are detailed in this section, as they stood out in their electoral importance: the creation of a pool of Adivasi leaders to tap as state-level political candidates, the funneling of the VKA's young recruits into the BJP to serve as party workers, and the efforts of the service activists themselves in shifting political opinions around elections.

The highest-profile benefit that service chapters have yielded for the BJP has been their recruitment of a small but important cadre of Adivasi politicians for the party. These members largely hail from cohorts of the first tribals integrated into the VKA by upper caste activists during the organization's initial expansion efforts. Many of these recruits have now moved to assume positions of prominence in the BJP's state political machine:

Look, they [the VKA and RSS] are our party's main backbone, the soul of the party. They are the tree; we are the fruit. They may work directly, indirectly, but ultimately we are a seed that had been sown by them ... our current ST [Scheduled Tribe/Adivasi] leadership have come from the grassroots, come up through the VKA system and are trained by them. Our ST leadership includes Vishnu Dev Sai (Member of Parliament, Raigarh), Nand Kumar Sai (MP Sarguja), Ganesh Ram Bhagat (MP Jashpur) all affiliated with the VKA.[56]

Many of these Adivasi leaders note that the success of the BJP in the district is pretty much entirely dependent on the work of the Sangh, specifically the VKA. Nand Kumar Sai, a member of Parliament from the constituency of Sarguja and an influential Adivasi within the BJP's state unit, noted that service activists went "where no one else has gone" and had really helped the BJP "establish a presence with these sections" and "consolidate through [the VKA's] extensive organization."[57]

---

[56] Interview with Satyanand Rathiya, BJP state cabinet minister (independent charge), Raipur, April 12, 2008.
[57] Interview with Nand Kumar Sai, New Delhi, April 28, 2008. Sai was also the first Adivasi president of a BJP state unit (Madhya Pradesh).

This dependence has led BJP politicians to take unusual steps to stay in the good graces of their movement partners. Dilip Singh Judeo, the putative *maharaja* (king) of Jashpur and a BJP party leader in the state, made sure every male member of his family attended the local VKA school for a short token period, even though his family is not Adivasi.[58] In joint meetings held between the Sangh and the BJP in Chhattisgarh, even senior party leaders are extremely deferential to their non-electoral partners, sitting on the floor while the movement activists are given chairs and allowing the latter to take the lead in these discussions.

The importance of the VKA's Adivasi recruitment is heightened in a state such as Chhattisgarh, where a high number of assembly seats are reserved for Scheduled Tribe candidates. Moreover, these bottom-up politicians (dubbed "everyday Adivasis" by one BJP leader) often had deeper political linkages with their constituencies than did previous generations of top-down tribal candidates.[59] The latter were often uninspiring leaders who had been picked solely on the basis of their connections with upper castes in Delhi and Raipur (the state capital). By contrast, everyday Adivasi candidates came up through a tradition of grassroots activism that helped make them more effective campaigners than their predecessors.

In addition to this core of political leaders picked from among its earliest members, the VKA has provided the BJP with a cadre of youthful party workers from among its later recruits. As the VKA's chapters proliferated across Chhattisgarh in the 1990s, many young Adivasis were recruited into the organization as service activists. Many of these recruits were then channeled into the BJP apparatus as village-level party workers. As one activist told me, "*seva karya se karyakarta mil rahein hain* [from our service work we are getting workers]."[60] For example, a good number of the full-time boarders in VKA residential hostels retain their connections with the organization after graduation. Many come to VKA schools from faraway villages, often because post-primary facilities are not available in their home villages. These residential facilities prove to be especially rich recruiting grounds for the Sangh:

See in the beginning, people were suspicious, but the best proof of the turn [in their opinions] has been that we have managed to recruit fifteen students from our school alone in the last few years to work as full-time party workers for *hamara bhajapa* [our BJP]. I'm not saying we can make this work for everyone ... [but] if we have thirty-eight students at a time in the *chatravaas* [student hostel] about half will work for us later in some capacity.[61]

Such high yield rates are less common among participants in the village day schools, but the expansiveness of this network ensures a sizeable number of recruits as well.

---

[58] Interview with Ranvijay Singh Judeo, BJP party member, Raipur, March 31, 2008.
[59] Interview with Krishna Rai, BJP leader, Jashpur, March 29, 2008.
[60] Interview with AF, Jashpur, July 24, 2010.
[61] Interview with AH, Bilaspur, July 27, 2010.

The BJP's growing youth cadre in Chhattisgarh is visible at the village level. In the twenty-four villages that were part of the voter survey described later in this chapter, the average age of the BJP's primary *karyakarta* (party worker) was 26.5, nearly a dozen years younger than the Congress average of 38 years. Moreover eighteen of the BJP's twenty-five party workers (one village had two workers) came to the party from the VKA network, and both Congress and BJP leaders openly stated that the party is similarly dependent on the Sangh across the state. A comparative advantage in cadre recruitment is especially valuable in places marked by low levels of literacy and technological infrastructure, where door-to-door activism is particularly vital. In addition to generating this cadre, the VKA's network itself provides a wealth of local information to the BJP's party workers. For example, Dhruva, who works as a VKA *nirakshak* (inspector) in the state, showed me the detailed information he keeps on villages within the local administrative block.[62] The log he maintains contains minutiae on the caste and occupational and economic profiles of all households in these villages. Sharing this information with the BJP helped the latter make tactical decisions, including those pertaining to candidate selection and canvassing strategy.

Although service wings clearly generate valuable political resources for the BJP's own apparatus, the VKA activists also constitute an important, separate shadow cadre for the party. This cadre has also expanded over time, both in the number and social composition of its activists. Whereas upper castes dominated the initial generations of VKA workers within the state, most subsequent recruits were Adivasis who came into the organization via various paths. For example, Harish was sent to a VKA boarding school by his parents because of the substandard quality of schooling available in his village. Unlike private schools, the VKA only asked for occasional donations of rice from his relatively poor parents. Immediately after graduating, Harish began working for the VKA and currently runs one of its boarding schools.[63] Another such story was that of Rajesh, who stayed in the VKA hostel from grades 10 through 12 because it was closer to the nearest government secondary school than his home village and now runs a day school himself.[64] Another example is Bhaskar, who began interacting with the VKA when he went to a government college in Jashpur in 1998 and needed a place to stay in town.[65] The VKA helped him at that time, and his gratitude compelled him into full-time service for the organization.

The political work performed by these nonpolitical activists was the least easily discernible mechanism uncovered by my qualitative fieldwork. The first glimpse of such electoral motivations came to me in an informal conversation with Harish, who described how villagers regarded Sangh teachers:

[62] Meeting with Dhruva, Anola April 1, 2008.
[63] Interview with Harish, Kutki March 22, 2008.
[64] Interview with Rajesh, Bael, March 16, 2008.
[65] Interview with Bhaskar, Sitanagar, July 23, 2010.

Our teachers are not respected at first, because people are not sure about what they are trying to do in the village. But over time they gain high social status in the village. VKA teachers are working with children, and even today teachers in tribal society command much respect, which is helpful for the Sangh.[66]

As the conversation progressed, the usefulness of such high social standing became more fully developed. Harish began describing how once they have been able to insert themselves into the fabric of village communities, Sangh activists form their own subtle mobilizing for the BJP to tap into during elections.

The depoliticized discourse surrounding service work was particularly crucial in enabling VKA activists to profess their removal from the dirty river of politics. This formally non-partisan status uniquely equipped service workers to perform delicate partisan tasks, such as spreading rumors about rival competitors from the Congress. Harish continued:

In addition to doing social work, the VKA has managed to do other work for the BJP such as telling people the truth about how [Congress Party leader and former chief minister] Ajit Jogi is trying to pass off as a real Adivasi while he was not one, as well as reassuring them that BJP candidates are friends of the VKA and will not engage in corruption.[67]

Jogi was the best-known victim of this efficient rumor network.[68] He was accused of falsely certifying himself as a member of the Kanwar Scheduled Tribe, allowing him to contest seats reserved for Adivasi candidates as well as gain popularity among the state's important tribal electorates. As Jogi's formal caste status was debated in the Indian courts, it was VKA activists who worked hard to plant seeds of doubt against the Congress leader among Adivasi communities.

Ordinary villagers saw these accusations as more credible precisely because they were voiced by actors outside the formal political arena.[69] The rumors were widely understood to have severely compromised Jogi's popularity among Adivasis, even after his status as a Scheduled Tribe (Adivasi) was formally certified. Indeed, a high-ranking Congress official in the state admitted that "the controversy over Jogi's status led many Adivasis to decide he wasn't one of them, and the Adivasi areas were where our party was hurt the most [in the 2008 state elections]."[70] This high-profile example is far from the only instance when the VKA deployed its effective politics of rumor. Service activists also routinely enacted similar strategies against far less heralded rivals, most often in

---

[66] Interview with Harish, Kutki. March 22, 2008.

[67] Ibid.

[68] The controversy made headlines following the 2001 ruling by the National Scheduled Tribe and Scheduled Caste Commission. The commission, which was headed by a BJP leader (Dilip Singh Bhuria), stated that Jogi was in fact a member of the Satnami (Dalit/Scheduled Caste) community, and not an Adivasi. The Bilaspur High Court overturned this decision in 2006, enabling Jogi to serve once more as a state legislator from an Adivasi constituency.

[69] See Zaidi 2003.

[70] Interview with Chandra Das Mahant, Congress state president, Raipur, March 28, 2008.

the form of voicing allegations of corruption against local Congress candidates before and during elections.

In addition to their effective use of rumor, VKA activists performed more direct mobilizing roles during electoral contests. Although most activists were initially reticent about admitting to any political involvements, over time they began to discuss their efforts more readily. One of them offered the following explanation of why welfare providers are regarded as particularly effective at political mobilization:

See when the students come to one of our schools, their parents also start getting affected. They see that the schooling is much stronger than in government schools. So their thoughts also turn toward our schools. Now if someone who we support enters politics, then because [the parents'] thoughts toward our school, toward our teachers, are favorable, they are open to listening to our views. We will not campaign for any party, but from an individual point of view, we will say who we think would do well. We even tell the candidates – we will try and help you, but we will never walk around with you or your campaign.[71]

This informative response begged a further question: how were such non-campaigns conducted?

Further conversations revealed that even as activists would deliberately recommend candidates in their capacity as nonpolitical individual citizens, local Sangh leaders systematically coordinated their electoral efforts. Numerous activists informed me that the Sangh "holds meetings before every election to make clear which candidates its service activists should be supporting."[72] During campaign seasons, workers are given responsibility for a cluster of villages (typically between twelve and twenty) close to the chapter they run. In their assigned villages, activists hold a series of *baithaks* (meetings) that are open to all residents. During these meetings, the activist will embed discussions about the upcoming election within a broader discussion of local issues. By doing so, they look to simultaneously canvass political opinions and advocate for particular candidates within the neutral framework of a public conversation:

See whenever I go, even for political work, if I'm holding a *baithak*, I start the meeting the same way that I do for normal meetings [not around elections], with a song or something to set a good mood. And I tell people at the meeting that all I want to do is talk about what is best for our Adivasi community. Then I tell them that I know about the personality, about the behavior of the candidates. I tell them look I am not from any political party, and so I am not in this to win an election – I just want us to choose the best person we can, that I can tell you who a good person is.[73]

[71] Interview with AH, Bilaspur, July 27, 2010.
[72] Ibid. A VKA worker in Bael village made a similar observation, noting "See our samiti tells us *kisko dena hai kisko nahi dena hai vote* [who to vote for and who not to vote for]. So they tell us we need to support this candidate and not this candidate – and we go around to nearby villages and talk to them about this." Interview on July 23, 2010.
[73] Interview with Laxmi, Ber village, July 24, 2010.

Many activists work in this vein, trying to maintain an air of non-partisanship by promoting particular candidates on the basis of their ability to serve Adivasis, rather than their adherence to Hindu nationalist views:

So for example villagers might ask us, which candidate do you like? Now first we always ask them – well who are you thinking of supporting? If they are thinking of the BJP, then we don't say much – why put more pressure [*dabav*]? But if they say Congress, then we ask – have you considered all the issues when making this decision? Then we *samjhao* [explain] why they should reconsider. If after hearing us they say we still want to vote for Congress, we don't insist they reconsider [*zabardasti nahi karte*] – we don't want them to think we are working for a party.[74]

A number of service workers told me the idea was not to aggressively compel voters but to sway them toward their side [*apne taraph jhukana hai*].[75]

Another electoral strategy used by the VKA (referred to by its workers as the *sanstha* or "institution") works slightly more indirectly: "We go to a village, and first sit with those villagers we have a good relationship with and make clear which candidate we want to win the election. We'll say – ok who does the most for their society – that is the person we have to help with the election."[76] A key point to note here is that the villagers with whom activists have a good relationship are most often not actively tied to the BJP. More often, these ties come from social connections and friendships service activists have independently forged through repeated interactions over the course of their own work.

These deep, but informal connections with ordinary villagers prove particularly useful for Hindu nationalists in central India: "We tell our friends to go and talk to their neighbors and try and convince them to support our preferred candidate. And we tell them how to explain their support – to make sure villagers understand the choice is best for the development of their community."[77] One illustration of this process came from a member of the Korva tribe whose daughter was enrolled in a VKA school. This resident told me that over time he developed a friendship with his child's teacher, which included regular conversations about political issues. This resident said he valued such discussions because the activist's views "are not coming from a political angle [*rajnaitik drishtikon*] but instead are concerned with *samaj ka bhala* [the overall well-being of the community]." Interestingly, this respondent said he did not agree with views associated with Hindu nationalism but trusts the teacher, "who has been working among us for nearly five years." Building on this friendship, he voluntarily participates in VKA discussions and efforts around elections to "get the right candidate to succeed."[78]

---

[74] Interview with Bhaskar, Sitanagar, July 23, 2010.
[75] Interview with Gopal, Kikar village, July 22, 2010.
[76] Interviews with Gopal and Mohan, Kikar village, July 22, 2010, August 2, 2010.
[77] Interviews with Mohan and Gopal, Kikar village, July 22, 2010, August 2, 2010.
[78] Interview with WC, Bael village, July 16, 2010.

Such friendships are especially valued by VKA leaders, who reason that villagers will view the opinions of their neighbors as even less tainted by partisan bias than those of service activists themselves. Further, this technique allows the VKA to reach a broader audience while enabling activists to retain a relatively non-partisan air. Clearly, conducting partisan work while trying to appear non-aligned requires constantly walking a political tightrope. As I detail in this book's Conclusion, although Hindu nationalists in Chhattisgarh have managed this equilibrium, several developments threaten their ability to continue doing so.

Close study of the VKA in Chhattisgarh has revealed how service provision enabled activists to first access distrustful communities, establish goodwill through regular provision of valued benefits, and finally convert that goodwill into political support for the BJP. Although the value of the VKA's services is undeniably important, my account also suggests the inadequacy of a solely material conceptualization of how service wins votes. Nor did support appear to be a reflection of subaltern false consciousness produced by ideological manipulation. Instead, micro-level research uncovered a complex interplay between discursive, material, and social factors that enabled the BJP to break through with disadvantaged electorates in the state.

Whereas qualitative fieldwork can reveal the multiple sources of service work's political influence, it is less well suited to more broadly test its effect on voting. The insights presented in this section are best distilled into two broad concerns for further analysis. First, the clear material appeal of services suggests that direct beneficiaries of the VKA's work should be more likely than non-beneficiaries to support the BJP. Yet, my analysis has suggested that service activists do also affect some non-beneficiaries within the broader community in which they are embedded. In this latter instance, the local standing of activists appears to crucially inform their political influence. Accordingly, a second expectation of my research is that the VKA should be more effective in shifting the electoral preferences of those non-beneficiaries who hold the organization in high esteem.

To assess if these expectations are realized, I conducted a voter survey across four Chhattisgarhi districts in 2008, the results of which are discussed in the next section.

DOES SERVICE WIN VOTES? TESTING THE ELECTORAL IMPACT OF PROVISION

According to the population-adjusted index of Sangh provisioning utilized earlier, the density of service networks in Chhattisgarh (.245) is the one of the highest in India. However, this formidable apparatus is not uniformly distributed within the state. To exploit this fact, I selected four districts for further study based on their marked variance on this key explanatory factor. The districts chosen were Bastar, Jashpur, Mahasamundh, and Raigarh, which are spread across the state, as Figure 5.4 shows. I was able to obtain data on the number of

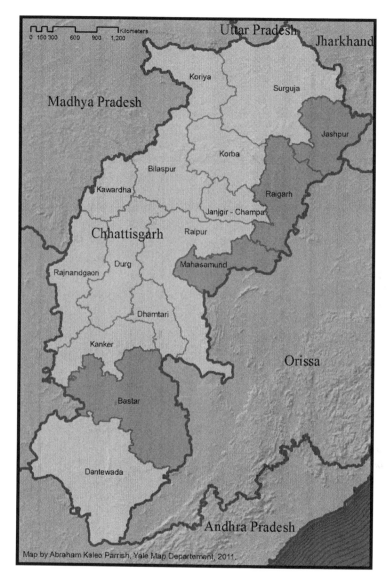

FIGURE 5.4. Survey districts (highlighted) in Chhattisgarh

service projects being run in 2007–2008 in each of these four districts through the written internal records made accessible to me by district chapters of Seva Bharati and the VKA.[79] As the survey instrument included sensitive questions

---

[79] Unfortunately, district-level disaggregations of Sangh service projects across India are not available.

and the survey area included fairly remote villages, it was especially vital that it was implemented according to the instrument design and sampling protocol. To ensure this, I personally administered the survey along with a single research assistant among 360 Dalit and Adivasi voters, spread equally across twenty-four villages, with the villages and respondents selected at random within these districts (for full details on the survey instrument, sampling techniques, and response rates, please see Appendix C).

Unlike the national sample, these districts clearly afford much more closely controlled comparisons of voter preferences. For example, all four districts have a comparable level of party competition, land area, population, and ethnolinguistic diversity. All of the districts chosen are predominantly rural (more than 90 percent) and have large Dalit and Adivasi populations (more than 40 percent). Further, all four districts have small Muslim populations (less than 2 percent) and have not experienced significant communal rioting since independence.[80] In short, the districts are remarkably similar across a number of measures conventionally thought to influence the chances for BJP success. These similarities enable us to better isolate the effects of service network strength on the party's performance.

District- and Village-Level Evidence

The survey found the BJP to have outperformed the Congress among subaltern voters across the four districts, garnering 46.76 percent of votes to the latter's 39.15 percent. Of greater analytic importance than this aggregate result is whether the party's district-level success corresponds to the local density of service networks. The middle two columns of Table 5.1 confirm the tremendous

TABLE 5.1. *Voting patterns across districts in Chhattisgarh*

District	Number of Sangh Service Projects	Per Capita Adjusted Index of Sangh Service Density	Percentage Voting for the BJP (2003)
Jashpur	545	1.07	59.55
Bastar	512	.619	67.78
Raigarh	20	.096	28.89
Mahasamundh	26	.059	19.77

Source: VKA Headquarters, Jashpur, Seva Bharati Office, Raipur, Chhattisgarh Author Survey, Chhattisgarh (2008).

[80] Indeed, the only district that experienced any rioting was Raigarh, which was one of the districts in which the BJP was not successful. Thus, the idea that the party could use rioting to garner votes appears not to have empirical support in the specific case of Dalit and Adivasi voters. Riot data from Varshney-Wilkinson Dataset on Hindu-Muslim Violence in India, 1950–1995, Version 2, Ashutosh Varshney and Steven Wilkinson, October 8, 2004.

within-state differences in the spread of Sangh networks. The rightmost column indicates that these differentials did correlate with variations in the party's performance. The BJP's vote share with Dalits and Adivasis in the high-strength districts of Bastar and Jashpur was more than twice as high as in the low-strength districts of Mahasamundh and Raigarh.[81] Such aggregate differences are telling. The neighboring districts of Jashpur and Raigarh are nearly identical across most major demographic, topographic, political, and economic factors, and yet they reveal strikingly disparate lower caste voting patterns.[82]

However, to fully examine whether services win votes, it is necessary to examine data at the level at which voting takes place. Accordingly, the analysis sought to assess two types of impacts that service organizations might have on individual voters. The first was more material *beneficiary linkages*, whereby these networks create support for the BJP among direct beneficiaries of Sangh service chapters. The expectation here was that these beneficiaries would be more likely than non-beneficiaries to support the BJP as a whole. However, service networks could also generate more indirect *opinion linkages*, whereby activists deploy their social standing within village communities to exert influence even on some non-beneficiaries. This second, more indirect effect carries two implications: that service wings are able to attract positive opinions of their work among some non-beneficiaries and that this shift is consequential enough to influence the latter's electoral decisions.

Based on these inquiry goals, the analysis worked with a tripartite conceptualization of voters: those who identified as members of service organizations, those who identified as beneficiaries of these organizations, and those who were neither (henceforth, non-beneficiaries). Respondents who had enrolled one of their children in a VKA school or had received medical treatment from a VKA doctor or health activist were considered beneficiaries. Only those respondents who also attended weekly *baithaks* or even worked for the VKA were classified as formal members. Disaggregating respondents into these three categories allowed me to examine how effective and extensive each type of linkage was in terms of helping the BJP at the polls.

---

[81] Congress politicians such as state leader Ajit Jogi have cried foul over the party's reversal in Bastar in the 2003 election, arguing that the result was the result of improper electoral procedures. Jogi maintains that the BJP, which was in power in New Delhi at the time, forcibly deployed the Central Reserve Police Force (CRPF) to the region under the guise of "keeping elections fair," when in reality they stuffed ballot boxes for the BJP in these areas. However Kumar (2004, http://www.india-seminar.com/2004/534/534%20sunil%20kumar.htm) notes that such allegations flew on both sides of the aisle, as some of his sources from Bastar informed him that the 1998 elections had not been fair, as "it was alleged that many booths were non-functional and district officials had gifted those seats to the then Congress Chief Minister Digvijay Singh on a platter." As a result, it is difficult to conclusively state that election irregularities hurt one party's performance systematically more than others'.

[82] The VKA's project totals in each of the four districts are 398 projects in Jashpur, 317 projects in Bastar, 13 projects in Raigarh, and 8 projects in Mahasamundh. Sewa Bharati runs the remaining projects in each district.

TABLE 5.2. *BJP support by respondent type in Chhattisgarh*

District	Members	Beneficiaries	Non-beneficiaries
High-Strength Districts	100% (27/27)	89.13% (41/46)	42.99% (46/107)
Low-Strength Districts	100% (4/4)	100% (12/12)	21.95% (36/164)

Source: Author Survey (2008).

Turning to the tabulations presented in Table 5.2, we see that the conditional probability of voting for the BJP was significantly higher among members and beneficiaries than among non-beneficiaries. The percentages of each type of respondent supporting the BJP provide a crude initial measure of the efficacy of each linkage type. The number of respondents falling in each category, reported in parentheses, indicates the extensiveness of this linkage. The results indicate that membership in a Sangh social service organization guarantees support for the BJP at the polls but also that relatively few voters fall into this category. The rest of this analysis is therefore devoted to examining the difference between the two larger remaining categories: nonmember beneficiaries and non-beneficiaries.

The results for the former group, reported in the third column of Table 5.2, are striking. First, they indicate an extremely high success rate for the BJP among those who have benefited from the Sangh's service activities. Although clearly preliminary, this disaggregation seems to provide some evidence that the influence of service organizations goes beyond a cadre of committed members to impact a wider community of those benefiting from their efforts. Second, whereas the efficacy of this material linkage remained high in all four districts, the extent of villager participation in Sangh activities did not. Service chapters were able to deliver the support of most of their beneficiaries to the BJP, even in the low-strength districts of Mahasmundh and Raigarh. However, service organizations in Jashpur and Bastar have encompassed more than four times as many respondents as they did in the other two districts. In these latter regions, the Sangh's organizational footprint proved simply insufficient for generating a significant electoral base for the BJP.

Third, although a high proportion of beneficiaries voted for the BJP across all four districts, the same constancy of support is not witnessed among non-beneficiaries. Respondents in this category are nearly twice as likely to support the BJP in Jashpur and Bastar as their counterparts in low-strength areas. This variation suggests the possibility that in communities where its organizations are dominant, the Sangh's activities produce a wider effect even on those voters who do not directly participate in their activities. Qualitative fieldwork suggested that such spillover effects may result from shifts in public opinion produced by service activists in areas where they are densely present. In a subsequent portion of this analysis, I statistically examine whether such broader opinion effects did in fact influence the voting decisions of non-beneficiaries.

Before proceeding to such analyses, it is useful to first pause and consider the possibility of selection effects operating at a level between that of the individual voter (the focus of Chapter 3) and that of the state (the focus of Chapter 4). We saw in Chapter 4 that demographic variables – notably the proportions of Dalits and Adivasis and of Christians – were the key determinants of where Hindu nationalists focused their service efforts. Of course, service organizations must also make decisions about where to place their activists within states where their activities are expanding. Yet, these local decisions cannot rely on the same selection criteria as used at the state level. Even within a given district such as Jashpur or Bastar, let alone the entire state of Chhattisgarh, there are a number of localities with comparably large subaltern populations. Thus, welfare providers must make choices about which villages to place their precious personnel on some other basis. If organizations such as the VKA choose to build chapters in localities that also share other characteristics correlated with BJP success, then such village-level selection effects might confound the electoral impact of welfare observed in Chhattisgarh.

Unfortunately, gaining access to information on village-level activities across all four districts was not possible. However, the Jashpur unit of the VKA, with whom I spent the most time during fieldwork, eventually gave me the records for its village-level activities for the entire district.[83] I was therefore able to code the roughly 700 villages within the district into one of three categories: those with a VKA project (including episodic activities such as health camps, described previously), those with a full-time resident VKA activist, and those with neither.[84] I then used logistic regression models to evaluate the impact of several variables that might confound a relationship between VKA presence and BJP performance.

It is conceivable for example that for their own comfort, service activists prefer to reside in better-developed villages or those closer to local towns. Such villages are also better connected to urban communities, where the BJP's primary base of support lies. It is therefore plausible that these localities might also be places of relatively strong BJP party organizations and electoral performance. To account for this, the analysis includes three measures of village development collected from the 2001 Indian national census: the per capita income of village residents (*Income*), the availability of tube wells (*Tubewell*), and the availability of electrical power for domestic use (*Electricity*).[85] Two additional variables measure a village's connectivity, including its distance from the nearest town (*Distance_Town*) and whether it has paved road access (*Roads*).

---

[83] I was given this information in my final visit to Jashpur in July-August 2010.

[84] Villages that were regularly visited by monthly medical camps described earlier but did not have a permanent resident activist were coded as having a project.

[85] All variables included were checked for potential multicollinearity, and none were found to have a variance inflation factor of more than 2.7, indicating that collinearity between the included explanatory variables was not a source of concern.

In addition to these potential confounders, I controlled for a few variables that might plausibly affect the VKA's allocation decisions. For example, it is possible that the organization avoids villages with strong public infrastructure of the kind that directly competes with the services it offers. To check whether this was the case, I included *Schooling*, a variable that measures the educational facilities available in a community, coded o for a village with no facilities, 1 for those with primary schools only, and 2 for those with both primary and middle schools. *Health* is a binary variable indicating if the village has either a primary health center or subcenter. Interviews with VKA elites also revealed that they preferred to locate some of their projects in larger villages with prominent *bazaars* to maximize the exposure their activities received. I therefore included variables measuring the geographic size (*Area*) and Adivasi population (*Adivasi_Pop*) of a village.

Overall, the logit models tested in Table 5.3 revealed that most of these factors had nonsignificant impacts on the likelihood of an activist (Column 1) or service

TABLE 5.3. *Village-level determinants of service activities*

	Resident Activist (1)	Service Project (2)
Income	−.001	.000
	(.001)	(.004)
Roads	−.505	−.593*
	(.339)	(.280)
Distance_Town	−.001	−.001
	(.002)	(.001)
Tubewell	.852	.497
	(.732)	(.717)
Electricity	−.555*	−.383
	(.256)	(.205)
Schooling	.169	−.225
	(.295)	(.246)
Health	.053	−.044
	(.325)	(.270)
Area	.161	.939***
	(.261)	(.255)
Adivasi_Pop ('000s)	−.001	−.003
	(.003)	(.003)
Constant	−2.066***	−1.421***
	(.400)	(.324)
N	764	764
Percent correctly predicted	89.14	82.33

Notes: *p<.05, **p<.01, ***p<.001 Results are from a random effects logistic regression model. Including sub-district (*tehsil*) or block-level fixed effects does not change the significance of the results for any of the variables.
Sources: 2001 National Census Village Profiles and Vanvasi Kalyan Ashram records.

project (Column 2) being present in a village. Activists were not more likely to be found in communities with richer populations, better water or road infrastructure, or greater proximity to urban centers. They also did not reside within communities with plausibly higher demand for their services, as neither *Schooling* nor *Health* variables registered a significant coefficient. Instead, the only significant finding in the results reported in Column 1 ran opposite to the direction expected, suggesting that activists were more likely to be found in villages lacking domestic electrification. The location of service projects was similarly unaffected by most village-level characteristics, including per capita income and distance to the nearest town. Once again, the availability of public service infrastructure that might directly compete with VKA provision did not appear to influence the Sangh's allocational decisions. The only significant results from the model tested in Column 2 suggests that projects are more likely to be found in larger villages and those lacking paved road access.

On balance, the nonsignificance of most variables in determining the placement of projects or activists improves our confidence that the electoral impact of service work is not a product of the systematic selection of particular types of villages. Indeed, to the extent that we can see any targeting at all, it appears that the Sangh prefers more remote villages with less developed roads and power infrastructure. However, given the BJP's urban middle-class base, we would expect residents of such villages to be if anything less likely to support the party. The minimal selection effects observed in Table 5.3 should therefore have a dampening rather than a confounding effect on any association between provision and voting.

Unfortunately, electoral data is not available at the village level in India. However, even looking at the villages included in the local survey is instructive. A simple difference of means tests comparing the ten villages with VKA projects with the fourteen villages without such projects shows no significant differences in *Area*, *Road*, and *Electricity* – the three variables with significant coefficients in the models tested in Table 5.3 – at the standard 95 percent confidence level. Thus, among this subsample, villages with VKA projects were not in fact larger or less connected with roads and power.

Further, the BJP did not enjoy systematically stronger prior support in villages with VKA projects. The voter survey asked respondents whom they had voted for in the prior state assembly elections in 1998. The responses indicated that the party won 23 percent of subaltern votes in the ten villages with service projects compared to 20 percent in the remaining fourteen villages.[86] Yet by 2003, the BJP's vote share among these same respondents was more than 40 percentage points higher in the villages with a VKA presence (67 percent to 25 percent).[87] This considerable divergence between 1998 and 2003 is especially telling because most other village-level factors – village size, social composition, average income – remained relatively stable during this time period. The far stronger

---

[86] The difference of means (two-tailed) was significant at the 95 percent level.
[87] This difference of means (two-tailed) was statistically significant at the 99 percent confidence level.

performance of the BJP in villages with VKA activists is therefore unlikely to be driven by underlying characteristics of these particular locations.

Qualitative evidence also suggested the lack of uniform criteria in the selection of villages. Numerous activists said the key to starting a project was the availability of a relatively well-educated resident willing to do service work.[88] However, the factors informing whether such a person was present in specific villages were far from systematic. For example, one of these educated activists planned to work in the state capital but came back to his home village after his father became ill. Needing a job within the village, he was quickly recruited by the VKA.[89] Similarly, another VKA teacher was a college graduate who had failed to get off the waiting list for a more lucrative position as a government schoolteacher. When he returned to his home village looking for employment, the Sangh's offer was his best opportunity.[90] Although instructive, these individual stories do not suggest some clear selection criteria that would confound the electoral impact of service work.

In sum, multiple forms of evidence from Chhattisgarhi villages suggest that the observed electoral effect of service is unlikely to be centrally driven by some other characteristic of the places where activists are located. However, as an added precaution against the influence of unobserved factors at the village level, the voter models tested in the next section include village fixed effects when evaluating individual-level patterns of electoral behavior.

Testing the Effects of Service: Voter-Level Evidence

To examine the impact of service provision on individual voters, I again specified logistic regression models with a dependent variable that was coded 1 for respondents who supported the BJP and 0 otherwise. I included in each model two variables designed to assess the electoral impact of service networks. *Service Beneficiary*, the first variable, is also a binary indicator coded 1 for respondents who directly benefited from Sangh service activities and 0 otherwise. *Service Opinion*, the second variable, measures how favorably a respondent views the activities of Sangh social service organizations on an increasing scale from 0 to 3. I also included the variable *Age*, measured in years, as many service activities have specifically targeted the youth, and consequently an observable implication of my argument is that the BJP will perform better among young respondents.

In addition to the new data on participation in and opinion of Sangh service networks, the surveys in Chhattisgarh replicated the questions used in the national survey instrument to construct comparable measures of the relevant control variables. In particular, the survey obtained identical measures of a respondent's

[88] Activists AG (July 20, 2010), AC (July 21, 2010), and AI (July 23, 2010) all cited such availability as the single most important factor in determining the location of VKA projects.

[89] Interview with AC, Anola village, March 20, 2008.

[90] Interview with Rajesh, Jashpur, July 25, 2010.

income, religiosity, affiliation to Hindu nationalism, and the influence of co-ethnic community leaders on their voting choice.[91] Given that Table 5.2 showed that all members of these service organizations voted for the BJP, I present the more substantively interesting results from a sample that excluded this subgroup and included only nonmember beneficiaries, and non-beneficiaries.

The results reported in Table 5.4 reveal that both key explanatory factors had highly significant impacts in the expected directions even after including

TABLE 5.4. *Assessing the influence of service on voting in Chhattisgarh*

	Voting for the BJP (2003)			
	(1)	(2)	(3)	(4)
Service Beneficiary	2.852***	2.466***	3.687***	4.909***
	(.506)	(.631)	(.658)	(1.236)
Service Opinion	.531***	.841***	.805***	1.492***
	(.189)	(.177)	(.204)	(.401)
Age	-.048***	-.070***	-.081*	-.151***
	(.011)	(.016)	(.033)	(.033)
Control Variables				
Religiosity			.393	.899*
			(.201)	(.376)
Communalism			.316*	.201
			(.109)	(.267)
Caste Influence			-.530	-2.558*
			(.583)	1.289*
Income			-.048	.341
			(.278)	(.905)
Male			-1.457*	-2.104**
			(.621)	(.803)
Education			-.023	-.023
			(.111)	(.243)
Constant	.636	1.834***	.695	-5.027
	(.433)	(.663)	(1.874)	(3.389)
Village Fixed Effects	No	Yes	No	Yes
No. of Villages	24	24	24	24
Observations	328	328	186	186
Percent predicted correctly	80.5	84.40	80.89	88.59
Log Likelihood	-67.048	-122.524	-74.071	-41.239

Notes: *p<.05, **p<.01, ***p<.001. Results are from logistic regression models with all data from Author Survey (2008). Sample excludes members (N=31).

---

[91] The only difference is that the measure of *Religiosity* uses an unweighted average instead of an index constructed using principal component analysis. Using such an index yielded no changes to any of the results in either statistical or substantive terms.

potential confounding effects (Models 3 and 4) and village-level fixed effects (Models 2 and 4).[92] Benefiting from service provision was found to significantly increase the likelihood of a respondent supporting the BJP in all four specifications. Respondent opinion of Sangh services was also found to have a strongly significant, positive impact on voting for the party.

Additionally, *Age* proved to be significant in all four models, with a substantial negative coefficient, suggesting that the BJP had made significant progress in recruiting young disadvantaged voters. Indeed, a stunning 65 percent of voters from the 18 to 29 category supported the party. Taken in conjunction with the qualitative evidence of the VKA's recruitment of young party workers for the BJP, this result suggests a strong generational dimension to the political dividends yielded by service work. This relative willingness of young subaltern voters to switch their allegiance to the BJP also makes sense given the wealth of scholarship demonstrating the stabilization of partisan preferences over time.[93] The focus of service activities on young people has therefore only served to enhance their electoral efficacy.

The analysis also found that earning a higher income did not increase the likelihood of BJP success, and the salience of co-ethnic leaders reduced support for the party (consistent with the national analysis in Chapter 3). Religiosity did appear to retain an impact in the fixed effects specification (Model 4), although its inclusion did not diminish the autonomous impact of participation, opinion, or age on BJP support. Perhaps most interestingly, respondents professing greater ideological proximity to Hindu nationalism were not found to be consistently more likely to vote for the BJP. These results echo similar findings from the national analysis, providing multiple levels of evidence that the appeal of Hindu nationalism, whether preexisting or constructed, is not central to the BJP's electoral expansion among the disadvantaged.

However, it would also be incorrect to suggest that service work has not produced attitudinal shifts. Despite their inability to forge attachments to Hindutva, service activists have shifted local perceptions of Hindu nationalism in more subtle ways. As I have argued in some detail, service workers won local standing within poor communities not only by providing valued benefits but also through discursively re-inventing their movement. Consequently, among Adivasis in places such as Jashpur, Hindu nationalism is no longer seen as simply the vehicle of radical firebrands or upper caste political interests but also as the home of patient providers of material benefits. The acceptance of service activists into these communities indicates an attitudinal shift that constitutes an ideological victory, albeit one more circumscribed than that for which the Sangh had originally hoped.

[92] The village was chosen as the unit for the fixed effects specification as it was the primary sampling unit for the survey. Changing the specification to use district-level fixed effects does not result in any statistical or substantive change to the results on any variable.
[93] For an elegant statement of this argument, see Converse 1969.

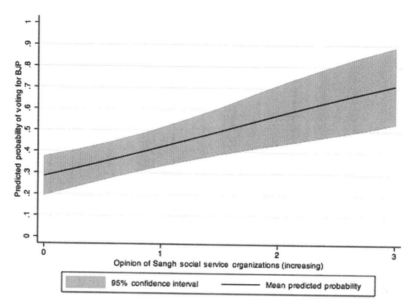

FIGURE 5.5. Effect of opinion of service organizations on voter preferences (non-beneficiaries only)
Source: Uses simulated predicted values from Model 4 in Table 5.4.

To assess the substantive impact of each key explanatory factor analyzed in Table 5.4, I examined how changes in their values affected the predicted probability of voting for the BJP. Dalit and Adivasi beneficiaries were found to be 54 percentage points more likely than non-beneficiaries to vote for the BJP. Similarly, those voters with the most favorable opinion of Sangh service networks were 52 percentage points more likely than those who rated these organizations least favorably to support the BJP.

However, with respect to opinion effects, I was more interested in determining whether positive opinions generated the kinds of spillover effects among non-beneficiaries suggested by my prior fieldwork. Figure 5.5 shows that a non-beneficiary with the most positive opinion of these organizations is two and a half times more likely to support the BJP as is one with the least favorable opinion possible, holding other variables at their mean values.[94] This striking difference indicates that the influence of service chapters does extend beyond the pool of direct beneficiaries and can impact a wider swathe of voters in communities in which activists are embedded.

Two familiar concerns remain. First, are beneficiaries different from non-beneficiaries in some fundamental way other than their participation in Sangh

[94] The figure uses predicted probabilities from Model 4 reported in Table 5.4.

TABLE 5.5. *Matching analysis among Chhattisgarh survey respondents*

Variable Name	Beneficiaries	Non-Beneficiaries	Means Difference	Means Difference (Post-Match)
Communalism	3.08	3.11	.03	.01
Income	2.25	2.47	.25	.13
Religiosity	4.94	4.49	.45**	.12
Ethnic Influence	.413	.502	.502	.502
Age	29.78	33.83	4.04*	.521
Gender	.53	.56	.03	.01
Education	7	5.355	1.645*	.48

Notes: *p<.05, **p<.01, ***p<.001.

service activities? Comparing the two subgroups in Chhattisgarh (Table 5.5) revealed no statistically significant difference in terms of income level, support for Hindu nationalism, or the degree to which respondents in each category are influenced by caste elites. However, the two subgroups appeared to significantly differ with respect to religiosity, age, and education, with beneficiaries emerging as slightly more pious, younger, and more educated.

A second concern is whether VKA beneficiaries were already prior supporters of the BJP. Qualitative evidence from this study runs counter to such a supposition in several respects. First, aggregate electoral evidence indicates the BJP never enjoyed the high level of support it has now attained in districts where these networks are strong. Further, the timing of the VKA's expansion in the early 1990s precedes the BJP's gains in the state during the late 1990s and early 2000s. Finally, although both BJP and Sangh leaders outlined many ways in which the party benefited from the efforts of its affiliates, no interviewee articulated any mechanisms through which the BJP funnels its supporters into service organizations.

In order to confirm the robustness of the beneficiary effect, I once again turned to matching preprocessing techniques and analyses of vote switching. I used propensity nearest neighbor matching (discussed in Chapter 3) to prune the sample to include only those non-beneficiaries who closely matched beneficiaries across age, gender, education, income, religiosity, communalism, and caste leader influence. The shaded column of Table 5.5 indicates that the pruning did reduce the significant differences between the two groups across religiosity, age, and education.

The results of the analysis found that the beneficiary effect was robust to the matching preprocessing. Beneficiaries were on average 41.3 percentage points more likely than matched beneficiaries to support the BJP (a difference that was significant at the p<.001 level). Again, this analysis is sensitive to the possibility of an omitted variable confounding the effect of welfare. However, a post-match sensitivity analysis found that beneficiaries would have to be 4.5 times more likely than matched non-beneficiaries to support the BJP to undermine the results here (at the p<.05 level). It seems extremely difficult to imagine a factor not accounted for in this analysis that would make otherwise similar voters so vastly different in their likelihood of supporting the BJP.

Finally, the survey asked respondents how they voted in the prior state assembly elections in 1998. A variable was then created from these responses, coded 1 for those voters who shifted to supporting the BJP between 1998 and 2003. Beneficiaries were found to be 25.4 percentage points more likely than their nearest neighbor non-beneficiary to have switched to voting for the BJP between 1998 and 2003 (again significant at the p<.001 level). These additional tests provide further confirmation that the electoral impact of service is unlikely to be a function of the underlying characteristics of beneficiaries or the result of service chapters simply targeting prior supporters of the BJP.

IS SERVICE PROVISION CLIENTELIST?

In answering important questions about how providing services can translate into votes, this chapter raises a further question about how this process is best conceptualized. One common view would be to see a welfare approach as a variant of clientelist exchange. The pervasiveness of clientelist transactions, especially among poor voters, is evident in the rapidly proliferating literature on machine politics in the global south. Yet, the temptation to classify any strategy predicated on non-programmatic material exchange as clientelist can result in unhelpful conceptual stretching.[95]

The empirical evidence presented in this chapter suggests numerous ways in which service does not conform to conventional definitions of clientelism.[96] First, services were not locally provided with discretion, as potential Dalit or Adivasi beneficiaries were never excluded from the Sangh's offerings. Second, continued access to services was not contingent on electoral reciprocity, as some residents openly confessed to voting for the Congress while continuing to avail themselves of the VKA's services. Finally, viewing service as individualized material exchange neglects the wider impacts Sangh activists have had on the communities in which they work. As both survey data and qualitative fieldwork revealed, the VKA has influenced the electoral decisions of many voters not directly benefiting from its labors.

The perspectives of villagers and activists further confirmed the inadequacy of viewing electorally motivated service as a species of clientelism. First, no villager interviewed reported ever being turned away from a VKA chapter, which interestingly could not be said for their experiences with some local government services (particularly in health care). Second, my research suggested that

---

[95] Sartori 1970.
[96] See Kitschelt and Wilkinson 2007; Stokes 2007.

villagers did harbor feelings of reciprocity toward Sangh activists but described such sentiments in terms of voluntary gratitude rather than of involuntary compulsion. For example, interviewees in five case study villages (N=80) were asked whether they felt they "had to" (*dena parhta hai*) give something back to the VKA in return for their services. The vast majority (87 percent, N=70) said they did not. However, when asked if they felt they "should" (*dena chahiye*) give something back in return for using the Ashram's services, 53 percent (N=42) responded in the affirmative.

Strikingly, not a single villager interviewed articulated such reciprocity in electoral terms. It is particularly significant that even non-beneficiaries who were Congress supporters – the most likely critics of the Sangh – disagreed that VKA activities were governed by an electoral quid pro quo. Among those who felt they should give something back to the VKA, two items emerged as the most common components of their reciprocity: attending meetings organized by the Ashram and making occasional gifts of rice (particularly around festivals). As many VKA meetings become sites of indirect political mobilization, especially during elections, the gratitude of beneficiaries clearly does still provide a channel for electoral influence. However, the mechanisms by which such goodwill is converted into votes differ substantially from the typical quid pro quo protocols of clientelism. Conflating the two processes would therefore fundamentally compromise our understanding of service as an electoral strategy.

Like ordinary villagers, service activists also emphasized that the VKA's efforts were not allocated on the basis of electoral outcomes, even as they made their involvement in electoral politics clear. When asked why they did not attach electoral conditions to their offerings, these activists did not cite problems with the morality of such demands or a lack of interest in political outcomes per se. Instead, they professed a concern with tarnishing their image as non-partisan service providers, which in turn would weaken their electoral efficacy. In part, these concerns stemmed from a patronizing view of subaltern voters:

Adivasis are not shrewd and cunning like us city people. When they put their trust in you, they will always trust you. And when that trust is broken that is complete as well. That is why we cannot risk pressuring them. By keeping their trust over time, we make sure our name is spread by word of mouth, and our work becomes easier.[97]

These essentializing views led Sangh leaders to avoid quid pro quo protocols that they believed would irreparably sever the trust they had laboriously earned among Adivasis.

Service activists also noted that monitoring voters – a key feature of clientelism – imposes prohibitive logistical costs, especially within populous Indian constituencies. Assuming such responsibilities would curtail the service work each activist could perform, reducing the number of poor voters within their

[97] Interview with AJ, Jashpur, March 27, 2008.

sphere of influence.[98] In addition to such practicalities, these providers also repeatedly reminded me that their primary goal was social transformation, which they understood as a long-term endeavor. It therefore made little sense to condition their efforts on the short cycles of electoral politics.[99]

WHITHER THE OPPOSITION?

Observing the extensive work done by Hindu nationalists to insert themselves into Adivasi communities raises the question of how the BJP's opposition has responded to these tactics. Given the evidence suggesting that service networks have keyed the BJP's electoral turnaround at the Congress's expense, it would be logical to assume the latter is making active attempts to win back its old support base. However, interviews with state and local leaders of the Congress revealed that the party has been extremely slow to even recognize the electoral impact of Sangh efforts in Chhattisgarh. Several older leaders confessed to me that they had not been able to fathom the BJP winning mass support from lower castes: how could a Brahmin-Bania party successfully court Adivasis?[100]

This complacency undoubtedly delayed efforts at recognizing and responding to the opposition's growing vote share. However, by now there is widespread agreement in the Congress that its rival's affiliates have been driving its rapid rise in Chhattisgarh. As a Congress Member of Legislative Assembly (MLA) candidate in Jashpur noted: "All the work for the BJP is done by the Sangh organizations only! The VKA takes on the name of development of tribals but really they are all working for the BJP full time as well. The day they stop working in this region, the BJP will be finished."[101]

Vikas Upadhyaya, who was the president of the Congress national student organization's (NSUI) Chhattisgarh chapter admitted his party was losing ground among young people: "See the BJP-*wallahs* [BJP people] have the help of the Sangh, and the Sangh employs and recruits teachers, and the teacher is more effective than a party worker because they are much better respected, and they [the Sangh] use teachers as a medium in every village."[102] After a belated start, Congress leaders in the state appear to be finally aware of the damage that service networks have inflicted on them.

---

[98] Interview with activist BF, Agra, January 8, 2010. These local claims appear to resonate with broader data from the national survey used in Chapter 3, as measures of monitoring efforts did not correlate with the BJP's success among associational members. Neither preelection contact with party activists nor attendance at campaign rallies increased the likelihood of nonparty members voting for the party in 2004.

[99] As one activist anonymously told me "*vo to neta log kar sakte hain, ham aisa nahin karte*" [that is for politicians to do, we don't act like that]. Interview in Jashpur, Chhattisgarh, July 30, 2010.

[100] Interview with Ramachandra Singhdev, former Chhattisgarh Congress finance minister, Raipur, April 11, 2008.

[101] Interview with Sarwan Bhagat, former Congress MLA candidate, Jashpur, March 28, 2008.

[102] Interview with Vikas Upadhyaya, Raipur, November 24, 2007.

Recognition however has not led to an effective response. A large part of the Congress's difficulties stem from its inability to change its strategy for incorporating lower caste voters. As discussed previously, the linkages the party had developed with the poor were loose vertical ties constructed through intermediaries and not deep direct linkages with voters. These patrons were usually local elites whose longtime hold on local constituencies was enabled by the latter's distinct lack of political self-mobilization.[103] This elite patronage system proved to be the ideal strategy for a service approach to compete against. First, the Congress's system ensured only a bare trickle of material benefits flowed to those on the lower levels of its patronage pyramid, enhancing the appeal of the Sangh's admittedly modest provisioning. Second, the party's patron-centered approach required little development of mass organizational networks, enabling Sangh activists to slowly embed themselves within communities strikingly free of associational opposition. Of all the types of political antagonists the Hindu nationalist combine might face in India, the strategies of the Congress in central India thus proved to be the most hospitable.

To recapture some measure of its lost support, the Congress clearly needed to be able to reorganize both its strategy and personnel, with a particular emphasis on local organization building. However, local leaders are pessimistic about the ability of their party to engineer a sudden renaissance in its organizational culture. Chandradas Mahant, the president of the Chhattisgarh Congress organization noted:

Congress has no cadre and no plan like the BJP – the Sangh has divided up society and wings for different social sections – women, NGOs, tribals – and this creates a huge advantage for the BJP. Congress should think about this, and we are thinking about opening our own schools, our own NGOs, but this hasn't happened yet – but we are seeing the need to engage in social work as well.[104]

Even with respect to its own fairly lackluster standards, the Congress's organization in Chhattisgarh is in a state of considerable decay. Party committees, which are meant to function at both the state and district levels, had not held meetings for more than three years between 2005 and 2008. Instead, the party's state unit has been wracked with factional disputes, leading one close observer of the region's politics to label it "a group of squabbling generals with no army."[105]

[103] Berthet, (2008, p. 23) notes: "After more than half a century of Independent political history the tribal political consciousness has not yet assumed the form of a distinctive movement either through a specific party or within the existing parties of Chhattisgarh." Indeed, Nand Kumar Sai, BJP MP from Sarguja and former state president of the Madhya Pradesh unit of the BJP, confessed that "Even the demands for 'a state for tribals,' the terms in which calls for a separate state of Chhattisgarh were often framed, came less from grassroots mobilization and 'largely from upper caste leaders who wanted to create their own political sphere of influence." Interview, New Delhi, April 28, 2008.
[104] Interview with Chandradas Mahant, Raipur, April 10, 2008.
[105] Interview with Sunil Kumar, editor *Daily Chattisgarh* newspaper, Raipur, July 21, 2010.

These problems were exacerbated by the fact that the channels for infusing new blood into the organization have been choked off. Since the early 2000s, the Congress has abolished internal elections for filling party posts, shifting instead to a system based entirely on centralized nominations. Mahant admitted to me that this shift was a tactical mistake committed because of the misgivings of powerful national and state elites seeking to consolidate their stranglehold on local units of the party.

However, by eradicating an important gesture toward democratic account-ability and upward mobility within the party, these leaders hampered their ability to select candidates capable of winning popular support. First, talented youth aspiring to a life in politics are deterred by a lack of clear advancement criteria. Second, local party workers grumbled to me that the removal of internal elections had ensured people who were "liked in Raipur and Delhi but not by their own their communities" staffed the organization.[106] These shortcomings have been thrown into even sharper relief as service networks have now given the BJP a mechanism to generate and recruit candidates with at least a modicum of grassroots experience and appeal.

CONCLUSION

This chapter has systematically outlined how service provision can help attract poor voters toward an elite party. Qualitative fieldwork revealed the multiple material and social mechanisms through which service activists help the BJP in Chhattisgarh. Materially, the VKA's offerings were especially appreciated for their dependability in an area devoid of reliable public alternatives. This good-will earned service activists a local standing that they could deploy to great effect politically. Through their local networks, welfare providers recruited subaltern cadres for the BJP to stock its candidate lists and worker rolls. Service activists also proved to be exceptionally effective electoral mobilizers, leveraging their non-partisan reputations to canvass their friends, collect information, and spread rumors against the BJP's partisan rivals.

The results of a local survey confirmed many of the insights of the qualitative fieldwork. The survey revealed that the density of service networks strongly correlated with BJP electoral success at the district level. Individual-level stat-istical analysis established that direct beneficiaries of Sangh services were far more likely than non-beneficiaries to support the BJP, even when accounting for a range of other factors, including past voting preferences. The survey also showed that service activists influence a wider community of voters, impacting the electoral decisions of many non-beneficiaries in areas where they worked.

Although this chapter has provided crucial evidence on how service won votes for the BJP in central India, it is unable to assess whether this strategy's success can be replicated elsewhere. Chhattisgarh clearly offered a highly

---

[106] Interview with Sarwan Bhagat, Congress Party worker, Jashpur, March 20, 2008.

facilitative environment for the Sangh, particularly given the vertical patronage strategy of the party's primary electoral rival. However, other local contexts in India need not prove as hospitable. The analysis therefore requires an investigation of the factors that might inhibit a service strategy from succeeding. To properly identify such conditions, the next chapter turns to investigate two cases in which welfare provision was actively attempted and yet failed to produce the spectacular returns it did in the forests of Chhattisgarh.

6

When Services Fail

Does service provision always succeed in enabling elite parties to appeal to poor voters? Or are there local features of a political arena that help or hinder this approach? How do the political strategies implemented by an elite party's rivals affect the electoral efficacy of welfare? The previous chapter focused on the state of Chhattisgarh, an on-the-line case of dense service provision and electoral success for the BJP. The analysis within Chhattisgarh was developed to test whether service activism actually produced those electoral shifts and to reveal the mechanisms through which it did so. By contrast, this chapter examines two off-the-line cases explicitly selected because service provision failed to generate electoral returns for the BJP. Analyzing such examples helps specify the conditions under which this strategy can succeed.[1] The motivations of this chapter precluded examining states such as West Bengal or Haryana, where Hindu nationalists have not actively attempted a service strategy. Instead, I selected areas within the northern state of Uttar Pradesh and the southern state of Kerala where the Sangh has actively provided services, but subaltern support for the BJP remains low.

Building on these two case studies, I argue that the political potency of service crucially depends on the strategies it competes against. Two features of these rival tactics prove extremely important: first, the degree to which they programmatically appeal to poor voter interests and second, whether they are based on horizontally or vertically mobilizing subaltern communities. In Chhattisgarh, the BJP's primary rival had been the catchall Indian National Congress, which largely pursued a vertical non-programmatic strategy to mobilize poor voters. Specifically, the party relied on indirectly incorporating subaltern communities through traditional elite intermediaries within its patronage network. Accordingly, subaltern voters received minimal material benefits and were vertically mobilized by traditional elites rather than horizontally mobilized against

[1] Lieberman 2005.

them. In this facilitative context, service activists found a grateful audience for their offerings and were unimpeded from using their local positions to deploy a range of political strategies.

In Uttar Pradesh and Kerala however, service activists found far less hospitable terrain for their endeavors. In Kerala, a long history of broad social mobilizations among lower caste communities prepared the ground for subsequent class-based mobilizations organized by communist activists. This rich history of activism produced deep *programmatic ties* between leftists and poor voters, which both compelled and were reinforced by the former's impressive record of public service provision. Relatively reliable public services, especially in the very fields of health and education in which Sangh benefits were concentrated, weakened the attractiveness of Hindu nationalist offerings for most poor voters. Unlike their counterparts in Chhattisgarh, Sangh activists complained of not even being able to attract enrollees into their service wings. Given a choice, poor voters appeared to prefer services provided by a government they voted for, rather than from an elite party's affiliates.

In Uttar Pradesh, the BJP did not compete against such broadly redistributive programmatic strategies. Subaltern self-mobilization occurred later in the state and was a more top-down process than in Kerala. The leaders of the Bahujan Samaj Party (BSP), India's most successful Dalit party, catalyzed such politicization. The BSP rose to prominence through ethnic appeals urging subaltern voters to unite against their upper caste antagonists and by redirecting patronage to members of these formerly excluded constituencies when in office. Although this *horizontal non-programmatic* strategy did directly channel material and symbolic benefits to lower castes, it did not involve the kind of broad provisioning effort witnessed in Kerala, especially in the fields of health and education. Sangh activists thus found a number of takers for the specific benefits they offered.

Yet, Hindu nationalists proved unable to translate this acceptance into votes for the BJP. I argue that this failure was the result of subaltern voters being sharply politicized along caste lines by the BSP's ethnocentric approach. By horizontally mobilizing lower castes, the BSP helped create an ethnically polarized arena where the BJP's elite image was especially detrimental to its project of subaltern recruitment. Under such conditions, the benefits provided by the Sangh were appreciated but simply insufficient to induce even direct beneficiaries to vote for a party socially identified with upper castes. Further, the BSP's horizontal strategy ensures that the party has its own network of operatives within Dalit communities. These lower caste personnel constantly and publicly questioned the political motivations of Sangh welfare providers and monitored the latter's activities. By doing so, local rivals prevented service activists from undertaking the range of mobilizing tasks they performed in Chhattisgarh.

Thus the programmatic strategies of a leftist party and the horizontal non-programmatic approach of an ethnic party proved more formidable than the tactics of the catchall Congress. The first robbed private welfare of its appeal among poor communities, whereas the second politically polarized elites and non-elites, widening the gap service providers had to bridge.

As in my study of central India, these arguments are supported by a blend of qualitative and quantitative analyses. I first compare the trajectory of lower caste politics in Kerala and Uttar Pradesh, primarily relying on the rich existing literature on the subject. Next, I draw on extensive fieldwork to compare the experiences of Hindu nationalist activists in each state. Finally, I use original survey data to test whether the observations from qualitative fieldwork aggregated into broader electoral patterns. The surveys results reveal both the common inability of service activists to win votes in Kerala and Uttar Pradesh and the different sources of their failures.

SOCIAL PROVISIONING AND LOWER CASTE ASSERTIVENESS IN KERALA

The source of Kerala's success in social development has understandably attracted a great deal of scholarly attention. It is beyond the scope of this book's argument to adjudicate among alternative emphases on a single factor most responsible for this success. Instead, this section provides a brief overview of Kerala's turbulent social history, with a view to identifying the blend of factors that most affected future Hindu nationalist efforts at expansion. I particularly focus on the sustained mobilization of non-elite communities in the state, first by caste-based social reform movements and later by communist cadres. These mobilizations politicized non-elite communities in a manner that created sustained pressures for strong social policies in the state. This political environment, marked by the interrelated traits of effective provisioning and broadly mobilized poor voters, proved particularly inhospitable terrain for a service-based expansionary strategy.

Early State Legacies

When newly independent India made the decision in 1956 to redraw the boundaries of its constituent states along linguistic lines, three provinces that were home to large majorities of Malayali-speaking residents were fused to make the new state of Kerala.[2] Two of the provinces, Travancore and Cochin, were formerly princely states ruled indirectly by the British during their Raj. The third major province of Malabar was directly administered by colonial

[2] Prior to the States Reorganization Act, Indian states were divided into different categories depending on their status under colonial rule. Whereas certain territories called "provinces" had been governed directly by British officials, others known as "princely states" had continued to be governed by local rulers, although these too were indirectly under British control. For a general account of the politics of linguistic mobilizations demanding the reorganization of Indian states, see Das Gupta 1970.

authorities and was originally a part of the Madras presidency (most of which later became part of the state of Tamil Nadu). However, contemporary politics in Kerala has been shaped by developments that far pre-date the state's formal creation. Indeed, regional caste and class relations have fueled political forces more locally influential than pan-Indian nationalism ever was, even during the early twentieth-century heyday of the anti-colonial independence movement.

The pre-independence local histories of the state's three constituent provinces were far from uniform, yet each region's experiences combined to forge a political arena markedly different from that of Chhattisgarh. The provinces of Travancore and Cochin were formally ruled by monarchs and overseen by colonial administrators. During the nineteenth and early twentieth centuries, a combination of colonial and indigenous rulers put in place an impressive set of social policies in these provinces, particularly in the sphere of primary education and land tenure.[3] In 1817, the local rani (queen) of Travancore issued a Royal Rescript formulated with substantial input from Colonel Munro, a colonial administrator who had recently commissioned a survey on the spread of education in the province. The Rescript stated that "the state should defray the whole cost of education of its people" and stipulated the need for primary education, a departure from the standard British emphasis on higher education for training select native administrators.[4]

It is important not to overstate the extent of government activism in the first half of the nineteenth century.[5] The vast majority of schools in this period were local, informal vernacular options.[6] Further, public schools did not live up to their name, as lower castes were not allowed entry until the end of the nineteenth century. Indeed, the inclusion of lower castes into educational institutions first came through an expansion of Christian missionary networks in the state.

[3] In the arena of land reform, the Pattom Proclamation proved especially significant. Often called the Magna Carta of the Travancore peasantry, the proclamation conferred ownership rights on tenants and was passed in 1865. See Desai 2007, pp. 53–61.

[4] Toward this end, the Rescript stipulated that the government treasury would pay for two teachers in every primary school. This local history of early state initiative in social policy has been popularized through the influential writings of Amartya Sen (e.g., 1990) on Kerala's social development.

[5] As Mathew (2001) notes, "the fact that the 'opposition to caste inequalities' in the state historically took a particularly pro-mass education form" helped compel the Kerala government into broader provision of social goods than most other poor Indians have enjoyed access to. There are heated disagreements over the principal source of the state's achievements in human development. Sen (1990) credits the enlightened policies of pre-independence rulers in Travancore-Cochin in sowing the seeds for progressive governance. Authors such as Desai (2007) have noted that early reform need not have translated into continued social policy success, as evidenced by reformist princely states that did not have postcolonial leftist governments and saw marked stagnation in their post-independence progress on human development indicators. Others such as Barbara Chasin and Richard Franke (1991) have sharply disagreed with Sen's line of argument, contending that postcolonial policies have played a far greater role than he acknowledges.

[6] By 1864, there were 270 schools in Travancore and a further 70 in Cochin, but only 20 of these were government schools. See Thakran 1984, p. 1917.

Groups such as the London Missionary Society (LMS) and Church Missionary Society (CMS) were operating in Travancore by the first part of the nineteenth century. The passage of the Charter Act of 1833, which centralized many parts of British administration under the East India Company, also ushered in the formal era of missionary activism in India.[7] A proliferation of missionary welfare chapters followed. In 1830, the LMS was running about 100 schools with 3,000 students; by 1890, this figure had risen to 300 and 14,000 respectively.[8]

Kooiman argues that missionaries, often themselves from working-class backgrounds, expressed sympathy for lower castes yet also articulated a position of moral superiority over local practices.[9] The combination spurred them to deplore caste-based hierarchies and emphasize universal access to their own system of social services. These efforts proved quite successful, with missionary schools for lower caste children in Alleppey and Kottyam enrolling hundreds of students.[10] Missionary activists also played a significant role in politicizing the subaltern communities they worked with against local upper castes. For example, Menon discusses the case of a Christian bishop who in the mid-nineteenth century published one of the first articulations of the view that Brahmins were not indigenous to southern India.[11] Later subaltern activists in the south would adapt this non-elite appropriation of regional identity for use in their own mobilizing efforts.

The strong tendency of missionary activists to advocate individual conversion and obedience to colonial civil authorities did limit the emancipatory potential of their work. Even so, scholars have argued that their service efforts still proved instrumental in prompting other elites into action. Local Brahmin communities began to fear that the appeal of missionary provisioning might succeed in converting large numbers of lower castes to Christianity. Realizing such mass defections would tear the social fabric on which their privilege had long depended, local elites relented from their prior opposition to making government schools accessible to lower caste children.[12]

Local rulers began to expand Malayalam-language government schools to attract students away from English-language missionary and colonial education. In 1862–1863, Travancore's budgetary allocation for education and health care was less than 1 percent; by the turn of the century, it had risen to nearly

---

[7] Menon 2006, p. 9.

[8] Kooiman 1989, p. 89.

[9] Ibid., p. 45.

[10] Thakran 1984, p. 1920.

[11] According to Menon (2006, p. 12), lower castes were "actively incorporated into the sphere of public debate through the missionary-led proliferation of print and the appearance of textbooks, journals and magazines." Later studies have shown lasting effects of missionary activity among lower castes. A 1968 Socio-Economic Survey on Caste/Communities in Kerala, commissioned by the Bureau of Economics and Statistics, found the literacy rates among Dalit converts (65.5 percent) to be considerable higher than among non-converts (47.1 percent). See Sivanandan 1979.

[12] Kooiman 1989, p. 254.

TABLE 6.1. *Literacy rates in Kerala and India (1911–1951)*

Year	Travancore	Cochin	Malabar	India
1911	15.0	15.1	11.1	N/A
1921	24.2	18.5	12.7	8.0
1931	23.9	28.2	14.4	N/A
1951	46.7	43.3	31.3	17.0

Source: Kerala figure from Kerala Human Development Report (2005), p. 13. India figures from Thakran (1990) in Desai (2007), p. 60.

10 percent.[13] The number of government schools expanded rapidly in the second half of the nineteenth century, growing to more than a thousand by the turn of the century. By 1895, Travancore began a small program of grants for low-caste children, and by 1908 the government of Cochin mandated free education in Malayalam for all. This competitiveness between local elites and missionaries thus had a salutary effect on overall literacy levels in the two provinces, which were higher than in neighboring Malabar, and far surpassed the all-India average by the time of national independence in 1947 (Table 6.1).[14]

Lower Caste Activism and Sociocultural Reform

A strong early legacy of service provision thus distinguished most of Kerala from the comparatively poor record of areas such as Chhattisgarh. The relative vibrancy of caste-based political activism also differentiated these two regions. Any account of the particular volatility of caste in Kerala has to begin by acknowledging that social hierarchies in the region were particularly pronounced, even by Indian standards. At the apex of this suffocating hierarchy was a tiny population of Namboodiri Brahmins, followed by members of the Nair caste, who were often given the responsibility of overseeing Brahmin estates. The Ezhavas were the largest caste community placed ritually below Namboodiris and Nairs and were classified as *sudras* or backward castes (OBCs). Ezhavas worked mostly in agricultural occupations including most famously the tapping and brewing of toddy. Dalit communities in the state were even more marginalized and were typically left the most stigmatizing and least remunerative of occupations. Members of Dalit castes such as Pulayas, Parayars, and Cherumas were not only regarded as untouchable but as

[13] Government of Kerala 2005, p. 37.
[14] In contrast to its arrangements with local rulers in Travancore and Cochin, the British Raj established direct rule in the province of Malabar. The level of social provisioning was considerably lower in the province, with the number of schools per capita less than half that of Travancore, as the government took no direct initiative in opening schools (Government of Kerala 2005, p. 37).

"unseeable" as well, their presence regarded by upper castes as polluting, even from a distance.[15]

Patterns of land ownership mirrored the inequities of this social hierarchy. Drawing on their ritual authority as priests, many Nambudiris accumulated large estates through the appropriation of surpluses generated by the cultivation of temple lands.[16] Brahmin landowners averaged about thirty acres of cultivable fields, whereas Ezhavas owned less than two, and Pulayas even less still.[17] Distributional inequities in landholding were particularly pronounced in Malabar, the province that fell under direct colonial rule. British administrators implemented a system that granted formal ownership to upper caste landlords, thereby enabling them to legally evict tenants and raise rents. Such overlapping patterns of economic and cultural marginalization produced great resentment against local upper castes among lower caste and minority communities.[18] These long-standing seeds of discontent fueled Malabar's emergence as a site of considerable agrarian unrest, most famously in the case of the Moplah (Mapilla) Rebellion of 1921.[19] The radical edge of these peasant protests also produced sharp regional critiques of the concurrent Indian nationalist movement, raising questions about the ability of Gandhian passive resistance to engineer sufficiently transformative social change.[20]

Non-elite communities in Kerala built on these local histories of protest. Spurred by their extreme marginalization in a state infamously labeled "a madhouse of caste" by Swami Vivekananda, lower castes began to systematically organize against their mistreatment.[21] Caste-based movements developed in the early twentieth century, mostly in response to specific discriminations each community experienced. For example, Ezhavas protested bans on their entering temples frequented by higher castes, as well as the reservation of government posts for elite Hindus. Ezhavas were particularly well positioned to protest their subjugation, as a great many had benefited from the previously mentioned expansion of public schooling. A small, but consequential Ezhava middle class began organizing collective demonstrations and found their spearhead in Sree Narayana Guru (1855–1928) and his organization, the Sree Narayana Dharma

---

[15] Menon 1994, p. 19.

[16] See Lemercinier 1983, especially ch. 3.

[17] Figures from 1931 Indian Census, Vol. 28, Travancore, Part I, Report Appendix IV, p. 472, reproduced in Sivanandan 1979, p. 475.

[18] Indeed, such resentment was even prevalent among the relatively prosperous Nair castes, which was at least in part explained by the Nambudiri matrimonial custom. Only the eldest son within Nambudiri households was permitted to marry, whereas the younger sons entered into "alliances" with women from Nair *tharavadus* (matrilineal households).

[19] Herring 1988, p. 393.

[20] Indeed, Gandhi actively condemned the Mapilla Rebellion; although he denounced the exploitative practices of certain landlords, he also reiterated his opposition to agrarian protest as a solution (see Herring 1988, p. 394).

[21] Quote from Sadasivan 2000, p. 611.

Paripalana Yogam (SNDP). The SNDP, founded in 1903, soon became the flagship association for articulating Ezhava demands for social reform.[22]

Although the SNDP receives the majority of scholarly attention, the activities of Pulaya (Dalit) social organizers were also critical in shaping lower caste political consciousness in Kerala. Pulaya subjugation was far more extreme than anything experienced by Ezhavas, as many Pulayas were even formally enslaved during the nineteenth century. In 1907, the Pulaya reformer Ayyankali founded the Sandhujana Paripalana Sangham (Association for Protection of the Poor, SJPS), followed in 1913 by the founding of an All Cochin Pulaya Maha Sabha (Pulaya Great Assembly). Both of these groups demanded the admission of lower castes into schools, and Ayyankali even organized strikes among Pulaya agricultural laborers until the schools were opened to them.[23] The SJPS also raised internal funds to start its own schools until the children of its members were granted access to public options. Pulaya and Ezhava associations formed alliances on occasion, most notably in an agitation demanding access for both communities to the famous Vaikam temple in Travancore.

These early agitations quickly punctured any chance of cultural solidarities among Hindus diffusing the tensions produced by stark inequities across the faith's internal divisions. By mobilizing subaltern populations in explicit opposition to elite discriminatory practices, these movements also began transforming caste from a signifier of place within a vertical social hierarchy into a more horizontal marker of political identity. In doing so, they helped politicize the cleavages separating elites from non-elites, attenuating the future possibilities of cross-caste, pan-Hindu unity.[24] These movements also added to regional critiques of the nationalist independence movement's consensual approach to dealing with caste-based differences. In 1924, the SNDP linked its efforts at Vaikam with the Congress, but Narayana Guru defied Gandhi's plea to restrict the protest tactics to nonviolent forms of civil disobedience. In doing so, the SNDP set an important precedent for subsequent regional efforts to break from the Congress's "big tent" politics.[25]

However, it is important to acknowledge the limits of these early movements as vehicles for social reform. Neither the SNDP nor Pulaya associations were radical organizations seeking to transform class relations or even eliminate caste

---

[22] Lemercinier 1983, pp. 247–51.

[23] Government of Kerala 2005, p. 12.

[24] Indeed, this divide was reinforced by the fact that upper caste communities developed their own influential caste associations (see Nossiter 1982, p. 29). The Nair Service Society (NSS), founded by Munnathu Padmanabhan in 1914, sought to push through social reforms within the relatively elite Nair community, including making the partition of properties in the traditional Nair joint family complexes legally recognized. Over time, the NSS expanded to take the lead in a number of social reform movements, on occasion linking up with the SNDP to challenge Namboodiri Brahmin sociocultural hegemony in the state, even as the Nairs and Ezhavas occupied very different spaces in the region's caste hierarchy.

[25] Desai 2007, p. 70.

categories. Instead, they fought the excesses of Brahminical discrimination and sought greater social status for their own communities. Despite offering trenchant critiques of upper castes, leaders of both groups would also exhort their followers to emulate Brahmin rituals and practices to gain parity, rather than reject them altogether.[26] For example, Narayana Guru called many lower caste temples "places of filth and superstition" and advocated the replacement of "offerings of toddy and blood [traditional lower caste offerings] with fruit and flowers [preferred by upper castes]."[27] Such aspirational conservatism inherently limited the ability of these movements to serve as sources of more fundamental reform. Yet, this early activism was indisputably important in sowing the seeds for more radical confrontations to the state's social order.

Communism and Social Provisioning

In Kerala, this later challenge came from the state's rapidly growing Communist movement. This movement drew on past legacies of non-elite protest but also transformed a narrow focus on sociocultural reform into demands for more fundamental redistributive change.[28] Communism became a national political presence in India in the 1920s with the founding of the Communist Party of India (CPI). However, the party's radical mandate for achieving independence earned its first ban from a wary imperial government in 1934, and CPI activists were subjected to "regular cycles of imprisonment" thereafter.[29] To continue their work, leftists began operating within the Congress Party's socialist wing, where many remained even after the reinstatement of the CPI in the late 1930s.[30] Initially working within the Congress umbrella, communists became firmly entrenched within Kerala in the first three decades of the twentieth century. The CPI competed in elections following independence and won a majority in Kerala in 1957, forming the first democratically elected Communist government in the country.[31] Subsequently, communists regularly competed with the

---

[26] These aspects of the SNDP's functioning challenges the sharp binary Jaffrelot (2000, pp. 756–66) posits between the "ethnicizing" character of caste movements in the south and their "sanskritizing" northern counterparts, who largely sought advancement through emulating upper caste practices.

[27] Quotations from Osella and Osella 2000, p. 155 and p. 163 respectively.

[28] Lemercinier 1983, pp. 250–60.

[29] Habib 1998, p. 14.

[30] For a more detailed analysis of the phases of the Indian Communist movement, see Rodriguez 2006.

[31] Nehru controversially dismissed this government in 1959. The Kerala wing of the Congress had organized a series of agitations, accusing the CPI of systematically filling administrative posts with their supporters. These protests combined with pressure from national Congress leaders, including then national party president Indira Gandhi, prompted Nehru's decision to dismiss the government and install President's Rule in the state.

Congress for power in the state, and they still anchor one of its two major electoral blocs.

Leftist leaders have acknowledged the foundation laid by prior lower caste activism for their own efforts.[32] However, it is important to note that communist activists pushed significantly beyond the cultural demands of caste organizations and sought widespread change in lower caste living conditions. The particularly strong overlap between class and caste status in Kerala heightened the popularity of these demands. Extreme concentrations of wealth among Brahmins allowed class-based demands to build on caste-based mobilizations and created widespread solidarity among lower caste tenants and laborers.[33] Even as they expanded their networks from within the Congress, communist workers began articulating the differences between their "Congress of the poor" and the more conservative "Congress of the rich."[34] The dedication of Congress socialists stood in marked contrast to the party's mainstream. This latter, more conservative wing was derisively labeled the "Sunday Congress," suggesting its personnel only graced villagers with their presence once a week.[35] Leftist leaders also strategically linked their demands to those for a separate linguistic state, enabling their efforts to benefit from the rising tide of ethnic Malayali sentiment in the late 1940s and early 1950s.

The mobilizing strategies through which the communists sought to achieve their demands proved crucial in shaping Kerala's political arena. Numerous accounts have detailed the tremendous proliferation of mass organizations by leftists that served to embed the party throughout the state. Socialists within the Congress used existing networks to their advantage, transforming philanthropic workers associations into trade unions and strengthening ties to lower caste associations.[36] At the same time, these embedded radicals began building up mass professional organizations of their own, most notably among elementary schoolteachers. Herring notes that "the radicals of the Congress patiently organized, village by village," and their incorporation of teachers was particularly impactful as the latter's "respect in village society enhanced [communist]

---

[32] EMS Namboodiripad (1977, p. 19), a longtime leader of the Communist Party of India (Marxist) in Kerala, cites the importance of these earlier movements in his analysis of Kerala's unique sociopolitical trajectory, noting "A significant difference between Kerala and the rest of India is the fact that the first form of political agitation and the corresponding organizations for carrying on such agitations were based on particular sub-castes and religious communities [as opposed to national mobilizations]."

[33] Desai (2001) compares Kerala caste relations with those in West Bengal, the other bastion of leftist politics in India, and notes that the caste system in the latter state was less hierarchical, and thus a preexisting reform movement spearheaded by lower caste associations did not exist. In contrast, the presence of these associations in Kerala fundamentally affected the development of communism in the region, giving it a grassroots character that the movement in Bengal did not possess.

[34] Communist leader P. Krishna Pillai coined this formulation during the late 1930s. See Nossiter 1982, p. 70.

[35] Heller 1999, p. 69.

[36] Isaac 1986, p. 63.

efforts."[37] These teachers "became the backbone of library and literacy movements and then chief organizers of political and mass activities in the village."[38] This strategic use of non-electoral figures (and specifically educators) for political mobilization foreshadowed the Sangh's strategy in Chhattisgarh. In Kerala, Hindu nationalists had been beaten to the organizational punch.[39]

Once in power in 1957, the Communist government implemented socioeconomic reforms of a scope unrivaled in India, particularly in the spheres of agrarian and educational policy. The Kerala Land Reform Act passed in 1969 was by far the most progressive piece of such legislation in the country. Most significantly, the act formally abolished tenancy and handed "land to the tiller."[40] M. A. Oomen notes that such radical reform clearly stemmed from the ruling government's political dependence on agricultural laborers and peasantry.[41] Further, many of those in the Communist government were themselves past campaigners of peasant and worker movements. Equally crucial was the fact that poor communities were sufficiently self-organized to stage continuous agitations to sustain the pressure required to overcome considerable opposition by local landlords to the act's implementation.

In addition to extensive land reform, Kerala under both Communist and Congress governments made impressive strides in human development, even as its macroeconomic growth remained unimpressive.[42] Indeed, as a result in part of competition with the communists, even the Congress Party unit in Kerala espoused far more progressive policies than its counterparts in other parts of India.[43] Although not one of India's wealthier states, Kerala has managed to remain among the leaders in per capita spending on development by devoting an above-average percentage of its resources toward education and health care.[44] The state has also routinely spent a high percentage of its budget on social security and welfare expenditures, ranking only below much wealthier states such as Punjab and Haryana.[45]

However, the entirety of Kerala's success cannot be understood on the basis of spending levels, as it routinely ranks outside the top five in aggregate expenditures on social development.[46] Much of its success is explained by the relative

---

[37] Herring 1988, p. 396.

[38] Isaac 1986, p. 64.

[39] Herring 1988, p. 396.

[40] Herring 1983.

[41] See Oomen 1971, p. 9.

[42] Well-known work on the Kerala model of development includes Franke and Chasin 1990. For a more critical appraisal of the Kerala model, see Tharamangalam 1998. Also see George 1993.

[43] Herring 1988, p. 411.

[44] The Human Development Report written on the state concluded that "Kerala's development experience has been pronouncedly more impressive in various non-income dimensions of well-being than in the income dimension." Government of Kerala 2005, p. 57.

[45] Ibid., p. 57.

[46] Per capita development spending figures available in *Handbook of Statistics on State Government Finances*, Reserve Bank of India, 2005–2006.

efficiency of provisioning, including what some analysts have called the most effectively run public distribution system in the country.[47] By 1981, the literacy rate in the state (81.6 percent) was nearly double the national average (43.6). The state currently has the highest human development index in the country, a reflection of its impressive literacy rate of 91 percent, as well as a rural infant mortality rate roughly one-seventh the national average.[48] Moreover, Kerala's social development gains have included its most marginalized populations, another rarity in India. The literacy rates among Dalits (79.66 percent) and Adivasis (57.22 percent) are the highest of the major Indian states by some margin, and nearly double the national averages in each case.[49]

Thus, communists carved out a position of dominance among subaltern voters in Kerala through a programmatic linkage rooted in basic social provisioning. Data from a 2001 survey of Kerala voters confirms the non-elite nature of the Communist support base. Figures 6.1A and B illustrate the responses of Dalits and Adivasis and the two other major caste communities in Kerala: upper caste Nairs and the politically influential backward Ezhavas.[50] The figures reveal clear differences between upper caste Nairs and less privileged voters in their evaluations of the left. Figure 6.1A shows that Nairs preferred the Congress manifesto to that of the Communist coalition by a two-to-one margin. However, this ratio is reversed among lower caste respondents, most of whom believed the Communist platform best addressed the needs of their caste community. Similarly, Figure 6.1B shows non-elite groups clearly rated the policy performance of communists in the field of education far more favorably than Nairs did. This relatively high approval of non-elite voters resonates with prior studies, which have noted how Kerala prioritized primary schooling over secondary education (in contrast to the national pattern).[51]

Further, the survey confirmed that the core Communist partisan support is clearly concentrated within Kerala's non-elite communities. Survey respondents were asked whether they considered themselves to be consistent supporters of the Communist coalition, the Congress coalition, or neither. Columns 1 and 2 of Table 6.2 show the distribution of responses within each major social grouping in Kerala. Among Dalits, Adivasis, and Ezhavas, the proportion of respondents

---

[47] As quoted in Suchitra 2004.
[48] Literacy and mortality data from Government of Kerala 2005.
[49] Data from United Nations Development Programme and Planning Commission of India, National Human Development Report, 2001, p. 191.
[50] Data is from the 2001 Kerala assembly election survey conducted by Lokniti. Dalits and Adivasis comprised 11 percent of all voters surveyed, and 80 percent of these respondents were Hindus. Nairs constituted approximately 10 percent of all voters, and just fewer than 69 percent of all upper caste Hindus. Ezhavas comprised 17 percent of all voters, and 58 percent of Hindu backward castes. This figure was significantly higher than that of the next biggest OBC community, Lohars, who constituted 12 percent of Hindu OBCs.
[51] Heller 2000, p. 497.

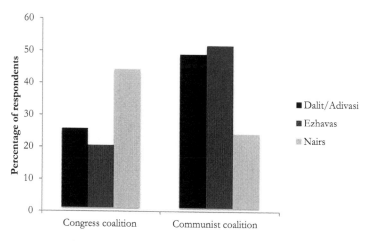

FIGURE 6.1A. Manifesto best addressing the problems of your community?
Source: Lokniti survey (2001).

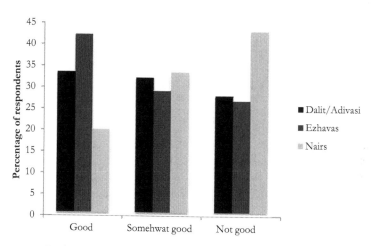

FIGURE 6.1B. Evaluations of Communist performance in education (1996–2001)
Source: Lokniti survey (2001).

identifying as consistently supporting the communists was between 30 and 45 percentage points higher than the proportion supporting the Congress coalition. The latter meanwhile enjoyed an advantage among upper caste Nairs, Christians, and Muslims. Within this base, the Congress traditionally won direct support from Nairs and Christians, while relying on its coalition partner, the Indian Union Muslim League, to deliver the support of Muslims.

TABLE 6.2. *Social bases of partisan support in Kerala*

| | Distribution of Partisan Support | | Predicted Probabilities of Partisan Support | |
	Communist Coalition (1)	Congress Coalition (2)	Communist Coalition (3)	Congress Coalition (4)
Dalit/Adivasi	58.22	26.03	47.98	26.16
Ezhava	61.54	17.65	47.94	26.20
Nair	31.34	42.54	34.80	37.98
Christian	31.60	50.40	24.56	50.10
Muslim	25.67	61.49	27.23	46.62
State Average	40.74	43.24	35.29	37.47

Note: Columns 1 and 2 report the simple distribution of partisan support among voters surveyed. Columns 3 and 4 report the predicted probability of a voter being a partisan of Communist or Congress coalitions derived from an ordered logistic regression model (full model reported in Appendix B). The outcome variable was coded 1 for voters identifying themselves as Communist supporters, -1 for Congress supporters, and 0 for those who did not consider themselves consistent supporters of any party. The binary measure identifying Dalits and Adivasis was statistically significant at the .05 level. In addition to the social categories listed in the table, the model controlled for age; gender; education; occupation; opinion of the Communist and Congress coalitions' policy manifestoes; and ratings of the incumbent Communist government's performance with respect to corruption, law and order, and education policy.

In addition to these simple distributions of support, I used ordered logistic regression models to assess how several factors impacted the likelihood of a respondent being a consistent Communist or Congress supporter. The dependent variable in these specifications was coded 1 for voters identifying themselves as Communist supporters, -1 for Congress supporters, and 0 for those who did not consider themselves consistent supporters of any party. Explanatory variables in the model included indicators of all the social groups listed in Table 6.2, as well as a respondent's age, gender, education, and occupation.[52] Further, the model controlled for a voter's evaluation of the Communist and Congress policy manifestos, and their specific ratings of the prior Communist government's performance in the areas of corruption, education policy, and law and order.[53]

The results of the model (reported in Appendix B) revealed that these evaluative preferences were clearly important determinants of support for the left.

[52] The occupation variable was a binary measure coded 1 for white-collar workers (which was defined to include thirty professions noted on the survey, mostly salaried professionals, public sector employees, and businesspeople). Unfortunately, the survey did not record information on respondent income, so this could not be included in the models tested.

[53] These individual issue ratings were combined using factor analysis to create a composite measure of a voter's opinion of Communist performance.

The predicted probability of a Dalit or Adivasi voter who prefers the Communist policy manifesto being a consistent supporter of the party was 68 percent, 32 percentage points higher than for an otherwise similar co-ethnic who does not share such a preference. Interestingly, this programmatic effect was weaker among subaltern supporters of the Congress. Dalit and Adivasi voters favoring the Congress manifesto were only 14 percentage points more likely to consistently support that party than their equivalent co-ethnics who did not. Indeed, the predicted probability of consistent subaltern support for the Congress, even among voters with favorable views of the party's platform, was only 35 percent.

These results have been reinforced by other surveys. Among the Kerala respondents on a 1996 national survey, a majority of respondents (59 percent) who identified the Communist Party (Marxist) as the party they felt closest to specified the party's "pro-poor policies" as the reason for their attachment. This proportion was even higher among Dalit and Adivasi respondents (62 percent). However, among respondents identifying the Congress, the reasons were more diffuse and less clearly rooted in policy preferences. In fact, the most popular reason given by Congress partisans in Kerala (cited by 29 percent of them) was simply that their preference was a "matter of personal taste."[54]

Thus, survey data confirms the communists as the primary barrier to the BJP's project of social expansion and the programmatic nature of subaltern support for the former. Yet, the results reported in columns 3 and 4 of Table 6.2 also suggest non-elite support for the communists in Kerala is not entirely reducible to how voters view the party's current policies or recent performance in office. Even when controlling for such evaluations, Dalit and Adivasi voters are more likely than respondents outside these communities to be consistent supporters of the left. Take the example of a Nair voter whose other characteristics (including his or her evaluation of contemporary Communist policies and performance) is set to the average values observed within the sample. The predicted probability of such a voter being a consistent Communist supporter is just less than 35 percent. If we switch the identity of this voter to the Dalit/Adivasi category while keeping all other characteristics constant, the likelihood of his or her being a Communist partisan jumps by a third to just less than 48 percent, whereas the equivalent probability of being a Congress partisan drops by a third to 26 percent.

Such differences between voters with similar policy preferences are consistent with arguments emphasizing how partisan attachments are not simply reflections of shared issue stances but are also shaped by the social images that voters associate with a party.[55] The evidence from Kerala supports the idea that subaltern partisan support for the left is rooted in both the progressive nature of Communist policies and the party's long-standing social image as an advocate for the disadvantaged.

---

[54] Data from Q22 and Q22a of the 1996 NES.
[55] Green et al. 2002.

Such overlapping motivations are also consistent with the historical trajectory of subaltern politics outlined in this section. The dominance of upper castes in the region was challenged early and often by social reform movements and class-based agitations led by communist activists. This robust history of activism compelled state governments to ensure broad and effective social services. Yet, as Heller notes, such provisioning has in turn enabled subaltern electorates "equipped with the basic human capabilities required of citizenship" to success-fully pressure governments to continue such pro-poor policies.[56] This virtuous cycle of grassroots mobilization and social development yielded the mixture of programmatic ties and social attachments that communists appear to enjoy with subaltern communities in Kerala.

SETTING THE CONTEXT: LATE LOWER CASTE ASSERTIVENESS IN UTTAR PRADESH

The state of Uttar Pradesh is India's most populous, with a population roughly equivalent to that of Brazil. The state is an integral part of the "Hindi heartland" conventionally considered to be the stronghold of Hindu nationalism. Lower caste politics in Uttar Pradesh developed along markedly different lines than in either south or central India. These dissimilar trajectories were informed by differences in caste demographics, linguistic profiles, land tenure patterns, and modes of colonial governance.[57] It is beyond the scope of this chapter to provide a full account of the divergence in subaltern experience between north and south India, which other studies have analyzed far more comprehensively.[58] Instead, I focus once more on identifying those political developments with particular significance for the expansionary efforts of Hindu nationalists.

I argue that lower castes in Uttar Pradesh were politically mobilized, but in a more top-down fashion than their southern counterparts. The state did not witness the waves of anti-elite subaltern collective action organized by social reformers and communists in Kerala. Instead, subaltern communities were politicized by lower caste political leaders seeking support for a new Dalit party. These efforts proved influential in politicizing lower caste identities but did not also compel an equivalent broadening of social provisioning. Thus, Uttar Pradesh constitutes a blend of a sharply politicized subaltern community (akin to Kerala's) and inadequate basic service provisioning (similar to Chhattisgarh's).

Early Elite Dominance in Uttar Pradesh

Whereas lower castes in Kerala began self-mobilizing efforts from an early juncture, initial social activism among non-elite communities in Uttar Pradesh

[56] Heller 2000, p. 497.
[57] Jaffrelot 2000.
[58] Varshney 2000; Jaffrelot 2000.

(formerly the United Provinces under British Raj) was largely spearheaded by social elites. A signature example was the Arya Samaj, a Hindu revivalist reform movement founded in the late nineteenth century in the nearby northern state of Punjab. The Arya Samaj soon spread to the United Provinces and by the early twentieth century had an estimated membership of more than 65,000.[59] The leaders of the Samaj articulated a need to reform Hinduism to unify its members into a community capable of withstanding the incursions of foreign religions. Toward this end, they rejected idolatry, the centrality of Brahmin priests, bans on widow remarriage, and pilgrimages. Samaj leaders campaigned actively for eradicating the practice of untouchability, arguing that "there are other people out to absorb them [Dalits]" and continual neglect would therefore be "simply suicidal" for the Hindu community.[60] Unlike in Kerala, these movements did not mobilize subaltern communities in direct opposition to local upper castes. Instead, groups such as the Arya Samaj functioned as pan-Hindu acculturative movements, focused on actively incorporating lower castes into a wider social mainstream.[61]

Early mobilizations within subaltern communities in Uttar Pradesh were neither as radical nor as organizationally robust as their southern counterparts. The relative quiescence of northern subaltern communities was clearly informed by contextual factors that complicated the task of forging unified opposition to local elites. Upper castes in the north were both far more numerous (more than 20 percent in Uttar Pradesh compared to less than 2 percent in Kerala) and less uniformly privileged than they were in the south, making them more challenging targets of subaltern grievances.[62] Caste-based discrimination in Uttar Pradesh was not as sharp as that in Kerala, neither were caste-class overlaps as strong, which prevented non-elites from binding into broad coalitions as they did in south India.[63]

Instead, political and economic elites in the north formed an effective alliance, ensuring the continued dominance of each. As one of the epicenters of British rule, the United Provinces were a central stage for the Indian nationalist movement's mobilizations, and the Indian National Congress developed a strong

---

[59] Jones 1989, p. 192.

[60] Lala Lajpat Rai (Arya Samaj leader and member of the Congress Party) in his presidential address to the Hindu Mahasabha's (a conservative wing of the Congress) annual meeting. Speech reproduced in Jaffrelot 2007, p. 76. The Arya Samaj also founded the *Jat Pat Todak Mandal* (the Society for the Abolition of Caste), which worked to facilitate the incorporation of untouchables into its ranks (Jones 1989, p. 195).

[61] Even the more radical offshoots of the Arya Samaj, such as the Adi Hindu (Original Hindu) movement (which proclaimed untouchables to be the original inhabitants of India) remained organizationally too circumscribed to broadly mobilize Dalits of the region. Further, Gooptu (1993) notes the Adi-Hindu leadership focused more on a fairly narrow agenda of organizing lower caste refusal to perform certain ritually unclean tasks (such as the handling of dead animals).

[62] Percentages according to the 1931 Indian Census.

[63] Heller 1999, p. 61.

network in the region. The colonial land tenure system in Uttar Pradesh facilitated the Congress's strategy of harnessing local elites, as the *zamindars* (landlords) had their positions kept largely intact by British authorities intent on utilizing them as tax-collecting intermediaries. The strong ties between landlords and the Congress enabled the latter to vertically integrate Dalits in a manner that had proved impossible to do in Kerala. During the 1920s and 1930s, several large landowners joined the Congress ranks in UP and actively helped mobilize the peasantry for Gandhi's civil disobedience agitations. Landlords were in turn reassured that their positions would be protected in the post-independence period by the consensual nature of Gandhian rhetoric.

This symbiotic relationship continued in the decades following independence and was reflected most clearly in the terms of the Uttar Pradesh Zamindari Abolition and Land Reform Act of 1951. Unlike its Kerala equivalent, this act did not outline a significant transfer of land rights to tenant cultivators. Instead, it focused on the abolition of a variety of taxes enacted by landlords on their tenants, a far less transformative measure than the actual redistribution of plots.[64] Whereas land in Kerala went expressly to the tiller, in Uttar Pradesh personal cultivation was not established as the primary criterion for establishing land rights. Instead, supervisory roles were included as a valid basis for claiming ownership, allowing landlords continued rights over most of their holdings. Further, cultivators were required to pay to acquire their own plots, and purchasing rates tended to be higher than most tenants could afford. Not surprisingly, these limited measures allowed the vast majority of the estimated 376,000 large landlords in Uttar Pradesh to face only "minor reductions in income."[65] Dalit sharecroppers, the most marginal of tenants, remained particularly unaffected by the act's provisions and continued to suffer from a lack of basic economic security.

This system of elite collusion remained remarkably robust in Uttar Pradesh for the first two decades of India's postcolonial era. During this period, more than 50 percent of the state's legislators came from upper caste backgrounds, more than twice their proportion in the population.[66] The first real cracks in the Congress's edifice were created by agrarian populists from within the party itself who sought to aggregate small and medium landowners into a coalition that challenged elite dominance in the state. Leaders such as Charan Singh sharply criticized "Nehru's Congress" for favoring the interests of big landowners and urban elites over the concerns of smaller farmers. This platform sought to unite middle caste communities into a coalition of peasant proprietors, many of whom continued to support Singh after he broke from the Congress to found his own

---

[64] See Elder 1962.
[65] Tenants were asked to pay rates set at ten times their annual land rent in one lump sum or twelve times the rent over four annual installments (Elder 1962, p. 21).
[66] Zerinini 2008, p. 35.

party in 1968.[67] This agrarian politics was focused on small and medium land-owners however, and excluded Dalits, most of whom were landless tenants.[68]

Dalits were also largely left out of subsequent non-elite movements within the state that were more explicitly centered on caste identities. These later mobilizations came from within the sprawling OBC category, placed between upper castes and Dalits in conventional caste hierarchies. In the late 1980s, OBCs successfully mobilized to win employment quotas within central government administrative institutions. However, because Dalits had already benefited from nationally mandated public sector quotas since independence, they were not incorporated into the political community produced by these OBC-led campaigns. In Kerala, reform movements had initiated an early alliance between OBCs (notably Ezhavas) and Dalit communities on the basis of shared social grievances, a relationship broadened and deepened by Communist activism around common class-based concerns. In Uttar Pradesh however, Dalits instead remained within the lower echelons of the Congress machine, often serving as a buffer against the electoral advancement of OBCs.

Autonomous political mobilization within the Dalit community thus remained low for most of this period.[69] It was only later, with the founding of a Dalit-led BSP in 1984 that Dalits signaled their arrival as an independent political force to be reckoned with in the region.

Late Lower Caste Assertion: The Rise of the BSP in Uttar Pradesh

The BSP was founded by Kanshi Ram, a Dalit from a Sikh Chamar *jati* (sub-caste), who was part of the small core of elites who benefited from mandated reservations for Dalit and Adivasi communities.[70] Initially, Ram worked in a government laboratory, a position that he left when his employers canceled their commemoration of the birth of B. R. Ambedkar, India's most significant Dalit leader.[71] Ram decided to devote himself to political activism but visualized a route for subaltern empowerment that was different from the southern Indian example. Instead of pressuring for change through grassroots agitations, Ram focused on using the tools of government institutions to affect a social

---

[67] For more detailed analyses on farmers' movements in India, see Omvedt 1993, especially ch. 5. See also Varshney 1999. On Charan Singh's political career specifically, see Brass 2011.

[68] Charan Singh's staunch opposition to lowering land ceilings reflected his support of middle-class farmer interests, even at the expense of marginal cultivators who stood to gain most from such reform (see Varshney 1999).

[69] Uttar Pradesh did have an active branch of the Republican Party of India, a legacy of the politicizing efforts in western India of Ambedkar, the preeminent Dalit politician of the independence era. However, the RPI was quickly thwarted in UP through a mixture of internal factional disputes and successful co-option of its leadership by the Congress, and it remained a marginal electoral player in the state. See Jaffrelot 2003, p. 387.

[70] On the centrality of these Dalit elites in catalyzing subaltern political assertion, see Chandra 2004 and Hasan 2002, pp. 370–96. For a critical view of these "new elites," see Jeffrey et al. 2008.

[71] Pai 2002, p. 87.

transformation "from above." However, he was heavily critical of legislative reservations as a sufficient means for providing Dalits access to these public institutions. He firmly believed that as the entire electorate selected legislators from reserved constituencies, upper caste voters could always ensure that the lower caste victors were their *chamchas* (puppets).[72]

Ram therefore believed that the only way to truly empower lower castes within the electoral arena was to create a successful political alternative led by subaltern politicians. This top-down strategic vision prioritized building networks between lower caste elites as a first step.[73] Toward this end, Ram founded the All India Backward and Minority Communities Employees Federation (BAMCEF), which primarily consisted of lower caste government employees like himself. By the 1980s, BAMCEF had more than 200,000 members, including approximately 500 members with PhDs.[74] BAMCEF then developed a separate electoral wing named the Dalit Shoshit Samaj Sangharsh Samiti (Committee for Fighting for the Dalit Community), popularly known as the DS-4. The DS-4 looked to politically mobilize lower caste voters through explicitly anti-elite rhetoric. One of its popular slogans was "*Brahmin, Bania, Thakur chor, baki sab hai DS-4*" (Brahmins, Banias, and Thakurs [three major upper castes] are all thieves, the rest are all with DS-4).[75] As a result of its need to carve out an electoral base, the DS-4 expanded BAMCEF's comparatively narrow organizational network into Uttar Pradesh's villages; by 1984, the party had managed to win more than a million votes.

Soon after the DS-4 emerged as a relevant political force, Kanshi Ram decided to dissolve the party to launch one with a name that more accurately reflected his electoral ambitions. Ram articulated the central problem of Indian democracy to be that 85 percent of the electorate allowed themselves to be ruled by the other 15 percent. The Bahujan Samaj Party replaced the DS-4's caste-specific moniker with the broader term *Bahujan* or "people of the majority." This shift in nomenclature signaled Ram's desire to craft a winning coalition out of a marginalized supermajority rather than be confined to leading a party of Dalits. The new party steadily improved its performance within UP during the 1990s, drawing enough support to become part of a ruling coalition within the state and then winning an outright majority in the 2007 assembly elections. Despite its expanded title, the BSP continued to draw its core support from Dalit constituencies, remaining unable to capture a plurality of votes from any other caste electorate.

---

[72] For this reason, Kanshi Ram was heavily critical of the Poona Pact signed by Ambedkar after a famous dispute with Gandhi discussed in Chapter 2. Ram articulated his critique in a volume published on the fiftieth anniversary of the pact's signing; Ram 1982 (especially p. 90).

[73] Pai 2002, ch. 2.

[74] Omvedt 1994, p. 163, cited in Jaffrelot 2003, p. 393.

[75] Interview with Suresh Chand Soni, former DS-4 and BSP member, current civil court advocate, Agra, Uttar Pradesh, January 6, 2011.

A full explanation of the BSP's ascent is not this chapter's mandate and has been the central focus of past studies.[76] My analysis is more concerned with how this support was won and what its impact was on subaltern politics in the state. Most observers agree that the BSP built its core support through a mixture of ethnocentric discursive and material strategies. The centerpiece of its material approach was a promise to lower caste constituencies of greater inclusion within circuits of patronage previously dominated by upper castes. As Chandra explains, the BSP initially signaled these intentions to Dalit voters by placing their co-ethnics in positions that would control patronage flows if the party were to come to power.[77]

When voted into government, primarily on the strength of lower caste support, the BSP reciprocated by channeling benefits to these constituencies. For example, Mayawati, Kanshi Ram's successor as the head of the BSP, issued orders during her first two stints as chief minister to divert social welfare funds toward selected villages with large Dalit populations. Local newspapers reported that "all officials were instructed to give maximum attention and priority" to such villages.[78] She also changed the requirements of a development program so that a larger number of villages with significant Dalit populations were eligible for the scheme. Available evidence suggests that the BSP did do better among recipients of such welfare programs. For example, a 2012 survey found the party won support from 72 percent of Dalit beneficiaries of a BSP-implemented scheme giving direct cash handouts to poor families. By contrast, among Dalit non-beneficiaries, the party's success rate was only 53 percent.[79] Although this evidence is unable to tease out whether such differences indicate ex post rewards or ex ante motivations for electoral support, it does point to the material basis of the BSP's appeal.

Yet, the breadth of the BSP's popularity among Dalits cannot solely be explained as a function of such limited material inducements. Unlike the broad social policy efforts of the left in Kerala, the narrower benefits distributed by the BSP reached a far smaller proportion of the party's Dalit supporters. For example, whereas a high proportion of subaltern beneficiaries of the cash handout scheme voted for the BSP, only 14 percent of Dalits surveyed had in fact benefited from the scheme itself. By comparison, 48 percent had not even heard of the scheme, and 31 percent had heard about it but had not benefited from it. In fact, a little more than four out of five Dalits supporting the BSP were not direct beneficiaries of this flagship scheme. Pai argues that the party's signature village-level development scheme for Dalits has been similarly narrowly targeted. She observed the party's local patronage networks capturing most of the scheme's resources, instead of disbursement being decided through

[76] Pai 2002; Chandra 2004.
[77] Chandra 2004.
[78] *Dainik Jagran* (Meerut edition), October 4 and 6, 1995 (as cited in Pai 2004, p. 1145).
[79] Heath and Kumar 2012, p. 46.

open village-level deliberations in line with official guidelines.[80] Meanwhile, the party has failed to put in place policies capable of affecting a broader swathe of the state's poor (including most Dalits), such as implementing agrarian reforms or appreciably expanding the provision of basic services.

Indeed, the BSP's success is all the more remarkable because many Dalits recognize that the party has not directly improved their material well-being. In a separate 2010 survey conducted for this study in the city of Agra (discussed in detail later in the chapter), one in three Dalit respondents *strongly* agreed that the BSP "only helps its workers and not the wider Dalit community."[81] Yet, even among these critical respondents, two out of three identified the BSP as the party that cared most for their caste community. In large part, this view was rooted in a belief that the party did more than its competitors to increase respect for Dalits within the state.[82] Similar patterns are evident in a recent survey conducted during the 2012 state elections in which the BSP lost power. Data from this survey suggests that many Dalits felt increasingly disgruntled with their party's track record while in office from 2007 to 2012.[83] Even so, Dalit voters still supported the party over any other by a huge margin (the BSP won 58 percent of the Dalit vote, beating its closest rival by more than 36 percentage points).[84] In sharp contrast, most non-Dalit beneficiaries of the BSP's cash schemes still largely preferred to support its rivals and were only marginally more supportive of the BSP (22 percent) than non-beneficiaries (17 percent).[85]

The sustained and specific appeal of the BSP for Dalits, even those who have not directly received material benefits from the party, compels recognition of the broader social attachments the party has forged among its base. A key driver of such attachments has been the BSP's ability to sharpen caste-based partisan fault lines, thereby solidifying its image as the "natural" party of Dalits. The BSP leaders deployed fiery oratory in identifying upper castes as their primary antagonists, whom they exhorted lower castes to unite against.[86] The campaign

[80] Pai 2002, p. 140.
[81] Percentages are calculated from responses to Question 16d on author survey (2010).
[82] Sixty-two percent of Dalit voters strongly agreed with this position, whereas only 12 percent strongly disagreed. Percentages are calculated from responses to Question 16b on author survey (2010).
[83] For example, 50 percent of Jatavs, the Dalit subcaste that is meant to be the absolute core of the BSP's support base, thought the party's expenditures on statues commemorating Dalit achievements while in office were "a waste of money" (Heath and Kumar 2012, p. 44).
[84] Data from Lokniti Survey 2012 reported in Heath and Kumar 2012. Recent arguments that the party's defeat was primarily the result of Dalits "deserting the BSP" (see Heath and Kumar 2012) are therefore overstated. The BSP did lose some support among Dalits in 2012, but this drop-off is largely the result of its 2007 vote share with these voters constituting "one of the highest recorded for a large social group *in any state in India since independence*" (Yadav and Kumar 2007a, emphasis added). Although lower than this historic performance, the 2012 result therefore hardly reflects an abandonment of the party by its Dalit core.
[85] Heath and Kumar 2012 p. 46.
[86] Pai 2002, p. 123.

speeches of Kanshi Ram and Mayawati, particularly during the party's early ascendancy, were peppered with these vociferous critiques.[87] In office, BSP leaders actively sought to capitalize on this rhetoric through numerous symbolic appeals, most famously by installing thousands of statues of B. R. Ambedkar across Uttar Pradesh. The party has also re-named both Agra University and a central park in Lucknow (the state capital) after the iconic Dalit leader, and it has named several public awards and sites after other prominent lower caste figures.

The BSP government also implemented policies that blended material benefits for lower castes with symbolic politics. For example, villages that qualified for special development schemes on the basis of a high Dalit population were designated as "Ambedkar villages." Another prominent and controversial example was the fast tracking of cases brought under the SC/ST (Prevention of Atrocities) Act, a centerpiece of the BSP's "politics of dignity" platform. The act is specifically designed to offer legal redress for Dalit and Adivasi victims of harassment and violence inflicted by upper castes. Whereas an accused had rarely been made to even face trial under prior administrations, the BSP made sure alleged perpetrators were sent to jail during the investigation and awarded funds for victims to pursue their case.[88]

These actions are not simply cosmetic and have permeated everyday life, even in rural parts of the state. Lerche's ethnographic study of two villages in Uttar Pradesh notes that during the BSP's rise, Dalit agricultural laborers began to sense for the first time "that the local police and court system would not act directly against their interests."[89] This confidence enabled laborers to organize strikes demanding higher wages. More controversially, Lerche notes that these laborers utilized the changed legal arena to their advantage, "pressing charges of assault and caste discrimination against a number of landowners (charges which they told me [Lerche] were as false as the ones the *Thakurs* [upper castes] used to press against them)."[90] The BSP's success had thus empowered lower castes to use and even misuse the legislative system to fight their elite antagonists. Evidence of this shift has been the rapid growth in the number of cases filed and convictions declared under the act's provisions, both of which are well above the national average.[91]

---

[87] As Chandra (2004, pp. 151–5) notes, "Kanshi Ram and other BSP activists typically called for the support of each Scheduled Caste (Dalit) category by name [and] did not shy away from identifying the category to which they themselves belonged."

[88] See Lerche 1999. I am also grateful to Dr. Mirza Asmer Beg, who made a similar observation in an informal conversation (Aligarh, January 8, 2011).

[89] Lerche 1999, p. 212.

[90] Ibid.

[91] In 2001, a total of 4,885 cases were registered in Uttar Pradesh under the act; by 2009, this number was 7,522, the highest in India. Moreover, the conviction rate in 2009 for UP was 52.6 percent, significantly higher than the national average of 29.6 percent. Statistics for 2001 and 2009 are from the National Crime Records Bureau annual report (ch. 7); 2001 statistics were downloaded from www.indiastat.com.

In sum, aggressively anti-elite political forces abruptly interrupted the narrative of upper caste dominance in Uttar Pradesh, albeit at a far later juncture than in Kerala. This rising lower caste assertiveness has led to some clear improvements for subaltern communities in Uttar Pradesh. However, the BSP's strategy for wooing the poor differed sharply from the more programmatic efforts of communists in the south. In Kerala, the left maintained its linkages to the poor through clear redistributive platforms that were implemented when the party won office. In Uttar Pradesh, observers have repeatedly found "striking evidence" that the BSP's support is independent of its positions on programmatic agenda items,[92] and that party leaders "rarely spelt out policies on basic issues: they consider them irrelevant to the bigger project of winning power."[93]

Instead, the party deployed an ethnocentric approach blending targeted patronage with measures advancing a politics of dignity. Yet, such strategies simply did not compel the robust associational life or systematic broadening of social services witnessed in Kerala. In fact, there has been little evidence of a deepening provision of basic services in Uttar Pradesh. A 2007 report issued by the Uttar Pradesh government itself ranked the state sixteenth out of the seventeen major states on the basis of its human development index score, a measure heavily weighted to reflect health and educational outcomes. The study also showed real per capita public expenditure on education actually decreased from 1997 to 2003 and ranked as the lowest among Indian states (and less than half that of Kerala).[94] Improvements in health care have been similarly anemic, with the state government noting a "meager" increase in infant vaccination coverage of 3 percent between 1997 and 2005 (from 20 percent to 23 percent).[95] Uttar Pradesh's physical health infrastructure has also remained far below even India's unimpressive national average.[96]

Although not significantly improving basic provisioning in the state, the BSP's modus operandi did serve to sharply politicize the divide between elites and nonelites to a high degree. First, by directly appealing to Dalits, the BSP forced these voters to think of themselves as an autonomous electoral community. In doing so, the party directly challenged the prior vertical incorporation of these voters by existing parties in the state.[97] As villagers in Lerche's study concluded, the chief legacy of the BSP's ascent within the state was "the politicization of untouchables" and not improvements in their basic material security.[98]

---

[92] Chandra 2004, p. 208.

[93] Hasan 2002, p. 392.

[94] Government of Uttar Pradesh, 2007, ch. 3, point 67.

[95] Ibid., ch. 4, figure 16.

[96] For instance, the average population and distance covered by a primary health subcenter in the state is 7,080 people and 3.4 kilometers respectively, considerably higher than the all-India averages of 5,109 people and 1.3 kilometers. Government of Uttar Pradesh 2007, ch. 4, point 69.

[97] In 2004, 56 percent of Dalit voters in the state agreed that they should vote in the same way as their co-ethnics, a third above the national average (see Question 24b on the 2004 NES).

[98] Lerche 1999, p. 213. For more recent work on the BSP's evolving strategies, see Guha 2007.

Second, by defining itself in opposition to upper castes, the BSP strengthened caste as a marker of partisan differences and helped Uttar Pradesh develop into a deeply divided ethnic party system. The state's ethnic voting index – which indicates the degree of dissimilarity in the electoral preferences of different caste communities – touched .45 by 2004, which was considerably above the national average (.294), and twice that of Chhattisgarh (.182).[99] In such a polarized environment, the BJP became increasingly pigeonholed as the party of the upper castes. In 1996, 33 percent of Hindu upper castes in Uttar Pradesh identified the BJP as the party they felt close to, whereas only 1 percent named the BSP. Meanwhile, the BSP held a 24 percent to 4 percent advantage among Dalit voters.[100] By 2004, this gap had widened further: the BJP enjoyed a 40 percent to 2 percent lead among upper castes, while trailing the BSP with Dalit voters by a 43 percent to 5 percent margin.[101] The late politicization of Dalits by the BSP thus created an electoral environment in which the BJP's elite partisan image that has so far stymied to its ability to reach out to subaltern voters.

HINDU NATIONALIST EFFORTS IN KERALA

In the prior two sections, I discussed the specific ways in which Kerala and Uttar Pradesh differed contextually from Chhattisgarh. In both northern and southern India, the Sangh Parivar encountered lower castes who had been significantly politicized by mobilizations with an explicitly anti-elite edge. However, only in Kerala did such mobilizations also compel effective public service infrastructure. In the next two sections, I draw on qualitative fieldwork conducted among Hindu nationalists in both states to outline how their experiences among subaltern communities were shaped by these contextual variations.

Limited Beginnings

Although the RSS, the Sangh's parent body, was formally established in 1925, its work in Kerala only began in 1942 and remained largely restricted to the Malabar region until the 1960s. Initially, the RSS sent three *pracharaks* (full-time activists) to Kerala: one to the city of Trivandrum (now Thiruvananthapuram) in the south, one to Ernakulam in the center, and one to Calicut (now Kozikhode) in the north of the state.[102] During these early years,

---

[99] The standard deviation across the seventeen states was .124.
[100] Percentages calculated from Question 22a on the 1996 NES.
[101] Percentages calculated from Question 15a on the 2004 NES. It is worth noting a slight difference in the question wording on the 1996 and 2004 instruments. The former asked responded which party they felt particularly close to, and the latter asked them if there was a party they particularly liked.
[102] One of these *pracharaks*, D. B. Thengadi, went on to establish the Sangh's labor union, the Bharatiya Mazdoor Sangh (BMS), a few years after his stint in Kerala (interview with R. Hari, Ernakulam, August 6, 2008).

the work of the RSS was confined to urban areas, and consequently its recruitment pools were circumscribed to upper caste Hindu personnel. Indeed, the very first RSS *shakha* (local branch) was located within the house of the local ruler of Calicut.

Ranga Hari, one of the first *pracharaks* from Kerala's dominant Malayali ethnolinguistic community, explained to me that this limited social reach was the product of multiple factors. He recalled that the RSS *pracharak* who recruited him could not speak Malayalam (the local language), and few locals spoke Hindi. Hari noted that "all three *pracharaks* contacted only the English-speaking classes. So their reach was limited ... At first *baithaks* [meetings] were in English, even joking was in English."[103] The Sangh's visible protection of upper caste interests during its early years in Kerala helped consolidate this elite bias. Local Brahmins viewed influential Muslim business owners as threats to their commercial interests in areas such as Thalassery, Kannur, and Kozikhode. Accordingly, several upper caste businesses began funding the RSS in return for the use of the organization's youth cadres to "protect them or indeed help them in setting up their own spheres of dominance."[104]

Not surprisingly, the Sangh in Kerala remained organizationally circumscribed to elite circles and grew slowly during its first two decades in the state. From 1950 to 1967, the RSS organization expanded marginally, from 250 to 650 *shakhas*.[105] However, in 1968, two political developments provided Hindu nationalists with opportunities to effectively expand their local support. First, the CPM-led state government made a decision to redraw internal borders, creating a new district of Mallapuram with a majority Muslim population. The RSS managed to somewhat effectively portray this move as pandering to minority communities, a charge that gained it broader support among local upper castes. The Sangh's second somewhat successful agitation centered on a call to restore the Thali Temple, which was allegedly destroyed by Tipu Sultan, a famous eighteenth-century Muslim monarch from nearby Mysore. Neither of these mobilizations radically transformed the local fortunes of the Sangh, but they did help the movement gain a firmer toehold into Kerala's political terrain.

In one of the only previous studies of Hindu nationalism in Kerala, Chiriyankandath notes that the Sangh experienced two other periods of political success in the state. The first phase was from 1975 to 1977, the years during which Indira Gandhi imposed emergency rule on the country. This draconian period saw many political organizations, including the RSS, forced underground following bans on their assembly.[106] Chiriyankandath argues that Hindu

---

[103] Ibid. There were early demographic exceptions to this elite base, primarily the result of the Sangh's early activities among poor fishing communities in Malabar. However, these outreach programs remained small in scope and were certainly not broad enough to substantively change the movement's profile (Jayaprasad 1991, p. 150).

[104] Interview with Ramesh Babu, Thiruvananthapuram, August 2, 2008.

[105] Figures from Jayaprasad 1991, pp. 150–60.

[106] Chiriyankandath 2001, p. 210.

nationalism's "martial ethos" allowed the movement to weather this political storm relatively well. Indeed, these clandestine capabilities enabled the Sangh to actually expand its organizational network in Kerala during the emergency, with the number of *shakhas* increasing from 900 to 1,500, and membership increasing from 25,000 to 35,000 in just two years (between 1975 and 1977).[107]

Indira Gandhi's mass imprisonment of her political opponents also brought Hindu nationalist activists together in conversation with cellmates from other political parties. In Kerala, her actions had the unintended consequence of creating a forced camaraderie between communists and the Sangh.[108] Such improbable solidarities laid the foundation for a broad national alliance against the Congress, which included both the Jana Sangh (the BJP's precursor) and parties of the left. The alliance swept into power in the post-emergency elections, and this victory had important local ramifications for Hindu nationalism in Kerala. Most significantly, participation in a winning coalition increased the Sangh's political stature by giving some of the party's leadership their first chance to assume positions of political importance in the state.[109] As Figure 6.2 charts, this upward momentum continued during the early 1980s, when the national Sangh organization held a massive convention in Kerala with

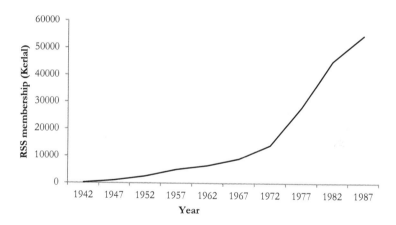

FIGURE 6.2. Expansion of RSS membership in Kerala (1942–1987)
Source: K. Jayaprasad (1991), p. 162.

---

[107] Jayaprasad 1991, p. 157.
[108] One Sangh worker noted that both Hindu nationalists and communists in Kerala were "classified as political prisoners, so we were free to move about and hold discussions" (interview with activist BA, Thiruvananthapuram, August 4, 2008). Another activist noted that "there was some sort of an understanding with the left and us because the fight was against the Emergency, not each other" (interview with O. Rajagopal, Thiruvananthapuram, August 4, 2008).
[109] For example, former Jana Sangh state president O. Rajagopal was given the position of Kerala state president of the governing coalition's internal organization.

the goal of creating a "Maha Mandalam" or "great association" of Hindu organizations.[110]

Despite this growing organizational presence, the BJP was unable to make any significant electoral headway with the state's voters. In fact, Kerala appears a particularly puzzling case, precisely because an extensive organizational network of the Sangh has consistently coexisted with only marginal support for the movement's electoral arm. Somewhat astoundingly, Kerala came to have the highest number of RSS chapters per capita in the country by the early 1990s. However, the BJP was never able to even position itself as an attractive local alliance partner within the state.

The party's primary difficulty was that the Sangh's impressive network remained highly socially confined, as most chapters offered no basic services and were principally located in upper caste areas. Recognizing these limitations, Hindu nationalists in Kerala began following the example of their saffron brothers in the north.[111] As Chapter 2 discussed, from the mid-1980s to early 1990s, the Sangh especially focused on sectarian agitations as the basis for building support.[112] The powerful reverberations of marches demanding the destruction of the Babri mosque in Ayodhya echoed across India. In Kerala, RSS activists began to focus their local attentions on protesting plans to build a church near a Hindu temple in the town of Nilakkal. The Nilakkal agitation successfully pressured the church to be moved and built at a nearby site acceptable to all parties. Given the dearth of its local triumphs, this victory was a huge boost to the Kerala cadre's morale.

The Sangh moved swiftly to capitalize on this precious momentum by launching the Hindu *Munnani*, a political front that began systematically organizing agitations around central components of the wider Hindu nationalist agenda. These concerns included the demand that public sector quotas for Dalits and Adivasis never be granted to Christian or Muslim converts from these communities. Additionally, the *Munnani* pressed for stronger anti-conversion legislation and for banning the slaughtering of cows in the state. However, these increased activities still did not yield electoral dividends for the BJP. The party actually saw its vote share dip from 5.56 percent to 4.76 percent between 1987 and 1991, the peak years of the Ayodhya mobilizations in the north.[113] Faced with successive dismal electoral outcomes despite their organizational growth, both BJP and Sangh leaders began realizing the necessity of a different form of outreach among poor voters.

---

[110] This convention was also centrally concerned with countering "the widespread perception that the Sangh Parivar institutions catered primarily to caste Hindus" (Chiriyankandath 2001, p. 213). See also Chiriyankandath 1996.

[111] I borrow this phrase from the title of a well-known book on the RSS by Anderson and Damle 1987.

[112] Jayaprasad 1991, p. 202.

[113] Data from the Electoral Commission of India.

Services Refused: The Struggles of Sangh Providers in Kerala

Hindu nationalists in Kerala believed that one way in which they could secure the support of influential non-Brahmin communities was by creating lasting relationships with the latter's major caste associations. The RSS even succeeded in building fairly cordial relations with the Nair Service Society (NSS) and Ezhava SNDP during the 1940s, on the grounds of their shared interests as "cultural organizations."[114] However, relations soured shortly after Hindu nationalists established a party arm in 1951. By making its independent electoral ambitions explicit, the RSS found it difficult to continue portraying itself as an apolitical, cultural organization to local caste associations in Kerala. For leaders of these latter associations, the emergence of this new party affiliate raised the political costs of linking with the RSS to an unacceptable level. As one BJP politician complained: "Then in these caste organizations political ambitions slowly crept in ... And so NSS and SNDP were also thinking that if we are connected with Sangh people, it might affect our political capabilities, particularly if they wanted to ally with either the Congress or the Marxists during elections."[115]

This rift became even more explicit when the NSS and SNDP attempted to form their own political parties. Although neither formation proved successful, their electoral ambitions created coalitional incentives for their founding caste associations to develop closer ties to the successful Congress and Communist parties, rather than with the inconsequential BJP and its affiliates. Thus, both Nair and Ezhava associations continue to remain linked to one of the major poles of Kerala's party system: the NSS with the Congress, and the SNDP with the CPM.[116]

Given this hostile landscape, Hindu nationalists felt particularly compelled to appeal more directly to Dalits and Adivasis. O. Rajagopal, a cabinet minister with the BJP-led national government in power from 1999 to 2004 and a leader of the Kerala party unit, explained the logic behind this compulsion:

[114] Initially, the relations between the RSS and both caste associations were actually quite strong. In fact, one of the NSS district presidents in the 1960s, Govinda Menon was also the state president of the RSS. Indeed, NSS founder M. Padmanabhan attended several RSS programs, a point RSS leaders liked to reiterate. Similarly, relations with erstwhile SNDP leader R. Sankar and the RSS were also quite cordial according to several RSS sources, and Sankar even extended formal support to the RSS resolution against cow slaughter during the 1950s (interview with Ba, Thiruvananthapuram, August 4, 2008).

[115] Interview with Bb, Thiruvananthapuram, August 5, 2008.

[116] There have of course been oscillations in the closeness of these ties. Reports of the SNDP accusing higher castes of dominating supposedly egalitarian Communist party structures have surfaced from time to time (Surendran 1994). Such tensions have been compounded by the fact that the majority of the Communist leadership in the state has been upper caste. Further, the Sangh and the SNDP have occasionally allied with each other, most significantly when they joined hands to critique the Left Front government's decision to take control over the organization responsible for overseeing the administration of temples and temple lands (see Verghese 1998). With respect to the BJP's recent overtures to the SNDP, O. Rajagopal was reported to have developed close ties to SNDP general secretary Vellappaly Natesan (Venugopal 2000).

I personally feel, I have been espousing this cause, that we have to concentrate on these SC/ST [Dalit/Adivasi] people – because they form 12 percent of the population [in Kerala] – that is the total amount of the vote we secured in the state in 2004 [national elections] ... now I told you, we don't have a special vote bank as such. Now how to compete in a popular democratic system without the support of a certain electorate? So taking into account these various aspects, we feel if we want to make a good quantum jump, we have to concentrate on these sections ... not [on] the Nairs or the Ezhavas [both higher in the caste hierarchy] because they already have groups for themselves to do this. See these Nair and Ezhava organizations are officially unaffiliated but have been working for so many years now that by now they are affiliated in practice with the Congress or the Communists. So in the Nair and Ezhava communities, we will have sympathizers, but their organization leaders will not be siding with you.[117]

Most importantly, Rajagopal notes the imperatives for the BJP to reach out to subaltern voters in the state. Kerala had a tiny number of upper castes, large religious minority populations, and self-mobilized backward caste communities. Any hope the BJP had of becoming a viable party therefore rested on its ability to attract non-elite support.[118]

As the Sangh began to emphasize basic provisioning as a cornerstone of its national strategy for expansion, its activists in Kerala also started to increasingly focus on expanding their service network to appeal to these crucial constituencies:

After 1989, especially after the centenary celebrations of [RSS founder] Dr. Hedgewar, there was a focus on service activities in Kerala ... more emphasis was given to building these service activities now. Colony work in SC/ST areas became much more important. We started so much work in Wayanad – Vivekananda Medical, and Attapady in Palakkad. And then we set up orphanages, and even taking children from parents who cannot afford to raise them – RSS front organizations are now running fifty-two orphanages in the state ... Regularly Seva Bharati is conducing so many activities, especially in these medical hospitals where they give out free food to patients and bystanders. In Trivandrum alone they were giving 2,000–2,500 meals everyday, and in Calicut, in Kasaragod.[119]

This buildup of service organizations in Kerala was indeed impressive, as reflected by the per capita index of Sangh service provision, which ranked second among the seventeen states analyzed in Chapter 4. However, we know from aggregate electoral statistics that this buildup did not succeed in dramatically shifting the tide for the BJP. How did Hindu nationalists themselves account for this apparent failure?

[117] Interview with O. Rajagopal, Thiruvananthapuram, August 4, 2008.
[118] Whereas Dalits and Adivasis comprised only 11 percent of Kerala's population, Hindu voters within these communities comprised more than 17 percent of the state's Hindu population. Moreover, the BJP viewed even Christian and Muslim Dalits as originally Hindu. From this perspective, the subaltern proportion of the state's Hindu population was more than 22 percent, a significant proportion, especially in a multiparty plurality institutional setting.
[119] Interview with Bc, RSS activist, Ernakulam, August 6, 2008.

In interviews, Sangh workers in Kerala repeatedly mentioned two factors responsible for their lack of success: the strength of basic government provisioning and the high degree of internal mobilization within lower caste communities. Hindu nationalists believed Kerala's strong social policy record had weakened demand for the services the Sangh offered, limiting their ability to ingratiate themselves with lower castes. "The thing is in Kerala that even service activities are competitive," complained one BJP operative.[120] He confessed that local schools tended to function comparatively well, preventing service activists from doing social work "in the way of getting results in Kerala," as they might be able to in other parts of the country. If poor residents did seek alternatives to public schools, they typically gravitated toward those run by Christian missionaries.[121] This activist was left to pessimistically conclude that "we are doing service anyway – if we get results good, but we know we may not."[122]

As I have already argued, Kerala's commitment to its poor was not the consequence of idiosyncratically benevolent leadership but was compelled by redistributive demands raised by leftist activists and an active subaltern citizenry. In central India, Hindu nationalist service workers were greeted with suspicion, but they had been able to slowly gain the confidence of villagers through service work unimpeded by associational competition.[123] By contrast, Sangh activists in Kerala found themselves to be relative latecomers within the state's lower caste villages and neighborhoods. In Kerala, the vibrancy of lower caste political life led these activists to complain that they were not even able to establish a regular presence among these communities.

However, the mere number of civic groups is not always a good indicator of their influence on political life.[124] What made Kerala's political terrain especially inhospitable for Sangh activists was not simply the density of subaltern associational life but the fact that groups with significant lower caste membership also fostered active ties to the BJP's electoral rivals.[125] Sangh interviewees complained of "the many obstacles provided by small-scale cooperatives – banks, milk societies, societies very close to the common man" because these groups

---

[120] Interview with Bd, Thiruvananthapuram, August 9, 2008.
[121] As Heller (2000, p. 498) observes of Kerala: "Overlapping an extensive public school network is a network of private and semiprivate schools sponsored by communal and caste organizations. The result is a school in every village and nearly universal primary school enrollment."
[122] Interview with activist Bd, Thiruvananthapuram, August 9, 2008.
[123] Interview with activist Be, Thiruvananthapuram, August 5, 2008.
[124] For an influential statement of this argument, see Berman 1997.
[125] In drawing attention to this political quality of associational life, I am not advocating the use of Chatterjee's (2008, p. 57) stylized distinction between "civil" and "political" society in India. Chatterjee broadly contrasts a civil society that operates in a formal-legal sphere accessible only to bourgeois urban middle classes with an informal, subaltern political society composed of "temporary, contextual and unstable arrangements" between poor publics and their governments. However, this dichotomy is not particularly useful for the central task of this analysis, which is to conceptualize the attempts to create a range of formal and informal ties between elite and subaltern political communities.

were almost always closely allied with local Communist cadres.[126] Regional lower caste associations also tended to ally with communists, whereas residents incorporated into the state's considerable Christian networks were most often linked with the Congress Party. Ketzer notes that in Bologna, the battle between "comrades and Christians" for political influence was "largely waged on social terrain."[127] A similar competitive dynamic had left Keral's social terrain too crowded for the Sangh to find any meaningful real estate.

Additionally, Hindu nationalists found the Pulaya Mahasabha – the main Dalit association in Kerala – had followed the example of Nair and Ezhava associations by fostering close ties with a major party (in this case, the communists). According to the BJP's senior *sanghathan mantri* (organizing secretary) in Kerala, "these allegiances made it difficult for the BJP to create a base among any community." Without equivalent organizational linkages of its own, the party was forced "to recruit lower castes at the individual level and go to each and every one to convince them to support us."[128] The BJP's problems were compounded by the fact that as a national party that purports to stand for all Hindus, "caste cannot be a major factor for us, so caste organizations … can become a major obstacle for us." Accordingly, service activists noted that the "main obstacle the Sangh faces is how to replace the social functions caste organizations played in Kerala society with our own activities," and they confessed that their own efforts "have failed in this work."[129]

To sum up, specific political developments in Kerala created a context that proved particularly treacherous for Hindu nationalists. A strong left party, dense associational life, and actively politicized subaltern electorate compelled strong social policies that weakened demand for Sangh services. Additionally, these factors combined to politicize the caste- and class-based divisions the BJP sought to downplay.[130] Instead of the facilitative environment found in Chhattisgarh's villages, Hindu nationalists in Kerala encountered self-mobilized lower castes with clear programmatic and organizational linkages to their political rivals.[131] Service activists had found themselves robbed of an opportunity to implement even the first step of a welfare-based strategy.

---

[126] Interview with activist Be, Thiruvananthapuram, August 5, 2008.
[127] Kertzer 1980, p. 4.
[128] Interview with K. Ummakanthan, Thiruvananthapuram (in English) August 5, 2008.
[129] Interview with K. Jayaprasad, an RSS-affiliated researcher at the Bharatiya Vichara Kendrum run by RSS leader P. Parameswaram in Thiruvananthapuram, August 9, 2008.
[130] Similar problems existed for the Sangh in neighboring Tamil Nadu. Sangh commentators themselves noted that the "long history of anti-Brahminism" in Tamil Nadu posed a problem for Sangh expansion given the movement's Brahmin base in the state (Kamath 1987).
[131] It cannot be asserted that the BJP's poor performance is purely the result of tactical voting by lower caste voters who would have supported the party if they thought it had a chance of winning. Respondents were asked whether they would have supported the BJP if it had a chance of winning the assembly polls, and more than 90 percent of non-BJP supporters said they would still not support the party.

HINDU NATIONALIST EFFORTS IN UTTAR PRADESH

Early Failures with Lower Castes

In this section, I turn to evaluating how service efforts by Hindu nationalists in northern Uttar Pradesh compare with the movement's experiences in south and central India. The state is home to the town of Ayodhya, which holds a central place in the Sangh Parivar's imagination as the mythological birthplace of the Hindu god Ram. Consequently, Uttar Pradesh has been the heart of the Sangh's central agitation, discussed in Chapter 2, which seeks to replace the Babri mosque in Ayodhya with a temple to Ram. This highly polarizing mobilization, which culminated with the mosque's destruction in 1992, did initially appear to yield the BJP some electoral success. The party emerged from relative marginality to strongly challenge the Congress in north India during the early 1990s.

However, the grisly theater produced by the mosque's destruction and its violent aftermath obscured the shallow roots of the BJP's appeal in Uttar Pradesh. On the one hand, the state was the site of Hindutva's most famous mobilization and also housed the highest number of Sangh *shakhas* in the country.[132] However, once again these branches were primarily located within upper caste neighborhoods and did little to expand the party's presence among subaltern communities. Moreover, as Chapter 2 detailed, the Ayodhya mobilizations were ineffectual in widening the Sangh's appeal among lower castes, who largely kept their distance from the campaign. This failure was brought home somewhat forcefully to the BJP in the 1993 assembly elections, the first held in Uttar Pradesh after the mosque's destruction. The electoral returns from these contests revealed the triumphalism of the early nineties to be short lived, as the party was swept from power by an alliance of the Bahujan Samaj Party (whose base was among Dalits) and the Samajwadi Party (whose base was among backward castes). The Hindutva agenda has since continued to decline in salience within Uttar Pradesh. According to a 2007 survey in the state, only 1 percent of respondents mentioned the Ayodhya dispute as the issue that mattered most to them while voting, far lower than standard economic concerns such as inflation (38 percent) and unemployment (16 percent).[133]

Figure 6.3 shows how the BJP's share of seats in the state legislature consistently declined from 1991, and how a large part of these losses came at the expense of the Dalit-led BSP. This abrupt end to its mercurial rise made the BJP realize that increasingly assertive lower castes in north India now demanded direct political attention. Yet, the BJP was unable to provide the kinds of

[132] As of 2005, the state had 10,417 *shakhas*. In comparison, Madhya Pradesh (the second most populous state in the country) had only 4,300. Maharashtra, where the RSS was founded, had 1,843. Figures are collected by the author from RSS office, Jhandewalan, New Delhi in October 2007.
[133] Yadav and Kumar 2007c.

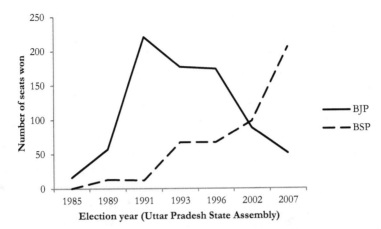

FIGURE 6.3. BJP and BSP electoral performances in Uttar Pradesh (1985–2007)
Source: Election Commission of India.

material and symbolic benefits the BSP provided to Dalit voters. For example, the BJP never systematically increased its internal representation of Dalits, as upper caste leaders rejected calls by some within the party to diversify the social profile of its candidate lists.[134]

Nor were party leaders able to mimic the discursive strategies of their subaltern-led competitors. The anti-elite rhetoric that had enabled the BSP's leaders, notably Kanshi Ram and Mayawati, to gain a foothold among lower castes in UP was simply not available to BJP campaigners. A former BJP MLA admitted that "the BSP can use anti-*savarna* [upper caste] rhetoric to recruit – and it is much easier to get people to your side that way."[135] The national head of the Scheduled Caste wing within the BJP explained this problem in Uttar Pradesh in greater detail:

---

[134] Here I disagree with the argument of Jaffrelot et al. (2003, p.158) who claim that there is "a striking difference" in the composition of the two BJP cabinets in 1991 and 1999. The authors argue this point on the basis of an increase in the percentage of backward castes in the cabinet (from 22 percent to nearly 32 percent). However, this increase came almost entirely at the expense of Dalit members of the cabinet (16.67 percent in 1999, 7.94 percent in 1999), whereas upper castes remained in the vast majority at more than 49 percent in both instances. It is true that the party did make a few token gestures to non-Dalit backward caste communities, most notably in appointing Kalyan Singh (a member of the OBC Lodhi community) as the chief minister of its UP state government in 1991. However, these non-elite appointees often complained of being sidelined by upper castes within the party, and Singh eventually quit the party, saying he was treated like "bonded labor" by party elites (see Khan 2009). Further, the BJP state unit flatly rejected calls by backward leaders such as Singh to broaden the social profile of the party's candidate lists.

[135] Interview with Ca, Agra, January 9, 2011.

See look at these smaller parties like the BSP. When they first mobilize lower castes, they are only looking to that section to build a base so they can spread hate against other sections of society with their propaganda – but we are a national party looking to build a "Hindu Rashtra" [Hindu nation] not a "Bahujan Samaj" [non-elite majority community]. We can't do what they do with this goal of integration in mind. Because we are more moderate, they [Dalits] won't come to us first. They will always go to these smaller parties first.[136]

Leaving aside the partisan rhetoric of this narrative, including the claim that the BJP is a "moderate" political force, this admission does reveal important contextual differences between the landscape faced by the party in Uttar Pradesh and in Chhattisgarh. In the former case, smaller caste-based political parties have actively mobilized subaltern communities as their primary base. Hindu nationalists were no match for such direct attention, and election results revealed the BJP was increasingly painted into a corner as the party of social elites. In the 1996 state elections, only 4 percent of Dalits in Uttar Pradesh voted for the BJP, compared to 62 percent of upper castes.[137]

Seemingly outmatched, BJP operatives began to consider the possibility of poaching lower caste votes through alliances with the very political forces inflicting the most damage on the party's expansionist ambitions. Insiders believed that forging a coalition with the BSP would enable the BJP to shed its image as a party of the privileged:

Now for whatever reason, Dalits thought that this party [BJP] is for upper castes, for Brahmins ... once an idea has stuck, it is hard to overcome ... So we thought that if we promoted Mayawati as a Dalit woman, then we will instill a faith inside that community that how can we be opposed to them if we help one of their own become a chief minister?[138]

Traditionally, Sangh activists had opposed forming alliances, fearing this approach would inevitably dilute the BJP's commitment to Hindutva's doctrine. However, even movement ideologues realized the desperate need to manufacture an opening for recruiting lower castes in Uttar Pradesh. The RSS's weekly newsletter, the *Organizer*, was actually enthusiastic about "the social fall-out" of an alliance with the BSP and argued that "the BJP-BSP alliance should lead to social harmony and Hindu consolidation. It ought to reduce the alienation of the deprived sections of the society. It is in this context that it [the alliance] is a pleasing development *from the RSS point of view*."[139]

Thus encouraged, the BJP decided to provide external support to the BSP in 1995, enabling the latter to form the government in Uttar Pradesh. Both parties appeared to be equally opportunistic in forging this seemingly unlikely coalition,

---

[136] Interview with Satya Narayan Jatiya, New Delhi, April 30, 2008.
[137] Figures from Yadav and Kumar 2007b.
[138] Interview with Cb, former BJP Agra president, Agra, January 9, 2011.
[139] Khosla 1997, p. 5, emphasis added.

with the BJP hoping to enhance its status with Dalits, and the BSP hungry for a chance to govern.[140] However, the nature of this alliance signaled the BJP's particular desperation, as it allowed the BSP leader Mayawati to head the coalition government despite her party's having won less than half as many seats as the BJP.[141] The two parties also formed alliances in 1997 and 2002, as each struggled to win outright majorities within the state.[142]

All three of these attempts proved short lived, with tensions between the coalition partners remaining high during each alliance period. One strategist for the BSP argued that his party always remained suspicious of the BJP's "greedy" motivations in seeking the partnership:

They honestly thought that if they helped to make Mayawati CM, then their [Dalit] mind-set about us will change – they will think look the BJP helped *behanji* [our sister], what we thought about them was wrong. Then the BJP thought we will then be able to get into their homes and recruit them.[143]

However, this BSP worker went on to explain that the superficiality of BJP support for Dalit causes was not difficult for his party to expose, concluding that "their viewpoint is *manuvadi* [casteist] and we can always show that."[144] He argued that such casteism was plainly evident in views of Hindutva's top leadership, citing the controversial comments of K. Sudarshan, the Sangh's supreme leader at the time: "when Sudarshan was asked whether caste should be abolished, he said no, who will do the sweeping? We [the BSP] can always point to [moments like] that."[145]

Although the BJP had hoped to gradually poach lower caste populations into its own vote bank, the party instead found itself outflanked by its smaller partner. Even from within alliances with the BJP, the BSP leadership skillfully exposed the contradictions inherent in the former's twin goals of protecting elite interests while appealing to lower castes.[146] In 1997, the coalition between the two parties specified a power-sharing arrangement whereby the BSP's Mayawati would serve as chief minister for a period of six months, to be followed by an equal stint for the BJP's Kalyan Singh. However, tensions surfaced when on assuming leadership, the BSP's leaders immediately began to voice their concerns

[140] Interview with Cc, BSP advisor, Agra, January 7, 2011.
[141] The BSP won 67 seats, compared to the BJP's 174. Data from Electoral Commission of India, www.eci.gov.in. Accessed on July 20, 2008.
[142] See Tripathi 2002.
[143] Interview with Cd, Agra BSP leader, Agra, January 7, 2011.
[144] Ibid.
[145] In the interview, what Sudarshan actually said was slightly different, although still open to a similar criticism by lower caste activists. He argued that caste in its original form "used to be like a fence around a farm. Those who violated its rules were ostracized. It was not discriminatory. Rather, it provided for job reservation. Every caste was given reservation [for] a particular job. A mason could not do a carpenter's job and carpenter could not do a sweeper's job" as quoted in "Old caste system" 2006.
[146] Gatade 2005.

about the partnership and indeed "gave the impression of not being unduly bothered about the longevity of the coalition."[147]

The situation deteriorated when the BJP, on assuming power, promptly issued a government order stating that the national act punishing atrocities committed against Dalits and Adivasis should not be misused. This order clearly reflected upper caste concerns that the act was enabling increasingly assertive Dalits to "unfairly" punish local elites on the basis of false accusations. Under the BJP government, upper castes accused under the act were no longer jailed during the investigation of the case, and Dalit plaintiffs no longer received financial compensation to fight the case in court.[148] Mayawati immediately seized on these moves to portray the BJP as anti-Dalit. The BSP subsequently organized several demonstrations against its own alliance partners and eventually broke the coalition before the BJP had a chance to complete its stint at the helm of government.

Overall, the alliance experiment backfired badly for the BJP in Uttar Pradesh. Instead of enhancing the party's appeal with lower castes, each coalition period enabled the BSP to expand its base with non-Dalits in the state, while continuing to pigeonhole its partner as representative of upper caste interests. BJP insiders themselves lamented this fact, noting that "we made a coalition with Mayawati, but she stole our strength and we were unable to get anything in return, and now she is in power."[149] From 1996 to 2007, the BSP significantly increased its vote share among upper castes from 4 percent to 16 percent. The party found particular success among financially less fortunate upper castes whom the BJP "rapidly lost the support of" during the 2000s.[150] These inroads were not transformative in the sense that upper castes remained only 10 percent of all BSP supporters. However, these selective inroads into the BJP's base did help deliver the additional boost the BSP needed to nose ahead of its rivals in a fragmented first-past-the-post system.

Meanwhile, the BJP's successive emphases on communal mobilizations and alliances appeared to have weakened efforts to systematically implement a service-based strategy in the state. Overall, the index of service provision in Uttar Pradesh (.088) is one of the lowest in India, and roughly one-third that of either Chhattisgarh or Kerala. However, the state provides several contextual features that make it a compelling site to study in conjunction with the other two cases examined here. First, poor voters supported distinct parties in all three states, with each of the three parties representing a significant larger category of political actors than in the global south. In Chhattisgarh, poor voters had

---

[147] Rajagopalan 1997.

[148] Lerche (1999, p. 215).

[149] Interview with Cb, former BJP Agra leader, Agra, January 9, 2011.

[150] Whereas the BSP won only 12 percent and 11 percent of the votes of rich Brahmins and Jats (two influential elite subcastes) in its winning 2007 campaign, it won 27 percent and 22 percent of votes from their poorer respective counterparts (Yadav and Kumar 2007c). "Rich" and "poor" here refer to either end of a fourfold division of class on the 2007 survey conducted by Lokniti.

primarily supported a catch-all party of national independence; in Kerala, they had united behind a leftist class-based party; and in Uttar Pradesh, they primarily rallied behind a rising ethnic party.

These variations informed important differences in the context in which service activists worked. Whereas Chhattisgarh was a case marked by inadequate public infrastructure and low levels of self-mobilization among subaltern communities, Kerala was distinguished by its history of strong social policies, as well as active lower caste involvement in political life. In contrast, Uttar Pradesh offers a somewhat intermediate case in which lower castes have been highly mobilized politically but service provisioning remains inadequate.

How did the experiences of service activists in this specific context compare with those of their counterparts in Kerala and Chhattisgarh? To meaningfully compare the experiences of Sangh providers across these three states, I concentrated my research within Uttar Pradesh in the city of Agra. Overall, Agra stands out as a pocket of strong service provision in a state where such efforts have in general been anemic. I have already discussed the types of activities performed by Seva Bharati in Agra (SBA), the primary Sangh service wing in the city, in some detail in Chapter 4 and will not repeat those descriptions here. My focus in the next section is instead on examining how successful these providers were in winning over Dalit communities in the city's impoverished slums.

Acceptance without Returns: Service Provision in Agra

According to a 2005 UNDP report, the human development index of the Agra district is comparable to that of Chhattisgarh (.621 compared to .627), both below the national average. Further, the literacy rate in Agra's slums is less than 50 percent, roughly one-third less than that of the city overall.[151] A USAID survey of Agra's slums classifies the vast majority as having severely inadequate public infrastructure, noting for example that most slum dwellers often resort to more costly private health facilities because of the greater proximity of these services and the better attention received in them.[152] However, as in central India, a lack of basic provisioning did not automatically generate support for the SBA's activists. Instead, providers faced many of the same challenges as the Vanvasi Kalyan Ashram (VKA) did in getting people to come to their service chapters in Chhattisgarh. One SBA worker confessed his disappointment with the suspiciousness with which he was first greeted, noting that "they just kept asking me why I was there – what fondness did I have for them and why?" He noted that among Dalit communities, "the first thought is to look for what is our [the Sangh's] *swarthik* [selfish] reason for being here, we cannot be here simply for their welfare."[153]

---

[151] Data from the 2001 Indian National Census, compiled by www.indiastat.com.
[152] USAID 2004, p. 10.
[153] Quote from Activist Ce, part of conversation with SBA workers, Madhav Bhavan, Agra, January 5, 2011.

SBA adopted many of the same strategies as their VKA counterparts in Chhattisgarh when dealing with such hostility. In initial visits to a particular slum, SBA activists focused on introducing themselves and inquiring about the needs of local communities. They often ran one-day events in the area they were targeting, at which activists provide free *khichdi* – lentils and rice cooked together – a dish meant to symbolize the "harmonious" mixing of different social groups that SBA purportedly sought to achieve. As one of SBA's founders noted:

Now we build our presence slowly – *khichdi* programs often provide initial contact. Then, slowly we ask – how many children go to school? People will say there are forty to fifty children in this area; only about three go to class. Then, later we will come back and ask – is there a place here for a small class? Then next time we ask – if we send a teacher will you help look after them? Will you give her a chair? Yes, we will, they say. Then, if things are going well, we ask for a couple of volunteers in the area to make a *samiti* [association] The *samiti* will help organize the details for running the class. Then, this becomes the medium – see we cannot go into the *bastis* as ourselves, but we can go as teachers.[154]

As in central India, SBA workers must work hard to ingratiate themselves with local communities, not "as themselves" (i.e., upper caste Hindu nationalists) but "as teachers."

Other service workers have had even tougher experiences than the one just quoted. One activist told me of the hostilities he faced while setting up his one-teacher school, which enrolls thirty students.[155] Initially, local residents told him that there were no students available for this center, even though he could see many school-age children at home during daytime hours. Lower caste residents even went so far as to tell him he was not welcome within the slum. In response, the activist began sitting just outside the narrow entryway of the locality and asked passing children to come sit with him. After six weeks, the residents invited him gradually "inside," first giving him a spot under a tree on the edge of the slum. Eventually, he received a vacant plot deeper in the neighborhood's interior, where class was being held during my visits in early 2011.

Other activists corroborated that their initial attempts centered on simply enrolling enough recipients to give their chapter some local credibility. Yet over time, the SBA has managed to win appreciation for its efforts, and activists have found a high demand for their services. Activists were keenly aware of the importance of using their efforts as the basis for creating social connections, confessing that "squeezing into someone's home is a difficult task, but that is what makes service effective, that is what it enables us to do, and that is what service can give the Sangh."[156]

[154] Interview with Cf, co-founder of Seva Bharati Agra, January 11, 2011.
[155] Interview with teacher activist Cg, Ravinagar locality, Agra, January 15, 2011.
[156] Interview with Ce, Seva Bharati *sachiv* (secretary), Agra, January 12, 2011.

As in central India, locals voiced appreciation of the greater reliability of service provision by Sangh chapters. A Dalit resident of a slum in the neighborhood of Shastripuram complained that in the nearby government school, "out of three teachers, only one actually shows up. There is no atmosphere for learning." He continued, "compared to the [local] Seva Bharati school, the work in government schools is third rate – it is just a salary collection business."[157] Residents of other areas, such as the slums clustering in the Tajganj area, echoed these complaints of inadequate infrastructure and absenteeism in nearby public facilities.

However, SBA workers openly admitted that they had been unable to translate the goodwill they accrued through service work into electoral results. In Chhattisgarh, Sangh activists were able to capitalize on the access provided by service work, embedding themselves within communities and using their influence to shift voting patterns at the local level. In Agra however, SBA workers complained that local political rivals, principally BSP party workers and supporters, "go around spreading the word that the goal of our work is to give the BJP an advantage."[158] Welfare activists explained that even as they were providing services, their opponents would caution residents that "these people belong to the Brahmins of the BJP and will later come and ask us for votes"[159] or that "people from the BSP and other caste-based parties like the Samajwadi Party go around telling everyone that we are just BJP workers."[160]

This repeated calling out of political motivations and caste affiliations was recognized by service workers to be especially harmful in Uttar Pradesh's ethnically polarized system. Such episodes also sharply differentiated their experiences from those of their Chhattisgarhi counterparts. A key aspect of service's strategic success in central India was the ability of Sangh activists to use their removal from the electoral arena to undertake a range of invaluable political work for the BJP. In Agra however, service workers found themselves constrained from engaging in recruiting candidates and party workers, spreading rumors about rival candidates, or attempting to sway voters directly at election time. One longtime SBA activist observed that "politics in UP is about caste, and the people of the BJP tend to be of higher caste, so we don't talk about politics; we only go for service."[161] Another worker noted that "because of the active rumors spread against us as working for the BJP, we have to tell our workers not to engage in political discussions and not to advocate for any particular candidate."[162] Indeed, SBA activists are so concerned about being labeled BJP

[157] Focus group discussion, Chottanagar, January 11, 2011.
[158] Interview with activist Ch, January 6, 2011.
[159] Ibid.
[160] Quote from activist Ci, worker in the Braj region, as part of conversation with SBA activists, Madhav Bhavan, Agra, January 5, 2011.
[161] Seva Bharati activist (name withheld by request), conversation with SBA workers, Madhav Bhavan, Agra, January 5, 2011.
[162] Interview with activist Ch, Agra, January 6, 2011.

workers that new recruits are instructed "to not even take party names ... because if as Seva Bharati activists we talk about politics, people will think we are part of the BJP and we won't get access to them again ... Now of course I am with the BJP – but I can't force that opinion on others."[163] Whereas VKA activists in Jashpur had discussed the implicit and explicit ways in which they had mobilized support for *hamara bhajpa* (our BJP), SBA workers worried that "we have to be careful not to talk about politics in the public domain – we do not want to be seen as politicians."[164]

Comparing field interviews in Kerala and Uttar Pradesh thus reveals important differences in the juncture at which activists encountered obstacles. In southern India, the Sangh seemed unable to even find takers for its services, let alone use provisioning as an entry point for more political efforts. In Agra however, as in Chhattisgarh, inadequate public infrastructure seemed to have provided an opening for Hindu nationalists to insert themselves within initially hostile lower caste communities. However, the deeply politicized divide between elites and non-elites in the state hampered the Sangh's ability to convert this social presence into electoral influence. In such a polarized arena, the BJP's social image as an upper caste party widened the divide service activists had to bridge. At the same time, the presence of lower caste political rivals prevented service workers from engaging in political mobilization. As one of the local leaders of the BJP within Uttar Pradesh noted, "the problem was that all these castes here formed their own groups and organizations."[165] SBA leaders were left to despondently conclude that even though their own organization had created strong networks within the city, "Dalits remained blindly wedded to Mayawati and the BSP." Unable to deliver electoral dividends, service activists saw no way for the BJP to "match the satisfaction Dalits received from seeing their own in government."[166]

SURVEY ANALYSIS: COMPARING SERVICE PROVISION IN KERALA AND UTTAR PRADESH

Are these qualitative insights about the challenges welfare activists faced in Kerala and Uttar Pradesh confirmed by quantitative data on electoral behavior? To address this question, I conducted local surveys similar to those carried out in Chhattisgarh with nearly 700 Dalit and Adivasi voters in both states (for survey details, see Appendix C).[167] As in central India, localities were deliberately chosen according to the density of service networks they housed, but with a different logic informing this selection. In Chhattisgarh, I sought to assess the impact of varying

[163] Interview with Ce, Agra, January 6, 2011.
[164] Interview with Cf, co-founder of Seva Bharati, Agra, January 11, 2011.
[165] Interview with Ca, former BJP MLA, Agra, January 9, 2011.
[166] Conversation with Ch and Ce, Seva Bharati activists, Agra, January 12, 2011.
[167] The survey in Kerala was carried out in April-May 2008, and the Agra survey was conducted during February 2011.

service network strength across highly comparable localities and therefore selected an equal number of high- and low-intensity districts. This chapter's analytic focus is on examining how *different contextual backgrounds* influence the success of a service-based approach, controlling for a common level of effort. Accordingly, for this portion of the analysis, I primarily selected areas with levels of service provision comparable to the high-intensity regions in Chhattisgarh.

In Kerala, I selected two districts with a strong Sangh service presence (Wayanad and Thiruvananthapuram) along with one low-strength district (Palakkad) for reference (Figure 6.4).[168] Within Agra, the survey was conducted across four major slum areas within the city (Figure 6.5), three of which have a high number of service chapters (Jagdishpura, Shastripuram, Tajganj), with a fourth low-strength locality (Shahganj) again included for reference.

The surveys confirmed that the BJP performed poorly with marginalized voters in both states. In Kerala, 46 percent of respondents said they voted for the CPM during the 2006 assembly elections, with the Congress placing second with 36 percent and the BJP a distant third with only 12 percent of the vote. These differentials were broadly in line with the findings of other polls conducted in the state during national and assembly elections.[169] The BJP performed similarly poorly among respondents in Agra, winning only 14 percent of their vote in the 2007 assembly election, compared to the BSP's overwhelming 78.75 percent share.

However, the variations across localities within each survey sample are of more importance for my analysis. Table 6.3 outlines the internal distribution of BJP support and broadly finds that the party performed poorly in each area surveyed. Unlike in Chhattisgarh, dense service networks did not correlate with strong party performance in specific districts within either state.

Further disaggregating the results according to the level of respondent involvement with the Sangh revealed some striking information on how service chapters were locally received. As in Chhattisgarh, I distinguished between respondents who were members of Sangh service organizations, nonmember beneficiaries of these chapters, and those who were neither (non-beneficiaries). Only one respondent was a formal member of Sangh service organizations in Kerala, and only two in Uttar Pradesh. All three of these members voted for the BJP. As I argued in this book's Introduction, such loyalty is not surprising, even

---

[168] In Kerala, each district is further subdivided into *taluks* corresponding to the *tehsil* level in Chhattisgarh. One village was randomly selected from a list of villages in each *taluk*, and as each district had fewer than six *taluks*, the remaining villages for each district were picked from *taluks* selected at random. This process ensured that each portion of the district was covered in the sample. Within each village, individual Dalit and Adivasi respondents were selected using the same random sampling procedure used in the Chhattisgarh surveys.

[169] Lokniti conducted a survey during the 2001 state assembly elections and had a sample that included 125 Dalit respondents, a little less than half the number surveyed for this study. The Lokniti survey found 37 percent of Dalits voting for the communists, 15 percent for the Congress, and only 2 percent voting for the BJP.

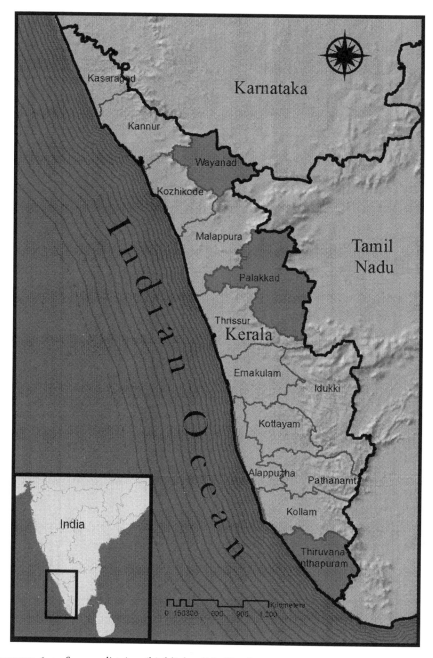

FIGURE 6.4. Survey districts (highlighted) in Kerala
Source: Map by Abraham Kaleo Parrish, Yale Map Department, 2011.

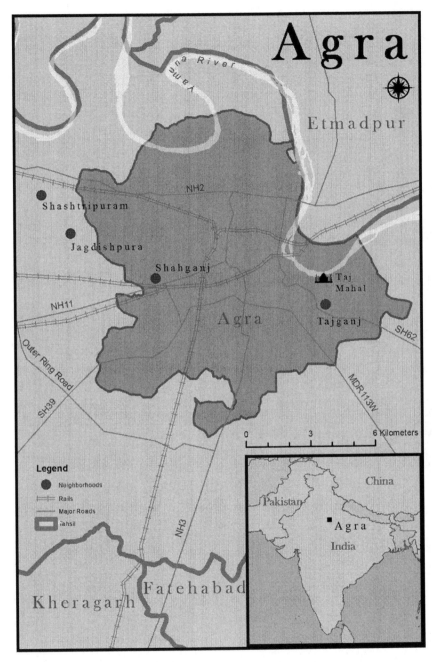

FIGURE 6.5. Survey localities in Agra
Source: Map by Abraham Kaleo Parrish and Maria Haras, Yale Map Department 2012.

TABLE 6.3. *Sangh service and BJP support in Kerala and UP*

State	District/Locality	Sangh Service Index	BJP Vote Share
Kerala	Palakkad	.169	17.07%
	Wayanad	.501	6.67%
	Thiruvananthapuram	.459	13.64%
UP (Agra)	Shahganj	.075	9.00%
	Shastripuram	.391	19.00%
	Tajganj	.341	5.00%
	Jagdishpura	.402	12.00%

Source: Author surveys (Kerala 2008, Agra 2011).

TABLE 6.4. *BJP support by respondent type in Kerala and UP*

State	District/Locality	Percentage of beneficiaries voting for the BJP	Percentage of non-beneficiaries voting for the BJP
Kerala	Palakkad	75% (N=3/4)	14.10% (N=11/78)
	Wayanad	25% (N=1/4)	5.81% (N=5/86)
	Thiruvananthapuram	100% (N=4/4)	9.52% (N=8/86)
UP (Agra)	Shahganj	10.00% (1/10)	9.64 (8/90)
	Shastripuram	19.35% (6/31)	18.84 (13/69)
	Tajganj	3.70% (1/27)	5.48 (4/73)
	Jagdishpura	20.00% (5/32)	10.29 (7/68)

Source: Author surveys (Kerala 2008; Agra 2011).

where the BJP is not competitive. Full-time recruits receive considerable benefits from their inclusion in Sangh networks and are fearful of being replaced if they do not display a commitment to the movement, including voting for the BJP. Yet, as in Chhattisgarh, such members are too few in number to serve as the basis for electoral expansion.

The survey results for respondents in the remaining two categories of affiliation reveal how the contextual differences between Kerala and Uttar Pradesh led to distinct forms of failure. It is true that as in Chhattisgarh, beneficiaries in Kerala support the BJP at higher rates than non-beneficiaries, even after accounting for the small number of positive responses.[170] However, this differential is rendered substantively inconsequential because of the tiny number of respondents who used these services in the first place. Table 6.4 reveals that in Kerala, Sangh activists were not even able to find takers for the services they sought to

---

[170] The chi-square test results using the Yates correction for small cell counts confirmed that this differential was significant in Palakkad and Thiruvananthapuram, but not in Wayanad.

furnish. Fewer than 5 percent of voters sampled were beneficiaries of Hindu nationalist welfare, compared to 23.33 percent of the Chhattisgarhi sample. Indeed, individual service chapters in central India were able to attract 3.5 times as many beneficiaries on average as their southern counterparts. Further, unlike the patterns of support witnessed in central India, beneficiaries in Kerala tended to be significantly more communal than non-beneficiaries. Additionally, all of the respondents who voted for the BJP in 2006 had also supported the party in previous elections, again in sharp contrast with the Chhattisgarh results.

Collectively, this evidence suggests that service wings are attracting a small pool of prior BJP supporters committed to Hindutva, rather than enhancing the party's appeal with previously unsupportive voters. The survey also provided evidence that the strength of social policies and subaltern political life in Kerala specifically blocked the ability of the BJP to expand its appeal. First, the state's relatively strong provisioning does indeed appear to have attenuated local demand for Sangh services. Respondents were asked how they thought their state compared to the rest of India in terms of public health and educational services – 80.84 percent of those surveyed in Kerala said they thought their state performed "Better" or "Much Better" compared to only 0.77 percent who said they thought the state performed "Worse" than other Indian states. The responses fit the admissions of BJP leaders quoted earlier, who complained that they had "not been able to do very much in the social service sector" because of the relative strength of public policy in that area.[171]

Second, the high degree of political self-mobilization among lower castes also hamstrung Hindu nationalist efforts to create cross-caste electoral coalitions. The survey results identified 35.5 percent of respondents to be members of lower caste associations, roughly double the proportion of the Chhattisgarh sample (17.5 percent). The pattern of voting among these members also indicates the partisan allegiances of these groups, with more than 52 percent of Pulaya Mahasabha (the largest Dalit association in the state) members voting for the communist CPM, more than double the proportion supporting any other party.[172]

Unlike Kerala, Uttar Pradesh continues to perform poorly across a range of social indicators, even by the comparatively low bar set by most Indian states. Levels of participation in associational life are also a fraction of those found in Kerala.[173] On the surveys conducted for this chapter, 38 percent of Dalits in Kerala are associationally active, compared to just 6 percent in Uttar Pradesh. Qualitative evidence suggested that these features, which more closely resemble

---

[171] Interview with Bb, BJP leader, Thiruvananthapuram, August 5, 2008.

[172] This figure was also roughly ten percentage points higher than the CPM's vote share among Dalits who were not part of this association.

[173] Dreze and Sen (1996, p. 93) note similar discrepancies in their well-known study of social development in India. The authors find that 50 percent of respondents in Kerala reported that they actively participate in at least one association, compared to just 4 percent in Uttar Pradesh.

the context of Chhattisgarh than Kerala, appear to have allowed Sangh activists to gain acceptance within communities in Agra as service providers.

The survey results supported this argument, revealing that in sharp contrast to their southern counterparts, service activists in Agra did not appear to have any difficulty in persuading a large number of members of lower castes to use their services. In fact, more than 30 percent of respondents claimed to have benefited from Sangh welfare in the three slum areas with dense service networks. These rates are comparable to those recorded in the BJP's stronghold districts within Chhattisgarh. Moreover, as in central India, beneficiaries in Agra were not more likely to be prior BJP supporters and were in fact slightly less communal than non-beneficiaries. These results suggest that service chapters in Agra, as in Chhattisgarh, were not simply attracting voters with preexisting ideological affiliations to Hindutva.

However, the survey results also suggest that the Sangh in Agra failed to produce the electoral shifts witnessed in Chhattisgarh. In central India, activists had won high rates of support for the BJP among direct beneficiaries of their provisioning and had even managed to use their broad social influence to sway a great number of non-beneficiaries toward the party. Interviews in Agra had suggested that the politicization of subaltern communities in Uttar Pradesh by the Dalit-led BSP proved crucial in preventing activists from translating service into political support.

The survey data appears to confirm patterns anticipated by these complaints, showing service organizations in Agra to be unable to attract a wider following. Strikingly, not a single one of the nearly 300 non-beneficiaries sampled expressed a positive opinion of Sangh service organizations, even though many of them lived in close proximity to service chapters. This lack of influence stood in marked contrast to Chhattisgarh, where Sangh activists were able to gradually sway the electoral decisions of a broader community of voters. Even more disappointingly for the Sangh, service activists did not fare much better even with direct beneficiaries who supported the party at the same negligible rates as non-beneficiaries.[174] Indeed, Sangh service activists could not even unsettle the BJP's elitist reputation among their direct beneficiaries, 63 percent of whom agreed with the statement that "the BJP mainly looks after upper caste interests." Indeed, only 17 percent of voters using Sangh services identified the BJP as the party that most looked after the interests of their caste community, compared to 74 percent of this subsample who still chose the BSP.

A replication of the statistical tests conducted on the Chhattisgarhi sample with those from Kerala and Uttar Pradesh further confirms the failure of service in each of the latter two states. Table 6.5 shows that beneficiaries of service were no more likely than non-beneficiaries to support the BJP in either Kerala or Uttar

---

[174] This insignificance was again confirmed by chi-square test results using the Yates correction for small cell counts. The tests found no difference between the conditional probability of beneficiaries and non-beneficiaries supporting the BJP in any of the four localities surveyed in Agra.

TABLE 6.5. *Assessing the influence of service on voting in Kerala and UP*

	KERALA		UP (AGRA)	
	(1)	(2)	(3)	(4)
Service Beneficiary	1.541	.801	−1.362	−1.527
	(2.580)	(1.076)	(1.016)	(1.049)
Service Opinion	4.145***	3.627***	.419	.474
	(.677)	(.676)	(.285)	(.297)
Age	−.017	.022	−.001	−.004
	(.018)	(022)	(.013)	(.012)
Control Variables				
Religiosity		.745		.305*
		(.418)		(.145)
Communalism		1.028***		−.072
		(.314)		(.121)
Caste Influence		.613		−.994**
		(1.783)		(.206)
Income		.089		−.006
		(.731)		(.147)
Male		−.352		.134
		(.626)		(.251)
Education		.034		.083
		(.085)		(.127)
Constant	−2.025**	−12.279***	−1.727***	−3.457**
	(.698)	(3.584)	(.251)	(.368)
Villages/Slum subsections	18	18	16	16
Observations	262	259	399	399
percent predicted correctly	92.75	93.82	86.00	86.47
Log Likelihoood	−67.048	−50.469	−160.874	−139.798

Note: **p<.01, ***p<.001. Robust standard errors clustered by village or slum quadrant.
Source: Data from author-conducted surveys (2008, 2011).

Pradesh, a sharp contrast with the results from Chhattisgarh. This inability of local chapters to win the votes even of direct beneficiaries once again suggests the inadequacy of understanding service working as a variant of clientelist exchange. Such a view would be equally unable to account for why many non-beneficiaries in Chhattisgarh supported the BJP, as well as why many beneficiaries in Uttar Pradesh did not vote for the party.

Models 3 and 4 also found that positive opinions of service chapters do not independently correlate with support for the BJP in Agra. Instead, higher levels of piety distinguished lower caste supporters of the party from their co-ethnics who supported other alternatives. By contrast, opinions of service wings in Kerala did appear to exert a positive and statistically significant impact on voting for the BJP (Models 1 and 2). However, this result was again of marginal substantive significance because of its limited scope: only fifteen respondents (6.5 percent of the sample) expressed positive views of Sangh service chapters, compared to 40 percent of Chhattisgarhi voters.

Most importantly, unlike in central India, positive views seemed to be strongly informed by underlying ideological orientations in Kerala. The few southern respondents who rated service wings favorably also tended to be significantly more communal than those who did not.[175] In Kerala, *Communalism* also had an independent, positive, and statistically significant impact on the likelihood of a subaltern voter voting for the BJP (Model 2). These results indicate that in sharp contrast to the Chhattisgarhi and national sample, ideological support for Hindutva played a primary role in distinguishing the small group of lower caste BJP voters in Kerala.

An intriguing difference between respondents from Kerala and Uttar Pradesh was their prioritization of caste identities when making electoral decisions. In Agra, the likelihood of subaltern support for the BJP significantly decreased by 9.15 percentage points if a voter cited co-ethnic leaders as having the greatest impact on their electoral decisions. However, this variable had no discernible impact among voters in Kerala. This difference resonates with the varying ways in which disadvantaged communities were politicized in north and south India. Even as subaltern voters largely assembled behind one of the BJP's rivals in both Kerala and Uttar Pradesh, the role of caste within such processes of aggregation varied.

In Uttar Pradesh, the BSP's success was heavily reliant on mobilizing Dalits as an autonomous political community and continually reinforcing the importance of caste-based bloc voting. Not surprisingly, most Dalit respondents in Uttar Pradesh (67 percent) *strongly agreed* with that they should vote for the same party as members of their caste community.[176] In Kerala, lower castes were certainly collectively mobilized by the communists, but their continuing loyalty to the party was also significantly predicated on the CPM's pro-poor policy record. The strong correspondence between class and caste in Kerala enabled the left to win the support of subaltern castes without relying on an explicitly ethnic mobilizing strategy. In line with this form of political incorporation, most subaltern voters (70 percent) in Kerala *strongly disagreed* with the idea that they should vote for the same party as their co-ethnics, even as they did largely vote for the same party.

CONCLUSION

Through examining instances where a service-based electoral strategy was tried and failed, this chapter has sought to refine my central argument. Where the

---

[175] Respondents with favorable opinions averaged 3.27 on the 4-point *Communalism* index, compared to 2.15 for those with non-favorable ratings, a differential that was significant at the .001 level.

[176] This finding was not an artifact of one survey, as similar differences emerged between subaltern voters in the two states on numerous national surveys. For example, on the 2004 NES, 46 percent of Dalits agreed with this position in Uttar Pradesh, compared to only 14 percent of Dalit respondents in Kerala.

Sangh's success in Chhattisgarh helped explain *how* service wins votes, its struggles in Uttar Pradesh and Kerala shed light on *when* this approach is more or less likely to succeed.

I find that two features of rival strategies heavily influence the electoral efficacy of welfare. First, if such tactics are premised on programmatic linkages with poor voters, as they were in Kerala, service activists are likely to fail, even in the initial step of attracting citizens to their chapters. In Kerala, subaltern communities had mobilized early and often to voice their grievances against economic and social persecution. Lower castes were deeply politicized, first by caste-based social reform movements and later by class-based agitations spearheaded by Communist organizations. Compelled by these actions, local governments in Kerala implemented far stronger social policies than most of their counterparts across India. These social processes thus produced both strong programmatic linkages that attenuated demand for Hindu nationalist services and a vibrant associational life that crowded out Sangh operatives. Service activists were simply never able to gain a foothold in this inhospitable terrain.

Such programmatic linkages among the poor are rare in India and elsewhere across the global south. The Sangh's struggles in Uttar Pradesh revealed that services could also fail to win votes when competing against non-programmatic alternatives. Within such scenarios, a second factor influences the efficacy of service: whether rival parties look to vertically or horizontally mobilize poor voters. Unlike their vertical incorporation by Congress elites in Chhattisgarh, subaltern voters in Uttar Pradesh have been horizontally mobilized by an ethnic party. The Dalit-led BSP's strategy of ethnically targeted patronage and discursive appeals was certainly not programmatic, neither was it accompanied by the implementation of strong social policies. Sangh workers in the city of Agra thus found a grateful audience for their offerings, much as they had in Chhattisgarh. Yet, the BSP's horizontal ethnic strategy politicized the divide between elites and non-elites in the state along caste lines. In this polarized context, the BJP's elite partisan image proved a particularly large liability against which the Sangh's service offerings proved insufficient. Further, the BSP's lower caste operatives forced Sangh workers to remain confined to their role as service providers within Dalit communities, preventing them from performing more political tasks. For now, service activists thus found themselves unable to convert their own acceptance into electoral support for their party arm. However, the BSP's non-programmatic approach may frustrate its supporters in the long run, and provide at least a window of opportunity for the BJP. In Kerala, such windows remain firmly shut.

7

The Argument in Comparative Perspective

I have no wish to push my argument's reach to exceed its grasp. Indeed, one of the aims of this analysis has been to demonstrate the empirical effort needed to determine how private welfare affects electoral behavior. Assessing the extent to which the arguments I have developed apply outside India would require equivalently substantial additional investigations. Such labors are beyond the scope of this project. My aims in this chapter are more modest, namely to illustrate how specific insights from this book can contribute to our understanding of political parties outside India.

Empirically, I focus on comparing the BJP's experience with that of parties inspired by the Muslim Brotherhood (MB), the Islamist organization founded in Egypt in 1928.[1] I selected the family of Brotherhood (or *ikhwan*) parties because they exemplify the type of actors my argument expects to be attracted to a welfare-based approach (see Table 1.2 in Chapter 1). First, like the BJP, these parties are embedded within the thick organizational networks of their founding religious movements. Second, unlike some other Islamist formations (notably some Salafist parties), *ikhwan* parties have been understood to have relatively privileged core constituencies.[2] Finally, these parties are substantively important and constitute a widespread and increasingly influential set of electoral actors across Asia and Africa.

Within this broader family, I focused on *ikhwan* parties in three countries: Egypt, Yemen, and Indonesia. Egypt is home to the original Brotherhood party and therefore is a theoretically important case to examine. Drawing primarily on this iconic example, the first section of this chapter details a number of intriguing

---

[1] I follow convention in defining "Islamist" to refer groups and practices that share a commitment to the implementation of Islamic Law (*shari'ah*) in all spheres of political, cultural, and economic life (Schwedler 2006, p. 8).

[2] An example here is the Salafist Egyptian Al-Nour party. An ACPSS/DEDI Egyptian Post-Election Survey conducted in 2011 found that supporters of Al-Nour were systematically more rural and less educated than the average Egyptian (see Malouche et al. 2013).

conceptual parallels between the BJP and Brotherhood parties: in their ideological motivations, organizational philosophy, social profile, and programmatic
orientation. However, I also detail some important distinctions between *ikhwan*
parties and the BJP, and how these inform divergences in their strategic capabilities and constraints. I conclude this section with a brief discussion of how
Egypt's short-lived period of post-Mubarak competitive electoral politics
affected the likelihood of the Egyptian Brotherhood deploying a welfare-based
electoral strategy.

The framework developed in this conceptual section hints at the potential
benefits of comparing Hindu nationalists with similarly situated parties outside
India. To further illustrate such potential, the remainder of the chapter empirically analyzes two additional *ikhwan* parties: Islah in Yemen and the Prosperous
Justice Party (PKS) in Indonesia. These countries offer interesting cross-sectional
and temporal variation across institutional features (including levels of democratic competition), salient social cleavages, and political factors (including the
nature of rival strategies among poor voters). Thus, together with the Egyptian
example, these cases offer interesting variation across features my argument
anticipates as important in shaping whether elite parties decide to undertake a
service-based strategy and the efficacy of this approach if implemented.

Before proceeding, it is imperative to note an important caveat: these brief
analyses are not meant to serve as the basis for ad hoc claims of my argument's
generalizability. Instead, they are meant to suggest the potential benefits of
examining political processes outside the subcontinent through the lens of the
Indian experience.

COMPARING HINDU NATIONALISTS AND IKHWAN PARTIES

At the outset of this comparative effort, it is worth noting the instructive parallels
in the social problems motivating Hindu nationalists and Muslim Brotherhood
parties, and the manner in which each seeks to address them. First, like Savarkar,
Hasan al-Banna (the founder of the Brotherhood) was preoccupied with examining the reasons for what he perceived to be the deterioration in his faith's
global stature and finding solutions for restoring it to its former glory. Mirroring
Savarkar's diagnosis, al-Banna saw this decline as rooted in pernicious intra-
faith disunity, which enabled the dominance of foreign political forces (notably
colonial governments) and the growing geopolitical clout of rival faiths.[3]

Second, like Hindu nationalists, Brotherhood members also believed that
their faith's decline could only be reversed through a painstaking bottom-up
process of societal transformation. Both movements remained fundamentally
suspicious of political parties as divisive institutions fostering electoral oppor-
tunism rather than ideological commitment. Accordingly, both also initially

---

[3] See discussion in Mitchell 1969, pp. 216–7.

focused on developing thick networks of non-electoral organizations to propagate their social vision one individual at a time.[4]

Third and perhaps most crucially for this analysis, the MB also originated within relatively privileged communities in Egypt. After founding the Brotherhood in 1928, al-Banna looked to first incorporate socially influential locals within his network, ranging from leading families to powerful religious clerics. The Brotherhood's first major organizational successes came from the occupational associations it founded among white-collar professionals – notably teachers and civil servants – whom al-Banna targeted because of their role as molders of sociocultural opinion.[5] Mitchell notes that the mutual affinity between relatively privileged Egyptians and the MB was further aided by the latter's self-conscious attempts to promote a culturally elite, *effendi* image, partly in an effort to dissociate itself from the "dervishism" of Sufi Islam.[6]

Not surprisingly, these tactical imperatives and ideological commitments combined to produce a membership base that was disproportionately stocked with highly educated, urban, middle-class professionals in Egypt.[7] Further, this elite bias has persisted over time, with recent analyses reporting a higher percentage of Brotherhood parliamentarians coming from highly educated backgrounds than their counterparts from other parties.[8] Such tendencies are not confined to Egypt, as they have been largely replicated within Brotherhood offshoot organizations from Jordan to Indonesia. For example, 59 percent of the founding members of the Islamic Action Front – Jordan's *ikhwan* party – were teachers, doctors, or merchants, whereas just 21 percent were farmers or employees.[9] I discuss similar elite biases in the personnel profiles of *ikhwan* parties in Yemen and Indonesia later in this chapter.

In drawing attention to these important parallels, I do not seek to paper over the significant differences between Hindu nationalists and Brotherhood parties. For example, the cult of personality around the figure of Hasan al-Banna has no equivalent within Hindu nationalism. Although the latter does revere its pantheon of past leaders, it does not deify one single individual to the same degree as does the Brotherhood (not even Savarkar, Hindutva's original architect). For my analysis however, the most important distinction between Brotherhood parties

---

[4] Mitchell (1969, p. 234) notes that according to al-Banna: "A people cannot be saved until individuals are ... Once the individual regains his spiritual balance, then the effect of his reform will find its way to his family and thence to the nation at large."

[5] Ibid., p. 7.

[6] Ibid., p. 329, quotes a member of the Brotherhood who claimed that "the primary manifestation of the message of the Muslim Brothers ... is that it is the message of the *effendi*."

[7] As in India, middle-class professionals are typically far closer to the upper end of the national income distribution than the middle.

[8] Masoud 2010, p. 187.

[9] Azem 1997, pp. 101–3.

and the BJP is a function of the idiosyncrasies of caste within Hinduism.[10] I have discussed at length why the economic and social asymmetries produced and maintained by caste practice made the task of constructing a pan-Hindu coalition particularly difficult. This task was rendered even harder by Hindutva's staunch cultural defense of Brahminical Hinduism, which included support for the moral legitimacy of caste.

By contrast, Islamists are both free of the specific asymmetries of caste and aided by the egalitarianism of key foundational concepts within Islam, including that of the *umma* – a classless transnational community of Muslims who are all equal before God. Hasan al-Banna illustrated the discursive potential of these concepts in his public rebuttal of an Egyptian royal's defense of class differences in 1939. Al-Banna argued that "Islam is equal for all people and prefers nobody to others ... thus we see Islam does not approve of the class system."[11] Enabled by such principles, *ikhwan*-affiliated parties should in theory be more easily able to incorporate strong rhetorical commitments to social justice and critiques of labor and class-based inequalities than the BJP has ever managed.[12]

Recognizing this distinction is important, but so is not overstating it. The discursive potential of key Islamic principles has often not been realized in the practice of Islamist parties. There may be several possible reasons for this failure. First, Islam hardly lacks its own forms of internal hierarchies, which are also often predicated on overlapping differentials in material prosperity and ritual textual knowledge. For example, Tugal notes the occasional condescension with which middle-class Islamists in Istanbul would speak about their poor neighbors, criticizing their lack of cultural refinement, textual knowledge, and capacity for ideological commitment.[13] Similarly, Dresch and Haykel find educated Brotherhood activists in Yemen voicing their contempt for the coarse unrefined style of local tribal leaders.[14]

Second, we cannot assume that elite Islamists always interpret egalitarian Islamic principles in an explicitly equalizing manner. Rather than challenge class hierarchies, the Islamists Tugal interviewed sought to "teach the poor to be content with their situation, despite the wealth and luxury of others, and spend their energies trying to gain religious status instead of wealth."[15] Here, the classless discourse of the *umma* is not leveraged to attack social inequities but to accept them, a strategy Hindu nationalists would strongly endorse. Similarly, Carapico discusses how *zakat*, religiously obligated charity meant to provide

---

[10] It should be noted that variants of caste practices do exist among some Muslim communities within South Asia.

[11] Lia 1998, p. 204.

[12] For just one example, see Tugal's (2009, p. 50) discussion of the Just Economic Order plan proposed by the Turkish Welfare Party (RP) – the precursor to the ruling Justice and Development Party (AKP).

[13] Tugal 2009, pp. 65–7.

[14] Dresch and Haykel 1995, p. 418.

[15] Tugal 2009, p. 130.

succor to poor Muslims, has often been deployed by Yemeni elites for their own enrichment.[16]

Third, like the BJP, the preponderance of relatively privileged citizens within the initial membership of *ikhwan* parties has unsurprisingly shaped their policy profile. This bias within initial party memberships often prompted Brotherhood parties to resolve programmatic conflicts in favor of more privileged interests. Take for example the inherent tension between any efforts at redistribution and the fierce defense of private property and valorization of individual effort that was also central to Islamist doctrine.[17] During debates on land reform in Egypt, the Brotherhood chose to support *infitah* (returning plots given to peasants under Nasser's land reforms back to landlords), largely because "the organization was dominated by wealthy conservative Islamists whose outlooks and class background predisposed them to support landowners."[18]

Likewise, Lia notes that the Brotherhood focused on protecting the economic position of the urban middle classes, prioritizing wage increases for junior civil servants and professionals in its platform.[19] Masoud finds evidence of continuity in this elite-friendly orientation, as Brotherhood candidates during Mubarak-era elections were more likely to be fielded in wealthier districts, and Brotherhood parliamentarians focused on providing goods that appeal specifically to middle-class voters."[20] Indeed, even in the 2011 post-Mubarak elections, none of the five top priorities in the Brotherhood's official platform emphasized the need for redistribution, increased government spending on basic public services, or reducing inequality.[21]

In short, the important differences between Hindu nationalists and Brotherhood parties should not obscure the commonalities discussed in this section, be it in their philosophical motivations, organizational strategies, comparatively privileged urban bases, or programmatic orientation. These parallels in turn inform a set of shared strategic capabilities and constraints, which might lead us to expect private welfare to be as appealing for *ikhwan* parties as it was for Hindu nationalists. Is this in fact the case?

Empirically, we do observe Brotherhood parties often framing their discussions of social justice in terms of the need for voluntary charity rather than enforced redistribution. The twin conceptual pillars of this approach are *zakat*

---

[16] Carapico 1998, p. 69.

[17] For example, Wedeen (2008, p. 191) argues that Islamists have tended to offer visions of social justice that are "able to avoid the radical land reform language of old while lending approval to private property and entrepreneurial profit."

[18] Springborg 1991 as quoted in Fandy 1994, p. 611.

[19] Lia 1998, pp. 208–9.

[20] Masoud 2010, pp. 183–4.

[21] 2011 Election Program, Freedom and Justice Party, p. 5 (accessed via website of Charles Kurzman, http://kurzman.unc.edu/). The five top priorities were establishing stability, eradicating corruption, balancing the budget, implementing Sharia, and safeguarding national security.

and *da'wa* (religiously inspired calls to service).[22] For example, in the "proposed solutions" to Egypt's economic problems offered in the 2011 electoral platform of the Brotherhood-affiliated Freedom and Justice Party (FJP), the only agenda specifically targeting poor voters called for "activating charitable work, encouraging compliance with the obligation of *zakat* and reforming national charitable trust system."[23]

This emphasis is not surprising. As with Hindu nationalist discourse regarding *seva* (service) discussed in Chapter 4, the language of Islamic philanthropy is well suited for resolving the tensions faced by elite Islamist parties. Fundamentally, philanthropic frameworks are clearly more compatible with a defense of private property and individual entrepreneurship and the promotion of class conciliation over conflict. The *noblesse oblige* language of charitable giving does not critique privilege; neither does it seek to overturn existing economic and political asymmetries. Indeed, it valorizes the voluntary donations of wealthy citizens and is therefore far less threatening to their material interests than demands for involuntary, equalizing, policy-based redistributions of land or income.

Yet, despite such affinities, the extent of the Brotherhood's welfare activities in the foundational case of Egypt were described as more circumscribed than the BJP's efforts in India. Some analyses have even argued that Brotherhood service organizations during the Mubarak era were biased toward providing fee-charging services to middle-class constituencies instead of free welfare to the poor.[24] Why might this be the case?

A definitive answer to this question is beyond the purview of this study, but a comparison with the Indian case points to the importance of underlying institutional conditions. As outlined in Chapter 1, several key features of India's institutional environment enabled the BJP's welfare-based strategy. Electoral competition incentivized outreach, whereas associational freedoms enabled service activism. Additionally, India's large electoral constituencies raised the monitoring costs of clientelism and incentivized the non-clientelist provision of local public goods.

By contrast, the Egyptian Muslim Brotherhood has both operated in a far less open political setting and had harsh restrictions placed on its activities by successive authoritarian rulers. The country was also divided into 222 small electoral districts, whose limited size enabled a candidate-centric, patronage-heavy system dominated by local notables allied to the incumbent regime. Consequently, the Brotherhood's focus, especially during the Mubarak era, understandably appears to have been on organizational survival rather than on electoral expansion. Given this focus, the fact the movement and its candidate affiliates prioritized the retention of their elite core supporters is understandable.

---

[22] See Pahwa 2013.
[23] 2011 Election Program, Freedom and Justice Party, p. 9, Part 1, point c, under "Proposed solutions to restore confidence to the Egyptian economy."
[24] Clark 2004.

Yet, with Mubarak's ouster suggesting the potential for more competitive politics, my argument would anticipate service to have become a more important component of the Brotherhood's strategic portfolio in post-Mubarak elections. During the transition, all three institutional factors listed earlier briefly shifted in ways that increased the incentives for service provision. Electoral incentives were clearly heightened, and associational life was less prone to authoritarian anti-Brotherhood crackdowns. At the same time, Egypt's interim military rulers reduced the country's electoral districts by more than half. Each new constituency was now 2.6 times larger than under the previous system, raising the costs of a patronage-based approach to construct a winning plurality.[25]

Consistent with my theory's expectations, recent accounts describe the Brotherhood's emphasis on private welfare over mandated public redistribution, both during its electoral campaign and when in office following its 2011 victory. As mentioned earlier, the FJP's 2011 election platform emphasized charitable giving as a cornerstone for social policy. An analysis of the Brotherhood's campaign rhetoric during those elections also found it to foreground the movement's "service tradition far more than religious rhetoric."[26] Perhaps most strikingly, even when the FJP was in government, it was reported to focus on enabling Brotherhood-linked non-governmental organization (NGOs) to provide basic services (including bread), rather than improving public distribution channels. Such initiatives were seen to "play to the Brotherhood's strengths: voluntary community work … and its capacity to out-organize its opponents."[27] But my analysis suggests they also point to the importance of private welfare in an elite party's efforts to build and maintain a broad social coalition.

Masoud's analysis of a nationally representative survey of 1,675 Egyptians, conducted during the 2011 elections, also provides some compelling evidence of the importance of welfare to the FJP's victory.[28] His study tried to ascertain reasons for the popularity of the FJP in the 2011 polls by examining the determinants of how favorably a respondent viewed the party's economic platform.[29] Using logistic regressions broadly comparable to those used in this book, his analysis finds beneficiaries of Islamic charity are significantly (between 17.5 percent and 36 percent) more likely to report favorable views of the FJP. Equally interesting, regular mosque attendance has no comparable effect.[30] These findings broadly resonate with the Indian case in emphasizing the specific importance of welfare over piety in shaping political support for elite parties with religious roots.

[25] Masoud 2013, p. 20.
[26] Pahwa 2013, p. 21.
[27] Perry and Yousseff 2013.
[28] Masoud 2013.
[29] In the analysis, this meant examining how redistributive a respondent believed the FJP was, as most Egyptian respondents were found to support a strongly redistributive role for their government.
[30] Masoud 2013, p. 39.

Chapter 1 also outlined why welfare would be less appealing to religious parties with non-elite core constituencies. In that discussion, I cited the Egyptian Salafist Al-Nour party as an example. I reasoned that having an underprivileged core allows Salafists to take programmatic positions that appeal to poor voters, reducing their demand for an electoral approach based on private welfare. In line with this argument, Masoud's analysis of Egyptian voters found no comparable effect of welfare on favorable opinions of Al-Nour.[31]

Clearly, it is difficult draw strong inferences from the 2011 polls, given their particular status as transitional elections. Moreover, the enabling shifts of 2011 have just as quickly evaporated following the removal of the FJP-led elected government by the Egyptian military. The return of harsh crackdowns against the Brotherhood and its supporters will require a re-prioritization of survival over expansion and will likely lead to an attenuation of welfare-based efforts. Given the current fluidity of the Egyptian political arena, any efforts at prediction are even more fraught with peril than usual.

THE ISLAH PARTY IN YEMEN

The prior section's broad conceptual comparison of Hindu nationalism and the iconic Muslim Brotherhood organization in Egypt has helped outline the contours along which more fine-grained comparisons might be productive. To further illustrate such potential, the next two sections develop brief empirical "shadow" case studies of *ikhwan* parties in Yemen and Indonesia.

In Yemen, the Yemeni Congregation for Reform (Tajamma' al-Yamani li al-Islah, more commonly known as Islah) has been an important political player following the unification of North and South Yemen in 1990. Unified Yemen is clearly not a fully democratic state, and indeed elections appear to have become less free and fair since the relatively open contest held in 1993. Presidential elections were not held for the first decade following unification in 1990, and former president Ali Abd Allah Salih (who was president of unified Yemen until 2012, and of North Yemen since 1978) made subsequent changes to legally lengthen his term even further. The current president, Abd Rabbuh Mansur al-Hadi, was Salih's vice-president and took over power in a carefully orchestrated transfer highlighted by an election in which he was the only candidate. Even in non-presidential parliamentary elections, Salih and the ruling General People's Congress (GPC) routinely made improper use of their extensive access to government personnel and funds to ensure comfortable majorities.[32]

---

[31] Masoud 2013.

[32] Longley (2007, p. 244) notes such tactics included "giving direct instructions to teachers and university professors on how they should vote," using state intelligence operatives "to spy on and spread rumors about the opposition," and even "moving military units to competitive areas such as Aden so that they could vote for the President and GPC candidates."

Despite the prevalence of such practices, Yemen defies many stereotypes of political life in nondemocratic settings. The country has had a vibrant history of associational life, and "Yemenis from a variety of regional and class backgrounds routinely criticize the regime without the fear of repercussions usually found in regimes classified as 'authoritarian.'"[33] Carapico outlines the long history of politicized civic participation in the country, from union-led, class-based mobilizations concentrated in the southern city of Aden during 1950s and 1960s, to local civic activism in the north in the late 1970s and early 1980s, to the proliferation of political and cultural organizations across the country following the unification of North and South Yemen in 1990.[34] These waves had an additive quality, as the diverse array of parties that emerged in unified Yemen built on the issues and cleavages politicized during prior surges of participation.

Islah was one of the parties formed during the period of political liberalization following unification and was officially launched on September 13, 1990. The party has competed in parliamentary elections held in 1993, 1997, and 2003 and emerged each time as the second largest party in terms of seats won, albeit far behind the dominant GPC. Unlike many other *ikhwan* parties, Islah is not simply an Islamist party, although the "character of its political agenda has been overwhelmingly and consistently Islamic."[35] Instead, Islamists form one of the major streams within the party, which also include an influential tribal segment and a smaller constituency of urban merchants.[36] Although Islah's factions cannot be reified into cohesive, unitary wings, they still reference important ideological and social divisions within the party.

Islah's tribal faction has been particularly influential in informing the party's actions and positioning within Yemeni politics. Tribal leaders within Islah have been closely tied to the patronage structures of the ruling GPC, and these connections (along with a common antipathy toward the Yemeni Socialist Party) have provided the basis for several GPC-Islah alliances.[37] This tribal section was headed by Shaykh Abdallah al-Ahmar, who until his death in 2007 was also the head of the powerful Hashid tribal confederation that included Salih's own tribe. Indeed, al-Ahmar's relationship with Yemen's longtime premier enabled him to hold the position of speaker of parliament

---

[33] Wedeen 2008, p. 76.

[34] Carapico 1998.

[35] Schwedler 2004, p. 210.

[36] For descriptions of how these internal factions have evolved over time, see Dresch and Haykel 1995; Schwedler 2006; and Longley 2007.

[37] For example, in 1993, Islah was given six portfolios: legal affairs, local governance, health, religious affairs, supply and trade, and deputy prime minister. Ministries opened more direct channels for Islah to influence public policies but also revealed to them the extent of corruption within government structures and the difficulty of actual policy implementation (Schwedler 2004, p. 217).

for fourteen years and earned him a reputation as the country's second most influential man.[38]

The Yemeni Muslim Brotherhood dominates the Islamist wing of the party. Dresch notes that the Brotherhood in Egypt had always been intrigued by Yemen, a Muslim country they viewed as untouched by Western colonial influence (at least in the north). The Brotherhood began efforts to expand its operation from the 1950s onward.[39] The Yemeni Brotherhood closely follows the structure and orientation of its Egyptian progenitor and is also supportive of pluralist political processes and a gradualist approach to achieving social change. Islah also includes a more radical Salafi wing, headed by the controversial Shaykh Abd al-Majid al-Zindani. However, although al-Zindani remains one of the party's "spiritual guides" and has held numerous leadership positions within the Yemeni Muslim Brotherhood, he is seen as "increasingly out of step with the pragmatic, moderate center of Islah"[40] and is said to have "little influence over routine party activities."[41]

The social profile of the membership of Islah's Islamist wing also mirrors that of its Egyptian counterpart and is staunchly urban, and middle class. Clark quotes a 1993 survey conducted among 190 of the party's 196 candidates, which showed nearly half (81) had university degrees.[42] Further, those without degrees tended to come from the party's tribal factions, whereas Islamists in the party have tended to be middle-class professionals. However, as discussed in the prior section, some Islamist positions did hold potential for appearing more inclusive than Hindutva's core doctrine. Take for example the opposition of mostly Sunni Islamists to northern Yemen's entrenched Zaydi Shia imamate. Although driven by sectarian differences, this resistance nevertheless gave Islamists an anti-hierarchical image in parts of the country that upper caste Hindu nationalists have never come close to acquiring in any part of India.[43]

Yet, the Yemeni experience also illustrates the challenges Islamists face in realizing their vision of a unified Muslim community. The country is divided into a number of tribal communities, which also often overlap with (and are thus reinforced by) regional divides.[44] Further, within each region, citizens are often arranged into a social hierarchy from *sayyid* families regarded as religious

---

[38] Another major tribal leader within Islah is al-Shaif of the Bakil confederation, although the two factions have themselves not always been united (Schwedler 2004, p. 212).

[39] Dresch 2000, p. 141.

[40] Burrowes 2010, p. 458

[41] Schwedler 2002, p. 52.

[42] See Clark 2004, p. 17.

[43] Weir (2007, p.22) notes for example that this "anti-sayyid thrust" of Islamists made the movement appear less hierarchical and appealing to low-status families in areas such as Sa'dah within the Zaydi heartlands.

[44] The term *tribe* in Yemen is "a vexed category," reflecting legacies of colonial taxonomy and reified by generations of misuse (Wedeen 2008, pp. 29–30, 170). In a Yemeni context, the term indicates territorial political arrangements or networks of political obligation in which leaders are chosen from local elite families, rather than lineage-based kinship networks. About 25 percent of Yemenis

aristocracy to low-status service groups. These divisions are marked by a blend of economic and social difference in a manner that at least broadly resonates with caste (which is in fact the exact term used by some Yemen scholars).[45] The salience of these intra-faith divisions constantly problematizes the Islamist vision of Muslim unity.

Islah's efforts were further complicated by the fact that religious appeals have been fairly muted within Yemeni politics. Political leaders worried that any such appeals might invoke visions of unpopular Zaydi rulers who had governed the north in the name of Islam until Egypt-backed republican forces overthrew them in 1962.[46] Further, the specific appeal of Islamists was circumscribed by their zeal for "purifying" social life. For example, Longley interviewed locals in the city of Mahwit who told her they had welcomed Islah into the community following the civil war in 1994. However, these residents began to resent Islah's attempt to forbid music and singing, particularly around wedding celebrations.[47] Such descriptions resonate with the resentment Sangh activists encountered when they attempted to pressure Adivasi communities into worshiping conventional Hindu deities, observing a standardized set of ritual occasions, or embracing vegetarianism.

Not only did Islah's particular ideological vision have limited mobilizing potential; poor voters also had few material incentives to support the party. With a few localized exceptions, the party could not compete with the patronage offerings of the dominant GPC. Nor did the party distinguish itself as an advocate of the material interests of poor voters in the policy arena. As previously discussed, Islamist organizations often mirror Hindutva's avoidance of radical demands that might unsettle the status quo. Accordingly, they advocate reforms "that are about everyday social practices rather than about establishing an economic balance between a rich minority and an impoverished majority."[48]

Islah exemplified this argument in its massive conference held prior to the post-unification 1993 elections. The conference, which was designed to popularize the party's positions, included statements on the economy that "valorized private economic initiative, restoration of nationalized property to former owners, and establishment of Islamic financial institutions."[49] These were positions that reflected the interests of middle-class entrepreneurs and large landowners, not the bulk of Yemen's poor. Elected members of Parliament from Islah did little better and appeared preoccupied with raising parliamentary questions on Islamic teaching and morality,[50] while displaying an "inability to develop

---

fall under the "tribal" category, almost all of them living within the country's northern highlands (Wedeen 2008, p. 172).

[45] Carapico 1988, p. 61.

[46] Schwedler 2006, p. 141.

[47] Longley 2007, p. 254.

[48] Wedeen 2008, p. 191.

[49] Carapico 1998, p. 169.

[50] Brown and Hamzawy (2010, p. 154) report that 41 out of 119 questions raised by Islah MPs between 2003 and 2009 were on this subject.

concrete policy platforms that address issues such as poverty, unemployment, and [public] social services."[51]

The limited direct appeal of Islamists with poor voters was compounded by the cultural elitism of Islah's activists, which compromised their ability to indirectly woo the poor through the more successful tribal wing of the party. As the Egyptian Brothers self-consciously cultivated an *effendi* image distinct from Sufi Islam, Islamists in Yemen sought to distinguish themselves from the unrefined style of tribal politicians and were said to "despise the tribal style or at best treat it condescendingly."[52] For their part, tribal leaders have been said to "find the style of the urban Islamist often inappropriate, even foolishly offensive."[53] This internal friction was exacerbated by inconsistent commitment of opportunistic tribal leaders to an Islamist sociopolitical vision. The relationship between these two wings has therefore been dubbed "a marriage of convenience"[54] in which Muslim Brothers have been routinely frustrated by tribal leaders contradicting the party's official positions.[55]

Matters have been made worse because the key to Islah's tribal leaders' success among the poor is also the reason they prove to be particularly ripe targets for defection. Specifically, the dependence of tribal leaders on state patronage to win votes made them particularly receptive to the dominant GPC's poaching efforts.[56] The consequence of these defections was "a flip in representation whereby most of Islah's electoral wins in 2003 came from the urban areas" where the Islamist wings are notably stronger.[57]

These tensions between urban Islamist activists and rural tribal leaders within the party gave the former incentives to develop an autonomous base of support beyond their urban middle-class core. At the same time, Islah's participation in parliamentary elections following unification gave the party electoral incentives to expand its appeal among the poor. Although parliamentary contests in Yemen were by no means as open and competitive as those in which the BJP participated in, they were held with some regularity and regulated access to posts of material and political value. Further, as in India, Yemen's single-member plurality electoral system accentuated the incentives to expand beyond an elite core within individual constituencies.

As anticipated by my argument, welfare provision does appear to have become an important component of Islah's strategic approach, at least among

---

[51] Brown and Hamzawy 2010, p. 153.
[52] Dresch and Haykel 1995, p. 418.
[53] Ibid.
[54] Carapico 1993, p. 3.
[55] Schwedler 2006, p. 178.
[56] Corstange (2008, pp. 146–7) quotes a local Islah activist who observed that after the GPC won an outright majority of seats in 1997, they "went and bought off the shaykhs in the countryside, and now they're [GPC] MPs [members of Parliament]."
[57] Ibid.

the urban poor.[58] In Yemen, the Islah Charitable Society (ICS) is the primary wing that furnishes such services.[59] As with Hindu nationalists, this provider was technically autonomous from its electoral affiliate but was financially and organizationally closely linked to it. In line with the shifts in political incentives faced by Islamists, the growth of mass religious welfare associations, headlined by ICS, was "very much a 1990s phenomenon."[60]

By national standards, the ICS's efforts appear to be quite significant. A report on charitable associations in Yemen commissioned by the World Bank found at least as many respondents benefited from private charitable groups as from the Yemeni Ministry of Social Affairs. During Ramadan, the report estimates that the ICS alone provided assistance to roughly one-fifth of the country's population (more than 1 million poor Yemenis), a sizeable proportion by any standard.[61] By 1994, the group was receiving annual contributions of approximately $8 million.[62] Even Clark's skeptical account of Islamist welfare, which stresses that Brotherhood-affiliated service wings in Egypt and Jordan are "by and for middle classes," calls the ICS "the most successful humanitarian nongovernmental organization helping the *poor* in Yemen."[63] For example, she observes the ICS branch in the governorate of Hodeidah engaging in six primary activities, five of which explicitly target poor communities.[64]

The specific appeal of service for Islah was the result of a number of factors. Importantly, the increased civic freedoms of the post-unification period (particularly for non-socialist organizations) enabled an associational approach. Further, the approach aligned well with wealthier supporters of Islah. As Carapico notes, although service did provide some measure of redistribution, it also "left discretion in the sort, size, and location of innovations to the conscience of the rich and powerful."[65] Perhaps it is not then surprising that the Hodeidah branch that Clark observed collected most of its operating budget from local merchants who are supportive of the movement, much as Seva

---

[58] Carapico (1998, p. 168) notes that in a preelection conference held by Islah in 1992, social services were the primary issue focused on by twenty-nine unsigned working papers attempting to formulate the party's positions on a range of issues.

[59] The ICS was also founded in 1990, just shortly before the founding of the formal party itself.

[60] Carapico 1998, p. 156. Of course, like Hindu nationalists, the ICS built on a longer tradition of private religious charity. However, such activities were few and far between, especially as the finances raised through *zakat* for providing such welfare were largely retained by elites (ibid.: p. 69).

[61] World Bank 2000, p. 12.

[62] Carapico 1998, p. 156.

[63] Clark 2004, p. 124, emphasis added.

[64] Ibid., p. 195, fn 45. This branch surveys poor neighborhoods to identify orphans (classified as children without a father) to whom it provides monthly financial support. At the time of Clark's study, it had also built two health care centers adjacent to slum areas and was in the process of building a third.

[65] Carapico 1998, p. 73.

Bharati did in Agra.[66] At the same time, welfare interventions could easily be designed to align with the ideological interests of Brotherhood activists who served as providers. For example, Islah ran community centers that took care of poor adolescent girls, training them to be frugal, obedient, modem homemakers (again echoing Seva Bharati's vocational training efforts).

In addition to these supply-side incentives for pursuing a welfare-based approach, the demand for basic services among the Yemeni poor – always high – steadily increased during the 1990s. Ballooning fiscal debts forced a period of structural adjustment, during which the government began to privatize its increasingly run-down public services. This demand was given a further boost with the mass repatriation of Yemeni migrants in Saudi Arabia, following their government's support for Iraq during the first Gulf War in 1990. Not only did this involuntary return rob families of much needed remittance incomes but migrants themselves also populated emergent shantytowns in desperate need of amenities.[67]

This blend of dedicated activists, middle-class financial resources, and poor communities in need resonates strongly with the configurations that drove electorally motivated service provision in India. The BJP's experience further suggests that the rival GPC's reliance on elite patronage networks to incorporate the poor (similar to the Congress in Chhattisgarh) should enhance the efficacy of Islah's service-based efforts.

It is beyond the scope of this project to collect the micro-level evidence needed to rigorously examine whether the ICS's service activities do actually translate into electoral support for Islah. Indeed, disaggregated data on electoral behavior in Yemen is not easily available or collectible, even for regional experts. However, responses from an Arab Barometer survey conducted in 2006 do provide the basis for a preliminary assessment. Although the survey did not report the specific electoral preferences of respondents, it did ask them whether they thought it "suitable to have a parliamentary system in which only Islamic political parties and factions compete."[68] Although clearly far from a perfect measure, this question does identify respondents who are more likely to express a political preference for Islamists. It seems reasonable to assume that Yemeni respondents who favor a system exclusively composed of Islamic parties are more likely to support Islah than those who do not.[69]

[66] See Clark 2004, pp. 125, 195, fn 45.
[67] Dresch 2000, p. 200.
[68] Question 246, part 2 on the 2006 Arab Barometer Survey Instrument. The survey was conducted in Jordan, Palestine, Algeria, Morocco, Kuwait, and Yemen.
[69] Interestingly, about 18 percent of Yemeni respondents agreed that such a system would be suitable, whereas Islah's support in the 1993, 1997, and 2003 parliamentary elections has been between 18 percent and 22 percent. Of course, this correspondence is helpful to the extent it suggests that the distribution of responses to the survey question is not markedly different from the level of Islah's support, although it is clearly not a rigorous test of the indicator's accuracy.

TABLE 7.1. *Determinants of support for Islamic party system in Yemen (2006)*

	Support for Exclusively Islamic Party System			
	Low Income		High Income	
	(1)	(2)	(3)	(4)
Membership	1.044***	0.956**	0.137	−0.285
	(0.265)	(0.357)	(0.199)	(0.234)
Piety	−0.010	0.0319	0.374***	0.578***
	(0.141)	(0.173)	(0.099)	(0.115)
Rating of Government Economic Performance		−0.360		−0.090
		(0.215)		(0.135)
Influence of Tribe		0.217		−0.115
		(0.143)		(0.089)
Male		0.137		0.532*
		(0.347)		(0.213)
Support Democracy		0.215		0.079
		(0.193)		(0.132)
Age Group		0.479*		−0.361*
		(0.223)		(0.149)
Education		−0.026		0.108
		(0.118)		(0.079)
Constant	−1.708***	−3.223**	−2.229***	−2.461**
	(0.432)	(1.193)	(0.327)	(0.792)
Percentage correctly predicted	79.12	78.18	77.78	86.59
Log likelihood	−178.792	−132.919	−320.756	−188.294
Observations	364	275	639	507

Note: *p<.05, **p<.01, ***p<.001. Variables were coded from questions in the 2006 Arab Barometer Survey instrument.

The survey also recorded respondent participation in civil society associations, in a manner roughly similar to the Indian surveys used in this book. A little less than a third of Yemeni respondents identified as members within this sample. This figure is not altogether surprising given the country's vibrant associational life. Interestingly, the subsample of Yemeni respondents with self-reported incomes in the bottom six deciles of the sample actually reported slightly higher rates of membership (30 percent) than among the top four deciles (28 percent).

Table 7.1 presents results from logistic regression models testing the influence of associational activity on a voter's preference for a system composed solely of Islamic parties. The dependent variable was coded 1 for respondents supporting such a system and 0 otherwise. The key independent variable, *Membership*, was also a binary measure indicating a respondent's active incorporation in a number of civil society associations, including those run by religious and cultural organizations. I anticipated Islah's organizational affiliates to have built a comparative organizational advantage among the poor that helped the party at the polls. As with the analysis for the BJP in Chapter 3, one observable implication of this argument is an increased likelihood of success for Islah among poor respondents incorporated within these associational networks.

Columns 1 and 2 report results from specifications tested on the subsample of poorer voters (defined as those self-reporting in the bottom six income deciles).[70] Among these respondents, associationally active members were in fact significantly more likely than nonmembers to voice support for an exclusively Islamic party system. The substantive effects of organizational inclusion were also substantial, doubling the likelihood of such a preference being expressed (from 14 percent to 30 percent). Conversely, a respondent's religiosity (measured as the frequency of reading the Quran) did not significantly influence their opinions on this issue.[71] A number of additional control variables, including the influence of tribal leaders on a respondent's voting decision, rating of the government's (i.e., the rival GPC's) economic record, or support for democratic procedures, all failed to register a significant impact.

This revealed importance of nonparty networks in mobilizing poor voter support for an elite party clearly resonates with the Indian case, as well as with qualitative studies of Yemeni politics. Van Hear conducted an intriguing study of Yemeni returnees from Saudi Arabia following the Gulf War crisis. A government survey of these nearly 800,000 involuntary returnees found that about half were uneducated, and nearly nine in ten were unable to find employment on their return.[72] Most returnees subsequently settled in shantytowns but received little government assistance toward their rehabilitation. International aid programs directed toward these returning migrants were also "painfully slow in implementation."[73] Further, Van Hear notes "there was little evidence of formal returnee self-organization" to lobby for increased assistance.[74]

Returnee communities in these shantytowns thus suffered from a lack of basic provisioning and low levels of political organization: the very conditions my argument anticipates as most facilitative for a service-based political strategy. In line with these expectations, the ICS's efforts in furnishing food, water, and education appear to have been quite electorally effective. Wedeen notes that in the subsequent 1993 parliamentary elections, "residents of the shantytowns returned the favor, voting heavily for the main Islamic party [Islah]."[75]

Examining Islamist politics in Yemen through the BJP's experience also compels a comparison of elite and non-elite respondents. Columns 3 and 4 in

[70] The key results are not sensitive to a specific threshold, and do not change if we use the bottom five or seven deciles.
[71] I follow Jamal and Tessler (2008, p. 101) in using this measure of respondent piety.
[72] The survey was conducted by the Central Statistical Organization of the Ministry of Planning and Development (cited in Van Hear 1994, pp. 22–3).
[73] Ibid., p. 30.
[74] Van Hear 1994, p. 31.
[75] Wedeen 2008, p. 199.

Table 7.1 report the results for identically specified models tested on the sample of relatively privileged Yemeni respondents. Within this pool of voters, organizational inclusion is negatively and insignificantly correlated with support for Islamic parties. However, measures of piety do appear to correlate very strongly with elite political preferences.[76] A comparatively elite Yemeni who reads the Quran everyday is more than 38 percentage points more likely to voice support for such a system than one who rarely does so.[77] As in India, organizational inclusion was the strongest predictor of poor voter support for an elite religious party, whereas cultural values were the strongest predictor of elite voter support.

Of course, these results cannot be read as conclusive. As with the analysis in Chapter 3, the broad measure of associational membership afforded by the Arab Barometer survey could be capturing participation within a range of nonreligious organizations, especially given Yemen's vibrant associational life. Carapico's detailed study enumerates three major types of organizations populating contemporary Yemeni civil society. The first category is composed of associations for major professions, including lawyers, teachers, and farmers. These organizations were typically founded in the pre-unification era and were tied to either the GPC or Yemeni Socialist Party, the respective ruling parties of North and South Yemen. The second category refers to groups headed by urban, educated elites focused on issues ranging from human rights to freedom of the press to environmental conservation. The third is composed of charitable associations of the kind emphasized by my argument.

It is certainly conceivable that the membership variable could measure participation in any of these three major groupings. The typical social profile of members of each type of organization helps us assess how likely this possibility is. As stated, professional associations (the first category) have clear links to either the GPC or Yemeni Socialist Party (YSP), with membership highly concentrated among partisan supporters of Islah's rivals. It is thus difficult to see a measure largely indicating this kind of participation correlating with poor voter support for Islamist politics.

Between the remaining two categories, members coming from the poor subsample of Yemeni respondents are far less likely to be in rights-based organizations, whose memberships tend to be overwhelmingly elite. By contrast, Islamist charitable associations explicitly targeted the poor, making it more likely that among the poor subsample specifically, the membership variable identifies members of such associations.[78]

---

[76] These findings build on Wedeen's (2008, p. 200) observation that piety might drive support for Islah in some instances but not others.

[77] The likelihood increases from 2.4 percent to 41.1 percent. These effects of piety and membership do not change if we restrict the sample to the top one, two, or three income deciles.

[78] Carapico 1998, p. 205. Additionally, the overall proportion of poor members captured by charitable associations relative to other associations has likely increased during the past decade and a half. Since 1994, observers noted a narrowing of civic space for a range of secular organizations but the continued growth of religious charities. Indeed, Carapico even calls

Survey data strengthens the plausibility of these expectations. For example, statistical tests found associational members within the wealthy subsample to be distinguished by behavior more likely to be associated with right-based organizations (such as attending a protest).[79] Yet, no such result was found among poor respondents. Conversely, within the poor subsample, associational members were more likely than nonmembers to be marked by social attitudes expected of participants within Islamist organizations.[80] Rich members were not distinguished by such attitudes. These differences suggest that Islamist organizations are more likely to dominate membership within the poor subsample for whom the key result is obtained. The fact that participation in secular rights-based groups is likely to be higher among the rich might also help account for why we do not observe an equivalent association between membership and Islamist support among wealthier voters.

Although limited, even this brief shadow case study has revealed a strikingly similar divergence in how organizational inclusion and cultural values affect elite and non-elite political preferences in India and Yemen. In both cases, organizational inclusion correlates strongly with poor voter support for an elite party with religious roots, but religious cultural values do not. On the other hand, these results are inverted among comparatively elite respondents, among whom evidence of an ideological connection is much stronger. I do not wish to overstate the degree of commonality between the two cases, but it is my hope that revealing these intriguing parallels helps illustrate how insights from the BJP's experience can contribute to the study of similarly situated parties outside the subcontinent.

THE PKS IN INDONESIA

As in Egypt, Islamic political groups in Indonesia have had their activities heavily constrained by incumbent governments for the majority of the country's postcolonial period. Consequently, these actors have been at the margins of political life in a country that is home to the world's largest Muslim population. For the three decades during which President Suharto's "New Order" regime ruled Indonesia (1965–1998), only one Islamic party was legally permitted to contest elections. This party, the United Development Party (PPP), was therefore an enforced fusion of multiple factions required to coexist under one name. The PPP typically ran a distant second to Golkar, the Suharto government's official party, in highly limited elections held during the New Order era.

However, following the collapse of Suharto's regime in 1998, Indonesia has experienced a remarkably rapid transition to robust democracy that places far

---

charitable associations linked to Islamist organizations the "most significant locus of new social capital formation" in the country.

[79] This difference was significant at the p<.05 level (two-tailed).

[80] For example, poor members were more supportive than poor nonmembers of the core Islamist demand for a legal system solely based on Sharia (significant at the p<.05 level, two tailed).

fewer limitations on religious actors. The country has also witnessed a proliferation of political parties contesting the competitive elections that have been held between 1999 and 2009. Most of these actors have remained committed to the Indonesian state's religiously syncretic doctrine of *Pancasila*,[81] which was articulated in 1945 by Sukarno, the country's first president. Even the National Awakening Party (PKB) and the National Mandate Party (PAN), which were both founded by Muslim social organizations, have chosen to officially adopt *Pancasila*. In fact, only two of the country's seven major national parties have explicitly sought changes to this doctrine and have claimed Islam instead as their ideological foundation: the PPP (which continues to operate in the post–New Order era) and the Islamist Prosperous Justice Party (*Partai Keadilan Sejahtera* or PKS).

Of these two, the PKS offers the more compelling comparison with the BJP. The party was founded shortly before the country's first post-Suharto election in 1999 and has contested every election since then.[82] Like the BJP, the PKS has a distinctly urban middle-class core and remains tied to the thick networks of the religious social movements from which it emerged.[83] For the PKS, this founding movement was known as the Jemaah Tarbiyah, a group that formed in the mid-1980s and drew its ideological and organizational inspiration from the Egyptian Muslim Brotherhood. Ideologically, the Tarbiyah advocated a return to original sources of Islamic teaching and a greater influence of Islamic doctrine on the functioning of Indonesian political institutions.[84] Mirroring both Hindu nationalists and the Egyptian Brotherhood, the Tarbiyah movement initially sought to achieve its ideological goals through societal transformation, effected through the gradually accumulated individual efforts of its dedicated cadres.

However, unlike the Sangh in India, the Tarbiyah found permissive arenas for building this cadre hard to come by. Mosques were not able to serve as places of refuge, as they had for dissident Islamist networks in Egypt and elsewhere.[85] The Suharto government closely monitored the country's mosques, and even censored the content of Friday sermons. Nor was contestation within the party

---

[81] Pepinsky, Mujani, and Liddle (2012, pp. 13–14) define *Pancasila* as a "religiously syncretic political ideology based on five core values held to be common to all Indonesians." They note that although *Pancasila*'s interpretation is not static, "since the 1970s the five principles have commonly been understood to be the acceptance of a single God, humanitarianism, the unity of the Indonesian state, democracy guided by consensus, and social justice."

[82] The PKS was initially called the Justice Party (Partai Keadilan or PK) during the 1999 campaign. However, the PK won only 1.4 percent of the overall vote and failed to meet the 2 percent electoral threshold for participating in the next electoral contest. Consequently, the party was reconstituted under its current name to run in the 2004 national elections.

[83] The PPP does attract some support from Islamists, but "local patron-client relations, more than pro-Islamic state sentiments, appear to have been PPP's main source of support" during the New Order period (Mujani and Liddle 2009: 581 as cited in Pepinsky et al. 2012, p. 13).

[84] Machimudi 2008, p. xviii.

[85] See Wickham 2002, especially ch. 5.

system an alternative for Islamists, as they were forced to operate under the banner of the PPP, which had itself been required to embrace *Pancasila* in 1984.

Somewhat ironically, Islamist activists found officially secular universities to be the best places for building their networks. Universities were hardly free from the New Order's regulatory constraints and monitoring efforts, as the Suharto government placed severe restrictions on the political activities of college students.[86] However, informal spaces within university campuses offered Tarbiyah cadres invaluable, albeit modest opportunities. Rather than engage in public demonstrations, these activists organized religious circles (*halaqah*) held in small rooms and ran study clubs.[87] A further irony was that the New Order's relative successes in managing the Indonesian economy enabled increasing proportions of the country's growing middle classes to attend universities at home and abroad. While a rising population of domestic students swelled the pool from which the Jemaah Tarbiyah recruited at home, a growing number of Indonesian students attending college in the Middle East (especially in Saudi Arabia) strengthened the Tarbiyah's connections with *ikhwan* networks abroad.[88]

It is worth pausing here to compare the Tarbiyah's early experiences with those of Hindu nationalist activists in India. A key point of similarity is the relatively privileged profile of each movement's earliest supporters. However, the reasons for this social composition clearly varied between the two. Put simply, Hindu nationalism's elite bias was deeply rooted in its founding doctrine of Hindutva, which was articulated by upper castes in a manner that reflected and protected their social position. This Brahminical interpretation primarily attracted upper caste followers, and a philosophical bias became an organizational one. Elite bias among PKS supporters appears to have been less intrinsically tied to the party's guiding ideology, which was (as discussed earlier) informed by egalitarian conceptions of a classless Muslim society common to many Islamist parties. Instead, the PKS's elite profile was more dependent on the specific, restrictive institutional conditions within which the movement first took shape.

As the Suharto regime's strength began to wane in the late 1990s, Jemaah Tarbiyah activists began to increasingly engage in political activities, even organizing large student demonstrations against the government. The New Order regime's demise in 1998 prompted considerable discussion within the Tarbiyah over whether the movement should form a formal party arm. These deliberations included a survey of nearly 6,000 activists across Indonesia,

---

[86] Most notably, the government issued a decree, the Normalization of Campus Life (NKK) in 1978, which directed students to focus on academics and circumscribed the activities student associations were allowed to undertake (Porter 2002, p. 56).

[87] Machimudi (2008, p. 116) notes that the government's monitoring of mosques actually "inadvertently inflated *dakwah* [Islamic proselytizing] activities on campus," because activists found university residences to be the safest places to conduct their activities.

[88] Ibid., p. 93.

68 percent of whom thought that a party should be established.[89] This decision led to the formation of a political wing, the PKS, which has contested every election held during the post-Suharto era.

Since its formation in 1999, the PKS has won plaudits for its organizational prowess and has been repeatedly identified as Indonesia's preeminent cadre-based party. The party used its connections with Tarbiyah organizational networks to replicate the cellular organizational structure of other Brotherhood parties.[90] The growth of the PKS's cadre between 1999 and 2009 was indeed remarkable, increasing nearly tenfold to more than 700,000 members.[91] This massive increase is especially striking given the party's rigorous selection procedures. However, according to Hamayotsu, it was precisely the merit-based nature of the PKS's internal promotion process that won them new recruits. She argues that young Indonesians were attracted to the "fair and institutionalized political opportunities" the party offered, especially when compared to its rivals.[92]

Even so, this growing network has remained socially circumscribed and hence limited in its ability to integrate poor voters into the PKS's electoral base. As in the Sangh's early days, the majority of the PKS's expanding cadre remained "young, well educated, extremely pious, and located in urban areas."[93] This Tarbiyah-derived network primarily mobilizes support from areas near the university campuses where it is most deeply rooted or from urban upper middle classes more generally.[94] Survey data from the 2006 Asian Barometer confirm this continuing elite profile, as 82 percent of PKS partisan supporters were found to live in urban areas, and 75 percent self-identified as members of the country's top income quintile.[95] A 2005 World Values survey found that, like the BJP, the PKS was even able to capture a plurality of votes from relatively privileged voters. Although the party ranked first out of Indonesia's seven major parties among voters in the top three income deciles, it ranked only fourth among those in the bottom four deciles.[96] Unable to significantly expand past its elite core, the party's vote share has stagnated since 2004 and never crossed 8 percent of total votes cast.

This electoral plateau has been partly interpreted as a consequence of the limited electoral appeal of the PKS's platform for poor Indonesians. This platform in turn reflects the preferences of the party's privileged base, which

---

[89] Nurdin (2010, p. 4).
[90] The PKS cadres were mobilized within small cell units called *usra* (family), which aggregated into larger administrative divisions (Tomsa 2011, p. 4). The PKS also set up an executive committee and a consultative council, again mirroring *ikhwan* practice.
[91] See Hamayotsu 2011a, p. 229.
[92] Ibid p. 234.
[93] Ibid, p. 229.
[94] Hasan 2009, p. 17; Mujani and Liddle 2010, p. 79.
[95] Data from Asian Barometer Survey 2006, accessed at www.asianbarometer.org.
[96] Data from World Values Survey 2005.

unsurprisingly supports elite-friendly policies. For example, a 2005 World Values Survey found that only 38 percent of PKS supporters agreed that taxing the rich to subsidize the poor is an essential characteristic of a democracy.[97] This proportion is significantly lower than many of the party's secular rivals, even those with ties to Muslim social organizations.[98] Thus, whereas the PKS's formal doctrine may offer greater egalitarian potential than the BJP's, it is likely to face similar political constraints in any effort to craft progressive platforms.

The PKS is seen as considerably more flexible than other Islamist formations in its positions on sociocultural issues.[99] However, by the standards of Indonesia's political arena, the PKS still appears to offer an "orthodox interpretation of Islam as a comprehensive value system for all aspects of social, political, and economic life." Within Indonesia, such a stance is distinctive and even "highly controversial."[100] Most significantly, the party had supported a modification of the preamble to the Indonesian constitution, specifying an obligation for Muslim Indonesians to adhere to *shari'ah*. Even as competing in elections since 1999 has compelled the party to moderate this position, its leaders still avow that the PKS remains a "religious nationalist" party and that "Islam forms the party's philosophical foundation."[101] The party also remains involved in polarizing efforts at "purifying" Indonesian public life.[102] Scholars of the region therefore continue to distinguish the PKS from parties that have remained consistently committed to *Pancasila*, and even from those that retain close relations with Muslim social organizations.[103]

The cultural positions the PKS has staked out hold limited appeal even among the relatively privileged circles from which the party draws its strongest support. Surveys find a majority of Indonesians do not support politicians who would advocate the implementation of Islamic law,[104] and researchers have concluded that most Indonesians "are not attracted to parties based on religious and ethnic identities."[105] Consequently, Islamist politics remains "the province of a small

[97] Ibid., q. V152, accessed at www.worldvaluessurvey.org.
[98] By contrast, 56 percent of supporters of the National Awakening Party (PKB) and 47 percent of supporters of the National Mandate Party (PAN), which are PKS rivals that are also linked to Muslim social organizations, support such redistribution.
[99] Some important reform steps undertaken by the party include nominating both women and non-Muslims for legislative and executive positions in local elections, participating in coalitions and joint caucuses in local parliaments with an openly Christian party (the Prosperous Peace Party or *Partai Damai Sejahtera*), and organizing a major party event in Hindu-dominated Bali. See Tomsa 2010, p. 152.
[100] Tomsa 2011, p. 3.
[101] The first quote is from party leaders in Fealy 2010. The second is from former PKS president Tifatul Sembiring, as quoted in Hamayotsu 2011b, p. 979.
[102] The PKS's more polarizing efforts include its leading role in pushing for an anti-pornography bill (which was passed in 2008) and for the official disbandment of the "deviant" sect of Ahmadiyah Muslims.
[103] For an example, see the categorization used in Pepinsky, Mujani and Liddle 2012.
[104] Mujani and Liddle 2004, p. 114.
[105] Mujani and Liddle 2010, p. 95.

intellectual and activist urban elite" that holds the same distinctive positions as the PKS itself.[106]

The PKS is thus a party with extensive organizational resources stemming from a founding religious movement but a narrow elite base and niche ideological appeal. At the same time, the party lacked access to the patronage resources of the state with which to expand its following. In all these respects, the PKS's political position was broadly comparable to that of the BJP. Given these similarities, it is not surprising that the PKS also appears to be attempting to use private welfare as "an integral part of its outreach."[107] The party has recently sought to develop a service network that "especially focuses on healthcare and education as key strategic fields to further expand its constituencies."[108]

As in India, basic service provisioning was financially enabled by private donations from the party's middle-class urban base. A welfare-based strategy aligned with a vision of social justice these core supporters could appreciate: voluntary assistance to the poor rather than systematic redistribution. Further, an expansion of welfare was enabled by the PKS's committed cadre network. The strategy struck a chord with these rank-and-file activists, who were critical of the ideological dilution being pushed by more opportunistic factions within the party.[109] A service-based approach was particularly appealing to activists motivated by a goal of societal transformation, who saw it not simply as a means of providing benefits but also of offering a way to "depoliticize the PKS's social activities to circumvent suspicion among Muslim communities" and in doing so "expand informal long-term community ties between the party elites and supporters."[110]

In short, the arguments made in this book about why the BJP undertook service provisioning resonate remarkably with the PKS's experience. As with Hindu nationalism, the PKS's adoption of a service-based approach during a period of intensifying democratic competition was not coincidental. Instead, the timing of this decision reflects the particular appeal of service for the evolving demands, capabilities, and constraints of an elite party with religious roots, within an increasingly open electoral environment.

However, I have also argued that the factors prompting such a party to provide private services have to be distinguished from those ensuring the strategy's success. Did welfare provisioning lead to an expansion in the PKS's support? A few accounts have suggested that the PKS has been able to increase its support among sections of the urban poor and have even speculated that service provision is at the

---

[106] Quote from Mujani and Liddle 2004, p. 118. On the preferences of PKS supporters, Mietzner (2008, p. 450) cites a poll conducted in 2005 in which a high proportion (seven out of ten) PKS supporters were found to be suspicious of non-Muslims, to believe women should not become president, and to think that bank interest payments should be outlawed.

[107] Fealy in Machimudi 2008, p. xi.

[108] Hamayotsu 2011a, p. 240.

[109] Hamayotsu 2011b, p. 988.

[110] Hamayotsu 2011b, pp. 983, 974.

root of such success.[111] Establishing whether services have translated into electoral support would however again require a detailed micro-level assessment that is beyond the scope of this study and which has yet to be undertaken elsewhere. Yet the PKS's stagnating performances and continued inability to win substantial support outside urban areas caution against assuming that an expansion (or even an acceptance) of welfare will necessarily yield electoral dividends.

Insights from the Indian case can help assess how conducive the Indonesian arena might prove for a service-based strategy. First, my study has suggested that the adequacy of public services does inform how receptive poor voters are to religious welfare. By and large, the quality of Indonesian public service provision far outstrips that of India. This is not to idealize the Indonesian record of governance, as numerous studies have documented the massive graft and crony-ism that both Suharto's regime and recent governments indulged in.[112] The country's rate of macroeconomic growth has also suffered following the Asian financial crisis in the late 1990s.

Yet, Pepinsky notes that corruption and development have not proved mutually incompatible in Indonesia. Instead, "Suharto enriched himself and those around him while also presiding over decades of sustained economic development," with the country's material prosperity "grow[ing] at an aston-ishing rate."[113] A recent UNDP report concurs, noting that under Suharto's long-standing regime, "rapid growth was accompanied by a relatively equal distribution of income," which resulted in "a sustained fall" in the number of people living in poverty.[114] Indeed, even the most cautious assessment would have to conclude that Indonesia handily outperforms India on practically every measure of social development. In 2010, India's poverty rate was nearly double that of Indonesia (35 percent to 18 percent), as was its under 5 mortality rate (63 to 35 per 1,000 live births), and its literacy rate remained 30 percentage points lower (63 to 93).[115] Across these indicators, Indonesia more closely resembles Kerala than either Uttar Pradesh or Chhattisgarh. Such a difference in basic outcomes suggests that Indonesian public services, although far from perfect, still set a far higher bar than their Indian equivalents. Within this context, the PKS will presumably have to provide higher-quality offerings than Hindu nationalists to prove attractive to potential beneficiaries, which will in turn affect both the costs and scale of private provision.

---

[111] Machimudi 2008, p. 128; Hasan 2009, p. 3.
[112] Robertson-Snape 1999.
[113] Pepinsky 2012, pp. 5, 6.
[114] United Nations Development Programme, *Indonesia National Human Development Report*, 2004, p. 7.
[115] Literacy data from UNESCO Institute for Statistics 2012, mortality data from a joint 2012 UNICEF/WHO/World Bank report, and poverty data from World Bank Development Indicators 2012. All data accessed from www.undp.org.

Along with levels of basic service infrastructure, the second contextual factor I have emphasized is the nature of rival strategies service competes against. The BJP's experience in Kerala and Uttar Pradesh suggested that the potential of welfare to politically incorporate the poor is significantly reduced if these voters have already been mobilized along cleavages that service activists seek to bridge. Transposed onto the Indonesian context, this argument anticipates that major non-Islamist Muslim social organizations (notably the Nahdlatul Ulama [NU] and Muhammadiyah) will prove particularly disruptive to the PKS's expansionary efforts.

Both of these organizations have significant memberships built over their long involvement in Indonesian public life. Muhammadiyah, characterized as the more modernist of the two, began in 1912 and by 2004 reported a mostly urban membership of roughly 35 million.[116] The more traditionalist NU was founded in 1926 and by 2004 claimed to have 50 million members, most of whom come from rural, non-elite communities.[117] This massive membership was developed through incorporating a large network of local clerics (*kyai*) who enjoy close direct ties with the rural communities among whom they work. As opposed to the reformist impulses of Hindu nationalists and Islamists, these *kyai* have often displayed innovative flexibility in incorporating local rituals distinct from orthodox Islam into their own practices.[118]

The direct mobilizing efforts of these rival organizations pose several challenges to the PKS's expansionary efforts. First, these groups have seen the PKS as a direct challenger to their own local memberships. The PKS's aggressive expansion has encroached on the constituencies of both associations, thereby irking their leaders. Muhammadiyah's chairman has even circulated an internal memo warning of the PKS's poaching efforts and instructing his membership to take steps to restrict the latter's local organizing efforts. The NU leadership has also taken steps to "protect their mosques and educational institutions from being infiltrated by the PKS" and has actively attempted to block the efforts of the party in East Java, the NU's stronghold.[119]

Second, in combatting the PKS, the NU and Muhammadiyah have looked to reduce the appeal of the PKS's message. The culturally flexible networks of the NU have been particularly well placed to construct an image of the PKS as an urban, middle-class party trying to impose a rigid version of Islam on Indonesia's

---

[116] Dates from Machimudi 2008, pp. 56, 61. Membership figures from Mujani and Liddle, 2004, p. 111.

[117] Membership figures from Mujani and Liddle, 2004, p. 111. Put somewhat bluntly, the core distinction between NU and Muhammadiyah is that whereas the former advocates an acceptance of the traditional interpretations of Islamic doctrine by the *ulema* (clerics), the latter supports members developing individual interpretations of these texts.

[118] Machimudi (2008, p. 56–7) notes that Abdurahman Wahid, the NU's founder, proposed a concept of "indigenization of Islam" to enable the accommodation of local practices within the NU network.

[119] Hasan 2009, p. 19; Hamayotsu 2011b, p. 989.

poor. Indeed, Mujani and Liddle argue that the presence of the NU and Muhammadiyah pose "significant obstacles to the further growth of Islamism" precisely because the cultural pluralism of these organizations render their memberships "immune to Islamism's allure."[120]

Third, NU and Muhammadiyah have hurt the PKS's expansionary agenda by helping politicize the modernist-traditionalist divide between Indonesian Muslims. I do not mean to narrowly equate this cleavage with caste. However, such intra-faith divisions do complicate the project of Muslim unity so central to the mission of *ikhwan* parties, as caste did for Hindu nationalists. In mobilizing their supporters on either side of this cleavage, the NU and Muhammadiyah have broadened a division PKS activists would prefer not to have to acknowledge, far less bridge. This effect has been even more pronounced because both groups are connected to two of the PKS's electoral rivals – the NU with the PKB and Muhammadiyah with the PAN.[121]

The BJP's experiences suggest that the PKS will struggle to expand their appeal among non-elite voters when challenged by these dense, accommodative, and politically connected rivals. Data from the 2005 World Values Survey, which includes information on the electoral choices and associational profiles of respondents, permits a broader assessment of this argument.[122] Overall rates of participation in associational life were strikingly high across the Indonesian sample, with more than 38 percent of respondents identifying as active members of religious or charitable organizations specifically. The PKS and NU-affiliated PKB won the support of a similar proportion of these members (16 percent and 17 percent respectively).

However, the social composition of members supporting each party varied greatly. Of members supporting the PKS, 56 percent were in the top third of the overall sample in terms of percentage of their educational attainment (most were college graduates). By contrast, only 17 percent were in the bottom third of this category (almost all of whom had not completed secondary school). In sharp contrast, 49 percent of members supporting the PKB came from the least educated subsample, and only 22 percent from their more educated counterparts.

These descriptive differences point to the elite nature of the PKS's cadre and the organizational advantage enjoyed by its rivals among disadvantaged communities. Table 7.2 reports the results of three logistic regression models that more systematically compare the impact of organizational incorporation on the likelihood of a respondent supporting the Muhammadiyah-affiliated PAN (column 1), the NU-affiliated PKB (column 2), or the PKS itself (column 3). The wording of the instrument allows us to construct a key independent variable,

[120] Mujani and Liddle 2004, p. 110.
[121] Each of these parties further cemented its syncretic credentials by making a firm decision to adopt *Pancasila* over Islam as its ideological foundation. In the NU's case, this decision prompted considerable dissent among more conservative *kyai* (Mietzner 2009, p. 255).
[122] Data accessed at www.worldvaluessurvey.org.

TABLE 7.2. *Determinants of support for PAN, PKB, and PKS in Indonesia (2005)*

	Voted for PAN (1)	Voted for PKB (2)	Voted for PKS (3)
Membership	−0.0834	0.318***	−0.069
	(0.084)	(0.062)	(0.056)
Religiosity	−0.100	0.078	0.163***
	(0.067)	(0.057)	(0.051)
Education	0.180*	−0.382***	0.358***
	(0.081)	(0.063)	(0.059)
Unemployed	−0.481	0.792**	0.121
	(0.528)	(0.258)	(0.283)
Support Large Public Sector	−0.038	−0.003	0.0114
	(0.040)	(0.031)	(0.027)
Religious Leader Influence	−0.186*	−0.050	−0.315***
	(0.093)	(0.074)	(0.063)
Male	−0.077	−0.164	−0.036
	(0.213)	(0.165)	(0.143)
Town Size	0.095	−0.031	−0.120***
	(0.050)	(0.034)	(0.029)
Age	0.018*	−0.014*	−0.018**
	(0.008)	(0.007)	(0.006)
Constant	−3.313***	−0.229	−2.051***
	(0.787)	(0.606)	(0.540)
Log Likelihood	−356.815	−511.855	−648.053
Percentage correctly predicted	93.58	88.39	83.07
N	1,542	1,542	1,542

Notes: *p<.05, **p<.01, ***p<.001. Measures were coded from questions in the 2005 World Values Survey. Results do not change if the ordinal (0–4) index of membership coded from the survey instrument is replaced with a binary variable.

Membership, which measures a respondent's level of participation in religious or charitable associations specifically. In contrast to the Yemeni analysis, the specificity of this measure reduces concern that it might capture participation in a range of associations unrelated to my argument. Other questions on the survey allow for an inclusion of control variables similar to those used in the prior analyses of the BJP and Islah.

The results show some intriguing differences between the determinants of support for these three Indonesian parties, particularly between the NU-affiliated PKB and the PKS. The PKS's supposedly superior organization does not appear to have helped it at the polls. In fact, the party fared less well among voters incorporated by associational networks. Instead membership was significantly

TABLE 7.3. *Education and organization: Influence on PAN and PKS support*

Party	Organization	Education	
		College	*Primary School*
PKB	Member	10.97	36.27
	Nonmember	3.33	13.74
PKS	Member	20.89	5.93
	Nonmember	25.64	7.61

Note: Values in percentage points. Predicted values obtained through simulations while keeping other variables at their means.

and positively correlated with support for the rival PKB. These results were inverted with respect to the variable *Religiosity*, which significantly increased PKS support but had no effect on the PKB's likelihood of success. Overall, the results reveal that the average PKS supporter continues to be educated, pious, and youthful, confirming that the party's expansion from its Tarbiyah core constituencies has been limited (at least as of 2005).[123] By contrast, PKB supporters appear to be not especially pious, less likely than PKS supporters to be highly educated or employed, but more organizationally active than the latter.

Table 7.3 compares the substantive impact of education and membership on the simulated probability of a respondent voting for the PKB or PKS. It suggests that the positive effects of membership on the PKB's success are particularly pronounced among less educated respondents, even when controlling for a range of demographic and attitudinal factors. Among respondents with only a primary school education, membership increased the chance of PKB support by 22 percentage points, compared to only by 8 percentage points among college-educated respondents. This result strongly suggests the NU's organizational strength among less privileged constituencies has especially helped its political affiliate. By contrast, the PKS is far more likely to win the support of college students and continues to be unsuccessful among less educated voters, irrespective of their membership status. Collectively, these results suggest that the rural, culturally flexible, and partisan networks of the NU have managed to retain the upper hand in organizationally incorporating the poor.

As in India, examining regional patterns helps support and appropriately nuance this broad argument within the context of Indonesia's complex democracy. Subnational breakdowns indicate that the PKS's greatest success has consistently come from urban areas such as Jakarta (where the party won five seats in 2004 [good enough for first place] followed by winning four seats in 2009). Jakarta has a large concentration of university student and

---

[123] Interestingly, PKS supporters do not support a greater role for religious leaders in influencing government decisions, possibly a reflection of the organization's distaste for traditional clerical authorities.

middle-class voters – the cornerstones of the party's urban elite core. Furthermore, the PKS has done well in several of the outer islands of the Indonesian archipelago (including the Riau Islands and North Maluku), where the presence of both the NU and Muhammadiyah is relatively weak.[124] Conversely, the PKS has not done well in East or Central Java, where the NU networks – and consequently PKB support – have been most densely concentrated.[125] These patterns broadly conform to expectations drawn from the Hindu nationalist experience.

Yet, the volatility of Indonesian politics also illustrates how the prospects for elite parties can change over time. Most notably, recent power struggles between NU and PKB leaders have strained relations between the two organizations and curtailed the level of support the latter receives from the former.[126] The PKB has therefore lost some of its comparative organizational advantage, in a way that the communists the BJP competes against in Kerala have not. In addition, the PKB has suffered from internal factional disputes, which have further compromised its electoral abilities. A divided leadership has prevented the party from maintaining its effective machine even within its East Javanese core. Battered by these external and internal rifts, the PKB's overall vote share declined in 2009. Although the bulk of PKB seats (twenty-four of twenty-eight) were still concentrated in Java, it was no longer the automatic choice for poor voters even in this former stronghold.[127]

In the context of these changes, the PKS was able to gain a small number of seats (four) at the expense of the PKB in East and Central Java in 2009. In an argument consistent with mine, Williams attributes the PKS's gains "not only to the internal conflict within PKB but also to targeting efforts by PKS in these areas, most notably ... community development programs targeting rural farmers."[128] However, this observation only applies for a small number of constituencies and still requires more rigorous empirical testing before it can be accepted even for those areas.

Evidence from the 2009 elections also shows how difficult it is for private welfare to compete against pro-poor programmatic approaches. Despite selective gains, the PKS captured almost exactly the same vote share (7.9 percent) as it did in 2004 (7.3 percent). Moreover, the party only crossed a 10 percent threshold in five of Indonesia's thirty-six provinces (down from six in 2004). Instead,

---

[124] Ufen 2012, p. 46.
[125] Indeed, Tomsa (2012, p. 24) goes so far as to say that the PKB is "the only party that is effectively a regional party" in Indonesia. The PKB placed first in East Java by some margin in the first two elections following independence and won forty-one seats across East and Central Java in 2004, whereas the PKS managed just five. Data from General Election Commission of Indonesia as reported in Ananta et al. 2005, pp. 44–5.
[126] See Tomsa 2008, pp. 164–5.
[127] Hwang 2013, p. 93.
[128] Quoted in Hwang 2013 p. 94

the major gains in 2009, including in former PKB strongholds went to the Democratic Party (PD), the party of incumbent president Yudhoyono. The PD's victory was widely attributed to the popularity of several election-year schemes targeting the disadvantaged, including direct cash aid for about 19 million poor families and credit schemes for small- and medium-size enterprises.[129] Thus, the Indonesian experience aligns with evidence from India suggesting the limited efficacy of private welfare when competing against extensive and popular redistributive public policies.

CONCLUSION

This chapter has sought to evaluate this book's arguments from a perspective beyond that of the Indian case in which they were conceived and tested. I have placed the BJP within a larger family of elite parties blessed with the thick organizational assets of their founding religious movements. These religiously oriented elite parties constitute a wide-ranging and increasingly influential set of actors across the global south. I specifically focused my conceptual comparison of Hindu nationalists with the family of parties inspired by the Egyptian Muslim Brotherhood. This comparison hinted at several compelling parallels, the implications of which were then further explored with empirical evidence from Yemen and Indonesia. Of course, these analyses remain more illustrative than conclusive. Even so, they serve to demonstrate how a study of the BJP can help us understand why elite parties outside India might seek to provide welfare for electoral gain and how successful such efforts are likely to prove.

[129] The cash assistance program gave $10 a month to families whose monthly per capita expenditure was $17.50 (United Nations Economic and Social Commission for Asia and the Pacific 2012). The scheme was implemented to counter the effects of rising inflation and the phasing out of fuel subsidies, and Yudhoyono's opponents criticized the policy as a clear attempt at election-year populism ("SBY benefiting" March 28, 2009).

8

Conclusion: The Future of Service as an Electoral Strategy

Why did an elite party in India choose to woo the poor through the private provision of local public goods? In his influential analysis of patronage politics, Shefter identified three considerations a party must jointly consider when selecting its electoral approach: the demands of voters, the resources available to the party, and the interests of elites allied with the party.[1] In this book, I have revealed that a similar confluence of concerns informed Hindu nationalists" decision to expand their provision of basic services. The attraction of a service-based electoral strategy derived directly from the simultaneous appeal it held for a diverse set of actors. Through providing locally public basic services, the BJP was able to materially appeal to a relatively large number of poor voters for a relatively low financial cost. A service-based approach was also less threatening to the party's elite core than alternative approaches based on redistributive shifts in policies or patronage. By outsourcing recruitment to its movement partners, the BJP could continue its core-centric platform and preserve its valued party positions for entrenched elites. Service thus proved an ideal tactic through which to recruit the poor and retain the rich.

More broadly, this book has revealed the affinity between the BJP and a welfare-based strategy to be the joint product of two factors: its demand (as an elite party) for a non-threatening strategy of poor voter recruitment and its supply (as a party founded by a social movement) of thick organizational resources. My theoretical argument anticipates private welfare to prove similarly attractive to all political actors with elite core constituencies. However, only those elite formations that are also endowed with thick organizational resources will prove capable of implementing this painstaking approach. The most substantively important examples of such parties across Asia and Africa are those that are tied to religious social movements. Accordingly, Chapter 7 compared

[1] Shefter 1977, p. 410.

the BJP's experience with that of other elite parties with religious roots in Egypt, Yemen, and Indonesia.

The framework developed here also helps explain why other types of parties are either unwilling or unable to undertake a service-based approach. Leftist and low-rank ethnic parties (examined in Chapter 6) face no demand-side incentives to implement such a strategy. Poor citizens are the core constituencies of these parties, and consequently the latter can make direct (class-based or ethnic) appeals to win the former's votes. Thus, even those non-elite parties with the organizational capacity to deliver private welfare –such as the Communist party in Kerala – have no strategic need for it.

What about parties less explicitly oriented toward the poor, such as the Indian National Congress (the BJP's rival in Chhattisgarh and several other states)? The party had managed to win over large majorities, even as it offered poor voters few programmatic benefits and privileged local elites within its party structure. Its dominance was instead predicated on a vertical patronage network, which began to crumble under the pressure of increasing party competition. As the Congress's access to patronage became less secure, its need for strategic alternatives grew. In this context, a welfare-based approach should prove increasingly attractive. However, as Chapter 5 made clear, the Congress has been unable to mimic the BJP because it lacks the organizational thickness needed to enact a welfare-based approach.

Understanding why elite parties such as the BJP undertake electorally moti-vated service provision is important but does not explain *how* this strategy wins over poor voters. A second set of arguments made in this book explained the translation of service into votes as a multidimensional social process, rather than a dyadic exchange of goods for support. In India, this process has unfolded across several stages. The expansion of service networks created collateral roles in which non-elite personnel could serve without disturbing the positions of entrenched elites within the BJP itself. Beyond this narrow activist core lay a far larger number of ordinary citizens who came into contact with religious providers as beneficiaries of the latter's activities or as residents of the communities in which they worked. Activists in India have converted this everyday contact into electoral returns by patiently earning voter goodwill, rather than by enforcing quid pro quo clientelist protocols. Service providers converted this goodwill into electoral returns among beneficiaries and some non-beneficiaries through the networks of friends and associates they developed and through their own powers of rumor and suggestion as apolitical residents of high local standing.

In revealing the absence of quid pro quo arrangements in India, my work warns against assuming that electorally motivated welfare is always reducible to an exchange of goods for votes. It also suggests the pitfalls of viewing distributive strategies among poor voters in the global south as necessarily clientelist. Proceeding under such assumptions would have prevented my analysis from recognizing the diversity of mechanisms –friendship, rumor, and suggestion – through which welfare influences political choices in India. In outlining how these local mechanisms were rooted in everyday social relations, I hope to have illustrated the benefits of paying greater attention to such quotidian interactions between parties and voters, not only the episodic material transactions between them.

Finally, this book presented arguments about *when* service is likely to succeed electorally, with particular attention to the rival strategies it competes against. I argued that if the poor have forged programmatic ties with a rival party, as was the case in Kerala, public services are likely to be more robust, reducing the demand for private welfare from the outset. By contrast, in both Uttar Pradesh and Chhattisgarh, the absence of such programmatic ties informed inadequate social provisioning, boosting the demand for private welfare.

Only in Chhattisgarh did such demand translate into votes for the BJP. Why? The key to explaining this divergence was that in Uttar Pradesh, the BJP's Dalit-led rival looked to horizontally mobilize lower castes through ethnically targeted patronage and discursive appeals. This strategy sharply politicized the very social cleavages Hindu nationalists sought to bridge, rendering the goodwill garnered by service activists insufficient for producing electoral returns, at least for now. By contrast, the BJP's major rival in central India (the Congress) vertically mobilized poor voters through elite-centered patronage pyramids. In this scenario, common across India and much of the global south, poor voters are neither the systematic recipients of programmatic policy benefits nor self-mobilized in opposition to local elites. It will be in such environments, my argument suggests, that a welfare-based approach will be able to achieve its fullest electoral potential.

In the remainder of this concluding chapter, I build on these arguments by assessing the future of service as an electoral strategy. First, I examine recent Indian electoral trends that have emerged after my arguments were conceived and tested. Do these trends confirm or trouble the importance of welfare to the party's success among the poor? Second, I outline what the BJP's experiences reveal about the considerable internal and external obstacles elite parties can face in sustaining the hard-won electoral gains of service work, and the necessity of alternative approaches to consolidate these gains.

ANTICIPATING THE FUTURE? A LOOK AT RECENT ELECTORAL DATA FROM INDIA

How well do this book's arguments anticipate emerging trends within Indian politics? To tackle this question, I examine the BJP's pattern of performance in elections that were held after this argument was conceived and tested. The most obvious source of data for such ex post testing comes from the parliamentary elections held in 2009. Unfortunately, the raw data from the 2009 National Election Study was still not publicly available for scholarly use when this book went to press. However, a recent set of articles published by the team conducting the survey contains enough information to estimate the BJP's subaltern vote share in fifteen of the seventeen major states analyzed in this study.[2] Although not exact, this information does help provide a sense of general patterns in the BJP's performance among Dalits and Adivasis in these most recent polls.

The first obvious question to ask is whether the BJP has continued to perform strongly in states with dense service networks or whether the gains made between 1996 and 2004 dissipated within one electoral cycle. If the party's performance simply reverted to the mean in 2009, then one might suspect the initial gains to be a product of short-term, idiosyncratic factors, rather than the result of the systematic implementation of a particular strategy. However, Figure 8.1 shows a continued high correlation between the density of service networks in 2004 and the party's subsequent performance in these most recent elections.[3] In four of the five states with the densest service networks, the BJP won nearly 40 percent of votes cast by Dalits and Adivasis in 2009. By contrast, in four of the five states with the weakest networks, the party won less than 10 percent of these votes.

The stability of this correlation between service network strength and the BJP's subsequent performance is clearly encouraging for this book's central claims. This stability is all the more impressive because of the party's declining all-India vote share, from 23.75 percent in 1999 to 22.16 percent in 2004 to 18.8 percent in 2009. It would have been reasonable to anticipate this negative trajectory to manifest most strongly among the BJP's unexpected new Dalit and Adviasi backers. Instead, in states with dense service networks, the party has maintained and even expanded its following among these least likely supporters.

Where Service Succeeds: Comparing Two South Indian States

Data from this more recent period can also help assess my conclusions about where service is likely to succeed and fail. The neighboring states of Tamil Nadu and Karnataka in southern India provide good cases for such an evaluation. The Sangh has rapidly expanded its service network in both states

---

[2] Data was available in *Economic and Political Weekly* special issue, 44, No. 39, September 26, 2009. Data was not available for Kerala or Haryana. The BJP's vote share throughout this study has been computed as the number of respondents voting for the BJP divided by the number of respondents who voted for any party (i.e., excluding respondents who did not vote). However, the articles reporting 2009 returns did not include data on the number of abstaining respondents. To ensure comparability in the data, I therefore assumed the same state-wise rate of such responses among Dalits and Adivasis in each state in 2009 as each group recorded in 2004. The data for six states (Andhra Pradesh, Assam, Bihar, Jharkhand, Punjab, and Tamil Nadu) included the BJP within a larger category (either a coalition or a residual "Others" category). In each case, I assumed the party won the same proportion of votes within this larger category as it did in 2004. I then multiplied this ratio by the subaltern vote share won by this larger category to get an estimate of the BJP's specific performance. In Rajasthan and Chhattisgarh, the Lokniti reports did not include the sample size of Dalits and Adivasis in the survey, so I used the sampling weights from the 2004 survey to create a weighted average for the BJP's vote share among these groups.

[3] This correlation coefficient is .742. A simple bivariate regression showed the impact of service wings on BJP vote share in 2009 was statistically significant at the .002 level.

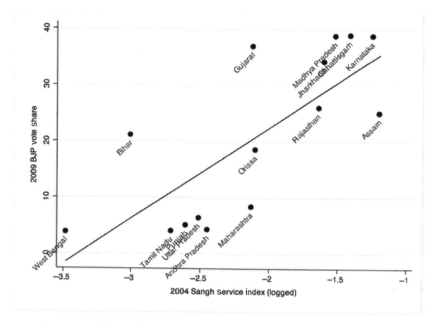

FIGURE 8.1. 2009 BJP performance and Sangh service activities
Source: Data from 2009 National Election Study as reported in *Economic and Political Weekly* special issue, 44, No. 39 (September 26, 2009).

since 2004. In Tamil Nadu, Seva Bharati (the main service organization in the state) had established nearly 10,000 projects in the state by 2009, most of them after 2004. These efforts produced one of the country's highest indices of service network strength (.67) in 2009.[4] This expansion itself was anticipated by my analysis in Chapter 4, which found the percentage of Christians in a state to strongly predict where service networks would be expanded. Figure 4.7 reports Tamil Nadu to have the second highest percentage of Christians (6.07 percent) of all states in the sample, trailing only Kerala. The Sangh's welfare network also expanded rapidly in Karnataka, which by 2009 boasted a comparable number of service projects (11,000) and per capita service index (.84).

Although the BJP's subaltern vote share in Karnataka significantly improved from 15 percent in 1996 to 39 percent in 2009, it stagnated during this period at less than 5 percent in Tamil Nadu. My argument expects such a divergence to reflect variations in levels of public provisioning and non-elite politicization between Tamil Nadu and Karnataka. Are such differences in fact apparent?

[4] The 2009 service index for Tamil Nadu and Karnataka was calculated using population figures from the 2011 Indian census and 2009 project totals from Rashtriya Seva Bharati, New Delhi.

The pattern of subaltern politics does differ quite dramatically between the two states. Tamil Nadu has a long history of active mobilizations by non-elite communities against local Hindu elites. Chapter 2 briefly discussed the efforts of E. V. Ramaswamy (a.k.a. Periyar), a politician who left the Congress Party in 1925 to direct a "self-respect movement" uniting a wide array of non-elite castes under the ethno-regional label of "Adi Dravidians," or original inhabitants of the south.[5] The efforts of Periyar and his followers culminated in the founding of an independent political party (the Dravida Kazagham, later the Dravida Munnetra Kazagham or DMK), which continues to be a major force in the state today. In 1972, a breakaway faction from the DMK founded the state's other major regional party, the All India Anna Dravida Munnetra Kazagham (AIADMK). The AIADMK replicated its progenitor's regionalist platform and primary support base among backward castes and Dalits. Together, these regional parties have established dominant positions among subaltern voters in the state, pushing national parties such as the BJP and Congress to the margins among these constituencies.[6]

Unlike Tamil Nadu, Karnataka does not have an arena where Dalits and Adivasis have been sharply politicized against local elites. The three major parties within the state are the Congress, the BJP, and the Janata Dal (Secular). The JD(S) is the only regional party of the three, in the sense that its electoral activities are largely confined to Karnataka. However, the party was never regionalist in its mobilizing strategy, nor did it especially look to mobilize subaltern electorates against local elites in the manner of the communists in Kerala, the DMK in Tamil Nadu, or the BSP in Uttar Pradesh. Instead, contemporary politics in the state is centrally defined by turf battles between the rival patronage networks of Lingayats and Vokkaligas, two dominant local caste communities.[7] In line with such vertical incorporation of subaltern voters, survey data shows upper and lower caste communities are not electorally polarized within Karnataka.[8]

[5] See Jaffrelot 2003.
[6] In 2004 for example, the DMK and AIADMK combined to win 57 percent of Dalit and Adivasi votes, compared to the 13.6 percent won by the BJP and Congress combined (National Election Study 2004).
[7] Hebsur 2011. Some scholars have argued that the tenure of Devraj Urs, who served as chief minister for most of the 1970s, constituted a partial exception to this pattern (Manor 1980). Urs was a Congress leader who came from outside these dominant communities and therefore was seen to challenge their grip on politics. However, even Urs's admirers (Manor 1980, p. 211) have noted that the "great weakness of his efforts ... is their failure to foster the *organization* of weaker sections of society for their own defence" (emphasis in original). More critical commentators have even argued that far from directly politicizing the poor, the Urs regime "revolved around the widespread use of patronage" that looked to accommodate elites and "not to be alienating to local notables" (Kohli 1982, pp. 313, 326).
[8] Indeed, between 1996 and 2004, Karnataka's ethnic voting index (measuring the dissimilarity in electoral preferences of major ethnic groups) was the second lowest among the seventeen major Indian states. Calculated by author using NES 1996, 1999, and 2004 data and the formula in Huber 2011.

Thus, rival party strategies among poor voters in Karnataka much more closely resembles the vertical patronage networks of Chhattisgarh than the horizontal linkages present in Kerala, Tamil Nadu, or Uttar Pradesh. These differences also correspond to variations in social policies between the two states. In a comparative analysis of Indian states, Teitelbaum and Thachil find the electoral performance of the DMK and AIADMK in Tamil Nadu positively correlated with spending on basic social services between 1960 and 2007.[9] The state's performance has also been quite strong when measured by social outcomes. Tamil Nadu ranks third out of India's seventeen major states in its human development index, and its literacy rate is second only to Kerala's.[10] The state was also a pioneer in providing midday meals to the mostly poor students who attend public schools, a scheme that has now been extended to the rest of the country.[11] One study found Tamil Nadu's performance in this important scheme to be exemplary: all schools surveyed had a separate kitchen for cooking the midday meal, compared to Karnataka, where nearly one in three did not.[12] A recent study of social policies across ten major states by the economists Jean Dreze and Reetika Khera praised Tamil Nadu for its "steady commitment to universal social policies" and ranked its social pension scheme as the best within the ten state sample.[13]

By comparison, Karnataka's record in basic provisioning has been decidedly mediocre, despite the state's role as a hub for India's booming information technology industry. The state's human development index and literacy rate are each exactly at India's unimpressive national average, placing Karnataka roughly between Tamil Nadu and Chhattisgarh on both measures.[14] Dalits and Adivasis have often been particularly excluded from the benefits yielded by redistributive policies within the state. One prominent example of such exclusion was in Karnataka's land reforms during the mid-1970s. The merits of these reforms have been hotly debated, but even its champions agree they were focused on tenant cultivators and were "an abject failure" in aiding landless laborers (the category under which many, if not most Dalits fell).[15]

In sum, Tamil Nadu and Karnataka broadly differ in the manner anticipated by my argument. The latter's comparatively weak social policy record ensured a

---

[9] Teitelbaum and Thachil 2012.

[10] Tamil Nadu's human development index is .53 on a scale from 0 to 1; its literacy rate is 80 percent. Data from National Human Development Report 2001, and the 2011 Indian Census.

[11] Swaminathan et al. 2004.

[12] Khera 2006.

[13] Dreze and Khera 2014.

[14] Karnataka's human development index is .47 and its literacy rate is 75 percent. Data from National Human Development Report 2001 and the 2011 Indian Census.

[15] Quote from Manor 1980, p. 205, who otherwise provides a laudatory appraisal of these reforms. For a more critical perspective, see Kohli 1982. Kohli notes that less than 1 percent of the landless agrarian population received an allotment of the surplus lands available for redistribution within the state.

strong local demand for Hindu nationalist offerings. Equally importantly, the BJP's rivals incorporated poor voters through vertical patronage networks, providing a facilitative context for service activists to translate welfare into votes. By contrast, Tamil Nadu's relatively strong social policies and self-mobilized subaltern communities prefigured the inefficacy of expanding service networks in the state.

Similarly, my analysis anticipates that Hindu nationalists will have limited success in exporting a service strategy to many other parts of India. For example, comparatively wealthy states such as Punjab and Haryana also have relatively robust public services, whereas others, such as West Bengal, have lower caste populations that have been horizontally mobilized by communists or co-ethnic leaders. Expanding service networks in these states are therefore unlikely to yield the electoral dividends Hindu nationalists have enjoyed across much of central India.

Does Violence Win Votes from the Poor? The Case of Gujarat

A final case that deserves mention within any broader discussion of the BJP's political future. The BJP has enjoyed tremendous success in the state, receiving a third successive mandate in 2012. The BJP in Gujarat is headed by the charismatic and controversial Narendra Modi, whose electoral victories fueled his rise to becoming his party's prime ministerial candidate in national elections scheduled for 2014. Yet, the BJP's successes have come in a state in which service networks were found to be relatively weak. How then does my explanation account for this famous case of Hindu nationalist success?

My argument suggests that with respect to the BJP's electoral success, Gujarat is very much the exception, and not the rule. Chapter 4 revealed the state was the only case of significant (>30 percent) subaltern support that was not also home to dense service networks. Chapter 2 also revealed another Gujarati idiosyncrasy that suggests an obvious solution to the party's success: communal violence. Gujarat was the only state in which a high incidence of Hindu-Muslim conflict co-occurred with significant subaltern support for the BJP.

This communal record included the infamous violence of 2002, which began when a train carrying Hindu nationalist activists was torched at a train station in the town of Godhra, killing fifty-eight people. In the days that followed, Gujarat witnessed communal violence on a massive scale, with organized killings of hundreds and possibly thousands of Muslims by groups of Hindus.[16] During

---

[16] The official Indian government figures report 790 Muslims and 254 Hindus died in the violence. However, there are a number of reasons to suspect these official figures undercount the number of people killed, as they are based on reported deaths at hospitals and police stations. As the Gujarati police were seen by many citizens (particularly Muslims) as complicit in the violence, it is reasonable to assume many deaths went unreported. A number of human rights organizations have estimated the death toll to be at least 2,000, the vast majority of whom were Muslims.

the violence, the Modi government was seen to be at best highly negligent in preventing the attacks. Indeed, human rights organizations have amassed substantial evidence of the complicity of state personnel in enabling and participating in the attacks on Gujarati Muslims.[17] Modi himself appeared to justify the violence by Hindus as a Newtonian response to the events of Godhra, stating that "every action has an equal and opposite reaction."[18] In polls held in the aftermath of the violence, Modi ran a highly polarizing, pro-Hindu campaign and won a convincing victory.

I have already demonstrated that communal violence does not explain the BJP's pattern of success with poor voters in the vast majority of Indian states. However, does Gujarat still serve as an example (albeit an exceptional one) of the fact that elite parties can sometimes use violent agitations to mobilize subaltern voters? This possibility can neither be confirmed nor dismissed without systematic micro-level analyses, which are beyond the scope of this book.[19] Yet, it is worth making a couple of observations regarding the possibility of violence as an electoral strategy in the context of the arguments made here.

First, even if violence did produce inroads for the BJP among subaltern voters, these gains appear to be dwindling. According to data from surveys conducted by CSDS, the BJP won roughly 37 percent of the combined Dalit and Adivasi vote in the 2007 Gujarat state elections. However, this figure had dropped to 30 percent by 2012. This decline, should it continue, begs the question of whether sporadic acts of violence produce gains that are equally transient. And if so, what explains why these inroads are episodic, whereas those forged through everyday service provision appear to be more lasting? Connecting this book's arguments with the Gujarati case thus helps suggest some intriguing questions for future research.

Second, the empirical analyses within this book reinforce the necessity of carefully parsing through *whom* violence really impacts at the polls. On this point, even simple descriptive data seems to suggest that the 2002 violence had more of an impact in distinguishing upper caste BJP supporters than lower caste ones. In a 2002 election survey, 26 percent of Dalit and Adivasi respondents who said the recent communal violence had a strong impact on their electoral decision reported voting for the BJP. By comparison, an almost identical percentage (25 percent) of those who said the violence did not matter at all in their ballot choice voted for the party.[20] By contrast, 65 percent of upper castes who were heavily influenced by the violence voted for the BJP, compared to 51 percent of those who said violence was not electorally important to them.

[17] Human Rights Watch 2002.

[18] Subrahmaniam 2011.

[19] To the best of my knowledge, analyses assessing the electoral impact of the 2002 violence have not yet been produced. However, for an excellent recent ethnographic analysis of how rioting produces and maintains social relations between Hindu nationalists and local communities in Gujarat, see Berenschot 2011.

[20] Data based on the 2002 Gujarat State Election Survey conducted by Lokniti.

Thus, future micro-level analyses will need to establish whether violence produces votes for the BJP and specify the communities within which it does so.

A final question raised by the Gujarati case is whether it attests to the possibility of BJP leaders developing direct populist links to voters, thereby eschewing their need to depend on movement affiliates (including service wings) altogether. Indeed, the BJP's electoral success in Gujarat has coincided with the shrinking footprint of its movement partners in the state.[21] Instead, many view the party's success as a function of the popularity of a single leader, Narendra Modi, rather than the collective efforts of Hindutva organizations.

Although the BJP's ascent in Gujarat pre-dates the rise of Modi, there is no question that he has developed a considerable personal following in Gujarat, and his specific appeal does currently outweigh that of the party and movement. His champions attribute this appeal to his economic policy record, which they view as the key to Gujarat's above-average growth since 2000. More skeptical observers argue that his dominance is at least equally the result of his ruthless marginalization of any potential challenger within the BJP and his deliberate severing of ties with the party's Sangh affiliates in the state. Modi's personal brand has also been lavishly developed through hi-tech campaigns crafted by an expensive American marketing firm, which include simultaneous rallies in multiple locations featuring 3-D holograms of Modi himself.

Discussions about Modi's appeal provoke important questions for further study. To what degree is his political appeal actually predicated on the popularity of his economic record? Are voter perceptions of his policies separable from their views on his visibly pro-Hindu rhetoric and actions or informed by them?[22] And has his appeal – programmatic or otherwise – percolated down to Gujarat's subaltern communities?

I confine myself here to addressing this last question, which is perhaps the most clearly linked to this book's concerns. Despite Modi's dominance in Gujarat, it is difficult to discern the degree of his popularity among Dalits and Adivasis specifically. The state's rapid growth has certainly been impressive, and has resulted in improved infrastructure that may positively affect these communities. Yet it has also been criticized for being exceedingly top heavy and for excluding its poorest citizens, especially those living in rural areas.[23] In fact, a recent UNDP report on Indian states argued Gujarat's high growth had "not yet

---

[21] It is by now common knowledge that a number of leaders within the Sangh and the BJP are wary of Modi's concentration of power, which they see as subverting the movement's prioritization of the collective over the individual (see Joshi 2013).

[22] For an analysis of the connections between Modi's commitments to liberalizing economic policies and Hindutva's cultural agenda, see Sud 2012.

[23] According to the recent India Human Development Report (Planning Commission 2011, p. 131), Gujarat's ranked thirteenth out of India's seventeen major states in an overall Hunger Index (which equally weights adult malnourishment, child malnourishment, and child mortality). Moreover, Gujarat was the only above-average income state in the bottom five of this category.

percolat[ed] to the marginalized sections of society, particularly STs (Adivasis) and SCs (Dalits)."[24]

Second, Modi's policy agenda has largely focused on the needs of urban Gujaratis, specifically cultivating what some have termed the "neo-middle class" vote.[25] Accordingly, his victories have been disproportionately fuelled by support from urban voters, mostly hailing from high or intermediate caste (OBC) backgrounds.[26] At the same time, as noted above, Modi's consecutive victories have come during a period of declining support from Dalit and Adivasi communities in the state. Yet such declines matter less in Gujarat than in other parts of India, given the relatively large size of the BJP's urban middle-class core in the state. Gujarat has always been a relatively prosperous and urbanized state by Indian standards, and recent economic and demographic growth has been heavily concentrated in cities.[27] In 2011, 42.58 percent of Gujarat's population resided in urban areas, well above the national average (31.16 percent).[28] In addition, the recent delimitation of electoral constituencies in 2008 increased the number of urban seats in the state. These developments have combined to make a core-centric strategy focused on the urban middle classes more feasible for the BJP in Gujarat than elsewhere in India.

Thus while Modi's individual appeal among the BJP's core is unquestionable, his personal popularity among poorer voters remains somewhat unclear, and of considerable importance in the run-up to the 2014 national election. Still, given the widespread displeasure with the incumbent Congress-led government, Modi and the BJP are likely to do extremely well in 2014, including with Dalits and Adivasis. The Congress has been battered by corruption scandals, betrayed by ineffective leadership, and hampered by weak local organizations. This book's arguments anticipate such a party to be the perfect opponent for enabling elite party success. Modi's personal popularity will be aided by his party's Sangh affiliates, who have made it clear they intend to campaign extremely hard for him during the 2014 campaign (albeit autonomously, as is their preference).[29] Thus if the BJP does win an expected victory, it will be imperative to avoid prisoner of the moment analyses that narrowly focus on the top of the ticket. Instead, this book's arguments suggest the need to pay equal attention to the full set of conditions that will enable such a victory, and to place it within the longer history of the party's efforts among the poor.

[24] Planning Commission 2011, p. 51. For example, health indicators for Adivasis (including younger than age 5 mortality rates and proportions of underweight children) are higher in Gujarat than the national average, despite the state's overall relative prosperity.

[25] See Jaffrelot 2013, especially p. 83.

[26] In 2012, the party's support among urban voters was 58 percent, and even higher (65 percent) among college-educated urban Gujaratis, compared to just 43 percent in rural areas. Data from CSDS Data Unit, as cited in Jaffrelot 2013, p. 89.

[27] Gujarat's urban communities added 6.7 million people between 2001 and 2011, compared to just 2.9 million people in rural areas (2011 Indian census).

[28] Data from 2011 Indian census.

[29] Rao 2014.

THE CHALLENGES TO SUSTAINING SERVICE'S SUCCESS

The prior section examined how well this book's arguments anticipated political trends within India that emerged after they were developed and tested. This section shifts to asking a slightly different anticipatory question, namely how sustainable are the gains generated by service provision? Although my research found that these inroads are not ephemeral, it also uncovered several obstacles to sustaining these victories over the long term. Such challenges are of two broad types: those resulting from internal tensions within an elite party and its affiliates and those resulting from major changes in the external environment in which service activists work. These potential pitfalls hint at the difficulties elite parties, both in India and elsewhere, will have in building sustainable coalitions through service. They further suggest that elite parties will need to undertake alternative approaches to consolidate the initial gains made through private welfare.

The first internal challenge service providers face is their ability to maintain a non-partisan image while engaging in political mobilization. Service activists in India deliberately avoided public collaborations with the BJP, as they understood their political influence to derive from reputations unsullied by the dirty river of politics. Evidence from India suggests walking such a tightrope is possible in the short to medium term. For example, more than three-quarters of households I interviewed in Chhattisgarh "strongly disagreed" that their local Sangh service activists worked for a political party.

Evidence from India also suggests that such apolitical political work may not be indefinitely sustainable. Even in the midst of the Sangh's successes in central India, murmurs of discontent have begun to surface, as some villagers are beginning to believe that service activists are "definitely working for the BJP."[30] It is certainly conceivable that these numbers will grow as successive elections more clearly establish partisan patterns in the efforts of service workers. Even if such shifts in perception take place, the BJP's electoral performance need not decline. Voters may well continue to support the party if their appreciation of the VKA's work outweighs any distaste for its increasingly apparent partisan nature or the appeal of any rival strategy.

The second major issue raised by a service strategy's success is how elite parties will transition from opposition to governing formations. I have argued that service activists helped project a more inclusive image for an elite formation in India within the communities in which they worked. The goodwill won by these cadres proved key in the BJP's electoral turnaround and helped propel the party to office in several central Indian states. Yet, poll victories have also ensured that the work of service activists can no longer serve as the exclusive indicator of Hindu nationalism's commitment to public welfare. Instead, BJP-led

[30] Jashpur household interview respondent, Ber village, August 4, 2010. Another respondent complained that VKA workers are clearly partisan, even though they claim not to be involved in politics. Jashpur household interview respondent, Kutki village, August 14, 2010.

governments have accumulated a policy record for voters to directly scrutinize. If this record is consistently devoid of any pro-poor schemes, the goodwill won by service activists may quickly become outweighed by renewed negative perceptions of the BJP's programmatic elitism. First-time Islamist-led governments in Egypt, Tunisia, and elsewhere have had to similarly negotiate the perils of incumbency.

If such updating does occur among poor voters, successful elite party regimes are likely to be those that find a way to consolidate the successes furnished by service activists, rather than continue to exclusively presume on them. Of course, sustained incumbency can also furnish new tools for such consolidation. Most importantly, newfound and sustained access to public monies can allow elite parties to offer some small policy gestures for poor supporters, without fundamentally disturbing the prioritization of their elite core. There is suggestive evidence of such solutions being implemented by second-term BJP governments in Chhattisgarh and Madhya Pradesh. In these states, the upper caste–dominated executive wing of the party continues to rely on its service network but has now supplemented private welfare efforts with selective schemes (such as subsidized rice) for the poor. For other BJP governments, notably in Karnataka, incumbency has only accelerated factional disputes and elite patronage grabs and has yielded incoherent policy regimes. Continued subaltern support for the party in these cases appears less likely.

A third difficulty a service-based approach faces is managing the growing aspirations of the non-elite personnel it successfully recruits. As I have argued, a key function of the organizational expansion of service chapters in India is to create an alternative low-status stream of employment through which to incorporate subaltern recruits. Such collateral roles protect the high-status positions of the party itself (executive positions in government, party candidacies, internal party positions, etc.) for entrenched social elites.[31] However, several young subaltern service activists in India have begun to express their desires to eventually work for the BJP and even to rise to prominence within the party. Such political ambitions are deeply troubling to upper castes, who are already worried about the growing autonomy of the non-elite activists they have helped transition into politics.[32] One such aggrieved elite leader, a descendent of a former royal family in central India, said such rogue protégés needed to be brought into line, and perhaps even demoted by upper castes. Continually blocking subaltern hopefuls will inevitably fuel their discontent and ask serious questions of service's continued ability to manage the competing aspirations of a diverse social coalition.

A fourth internal obstacle stems from the seeming inability of welfare providers to shift the ideological orientations of non-elite recipients. My study has cautioned against interpreting poor voter support for elite parties,

---

[31] On a similar point about the political benefits of expanding these collateral organizational positions, see Panebianco (1988, p.28).

[32] Interview with Dilip Singh Judeo, Jashpur, July 22, 2010.

particularly those tied to religious movements, as evidence of deeper ideological attachments. Ironically, whereas service activists in many parts of India have effectively mobilized electoral support, they have not sparked the social transformations they themselves prize most highly. This partial success has the potential to spark future disagreements between movement and party. For the BJP, service provision has achieved its primary goal of winning subaltern votes in many states. However, service activists may decide their painstaking efforts are better directed elsewhere if welfare remains unable to bring about the deeper ideological shifts they covet. Such a decision would clearly disturb the symbiotic equilibrium between movement and party that service itself has helped to foster.

A fifth and final internal challenge to sustaining service's success comes from ideological disagreements it sparks within the non-electoral affiliates of elite parties. These intra-movement divisions are not based on varying intensities of ideological commitment but on the means best suited to achieving social change. In India, a perceptible tension has emerged between the gradualist logic of service activism and the episodic violence enacted by Hindutva's more militant wings (such as the Vishva Hindu Parishad and Bajrang Dal). Service activists grumbled privately to me that the grisly, theatrical displays of intolerance and violence organized by these affiliates threatened to undermine their own efforts to present a more peaceful, inclusive image of the movement and party to subaltern communities.

Such rifts between equally motivated "gradualists" and "militants" are certainly not unique to Hindu nationalism. For example, Wickham interviews a gradualist Islamist activist with the Egyptian Muslim Brothers who complained that more militant *jihadis* are needlessly trying to achieve "by the hand" what he instead hoped to accomplish through "the heart" and "the tongue."[33] More analytical attention needs to be paid to the political implications of such intra-movement tensions between "hand" and "heart" wings. As a growing number of religiously oriented elite parties across the Middle East and Southern Asia face heightened electoral compulsions to expand their appeal, these tactical disagreements over how to achieve such an expansion are poised to grow in significance.

In addition to these internal tensions, shifts in the external environment in which voters make decisions can affect the electoral efficacy of private welfare. Most obviously, the expansion of public infrastructure, particularly in basic health and education, constitutes a major challenge to politically motivated service provision. Even though India's recent macroeconomic success has often been attributed to gradual pro-market reforms implemented since 1990, it would be erroneous to conclude that the footprint of the Indian state has diminished during this period. In fact, the country's rapid growth has fueled a swelling of public coffers, with government tax revenues increasing from $131 billion in 2006 to $225 billion in 2010.[34] Increasing revenues have in turn fed an expansion of the public sector in absolute terms. In fact, government

---

[33] Wickham 2002, p. 129.
[34] Data from the 2011 Economic Survey of India, p. 71.

expenditures on education alone increased from $21 billion to $36 billion during this period.[35]

Such developments threaten both the demand for and supply of religious welfare. Mohan, a Hindu nationalist service worker I repeatedly spoke with, worried aloud about how expansions in local public infrastructure would "take many of our students away." Mohan was especially concerned with the growing number of welfare schemes enacted by the Indian government through government schools. His organization would be unable to compete with the increasing incentives given to public schoolchildren ("not just midday meals, free books, uniforms, but soap and other incentives that we can't give").[36] However, he also admitted that his organization had withstood such expansions because they had not been accompanied by reductions in teacher absenteeism. Thus, the first-hand experience of private providers suggests that their efficacy is less threatened by the physical scale of public services than by the reliability of their delivery.

However, the Indian experience does suggest that even infrastructural expansion can affect a welfare-based strategy by disturbing the supply side incentives this tactic relies on. Hindu nationalists have depended on the continuing attractiveness of the relatively meager benefits paid to non-elite service providers recruited by upper caste activist cadres. So far, this strategy has worked in attracting educated villagers and slum residents facing a paucity of other employment options. However, the expansion of government infrastructure has created more remunerative public sector employment opportunities for these relatively qualified youth.[37] As these recent recruits were already less ideologically committed to the Hindutva movement than their elite predecessors, they have proved unable to resist such financial opportunities. Take the contrasting examples of an upper caste activist and a recent tribal recruit working for the VKA within the same state. The former told me he took a 50 percent pay cut in moving from a private sector job to become a teacher for the movement. He said the pinch hurt, "but he did it for the Sangh."[38] The latter meanwhile confessed that he immediately resigned his position as a VKA teacher once he managed to obtain a position as a public schoolteacher. It was, he noted, impossible to pass up a government job that offered "seven times the salary for less work."[39]

Such differences have fueled the fissiparous dynamics between older, upper caste, ideologically committed believers and younger, subaltern careerists. In one joint conversation, an upper caste Sangh activist took offense when his junior, non-elite colleague complained about how their wages paled in comparison

---

[35] This figure combines state and central government spending. Data from 2011 Economic Survey of India, p. 304.
[36] Interview with Mohan, Kikar village, July 22, 2010.
[37] Interview with informant AI, Sitanagar, July 23, 2010.
[38] Interview with informant AM, Ramnagar, 2010 (exact date withheld upon request).
[39] Interview with Rajesh, Anola village, July 25, 2010.

to the government school position that had recently become available in a neighboring village. The elder activist grumbled that even the Sangh has become "a *paise ki duniya*" (a world where only money matters).[40] In conjunction with the other challenges outlined here, such generational fissures suggest the initial successes of service, so painstakingly won, may also prove to be painfully short lived.

PARTY ORGANIZATIONS, ELECTORAL STRATEGIES, AND POOR VOTERS IN THE GLOBAL SOUTH

This book began by drawing attention to the compelling puzzle of poor voter support for an elite party in India. Through articulating and testing arguments about why, how, and when such support was won, I hope to contribute to our broader theoretical understanding of the relationship between party organizations and electoral strategies. Within the study of political parties, organizational prowess was initially seen as the purview of Duverger's "mass" parties, a concept clearly informed by the rise of socialist parties in Europe.[41] Duvergerian mass parties mobilized along class lines, were motivated by a powerful ideological vision, and formulated policies appealing to the material interests of their largely non-elite support base. Within this vision, organizational networks served to consolidate the programmatic ties between poor voters and leftist parties.[42] By contrast, Duverger viewed elite ("caucus") parties as organizationally thin formations, relying on powerful local patrons rather than on mass party structures to win votes.

In more contemporary accounts of party organizations, this typology has become somewhat inverted. With the shift from elite-centered patronage to more direct forms of mass clientelism among the poor in many countries, the discretionary strategies of many parties began to require increasing organizational resources. In such instances, party networks were theorized to primarily play a monitoring role, ensuring reciprocity at the polls within increasingly individualized clientelist pacts.[43] By contrast, parties with economically progressive policy stances that directly appealed to disadvantaged voters could create more programmatic linkages with the poor that did not require this monitoring apparatus.[44]

In the context of these evolving discussions, my account highlights a novel use of party organizations in crafting a winning coalition within a poor democracy. The organizational resources of an elite party in India did not consolidate the programmatic ties between poor voters and a party articulating their material

[40] Interviews with Gopal and Mohan, VKA workers, Kikar village, July 22, 2010.
[41] Duverger 1954.
[42] See Roberts 2002.
[43] Stokes 2005, Medina and Stokes 2002.
[44] Kitschelt and Wilkinson 2007.

interests. Nor did they serve to monitor reciprocity for a clientelist machine. Instead, the differentiated nature of these resources allowed an elite party to simultaneously deploy multiple electoral strategies. It was this division of labor that proved crucial for the simultaneous recruitment of poor voters and retention of rich ones. My argument here represents a shift from the dominant either-or focus of debates on whether parties prioritize new voters or longtime supporters.[45] Instead, I examine how parties can retain core supporters and recruit non-core electorates, as elite parties in poor polities must do in order to thrive.[46]

By detailing the BJP's reliance on these networks, my argument also qualifies prior conceptualizations of "movement-parties" that draw primarily on the experiences of advanced democracies. In this context, movement-parties have been defined as "making little investment in a formal organizational party structure" and as "lack[ing] extensive and intensive formal organizational coverage ... and a physical infrastructure of communication."[47] Such shallow capacities may indeed characterize parties emerging out of Western social movements. However, the robust presence of organizationally dense movement-parties across the global south (many of which are affiliated with religious social organizations) provides a powerful check on this definition's wider applicability.

The findings of this project also trouble a second set of claims stemming from the experience of wealthy democracies, namely that organizationally robust parties are being uniformly replaced by spare "electoral-professional" parties narrowly focused on developing techniques to win votes during elections.[48] These conclusions have been premised on trends of increasing affluence, post-industrial employment patterns, and technological advances that have compelled modern campaigns to put a premium on technical skills and personal charisma instead of on mass memberships. The arguments of this book highlight how the extension of such conclusions to less affluent arenas is premature. In contexts marked by continuing poverty, low levels of literacy, and uneven access to mass communication, a party's ability to utilize organizations embedded in the everyday lives of ordinary voters remains especially valuable.

While questioning the broader applicability of studies of political parties in Western democracies, my study also suggests the limitations of conventional portrayals of religious movement-parties within the global south itself. Such

---

[45] Core voter models predict that risk-averse political actors will channel benefits to loyal voters who are most likely to reciprocate at the polls (Cox and McCubbins 1986; Calvo and Murillo 2004; Nichter 2008). By contrast, swing voter theories argue that a party will not waste resources on voters whose backing they are already assured of and will instead target swayable voters who have remained outside their fold (Dixit and Londregan 1996; Stokes 2005).

[46] Relatively few analyses have focused on this important question, and those that have primarily outlined how incumbent parties can divide patronage among different segments of their support base. See Diaz-Cayeros, Estevez, and Magaloni 2010.

[47] Kitschelt 2006, p. 280.

[48] Panebianco 1988; Gunther and Diamond 2003, p. 174.

formations are often dichotomized as combinations of ideologically inflexible movement ideologues and Downsian party pragmatists. Hindu nationalism has itself been described as a blend of "movement activists who provoke riots against Muslims" and pragmatic party actors "who want to transform the party into a catch-all organization appealing to moderate voters."[49] Such frameworks assume movement activists will be uninterested in electoral success and only capable of mobilizing ideologically committed core supporters. Flexible party pragmatists are in turn assumed to compel and lead efforts among more distant non-core constituencies. However, evidence from India demonstrates that precisely the reverse arrangement is also possible, as movement radicals were revealed to have electoral interests and to spearhead efforts at non-core recruitment. Meanwhile, party personnel were found to retain ideological commitments and to play a leading role in retaining core voters. Such counter-intuitive arrangements suggest that if we wish to better anticipate the political strategies of such formations, we must develop more nuanced understandings of how electoral and ideological interests combine within them.

Finally, it is my hope that by examining the BJP's interactions with poor voters, this book has also helped complicate our understandings of how the latter engage with democratic politics. The literature on political parties often conceptualizes the poor, especially within non-Western settings, as citizens that parties prey on, rather than interact with. My research found that Dalits and Adivasis were neither simply the passive recipients of policies or patronage nor crowds easily manipulated by communal appeals. The considerable variation in how co-ethnics within these communities voted, even within the same village, also defied their portrayal as homogenous ethnic voting blocs. Instead, this project has tried to illustrate the value of studying how poor individuals make active political decisions, decisions that aggregate to shape the direction of national politics. In this account, poor voters often chose to support the BJP on the basis of definable material interests, social connections, and the continually shifting options available to them. Within these calculations, an elite party did occasionally emerge as a genuine choice of the poor in India but only when the latter in turn faced somewhat poor choices.

---

[49] Quote from McAdam and Tarrow 2010, p. 537. A similar description is in Hansen and Jaffrelot 2001, p. 1.

Afterword

As this book went to press, India held its 2014 general elections, which brought the BJP back to power in emphatic and unprecedented fashion. The BJP became the first non-Congress party in Indian history to win a majority of seats in the Indian parliament (282 out of 543).[1] Of course, these 2014 elections were far too recent for any systematic analysis of them to be included within this book. Yet, the party's historic victory does reinforce the importance of understanding its past efforts. How do the arguments made in this book help us contextualize and understand the largest election ever held?

The first point my analysis underscores is the need to resist rushing to broad conclusions after any single Indian election. The introductory chapter began by criticizing many media pundits who called the BJP a spent force after its 2004 defeat. Instead, I drew attention to the unlikely electoral coalition the party was building in several Indian states, even as it failed to win a national mandate. In the same spirit, assertions that the BJP will now become the focal point of future Indian elections are highly premature.[2] After all, this particular election was especially ripe for an anti-incumbent result, given the high inflation, slowing economic growth, and massive corruption scandals that have rocked the outgoing Congress-led government.[3]

Despite this caveat, it is important to briefly consider what this book's analysis can bring to bear on understanding the BJP's performance in 2014 and beyond. Toward this end, I focus here on identifying key areas where these elections displayed continuity and discontinuity with Hindu nationalism's past strategic efforts.

---

[1] The coalition led by the BJP won an impressive total of 336 seats.

[2] Pradeep Chhibber and Rahul Verma, "It is Modi, not BJP, that won this election." *The Hindu*, June 1, 2014.

[3] Adam Ziegfeld, "Does Modi get all the credit for BJP win? Jury's still out." *Times of India*, May 25, 2014.

The BJP's victory clearly built on three key aspects of its past successes high-lighted in this book: its disproportionate support from Hindu upper castes, its expanded appeal with poor voters in certain states, and its heightened success rate when directly competing against the Congress. The 2014 result was in no small part the result of the party's further elevating its performance across these areas of prior strength.

First, the 2014 results saw a massive concentration of elite support for the BJP, even relative to the party's traditionally strong performance with these groups. Hindu nationalists won about 30 percent of all votes cast in the election, but national survey data shows that they won roughly 60 percent of upper caste votes. By contrast, the BJP won just over 25 percent of Dalit votes.[4] Thus, even in the midst of a major victory, upper castes continued to support the party at disproportionately high rates.

Second, the BJP did better with subaltern voters in 2014 in those areas where it had already made initial breakthroughs via service. National Election Study data on caste-wise support for the BJP across these major states in 2014 is not yet publicly available. However, the breakdowns reported by the NES survey team in the popular press suggest important continuities with the evidence provided in this book. For example, in the eight major states with large Adivasi populations, the BJP beat or matched the Congress in all five in which Hindu nationalists had already built welfare networks (Assam, Chhattisgarh, Jharkhand, Madhya Pradesh, and Rajasthan).[5] By contrast, the BJP trailed the Congress among Adivasis in two of the remaining three states where Sangh service networks were weaker (Gujarat, Maharashtra, and Orissa).[6] A similar pattern was evident among Dalits.[7] Given these trends, it is not surprising that the BJP in 2014 proved especially successful in winning seats in states where welfare had helped them make inroads among poor voters in prior years. The BJP won 81 percent of seats across six of the seven high-service states examined in this book (the exception was Kerala once again).[8] Across the remaining ten major states in my sample, the party won just under 44 percent of seats.

---

[4] Sanjay Kumar, "Role of polarization in BJP's big victory." *Mint*, May 17, 2014.

[5] I define "large" here as those cases where Adviasis constitute more than 10 percent of the state's total population. Jyoti Mishra, "Voting patterns among scheduled tribes." *The Hindu*, June 9, 2014.

[6] The Gujarat result is particularly interesting, as it is considered a BJP stronghold and is the home state for Narendra Modi, the party's prime ministerial candidate. While the BJP dominated the polls, winning all 26 seats, surveys reported it still trailed the Congress in winning Adivasi voters (Mishra 2014).

[7] For example, 37 percent of Dalits in Chhattisgarh and 43 percent of Dalits in Madhya Pradesh voted for the BJP. Data from NES 2014 as reported in Anupama Saxena, "In Chhattisgarh, BJP builds on success of 2009." *The Hindu*, May 25, 2014; and Yatindra Singh Sisodia, "Educated, urban voters flocked to BJP in MP." *The Hindu*, May 25, 2014.

[8] Author calculations using data from the Election Commission of India. The party won 98 of a possible 121 seats across Assam, Chhattisgarh, Jharkhand, Karnataka, Madhya Pradesh, and Rajasthan.

Third, as anticipated by my argument, the BJP enjoyed far greater success in constituencies when it went against the Congress than when it was pitted against regional parties. In the 189 constituencies in which the BJP and Congress were the top two vote getters, the BJP won 88 percent of the time. In the remaining 239 seats it contested, the party won only 49 percent of the time.[9]

Thus, the BJP's historic victory in 2014 did not appear from nowhere but consolidated and expanded upon prior areas of strength. That said, the election also highlighted important new developments within the party for consideration. Geographically, the most significant discontinuity came in Uttar Pradesh, where the BJP reversed many years of failure to win a massive mandate (71 out of 80 seats). Once again, the party was extraordinarily successful among the state's large upper caste electorate, winning nearly three out of every four votes. Meanwhile the BJP (30 percent) continued to trail the BSP (46.5 percent) among Dalits, but it narrowed the gap between the two parties by more than enough to help ensure its decisive victory.[10]

This dramatic narrowing signals the weakening appeal of the BSP's ethnic patronage strategy. In Chapter 6, I argued that the party had managed to politicize Dalits against upper castes but did not broadly improve public provisioning for lower caste communities. Instead, the BSP used its time in office to deliver concentrated patronage benefits to its core cadre, specifically the Jatav Dalit subcaste from which its leadership came. Accordingly, I argued that the BSP had generated less robust linkages than the programmatic ties communists enjoy with poor voters in Kerala. While initially effective, this ethnic strategy indeed seems to have worn out the patience of the BSP's Dalit supporters, particularly those outside of the party's Jatav-dominated patronage network.[11]

However, a far bigger story than the BJP's performance in any one state was the emergence of Narendra Modi as the undisputed national leader of the party. Indeed, many election commentators viewed the victory as largely a consequence of Modi's individual popularity as a leader. Modi's campaign strategy certainly showed several signs of a centralization of control. He invested considerable effort and money into crafting an image of presidential authority with which to directly connect with voters. His campaign focused on building a personal brand, trumpeting his humble origins as a tea vendor as evidence of his self-reliance, and his *chhapen*-inch *chhata* (56-inch chest) as proof that he was the strongman India needed at its helm. This brand was advertised via elaborate preelection events orchestrated by expensive public relations firms, including

[9] Neelanjan Sircar, "The numbers game: An analysis of the 2014 general election.' *India in Transition*, June 16, 2014.
[10] A. K. Verma, Mirza Asmer Beg, and Sudhir Kumar, "A saffron sweep in Uttar Pradesh." *The Hindu*, May 23, 2014.
[11] NES data suggests the BJP's inroads in 2014 have specifically come among non-Jatav Dalits. The BSP won more than 68 percent of Jatav votes to the BJP's 18 percent. However, among non-Jatavs, the BJP led the BSP by a 45 percent to 18 percent margin. Verma et al., "A saffron sweep in Uttar Pradesh."

simultaneous rallies across the country where Modi appeared to attendees as a three-dimensional hologram. Such efforts proved successful, as Modi enjoyed large and consistent leads in direct comparisons with potential prime ministerial candidates from other parties.[12]

However, it is imperative to be cautious in attributing any result in such a massively complex parliamentary democracy to a single person, however charismatic. Some analysts supported such attributions by citing NES survey data reporting roughly 25 percent of BJP supporters saying they would have voted differently had Modi not led the party.[13] Yet, this figure is very much in line with those for past prime ministerial candidates in Indian national elections.[14] Further, "Modi wave" arguments have to account for the fact that most BJP victories came in areas where the party has done well in the pre-Modi era, whereas many of its failures came in areas where it has historically done poorly. Further, even in important exceptions to this pattern (such as Uttar Pradesh), a relatively low percentage of voters (17 percent) said their vote would have been affected were Modi not the BJP's prime ministerial candidate. It is therefore more prudent to avoid prisoner of the moment arguments focusing solely on Modi's popularity. Instead, the 2014 victory is best understood as one produced by new factors (such as an especially popular leader) building on the foundation laid by past efforts.

Quite aside from questions of how the BJP's triumph was achieved is how the victory itself will affect its future modus operandi. This book has shown how private welfare helped the BJP win office in several Indian states by moderating Hindu nationalism's elite image among many poor communities. Yet, Chapter 8 discussed why private welfare is more effective in helping elite parties win office than in retaining incumbency. When such parties head governments, private welfare no longer serves as the primary indicator of their intentions toward the poor's well-being. Instead, disadvantaged communities will now also examine how well the incumbent party serves their policy interests. Given this reality, I noted how crucial it was for elite parties like the BJP to consolidate the initial successes enabled by private welfare through public policy action. At the subnational level, I noted that BJP state governments in Madhya Pradesh and Chhattisgarh have made this transition by implementing limited but effective public welfare schemes. The Modi government's clear majority will only intensify the need for equivalent policy gestures at the all-India level to ensure the tide of poor voter sentiment does not turn against it.

---

[12] CNN-IBN CSDS voter poll: http://ibnlive.in.com/news/poll-tracker-modi-leads-pm-race-in-six-states-rahul-a-distant-second/456296-81.html. Pew Research Center poll: http://www.pewglobal.org/2014/02/26/indians-want-political-change/.

[13] Pradeep Chhibber and Rahul Verma, "It is Modi, not BJP, that won this election." *The Hindu*, June 1, 2014.

[14] In 2004, 29 percent of people who voted for the BJP expressed the same sentiment about Prime Minister Atal Behari Vajpayee (Question 38a on NES 2004), as did 22 percent of Congress voters about party leader Sonia Gandhi (Question 39a on NES 2004).

Yet, my analysis has also shown how such programmatic shifts are not easy for elite parties to undertake, as they risk alienating privileged core constituencies. The BJP's upper caste core supporters, who voted for it in record numbers in 2014, expect their policy interests to be served by the new government in ways that may not please poor electorates. Such tensions have already surfaced following the Modi government's suggestion that it might revise India's Land Acquisition Act to make it easier for private companies to override farmers opposing the acquisition of their land for development projects.[15] While such revisions are likely to please the party's corporate financiers and elite supporters, they are likely to be less well received by the rural poor.

A second issue this book's analytical framework highlights is how the BJP's victory will affect its future relationship with its movement affiliates. The Sangh cadres campaigned hard for Modi, who came to the party via the RSS and is seen as personally committed to Hindutva ideology. Consistent with the efforts described in this book, Sangh cadres were not formally part of the BJP's campaign but used their local influence to collect information, mobilize voters, and stymie opponents.[16] However, there is considerable disquiet within the Sangh's leadership over Modi's cult of personality.[17] Philosophically, such cults go against the movement's ethos, which privileges the collective over the individual. Politically, movement affiliates worry that Modi's personalist approach will render them increasingly politically redundant.

From the BJP's perspective, a reduced dependence on the Sangh could certainly emancipate the party from having to support electorally unpopular elements of the Hindutva platform. Yet, losing the Sangh's organizational heft could prove costly. The Modi government will not have much time to decide how to manage this familiar trade-off. The BJP's parliamentary majority has only increased pressure from its movement partners to implement key provisions of the Hindutva agenda immediately. Initial signs from the Modi government show it responding to this pressure, including an unexpectedly early push for Hindi as the official language of government (a Sangh favorite).[18] Yet, as this book has repeatedly argued, such polarizing agenda items are unlikely to help the BJP maintain its appeal beyond its core base.

Reading the 2014 results in light of this book's arguments thus shows how the BJP's victory does not alter the fundamental dilemmas the party has faced. How can an elite party simultaneously meet the expectations of poor voters without alienating their privileged core? How can such a party balance its own electoral

---

[15] Elizabeth Roche, "Nitin Gadkari hints at amendments to land acquisition act." *Mint*, June 27, 2014.

[16] Vinay Kumar and K. A. Shaji, "RSS going all out to campaign for Modi." *The Hindu*, October 26, 2013; Piyush Srivastava, "RSS campaigns for Narendra Modi in UP to ensure maximum Lok Sabha seats." *Mail Today*, April 5, 2014.

[17] Manjari Katju, "Why the Sangh fears Modi." *Indian Express*, April 16, 2014.

[18] 'Narendra Modi's push for Hindi struggles to translate in some states.' *Times of India*, June 19th, 2014.

ambitions with the ideological goals of its founding movement? If anything, unfettered incumbency throws such challenges into even starker relief. While the scale of the BJP's victory in 2014 is certainly unprecedented, the challenges it will face in maintaining this success will be all too familiar.

Tariq Thachil
New Delhi
June 28, 2014

Appendix A Variables, Sources, and Summary Statistics

TABLE A.I. *Variables Used for Voter-Level Analysis in Chapter 3 (all measures coded from 2004 NES)*

Concept	Measure	Source	Summary Statistics for non-elite Sample			
			MEAN	Standard Deviation	Min.	Max.
Electoral Support of the BJP (2004)	Did you vote for the BJP in 2004?	Question 2a	.189	.391	0	1
Switching to Support BJP	Did you vote for the BJP in 2004? (only voters who did not in 1999)	Questions 2a and 5a	.095	.293	0	1
Membership	Other than political parties, are you a member of: Any religious/caste association? Any other associations and organizations like co-operatives, farmers' association, trade unions, welfare organizations, cultural and sports organizations?	Questions 18 and 19	.190	.413	0	1
Religiosity	Now I will ask you about a few religious activities. You tell me how often do you practice them – daily, weekly, only on festivals, or never? a. Prayer b. Visiting temple, mosque, church, *gurdwara* (Sikh temple), etc.	Questions 34a, 34b.	2.841 2.343	1.046 .871	1 1	4 4
Communalism	To what extent do you agree with these options – fully agree, somewhat agree, somewhat disagree, or fully disagree: On the site of the Babri Masjid, only Ram temple should be built	Q34a.	2.758	1.059	1	4
Income	What is your total monthly household income?	QB19	2.15	1.529	1	8
Ethnic Influence	In deciding whom to vote for, whose opinion mattered to you most? (coded 1 only if response was "caste/community leader"	Q9	.106	.308	0	1

Support for Economic Liberalization					
Now I will read out a few statements regarding the economic policy of the country. You tell me, do you fully agree, somewhat agree, somewhat disagree, or fully disagree with these statements?	Q30b-e	9.475	2.312	4	16
The number of government employees should be reduced as paying for their salaries is costly for the country.	Q30b	2.379	1.042	1	4
The government factories and businesses should be sold/handed over to private companies.	Q30c	2.162	.964	1	4
Foreign companies should not be allowed free trade in India (coding was reversed for this question)	Q30d	2.625	1.002	1	4
People are responsible for their poverty and not their government.	Q30e	2.309	1.146	1	4

TABLE A.2a. *Variables Used for State-Level Analysis*

Concept	Measure	Source	Mean	Standard Deviation	Min.	Max.
BJP Dalit/ Adivasi Support	Percentage of a state's Dalit and Adivasi population supporting the BJP	National Election Study (1996, 1999, 2004)	17.75	14.14	0	54.5
Religious Welfare[1]	Total Service Projects/Combined Dalit and Adivasi Population Seva Bharati Service Data	Seva Disha reports (1997, 2004) collected by the author from Rashtriya Seva Bharati, New Delhi.	.096	.082	−.004	.303
	Vanvasi Kalyan Ashram Service Data	Collected by author from VKA headquarters, Jashpur, Chhattisgarh (2007, 2010).				
Party Fragmentation	Effective Number of Parties (Votes)	Election Commission of India Reports (1996, 1999, 2004 Lok Sabha editions)	4.287	1.361	2.07	7.75
Ethnic Voting	Index of Group-Based Ethnic Voting from Huber 2011	National Election Study (1996, 1999, 2004).	.293	.125	.128	.703
BJP Upper Caste Support	Percentage of a state's upper caste population supporting the BJP	National Election Study (1996, 1999, 2004)	33.48	23.06	0	78.22
Economic Development (logged)	Per capita income	Reserve Bank of India's Annual Bulletin	4.481	.518	3.369	5.242
Percentage Christian	Percentage of state population that is Christian	Census of India (1991, 2001 editions)	2.667	4.494	.064	19.319
Percentage Muslim	Percentage of state population that is Christian	Census of India (1991, 2001 editions)	11.692	8.441	1.180	30.915
Percentage Non-elite	Percentage of state population that is Dalit or Adivasi	Census of India (1991, 2001 editions)	25.728	8.844	10.9	44

[1] See Tables A.2b and A.2c for state-wise breakdown of service chapters

TABLE A.2b. *State-wise Breakdown of Sangh Service Chapters* (2004)

State	Seva Bharati Projects					Vanvasi Kalyan Ashram Service Projects
	Education	Health	Social Organization	Self-Reliance	Total	
Andhra Pradesh	453	171	263	15	902	604
Assam	43	834	63	56	1046	510
Bihar	98	9	4	3	114	572
Chhattisgarh	833	33	255	13	1134	1086
Gujarat	49	210	40	7	306	1013
Haryana	131	19	41	93	284	1
Jharkhand	152	119	56	20	238	1847
Karnataka	1634	463	1079	13	3189	479
Kerala	75	104	493	16	688	325
Madhya Pradesh	2044	300	536	135	3015	1703
Maharashtra	437	307	165	19	928	1260
Orissa	154	34	59	3	250	1494
Punjab	260	160	454	70	520	0
Rajasthan	192	85	182	52	911	2400
Tamil Nadu	384	105	4	33	527	306
Uttar Pradesh	1028	1127	454	181	2790	315
West Bengal	68	119	7	11	205	499

TABLE A.2C. *Per capita Index of Sangh Service Strength (2004)*

State	Total Projects	Dalit Population	Adivasi Population	Sangh Index
Andhra Pradesh	1506	12,339,496	5,024,104	0.087
Assam	1556	1,825,949	3,308,570	0.303
Bihar	686	13,048,608	758,351	0.050
Chhattisgarh	2220	2,418,722	6,616,596	0.246
Gujarat	1319	3,592,715	7,481,160	0.119
Haryana	285	4,091,110	0	0.070
Jharkhand	2085	3,189,320	7,087,068	0.203
Karnataka	3668	8,563,930	3,463,986	0.305
Kerala	1013	3,123,941	364,189	0.290
Madhya Pradesh	4718	9,155,177	12,233,474	0.221
Maharashtra	2188	9,881,656	8,577,276	0.119
Orissa	1744	6,082,063	8,145,081	0.123
Rajasthan	3311	9,694,462	7,097,706	0.197
Punjab	520	7,028,723	0	0.073
Tamil Nadu	833	11,857,504	651,321	0.067
Uttar Pradesh	3105	35,148,377	107,963	0.088
West Bengal	704	18,452,555	4,406,794	0.030

Source: Seva Bharati figures from Official Report: Seva Disha 2004, obtained from Sew Bharati office, Bhopal. Vanvasi Kalyan Ashram figures from VKA national headquarters, Jashpurnagar, Chhattisgarh (obtained on March 30, 2008). Population figures from 2001 Indian census. Index is computed as follows: (Sewa Bharati Projects + VKA Projects)/(Combined SC and ST population in the state), and this figure is then multiplied by 1,000 for easier readability.

TABLE A.3. *Summary Statistics for National Analysis (Chapter 3)*

TABLE A.3a. *Summary Statistics for Upper Caste Sample (NES 2004)*

Variable	Observations	Mean	Standard Deviation	Min.	Max.
Nonparty Member	3186	.210	.407	0	1
Liberalization	3264	9.573	2.627	4	16
Ethnic Influence	3264	.054	.226	0	1
Income	3245	3.734	2.038	1	8
Communalism	3264	2.962	1.139	1	4
ConversionBan	3264	2.936	1.185	1	4
Religiosity	3264	13.900	3.586	5	20
Age	3264	40.201	18.918	18	99
Male	3264	1.072	.997	0	2
Education	3264	3.222	2.270	0	9

TABLE A.3b. *Descriptive Statistics for Dalit and Adivasi Sample (NES 2004)*

Variable	Observations	Mean	Standard Deviation	Min.	Max.
Nonparty Member	5226	.190	.413	0	1
Liberalization	5460	9.475	2.312	4	16
Ethnic Influence	5460	.106	.308	0	1
Income	5409	2.15	1.529	1	8
Communalism	5460	2.758	1.059	1	4
Conversion Ban	5460	2.864	1.121	1	4
Religiosity	5460	12.573	3.507	5	20
Age	5460	38.897	15.356	18	99
Male	5460	.537	.498	0	1
Education	5460	1.632	2.011	0	9

TABLE A.4. *Summary Statistics for Case Studies (Chapters 5 and 6)*

TABLE A.4a. *Summary Statistics for Chhattisgarh Survey Analysis (Author Survey)*

Variable	Mean	Standard Deviation	Min.	Max.
Service Beneficiary	.171	.377	0	1
Service Opinion	.575	.939	0	3
Age	36.45	13.13	21	84
Ethnic Influence	.486	.501	0	1
Income	2.290	1.363	1	7
Communalism	3.090	1.077	1	4
Religiosity	4.562	1.254	2	8

TABLE A.4b. *Summary Statistics for Kerala Survey Analysis (Author Survey)*

Variable	Mean	Standard Deviation	Min.	Max.
Service Beneficiary	.031	.172	0	1
Service Opinion	.064	.247	0	1
Age	35.86	11.15	18	67
Ethnic Influence	.034	.182	0	1
Income	1.504	.531	1	3
Communalism	2.160	.77	1	4
Religiosity	4.612	.908	2	6

TABLE A.4C. *Summary Statistics for Agra Survey Analysis (Author Survey)*

Variable	Mean	Standard Deviation	Min.	Max.
Service Beneficiary	.268	.443	0	1
Service Opinion	.698	1.239	0	3
Age	41.572	12.614	19	80
Ethnic Influence	.283	.451	0	1
Income	4.285	1.201	1	7
Communalism	3.330	.74	1	4
Religiosity	6.568	1.473	2	8

Appendix B Additional Tables and Figures

Chapter 2

Words and phrases included in content analysis of **BJP** election manifestos and presidential speeches:

Cultural Nationalism	Poverty and Inequality	Social Justice for Dalits and Adivasis
Hindu Nationalism	Poverty	Ambedkar
Hindutva	Inequality	Untouchability
Ram/Ramrajya	Employment	Social Justice
Yatra	Employment for the poor	Dalits
Ayodhya	Jobs	Adivasis
Janmasthan	Land reform	Underprivileged
Cow slaughter	Income gap	Reservations
Article 370	Welfare	Affirmative action
Riots	Housing	Backwardness
Beef	Education	Quotas
Pakistan	Literacy	Scheduled Caste
Bangladesh	Anti-poverty	Scheduled Tribe
Minorities/Minorities Commission	Public distribution system	Other Backward Classes/ OBCs
Religious conversion	Farmer subsidy	Atrocities
Secularism	Food subsidy	Weaker sections
Pseudo-secularism	Antodaya	
Uniform Civil Code	Ration	
Population control		

Chapter 3

TABLE B.2. *Shifts in Simulated Probability of Supporting BJP among Upper Castes (Estimated from Models Reported in Table 3.1)*

VARIABLE NAME	UPPER CASTES		LOWER CASTES	
	Model 1	Model 2	Model 3	Model 4
Membership			15.55	9.27
Liberalization	12.59	14.38		
Caste Influence	−11.05		−5.64	
Income	8.90		5.78	
Communalism	9.98	11.08		
Religiosity	15.37	14.23	10.60	5.81
Education	19.43	19.66		

Note: Predicted values obtained through simulations using the *Clarify* software package while keeping other variables at their means. Only statistically significant determinants in each model are shown in table.

Chapter 6

TABLE B.3. *Determinants of Partisan Support for Communists in Kerala (Ordered Logit Model)*

	Regular Left Front Supporters	
	(1)	(2)
Dalit/Adivasi	.795***	.486*
	(.200)	(.249)
Ezhava	.886***	.518*
	(.189)	(.228)
Nair	−.271	−.128
	(.213)	(.258)
Christian	−.948***	−.839***
	(.159)	(.196)
Muslim	−.598***	−.585**
	(.174)	(.214)
White Collar	−.131	.167
	(.137)	(.164)
Age	−.012**	−.005
	(.004)	(.005)
Male	.200	.184
	(.113)	(.138)
Education	−.101*	.007
	(.041)	(.048)

TABLE B.3. (*continued*)

	Regular Left Front Supporters	
	(1)	(2)
Left Manifesto		1.317***
		(.184)
Congress Manifesto		-.701***
		(.163)
Left Performance		1.022***
		(.094)
Threshold alpha1	-1.217	-.629
	(.287)	(.356)
Threshold alpha2	-.489	.489
	(.286)	(.355)
N	1240	1158
Psuedo Rsq	.07	.29
Log Likelihood	-1181.635	-833/592

*** p<.001 ** p<.01 * p<.05

Appendix C Supplemental Survey Information

1. Sampling Procedures

The sampling for the surveys used in this study depended on several factors. First, the seven districts within Chhattisgarh and Kerala were chosen to vary on the key independent variable of Sangh service strength within each state. To select villages within each district, I consulted the Indian census directory of villages and randomly selected six villages within each district from the list. The next issue was the selection of fifteen Dalit or Adivasi individual respondents from each village. The first step in this selection was to make a list of the households within the village or where relevant within the Dalit *basti* or section of the village. This was done with the help of the local *sarpanch* (head of the village) or in some instances a *panch* (local council member) who supplied the necessary information on the number of households in the village or *basti*.

Once a list of the households had been generated, fifteen were selected at random and were visited in turn. In each case, the head of household was approached and asked to enumerate the members of the household. A member of the household was then selected based on gender (alternating between male and female) and age criteria (alternating between 18 and 35 or more than 35) and interviewed with both their permission and that of the head of household (if different). No more than one member per household was interviewed. If the respondent of the right age and gender was not available, we went directly to the next household on the list. At the end of this cycle, depending on how many further interviews were required to complete fifteen responses, another household was selected, and the process repeated until the requisite number of surveys had been completed. All surveys were anonymous.

With respect to asking about vote choices, the survey replicated a technique used on the National Election Study conducted by the Center for the Study of Developing Society to ensure comparability of results. Each respondent was supplied with a dummy ballot with the party's name and symbol and was asked to put the ballot in a sealed ballot box that was only opened after leaving the village (a respondent ID number was placed on each ballot to match it with the corresponding completed survey). Last, the survey in Chhattisgarh was carried out in Hindi (Chhattisgarh version translated by the author from the English version reproduced here) and in Kerala was carried out in Malayalam (translated by Dr. Sajad Ibrahim, the Department of Political Science, University of Kerala, Thiruvananthapuram).

Agra: As the survey in Agra was conducted in an urban setting, a slightly different sampling procedure was utilized. Each slum area (Jagdishpura, Shastripuram, Tajganj, and Shahganj) was divided into four equal-sized quadrants. Within each quadrant, a location was chosen at random, toward the middle of the slum, as the starting point. From that point, individual households were selected using the left-hand rule, skipping two dwellings between each interview. Again, only one respondent was selected within each household, and 25 respondents were selected within each quadrant (for a total of 100 respondents per slum area). Interviewees within households were again selected based on the gender and age-based criteria used in Kerala and Chhattisgarh. The survey instrument was again worded in Hindi, with additional questions for the UP questionnaire translated from English by Dr. Mirza Beg (Department of Political Science, Aligarh Muslim University, Aligarh).

2. Response Rates

Chhattisgarh (4 districts, 24 villages):

A. *Completed*:	360	
B. *Refused*:	169	
C. *Not at home*:	107	
D. *Communication/Language issues*:	24	
E. *Ineligible (No one of required gender/age)*:	62	
Response Rate (A/ A+B+C+D):		**54.54%**

Kerala (3 districts, 18 villages):

A. *Completed*:	262	
B. *Refused*:	112	
C. *Not at home*:	168	
D. *Communication/Language issues*:	40	
E. *Ineligible (No one of required gender/age)*:	71	
Response Rate (A/ A+B+C+D):		**45.02%**

Uttar Pradesh (Agra city, 4 slum areas):

A. *Completed*:	400	
B. *Refused*:	91	
C. *Not at home*:	73	
D. *Communication/Language issues*:	8	
E. *Ineligible (No one of required gender/age)*:	89	
Response Rate (A/ A+B+C+D):		**60.51%**

3. Sample Survey Instrument for Chhattisgarh (Kerala and Uttar Pradesh Survey Instruments Are Available in the Online Supplement)

Chhattisgarh Survey Questionnaire

District_____   Respondent Number: _____
Village Name_____

Interviewer's Introduction:
I have come from New Delhi and am working for a university located abroad that is interviewing people across Chhattisgarh as part of a study of voter choices here. This survey is an independent study for research and is not linked with any political party or government agency. You will not be asked for your name, and none of the information you give will be linked to you in any way. Please spare a few minutes to help us with our study.

1. Who did you vote for in the 2003 Vidhan Sabha Elections? Please mark your vote on this slip and put it in this box. (Supply dummy ballot and explain the procedure.)
2. Who did you vote for in the 1998 Vidhan Sabha election? Please mark your vote on this slip and put it in this box.
3. Did a candidate/party worker or canvasser come to your house during the campaign to ask for your vote?
     2. Yes   1. No   8. Don't remember
3a. If yes, do you remember for which party/alliance? (Circle all that apply)
     1. Congress   2. BJP   3. BSP   4. Other
     5. None   8. Don't remember
4. In deciding whom to vote for, whose opinion mattered to you most?
     1. Spouse   2. Other family members
     3. Caste community leaders   4. Friends/neighbours
     5. No one   6. Others   8. Don't know
5. While voting, what is the most important consideration for you, the candidate, your party, your caste community's interest or something else?
     1. Candidate   2. Party   3. Caste Community
     4. Something Else   8. Don't Know
6. For you, in this election, which were the biggest/most important issues?

(Record exactly in the order mentioned and probe for 2nd and 3rd response)
     1. _____
     2. _____
     3. _____

7. In your opinion, which party was the best at:

	Congress	BJP	BSP	Other	Don't Know
a. Curbing Corruption	1	2	3	4	8
b. Had Better Leaders	1	2	3	4	8
c. Providing Employment	1	2	3	4	8
d. Promoting Development	1	2	3	4	8

8. Other than political parties, are you a member of any religious/caste organization or association?
   1. No   2. Yes   8. Don't Know
8a. If yes, which ones? _____
9. Aside from caste and religious organizations, do you belong to any other associations like co-operatives, farmer's associations, or trade unions?
   1. No   2. Yes   8. Don't Know
9a. If yes, which ones? _____
10. In the past five years, has your financial situation improved, stayed the same, or got worse?
    1. Deteriorated   2. Stayed the same   3. Improved
    8. Don't know
11. Now I will ask you about a few religious activities. You tell me how often you practice them daily, weekly, only on festivals, or never?

	Daily	Weekly	On festivals	Never
a. Prayer (puja/namaz, etc.)	4	3	2	1
b. Visiting temple, mosque, church, gurudwara, etc.	4	3	2	1

12. Now I will read out a few options. Tell me to what extent you agree with these options – fully agree, somewhat agree, somewhat disagree, or fully disagree?

	Fully Agree	Somewhat Agree	Somewhat Disagree	Fully Disagree	Don't Know
a. One should vote the same way one's caste community votes.	4	3	2	1	8
b. On the site of *Babri Masjid* only Ram Temple should be built.	4	3	2	1	8
c. The problems and needs of Muslims in India have been neglected.	4	3	2	1	8
d. Religious conversions should be banned.	4	3	2	1	8
e. Caste community is more important than religious community.	4	3	2	1	8

13. Did you ever take part in a protest of any kind with members of your caste community?
    0. No   1. Yes   8. Don't Know
14. How happy are you with the performance of your local MLA?
    1. Not Happy   2. Little Happy   3. Quite Happy
    4. Very Happy   8. Don't Know
15. I am going to read you the name of a few organizations. Please tell me if you have taken part in their activities, and what you think of the work they are doing:

	Opinion of Work?	Took part in?
a. Rashtriya Swayamsevak Sangh (RSS)	3. Very good work 2. Good work 1. Neither good nor bad work 0. Poor work	1. Yes 0. No
b. Seva Bharati/ Vanvasi Kalyan Ashram (VKA)	3. Very good work 2. Good work 1. Neither good nor bad work 0. Poor work	1. Yes 0. No
c. Bharatiya Kisan Sangh	3. Very good work 2. Good work 1. Neither good nor bad work 0. Poor work	1. Yes 0. No
d. Bharatiya Mazdoor Sangh	3. Very good work 2. Good work 1. Neither good nor bad work 0. Poor work	1. Yes 0. No

Personal Information:

B1. Age: _____
B2. Gender:
    1. Male   2. Female
B3. Education Level: _____
B4. Jati: _____

B5. Caste Group:
    1. SC
    2. ST
    3. OBC
    4. Other
B6. Religion:
    1. Hindu   2. Muslim   3. Christian   4. Sikh
    5. Other   8. Don't Know
B7. Size of land owned: _____ acres
B8. I will read you a list – please tell me which of the following do you see
    yourself as **most** importantly: (IF MORE THAN ONE THEN MARK
    THE ORDER):

  If respondent is SC:
    1. Indian   2. Scheduled Caste   3. Harijan   4. Dalit
    5. Hindu/Muslim/Christian/Sikh   6. Chhattisgarhi
  If respondent is ST:
    1. Indian   2. Scheduled Tribe   3. Vanvasi   4. Adivasi
    5. Hindu/Muslim/Christian/Sikh   6. Chhattisgarhi

B9. What is your household's approximate monthly income?
    1. Below Rs. 1000
    2. Between Rs. 1001–2000

    3. Between Rs. 2001–3000
    4. Between Rs. 3001–4000

    5. Between Rs. 4001–5000
    6. Between Rs. 5001 to 10,000

    7. Above Rs. 10,000

Appendix D Information Available in Online Supplement

1. Section A: Additional tables and figures
   a. Table A.1: State effects from Table 2.1
   b. Table A.2: State effects from Table 3.1
   c. Table A.3: Results are not replicated among poor Muslims or Christians
   d. Table A.4: Party organizations are not responsible for non-elite recruitment
   e. Table A.5: Results are robust to controlling for Personal Satisfaction with BJP
   f. Table A.6: Results are robust to controlling for positive ratings of BJP
   g. Table A.7: Results show organizational effects correlate with switching to BJP between 1999 and 2004, not voting for BJP in 1999, and late deciders voting and switching to vote for the BJP
   h. Table A.8: Results robust to using alternative measure of communalism
   i. Table A.9: Exact matching analysis
   j. Table A.10: Does membership increase BJP support more in states with dense welfare networks?
   k. Figure A.1: Service*Member interaction effects after logit
   l. Figure A.2: Z-statistics of Service*Member interaction effects
   m. Table A.11a: Is membership driven by unions?
   n. Table A.11b: Is membership driven by caste associations?
   o. Table A.11c: Is membership driven by religious associations?

2. Section B: Additional survey sample instruments
   a. Kerala Survey Questionnaire
   b. Uttar Pradesh Survey Questionnaire

3. Section C: Why study Dalits and Adivasis together?

References

Books, Articles, Chapters, and Papers

Abu-Lughod, Lila. "Movie Stars and Islamic Moralism in Egypt." *Social Text*, No. 42 (Spring 1995): 53–67.

Acemoglu, Daron and James Robinson. *Economic Origins of Dictatorship and Democracy*. Cambridge: Cambridge University Press, 2006.

Achen, Christopher. "Let's Put Garbage-Can Regressions and Garbage-Can Probits Where They Belong." *Conflict Management and Peace Science* 22, 4 (January 2005): 327–39.

Ahir, D. C. *Dr. Babasaheb Ambedkar, Writings and Speeches*, Vol. 8. New Delhi: B. R. Publishing Corporation, 2007.

Ahuja, Amit and Pradeep Chhibber. "Why the Poor Vote in India: 'If I Don't Vote, I Am Dead to the State.'" *Studies in Comparative International Development* (June 2012): 1–22.

Aldrich, John. *Why Parties? The Origin and Transformation of Party Politics in America*. Chicago: University of Chicago Press, 1995.

Alesina, Alberto. "Credibility and Policy Convergence in a Two-Party System with Rational Voters." *American Economic Review* 78, 4 (September 1988): 796–805.

Ambedkar, B. R. *The Annihilation of Caste*. Bombay: B. R. Kadrekar, 1937.

Ananta, Aris, Evi Nurvidya Arifin, and Leo Suryadinata. *Emerging Democracy in Indonesia*. Singapore: Institute of Southeast Asian Studies, 2005.

Anderson, Benedict. *Imagined Communities*. London: Verso, 1983.

Anderson, Walter K. and Shridhar D. Damle. *The Brotherhood in Saffron: The Rashtriya Swayamsevak Sangh and Hindu Revivalism*. New Delhi: Vistaar Publications, 1987.

Angrist, Joshua and Jorn-Steffen Pischke. *Mostly Harmless Econometrics*. Princeton: Princeton University Press, 2009.

Auyero, Javier. *Poor People's Politics*. Durham: Duke University Press, 2000.

Azem, Ahmad Jamil. "The Islamic Action Front Party," in Hani Hourani. *Islamic Groups in Jordan*. Amman: Al-Urdin Al-Jadid Research Center, 1997:95–144.

Bacchetta, Paola. "Hindu Nationalist Women as Ideologues," in Christophe Jaffrelot, ed. *The Sangh Parivar*. New Delhi: Oxford University Press, 2005: 108–47.

Bakshi, Rajni. "A Year after Niyogi's Murder." *Economic and Political Weekly* 27, 40 (1992): 2157.

Baland, Jean-Marie and James Robinson. "How Does Vote-Buying Shape the Economy?," in Frederic Schaffer, ed. *Elections for Sale*. Boulder: Lynne Reinner, 2007: 123–41.

Banerjee, Abhijit and Esther Duflo. "Improving Health Care Delivery in India." Working paper, November 2009 draft.

Bartels, Larry. *Unequal Democracy: The Political Economy of the New Gilded Age*. Princeton: Princeton University Press, 2008.

Bartolini, Stefano and Peter Mair. *Identity, Competition, and Electoral Availability: The Stabilization of European Electorates 1885–1985*. Cambridge: Cambridge University Press, 1990.

Baxter, Craig. *The Jana Sangh: A Biography of an Indian Political Party*. Philadelphia: University of Pennsylvania Press, 1969.

Beck, Nathaniel and Jonathan Katz. "What to Do (and Not to Do) with Time-Series Cross-Section Data." *The American Political Science Review*, 89, 3 (September 1995): 634–47.

Becker, Gary. "A Theory of Competition among Pressure Groups for Political Influence." *The Quarterly Journal of Economics* 98, 3 (August 1983): 371–400.

Becker, Sascha O. and Marco Caliendo. "Sensitivity Analysis for Average Treatment Effects." *Stata Journal* 7, 1 (2007): 71–83.

Berenschot, Ward. *Riot Politics*. London: Hurst and Company, 2011.

Berman, Sheri. "Civil Society and the Collapse of the Weimar Republic." *World Politics* 49, 3 (April 1997): 401–29.

Berthet, Samuel. "Chhattisgarh: Tribals, OBCs, Reformist Movements and Mainstream Politics," in Christophe Jaffrelot, and Sanjay Kumar, eds. *Rise of Plebians: The Changing Face of the Indian Legislative Assemblies*. New Delhi: Routledge, 2008: 326–58.

Blaydes, Lisa. *Elections and Distributive Politics in Mubarak's Egypt*. Cambridge: Cambridge University Press, 2010.

Boix, Carles. *Democracy and Redistribution*. Cambridge: Cambridge University Press, 2003.

Bonoli, Giuliani and Martin Powell. *Social Democratic Party Policies in Contemporary Europe*. London: Routledge, 2004.

Brass, Paul. "The Rise of the BJP and the Future of Party Politics in Uttar Pradesh," in Harold Gould and Sumit Ganguly, eds. *India Votes: Alliance Politics and the Ninth and Tenth General Elections*. Boulder: Westview Press, 1993.

Brass, Paul. *An Indian Political Life: Charan Singh and Congress Politics, 1937–1961*. London: Sage, 2011.

Brown, Nathan and Amr Hamzawy. *Between Religion and Politics*. Washington, DC: United States Institute of Peace, 2010.

Brown, Nathan and Amr Hamzawy. "The Draft Party Platform of the Egyptian Muslim Brotherhood: Foray into Political Integration or Retreat into Old Positions." Washington: Carnegie Endowment for International Peace.

Burrowes, Robert D. *Historical Dictionary of Yemen*. Lanham: Scarecrow Press, 2010.

Calvo, Ernesto and Victoria Murillo. "Who Delivers? Partisan Clients in the Argentine Electoral Market." *American Journal of Political Science* 48, 4 (2004): 742–57.

Cammett, Melani and Lauren MacLean. "Introduction: The Political Consequences of Non-state Social Welfare in the Global South." *Studies in Comparative International Development* 46, No. 1 (January 2011): 1–21.

Cammett, Melani and Sukriti Issar. "Bricks and Mortar Clientelism: Sectarianism and the Logics of Welfare Allocation in Lebanon." *World Politics* 62, 3 (July 2010): 381–421.

Carapico, Sheila. "Elections and Mass Politics in Yemen." *Middle East Report* 185 (November 1993): 2–6.

Carapico, Sheila. *Civil Society in Yemen*. Cambridge: Cambridge University Press, 1998.

Cayeros, Alberto Diaz, Frederico Estevez, and Beatriz Magaloni. "The Core Voter Model: Some Evidence from Mexico." Working Paper, April 2010 draft.

Cayeros, Alberto Diaz and Beatriz Magaloni. "The Politics of Public Spending: The Logic of Vote-Buying." Draft Manuscript, 2010 draft.

Chandhoke, Neera. "Case Study of the Chhattisgarh Mukti Morcha," in R. Tandon, and R. Mohanty, eds. *Does Civil Society Matter*. New Delhi: Sage Publications, 2003.

Chandra, Kanchan. *Why Ethnic Parties Succeed*. Cambridge: Cambridge University Press, 2004.

Chaudhury, Pradipta. "The 'Creamy Layer': Political Economy of Reservations." *Economic and Political Weekly* (May 15, 2004).

Chhibber, Pradeep. "State Policy, Rent Seeking, and the Success of a Religious Party in Algeria." *Journal of Politics* 58, 1 (February 1996): 126–48.

Chhibber, Pradeep. "Who Voted for the Bharatiya Janata Party?" *British Journal of Political Science* 27, 4 (October 1997): 631–9.

Chhibber, Pradeep. *Democracy without Associations: Transformations of the Party System and Social Cleavages in India*. Ann Arbor: University of Michigan Press, 1999.

Chhibber, Pradeep and Irfan Nooruddin. "Do Party Systems Count? The Number of Parties and Government Performance in the Indian States," *Comparative Political Studies* 37, 2 (2004): 152–87.

Chhibber, Pradeep and Ken Kollman. "Party Aggregation and the Number of Parties in India and the United States." *American Political Science Review* 92, 2 (June 1998): 329–42.

Chiriyankandath, James. "Hindu Nationalism and Regional Political Culture in India: A Study of Kerala." *Nationalism and Ethnic Politics* 2, 1 (Spring 1996): 44–66.

Chiriyankandath, James. "Bounded Nationalism: Kerala and the Social Regional Limits of Hindutva," in Thomas Blom Hansen and Christophe Jaffrelot, eds. *The BJP and the Compulsions of Politics in India*. New Delhi: Oxford University Press, 2001: 202–27.

Chubb, Judith. "The Social Bases of an Urban Political Machine." *Political Science Quarterly* 96, 1 (Spring 1981): 107–25.

Clark, Janine. *Islam, Charity and Activism*. Bloomington: Indiana University Press, 2004.

Clark, William and Matt Golder. "Rehabilitating Duverger's Theory: Testing the Mechanical and Strategic Modifying Effects of Electoral Laws." *Comparative Political Studies* 39 (2006): 679–708.

Converse, Philip. "Of Time and Partisan Stability." *Comparative Political Studies*, 2, 2 (July 1969): 139–71.

Corbridge, Stuart. "Competing Inequalities: The Scheduled Tribes and the Reservations System in India's Jharkhand." *The Journal of Asian Studies* 59, 1 (February 2000): 62–85.

Corstange, Daniel. "Institutions and Ethnic Politics in Lebanon and Yemen." Dissertation Manuscript (2008).

Cox, Gary and Mathew D. McCubbins. "Electoral Politics as a Redistributive Game." *Journal of Politics* 48 (May 1986): 370–89.

Das Gupta, Jyotindra. *Language Conflict and National Development: Group Politics and National Language Policy in India*. Berkeley: University of California Press, 1970.

De La O, Ana L. and Jonathan A. Rodden. "Does Religion Distract the Poor? Income and Issue Voting Around the World." *Comparative Political Studies* 41, 4/5 (April-May 2008): 437–76.

Desai, Manali. "Party Formation, Political Power, and the Capacity for Reform: Comparing Left Parties in Kerala and West Bengal, India." *Social Forces* 80, 1 (September 2001): 37–60.

Desai, Manali. *State Formation and Radical Democracy in India*. London: Routledge, 2007.

Dixit, Avinash and John Londregan. "The Determinants of Success of Special Interests in Redistributive Politics." *Journal of Politics* 58 (November 1996): 1132–55.

Downs, Anthony. *An Economic Theory of Democracy*. New York: HarperCollins, 1957.

Dresch, Paul. *A History of Modern Yemen*. Cambridge: Cambridge University Press, 2000.

Dresch, Paul and Bernard Haykel. "Stereotypes and Political Styles: Islamists and Tribesfolk in Yemen." *International Journal of Middle East Studies* 27, 4 (November 1995): 405–31.

Dreze, Jean and Reetika Khera. "Water for the Leeward India." *Outlook*, 2014, available at http://www.outlookindia.com/article.aspx?289801.

Dreze, Jean and Amartya Sen. *India: Development and Participation*. New Delhi: Oxford University Press, 1996.

Durkheim, Emile. *The Elementary Forms of Religious Life*. New York: Free Press, 1912 (translation by Karen Fields, 1995).

Duverger, Maurice. *Political Parties*. New York: Wiley, 1954.

Eckstein, Harry. "Case Studies and Theory in Political Ccience," in F. I. Greenstein and N. W. Polsby, eds. *Handbook of Political Science*. Reading, MA: Addison-Wesley, 1975: Vol. 7, pp. 94–137.

Elder, Joeseph. "Land Consolidation in an Indian Village: A Case Study of the Consolidation of Holdings Act in Uttar Pradesh." *Economic Development and Cultural Change* 11, 1 (October 1962): 16–40.

Fandy, Mamoun. "Egypt's Islamic Group: Regional Revenge?" *The Middle East Journal*, 48, 4 (Autumn 1994): 607–25.

Fealy, Greg. "Front Stage with the PKS." *Inside Indonesia* 101 (July-September 2010).

Frank, Thomas. *What's the Matter with Kansas*. New York: Metropolitan Press, 2004.

Franke, Richard W. and Barbara H. Chasin. "The Kerala Experiment: Development without Growth." *Technology Review* 95, 3 (1990): 42–51.

Frankel, Francine. *India's Political Economy 1947–2004*. New Delhi: Oxford University Press, 2005.

Froerer, Peggy. "Emphasizing Others: The Emergence of Hindu Nationalism in a Central Indian Tribal Community." *Journal of the Royal Anthropological Institute* 12 (2006): 39–59.

Froerer, Peggy. *Religious Division and Social Conflict*. New Delhi: Orient Longman, 2007.

Gandhi, M. K. *Caste Must Go and the Sin of Untouchability* (compiled by R. K. Prabhu). Ahmedabad: Navajivan, 1964.

Gatade, Subhash. "Subverting the Sudra-Ati Sudra Revolution: The Uttar Pradesh Way," in Anand Teltumbde, ed. *Hindutva and Dalits*. Delhi: Samya, 2005: 187–207.

Gelman, Andrew, David Park, Boris Shor, and Jeronimo Cortina. *Red State, Blue State, Rich State, Poor State*. Princeton: Princeton University Press, 2008.

George, K. K. *Limits to the Kerala Model of Development: An Analysis of Fiscal Crisis and Its Implications*. Thiruvananthapuram: Center for Development Studies, 1993.

Gerring, John. "Is There a (Viable) Crucial-Case Method?" *Comparative Political Studies*, 40, 3 (March 2007): 231–53.

Gibson, Edward. *Class and Conservative Parties*. Baltimore: Johns Hopkins University Press, 1996.

Gilens, Martin. "Inequality and Democratic Responsiveness." *Public Opinion Quarterly* 69, 5 (2005): 778–96.

Golwalkar, Madhav Shadashiv. *We or Our Nationhood Defined*. Nagpur: Bharat Publications, 1939.

Golwalkar, Madhav Shadashiv. *Bunch of Thoughts*. Bangalore: Vikrama Prakashan, 1966.

Gooptu, Nandini. "Caste and Labor: Untouchable Social Movements in Urban Uttar Pradesh in the Early 20th Century," in Peter G. Robb, ed. *Dalit Movements and the Meanings of Labour in India*. Delhi: Oxford University Press 1993: 277–98.

Gooptu, Nandini. *The Politics of the Urban Poor in Early Twentieth-Century India*. Cambridge: Cambridge University Press, 2005.

Graham, Bruce. *Hindu Nationalism and Indian Politics: The Origins and Development of the Bharatiya Jana Sangh*. Cambridge: Cambridge University Press, 1990.

Graham, Bruce. "The Leadership and Organization of the Jana Sangh: 1957 to 1967," in Christophe Jaffrelot, ed. *The Sangh Parivar*. New Delhi: Oxford University Press, 2005: 225–67.

Green, Donald, Bradley Palmquist, and Eric Schickler. *Partisan Hearts and Minds*. New Haven: Yale University Press, 2002.

Grossman, Gene and Elhanan Helpman. "Electoral Competition and Special Interest Politics." *The Review of Economic Studies* 63, 2 (April 1996): 265–86.

Guha, Sohini. "Assymmetric Representation and the BSP in U.P." *Seminar* 571 (March 2007).

Gunther, Richard and Larry Diamond. "Species of Political Parties." *Party Politics* 9, 2 (2003): 167–99.

Habib, Irfan. "The Left and the National Movement." *Social Scientist* 26, 5/6 (May-June 1998): 3–33.

Hagiopan, Frances. "Parties and Voters in Emerging Democracies," in Carles Boix and Susan Stokes, eds. *The Oxford Handbook of Comparative Politics*. Oxford: Oxford University Press, 2007: 582–603.

Hamayotsu, Kikue. "Crisis of Identity in PAS and Beyond." *The Round Table* 99, 407 (April 2010): 163–75.

Hamayotsu, Kikue. "Beyond Faith and Identity: Mobilizing Islamic Youth in Democratic Indonesia." *The Pacific Review* 24, 2 (2011a): 225–47.

Hamayotsu, Kikue. "The Political Rise of the Prosperous Justice Party in Post-Authoritarian Indonesia." *Asian Survey* 51, 5 (2011b): 971–92.

Hansen, Thomas Blom. *The Saffron Wave*. Princeton: Princeton University Press, 1999.

Hansen, Thomas and Christophe Jaffrelot. "Introduction: The Rise to Power of the BJP," in Thomas Blom Hansen and Christophe Jaffrelot, eds. *The BJP and the Compulsions of Politics in India*. New Delhi: Oxford University Press, 2001: 1–21.

Hasan, Noorhaidi. "Islamist Party, Electoral Politics, and *Da'wa* Mobilization among Youth." RSIS Working Paper No. 194, October 2009.

Hasan, Zoya, ed. *Parties and Party Politics*. New Delhi: Oxford University Press, 2002a.

Hasan, Zoya. "Representation and Redistribution: The New Lower Caste Politics of North India," in Hasan, Zoya, ed. *Parties and Party Politics*. New Delhi: Oxford University Press, 2002b: 370–96.

Heath, Oliver and Sanjay Kumar. "Why Did Dalits Desert the Bahujan Samaj Party in Uttar Pradesh." *Economic and Political Weekly*, 47, 28 (July 14, 2012): 41–49.

Hebsur, Raghavendra Keshavarao. "Karnataka: The Surge of Saffron," in Paul Wallace and Ramashray Roy, eds. *India's 2009 Elections*. New Delhi: Sage, 2011, 270–285.

Heller, Patrick. *The Labor of Development*. Ithaca: Cornell University Press, 1999.

Heller, Patrick. "Degrees of Democracy: Some Comparative Lessons from India." *World Politics*, 52, 4 (July 2000): 484–519.

Herring, Ronald. *Land to the Tiller*. New Haven: Yale University Press, 1983.

Herring, Ronald. "Stealing Congress' Thunder: The Rise to Power of a Communist Movement in South India," in Kay Lawson and Peter Merkl, eds. *When Parties Fail: Emerging Alternative Organizations*. Princeton: Princeton University Press, 1988: 389–418.

Herring, Ronald and Rina Agarwala. "Restoring Agency to Class: Puzzles from the Subcontinent." *Critical Asian Studies* 38, 4 (2006): 323–56.

Ho, D., K. Imai, G. King, and E. Stuart. "Matching as Nonparametric Preprocessing for Reducing Model Dependence in Parametric Causal Inference." *Political Analysis* 15 (January 2007): 199–236.

Ho, D., K. Imai, G. and King, E. Stuart. "Matchit: Nonparametric Preprocessing for Parametric Causal Inference." Software documentation, February 2, 2009.

Honaker, James, Gary King, and Matthew Blackwell. "Amelia II: A Program for Missing Data." February 19, 2009.

Horowitz, Donald. *Ethnic Groups in Conflict*. Berkeley: University of California Press, 1985.

Huber, John. "Religious Belief, Religious Participation, and Social Policy Attitudes in Countries." Working paper, September 29, 2005 draft.

Huber, John. "Measuring Ethnic Voting: The Political Context and the Politicization of Ethnicity." Working Paper, January 13, 2011 draft.

Huber, John and Piero Stanig. "Individual Income and Voting for Redistribution." Working Paper, September 9, 2009 draft.

Huber, John and Piero Stanig. "Church-State Separation and Redistribution." Working Paper, September 20, 2010 draft.

Hwang, Julie. "Islamic Identity, Yes, Islamist Parties, No: The Mainstreaming of Political Islam and Its Challenge for Islamist Parties," in Michelle Williams, ed. *The Multicultural Dilemma*. London: Routledge, 2013, 84–99.

Illiah, Kancha. *Why I Am Not a Hindu*. Calcutta: Samya, 1996.

Ingelhart, Ronald. "The Silent Revolution in Europe: Intergenerational Change in Post-Industrial Societies." *American Political Science Review* 65, 4 (December 1971): 991–1017.

Inglehart, Ronald and Scott Flanagan. "Value Change in Industrial Societies." *American Political Science Review* 81, 4 (December 1987): 1289–1319.

Isaac, Thomas. "The National Movement and Communist Party in Kerala." *Social Scientist* 14, 8/9 (August-September 1986): 59–80.

Islam, Shamsul. "Dalits in Theory and Practice of Hindutva," in Anand Teltumbde, ed. *Hindutva and Dalits*. Delhi: Samya, 2005, 23–45.

Iverson, Torben and David Soskice. "Electoral Institutions and the Politics of Coalitions: Why Some Democracies Redistribute More Than Others." *American Political Science Review* 100, 2 (May 2006): 165–81.

Jaffrelot, Christophe. *The Hindu Nationalist Movement in India*. New York: Columbia University Press, 1993.

Jaffrelot, Christophe. "Sanskritization vs. Ethnicization in India." *Asian Survey* 40, 5 (September 2000): 756–66.

Jaffrelot, Christophe. "The Sangh Parivar Between Sanskritization and Social Engineering," in Thomas Blom Hansen and Christophe Jaffrelot, eds. *The BJP and the Compulsions of Politics in India*, New Delhi: Oxford University Press, 2001, pp. 22–71.

Jaffrelot, Christophe. *India's Silent Revolution*. New York: Columbia University Press, 2003.

Jaffrelot, Christophe, ed. *The Sangh Parivar*. New Delhi: Oxford University Press, 2005.

Jaffrelot, Christophe, ed. *Hindu Nationalism: A Reader*. New Delhi: Permanent Black, 2007.

Jaffrelot, Christophe. "Why Should We Vote?" in Christophe Jaffrelot and Peter Van de Weer, eds. *Patterns of Middle Class Consumption in India and China*. New Delhi: Sage, 2008: 35–54.

Jaffrelot, Christophe. *Religion, Caste, and Politics in India*. London: Hurst and Company, 2010.

Jaffrelot, Christophe. "Gujarat Elections: The Sub-Text of Modi's 'Hattrick'– High Tech Populism and the 'Neo-middle Class.'" *Studies in Indian Politics*, 1, 1 (June 2013): 79–95.

Jaffrelot, Christophe, Jasmone Zerinini Brotel, and Jayati Chaturvedi. "The BJP and the Rise of Dalits in Uttar Pradesh," in Roger Jeffery and Jens Lerche, eds. *Social and Political Change in Uttar Pradesh: European Perspectives*. New Delhi: Manohar, 2003: 151–80.

Jalal, Ayesha. *Democracy and Authoritarianism in South Asia*. Cambridge: Cambridge University Press, 2005.

Jamal, Amaney and Mark Tessler. "Attitudes in the Arab World." *Journal of Democracy* 19, 1 (January 2008): 97–110.

Jayaprasad, K. *RSS and Hindu Nationalism: Inroads into a Leftist Stronghold*. New Delhi: Deep and Deep Publications, 1991.

Jeffrey, Craig, Patricia Jeffery, and Robert Jeffery. "Dalit Revolution? New Politicians in Uttar Pradesh, India." *The Journal of Asian Studies*, 67, 4 (Nov. 2008): 1365–96.

Johnston, Hank. "Verification and Proof in Frame and Discourse Analysis," in Bert Klandermans and Suzanne Staggenborg, eds. *Methods of Social Movement Research*. Minneapolis: University of Minnesota Press, 2002: 62, 91.

Jones, Kenneth W. *Socio-religious Movements in British India*. Cambridge: Cambridge University Press, 1989.

Kadera, Kelly M. and Sara M. Mitchell. "Heeding Ray's Advice: An Exegesis on Control Variables in Systemic Democratic Peace Research." *Conflict Management and Peace Science* 22, 4 (January 2005): 311–26.

Kalyvas, Stathis. *The Rise of Christian Democracy in Europe*. Ithaca: Cornell University Press, 1996.

Kalyvas, Stathis. "Commitment Problems in Emerging Democracies." *Comparative Politics* 32, 4 (2000): 379–99.

Karabarbounis, Loukas. "One Dollar, One Vote." *The Economic Journal* 21, 553 (June 2011): 621–51.

Kertzer, David. *Comrades and Christians*. Cambridge: Cambridge University Press, 1980.

Khemani, Stuti. "Political Cycles in a Developing Economy: Effect of Elections in the Indian States." *Journal of Development Economics* 73 (2004): 125–54.

Khera, Reetika. "Mid-Day Meals in Primary Schools: Achievements and Challenges." *Economic and Political Weekly*, 41, 46 (November 18, 2006): 4742–50.

King, Gary, James Honaker, Anne Joseph, and Kenneth Scheve. "Analyzing Incomplete Political Science Data: An Alternative Algorithm for Multiple Imputation." *American Political Science Review* 95, 1 (March 2001): 49–69.

King, Gary, Michael Tomz, and Jason Wittenberg. "Making the Most of Statistical Analyses: Improving Interpretation and Presentation." *American Journal of Political Science* 44, 2 (April 2000): 347–61.

Kitschelt, Herbert. "Linkages between Citizens and Politicians in Democratic Politics." *Comparative Political Studies* 33, 6/7 (August-September 2000): 845–79.

Kitschelt, Herbert. "Movement Parties," in Richard S. Katz and William J. Crotty, eds. *Handbook of Party Politics*. London: Sage, 2006: 278–89.

Kitschelt, Herbert. "Party Competition in India: Continued Weak Programmatic Structuration of Partisan Alternatives." Unpublished report, 2011 draft.

Kitschelt, Herbert and Steven Wilkinson, eds. *Patrons, Clients, and Policies: Patterns of Democratic Accountability and Political Competition*. New York: Cambridge University Press, 2007.

Kochanek, Stanley. *The Congress Party in India*. Princeton: Princeton University Press, 1968.

Kochanek, Stanley. "Mrs. Gandhi's Pyramid," in Zoya Hasan, ed. *Parties and Party Politics*. New Delhi: Oxford University Press, 2002: 76–106.

Kohli, Atul. "The State and Agrarian Policy." *Journal of Commonwealth and Comparative Politics*, 20, 3 (1982): 309–28.

Kohli, Atul. *The State and Poverty in India*. Cambridge: Cambridge University Press, 1987.

Kohli, Atul. *Democracy and Discontent*. Cambridge: Cambridge University Press, 1990.

Kohli, Atul, ed. *The Success of India's Democracy*. Cambridge: Cambridge University Press, 2001.

Kohli, Atul. *State-Directed Development*. Cambridge: Cambridge University Press, 2006.

Kooiman, Dick. *Conversion and Social Equality in India*. New Delhi: Manohar, 1989.

Kothari, Rajni. "The Congress 'System' in India." *Asian Survey* 4, 12 (December 1964): 1161–73.

Kremer, Michael, Nazmul Chaudhury, F. Halsey Rogers, Karthik Muralidharan, and Jeffrey Hammer. "Teacher Absence in India: A Snapshot." *Journal of European Economic Association* 3, 2/3 (April 2005): 658–67.

Krishna, Anirudh. "What's Happening to Caste? A View from Some North Indian Villages." *The Journal of Asian Studies* 62, 4 (November 2003): 1171–93.

Kumar, Sanjay. "Patterns of Political Participation: Trends and Perspective." *Economic and Political Weekly* (September 26, 2009a): 47–51.

Kumar, Sanjay. "Training Workshop: National Election Study 2009." Unpublished paper, 2009b.

Lakha, Salim. "From Swadeshi to Globalization: The Bharatiya Janata Party's Shifting Economic Agenda," in John McGuire and Ian Copland, eds. *Hindu Nationalism and Governance*. New Delhi: Oxford University Press, 2007: 106–31.

Lemercinier, Genevieve. *Religion and Ideology in Kerala*. Louvain: University Catholique de Louvain, 1983.

Lerche, Jens. "Politics of the Poor: Agriculture Labourers and Political Transformations in North India." *Journal of Peasant Studies* 26, 2 (1999): 182–241.

Leuven, Edwin and Barbara Sianes. "PSMATCH2: Stata Module to Perform Full Mahalanobis and Propensity Score Matching, Common Support Graphing, and Covariate Imbalance Testing. Statistical Software Components S432001, Boston College Department of Economics, 2003.

Levitsky, Steven. *Transforming Labor-Based Parties in Latin America*. Cambridge: Cambridge University Press, 2003.

Levitsky, Steven. "From Populism to Clientelism? The Transformation of Labor-Based Party Linkages in Latin America," in Herbert Kitschelt and Steven Wilkinson, eds. *Patrons, Clients, and Policies: Patterns of Democratic Accountability and Political Competition*. New York: Cambridge University Press, 2007: 206–26.

Lia, Brynjar. *The Society of Muslim Brothers in Egypt*. Reading: Garnet, 1998.

Liang Kung-Lee and Scott Zeger. "Longitudinal Data Analysis Using Generalized Linear Models." *Biometrika* 73, 1 (April 1986): 13–22.

Lieberman, Evan. "Nested Analysis as a Mixed-Method Strategy for Comparative Research." *American Political Science Review* 99, 3 (August 2005): 435–52.

Linz, Juan and Alfred Stepan. *Problems of Democratic Consolidation*. Baltimore: Johns Hopkins University Press, 1996.

Linzer, Drew. "The Left-Right Ideological Spectrum in Global Mass Opinion." Working Paper, 2010 draft.

Lipset, Seymour Martin. *Political Man*. Baltimore: Johns Hopkins University Press, 1981.

Lipset, Seymour Martin and Stein Rokkan. "Cleavage Structures, Party Systems, and Voter Alignments: An Introduction," in Lipset, Seymour Martin and Stein Rokkan, eds. *Party Systems and Voter Alignments: Cross-National Perspectives*. New York: Free Press, 1967: 1–56,

Lokniti Team. "National Election Study 2004." *Economic and Political Weekly* (December 18, 2004): 5373–81.

Long, Scott. "Group Comparisons in Logit and Probit Using Predicted Probabilities." Draft manuscript, 2009.

Longley, April. "The High Water Mark of Islamist Politics? The Case of Yemen." *Middle East Journal* 61, 2 (Spring 2007): 240–60.

Loomba, Ania. *Colonialism and Postcolonialism*. Oxon: Routledge, 2005.

Luna, Juan Pablo. "Segmented Party-Voter Linkages in Latin America: The Case of the UDI." *Journal of Latin American Studies* 42 (2010): 325–56.

Luna, Juan Pablo. "The Weakest Link: Inequality, Political Representation and Democracy in Latin America." Draft manuscript, 2011.

Machmudi, Yon. *Islamising Indonesia*. Canberra: ANU Press, 2008.

Madrid, Raul. "Indigenous Voters and Party System Fragmentation in Latin America," *Electoral Studies*, 24, 2 (April 2005): 689–707.

Madrid, Raul. "The Rise of Ethnopopulism in Latin America," *World Politics*, 60 (April 2008): 475–508.

Malouche, Dhafer, Lindsay Benstead, Ellen Lust, Gamal Soltane, and Jacob Wichmann. "Who Voted and Why? An Analysis of 'New' and 'Old' Voters in Tunisia and Egypt." Unpublished paper, 2013.

Manza, Jeff and Clem Brooks. "The Religious Factor in U.S. Presidential Elections, 1960–1992." *American Journal of Sociology* 103, 1 (1997): 38–81.

Magaloni, Beatriz. *Voting for Autocracy*. Cambridge: Cambridge University Press, 2007.

Mair, Peter and Cas Mudde. "The Party Family and Its Study." *Annual Review of Political Science* 1 (1998): 211–29.

Mair, Peter, Wolfgang Müller, and Fritz Plasser. *Political Parties and Electoral Change: Party Responses to Electoral Markets*. London: Sage, 2004.

Malaviya, Madan Mohan. "Presidential Address (1923)," in Christophe Jaffrelot, ed. *Hindu Nationalism: A Reader*. New Delhi: Permanent Black, 2007: 64–9.

Malkani, K.R. *The RSS Story*. New Delhi: Impex India, 1980.

Manor, James. "Pragmatic Progressives in Regional Politics: The Case of Devraj Urs." *Economic and Political Weeklyi*, 15, 5/7 (February 1980): 201–3, 205, 207, 209, 211, 213.

Marx, Karl. *A Contribution to the Critique of Hegel's Philosophy of Right*. Deutsch-Französische Jahrbücher, 1844 (translation by A. Jolin and J. O'Malley). Cambridge: Cambridge University Press, 1970.

Masoud, Tarek. "Why Islam Wins." Draft manuscript, 2010 version.

Masoud, Tarek. "Arabs Want Redistribution, So Why Don't They Vote Left?" Harvard Kennedy School Faculty Research Working Paper Series, 2013.

Mathur, Shubh. *The Everyday Life of Hindu Nationalism*. Gurgaon: Three Essays Collective, 2008.

Mawdsley, Emma. "Re-drawing the Body Politic: Federalism, Regionalism, and the Creation of New States in India." *Journal of Commonwealth and Comparative Politics* 40, 3 (2002): 34–54.

McAdam, Doug and Sidney Tarrow. "Ballots and Barricades: On the Reciprocal Relationship between Elections and Social Movements." *Perspectives on Politics* 8, 2 (June 2010): 529–42.

Medina, Luis Fernando and Susan Stokes. "Clientelism and Political Monopoly." Unpublished paper, 2002.

Meltzer, Allan and Scott Richard. "A Rational Theory of the Size of Government." *The Journal of Political Economy* 89, 5 (October 1981): 914–27.

Menon, Dilip. *Caste, Nationalism, and Communism in South India: Malabar 1900–1948*. Cambridge: Cambridge University Press, 1994.

Menon, Dilip. *The Blindness of Insight*. New Delhi: Navayana, 2006.

Menon, Kalyani. *Everyday Nationalism*. Philadelphia: University of Pennsylvania Press, 2010.

Merton, Robert K. *Social Theory and Social Structure*. New York: Free Press, 1949.

Middlebrook, Kevin. "Party Politics and Democratization in Mexico: The Partido Acción Nacional in Comparative Perspective," in Kevin Middlebrook, *Party Politics and the Struggles for Democracy in Mexico*. La Jolla: University of California San Diego Press, 2001: 3–46.

Mietzner, Marcus. "Comparing Indonesia's Party Systems of the 1950s and the Post-Suharto Era." *Journal of Southeast Asian Studies* 39, 3 (October 2008): 431–53.

Mietzner, Marcus. *Military Politics, Islam, and the State in Indonesia.* Singapore: ISEAS, 2009.

Milanovic, Branko. "The Median-Voter Hypothesis, Income Inequality, and Income Redistribution: An Empirical Test with the Required Data." *European Journal of Political Economy* 16, 3 (September 2000): 367–410.

Mitchell, Richard. *The Society of the Muslim Brothers.* Oxford: Oxford University Press, 1969.

Mueller, F. Max, ed. *The Laws of Manu.* New Delhi: Low Price Publication, 1996 (first edition 1886).

Mujani, Saiful and William Liddle. "Politics, Islam, and Public Opinion." *Journal of Democracy* 15, 1 (January 2004): 109–23.

Mujani, Saiful and William Liddle. "Voters and the New Indonesian Democracy," in Edward Aspinall and Marcus Mietzner, eds. *Problems of Democratisation in Indonesia.* Singapore: ISEAS Press, 2010: 75–99.

Nagaraj, D. R. *Flaming Feet and Other Essays.* New Delhi: Permanent Black, 2010: 23–60.

Namboodiripad, E. M. S. "Castes, Classes, and Parties in Modern Political Development." *Social Scientist* 6, 4 (November 1977): 3–25.

Nichter, Simeon. "Vote Buying or Turnout Buying." *American Political Science Review* 102, 1 (February 2008): 19–31.

Norris, Pippa. *Electoral Engineering: Voting Rules and Political Behavior.* New York: Cambridge University Press, 2004.

Norton, Augustus. *Hezbollah.* Princeton: Princeton University Press, 2007.

Norton, Edward, Hua Wang, and Chunrong Ai. "Computing Interaction Effects and Standard Errors in Logit and Probit Models." *The State Journal* 4, 2 (2004): 154–67.

Nossiter, T. J. *Communism in Kerala: A Study in Political Adaptation.* Berkeley: University of California Press, 1982.

Nurdin, Ahmad Ali. "Islamic Party and Democracy: The Experience of the PKS during 1999, 2004 and 2009 Elections." Working Paper, 2010.

Omvedt, Gail. *Reinventing Revolution: New Social Movements and the Socialist Tradition in India.* Armonk: M. E. Sharpe, 1993.

Oomen, M. A. *Kerala Land Reform: Essays on the Kerala Economy.* Madras: Christian Institute for Study of Religion and Society, 1971.

Osella, Filippo and Caroline Osella. *Social Mobility in Kerala.* London: Pluto Press, 2000.

Pahwa, Sumita. "Secularizing Islamism and Islamizing Democracy: The Political and Ideational Evolution of the Egyptian Muslim Brothers 1984–2012." Working Paper, 2013.

Pai, Sudha. *Dalit Assertion and the Unfinished Democratic Revolution.* New Delhi: Sage, 2002.

Pai, Sudha. "Dalit Question and Political Response: Comparative Study of Uttar Pradesh and Madhya Pradesh." *Economic and Political Weekly* 39, 11 (March 13–19, 2004): 1141–50.

Paige, Jeffery. "Land Reform and Agrarian Revolution in El Salvador." *Latin American Research Review* 31, 2 (1996): 127–39.

Palshikar, Suhas. "Politics of India's Middle Classes," in Imtiaz Ahmad and Helmut Reifeld, (eds.), *Middle Class Values in India and Western Europe.* New Delhi: Social Science Press, 2001: 171–193.

Pandey, Saumya. "Communalism: Narratives in Chhattisgarh." *Economic and Political Weekly* (January 12, 2008).

Panebianco, Angelo. *Political Parties: Organization and Power.* New York: Cambridge University Press, 1988.

Pendse, Sandeep. "Dalits and Hindutva: Gainers and Losers," in Anand Teltumbde, ed. *Hindutva and Dalits.* Delhi: Samya, 2005: 75–91.

Pepinsky, Thomas. "The Limits of the Indonesian Model." Unpublished Working Paper, July 2012 draft.

Pepinksy, Thomas, R. William Liddle, and Saiful Mujani. "Testing Islam's Political Advantage: Evidence from Indonesia." *American Journal of Political Science* 56, 3 (July 2012): 584–600.

Petras, James and Maurice Zeitlin. "Agrarian Radicalism in Chile." *British Journal of Sociology* 19 (1968): 503–31.

Porter, Donald J. *Making Politics and Islam in Indonesia.* London: Routledge, 2002.

Posner, Daniel. *Institutions and Ethnic Politics in Africa.* Cambridge: Cambridge University Press, 2006

Prasad, Vijay. *Untouchable Freedom: A Social History of the Dalit Community.* Delhi: Oxford University Press, 2000.

Przeworski, Adam and John Sprague. *Paper Stones: A History of Electoral Socialism.* Chicago: Chicago University Press, 1986.

Putnam, Robert. *Making Democracy Work: Civic Traditions in Modern Italy.* Princeton: Princeton University Press, 1993.

Qassem, Na'im. *Hizbullah: The Story from Within.* London: SAQI Books, 2005.

Rajagopal, Arvind. *Politics after Television.* Cambridge: Cambridge University Press, 2001.

Ram, Kanshi. *The Chamcha Age: An Era of Stooges.* New Delhi, 1982.

Rao, Anupama. *The Caste Question.* Berkeley: University of California Press, 2009.

Ray, James Lee. "Explaining Interstate Conflict and War: What Should Be Controlled For?" *Conflict Management and Peace Science* 20 (2003): 1–31.

Ray, James Lee. "Constructing Multivariate Analyses (of Dangerous Dyads)." *Conflict Management and Peace Science* 22, 4 (January 2005): 277–92.

Richards, Alan and John Waterbury. *A Political Economy of the Middle East.* Boulder: Westview Press, 2008.

Roberts, Kenneth. "Social Inequalities without Class Cleavages in Latin America's Neoliberal Era." *Studies in Comparative International Development* 36, 2 (Winter 2002): 3–33.

Robertson-Snape, Fiona. "Corruption, Collusion and Nepotism in Indonesia." *Third World Quarterly* 20, 3 (1999): 589–602.

Robinson, Glenn E. "Hamas as Social Movement," in Quintan Wiktorowicz. *Islamic Activism: A Social Movement Theory Approach.* Bloomington: Indiana University Press, 2004: 112–39.

Rodriguez, Valerian. "The Communist Parties in India," in Peter Ronald deSouza and E. Sridharan, eds. *India's Political Parties.* New Delhi: Sage, 2006: 199–252.

Roemer, John. "Why the Poor Do Not Expropriate the Rich." *Journal of Public Economics* 70 (1998): 399–424.

Rosenbaum, Paul R. *Observational Studies.* New York: Springer, 2002.

Rosenblum, Nancy. "Religious Parties, Religious Political Identity, and the Cold Shoulder of Liberal Democratic Thought." *Ethical Theory and Moral Practice* 6, 1 (March 2003): 23–53.

Rosenblum, Nancy. "Banning Parties: Religious and Ethnic Partisanship in Multicultural Democracies." *Law and Ethics of Human Rights* 1, 1 (2007): 17–59.

Roy, Ramashray. "The Text and Context of the 2004 Lok Sabha Elections in India," in Ramashray Roy and Paul Wallace, eds. *India's 2004 Elections: Grass-roots and National Perspectives*. Sage: New Delhi, 2007: 9–34.

Rudolph, Lloyd and Suzanne Rudolph. *In Pursuit of Lakshmi*. Chicago: Chicago University Press, 1987.

Sadasivan, S. N. *A Social History of India*. New Delhi: APH Publications, 2000.

Saez, Lawrence and Aseema Sinha. "Political Cycles, Political Institutions, and Public Expenditure in India, 1980–2000." *British Journal of Political Science* 40 (November 2009): 91–113.

Sarkar, Tanika. "Heroic Women, Mother Goddesses: Family and Organization in Hindutva Politics," in Christophe Jaffrelot, ed. *The Sangh Parivar*. New Delhi: Oxford University Press, 2005a: 148–77.

Sarkar, Tanika. "The Gender Predicament of the Hindu Right," in Christophe Jaffrelot, ed. *The Sangh Parivar*. New Delhi: Oxford University Press, 2005b: 178–93.

Sartori, Giovanni. "Concept Misinformation in Comparative Politics." *American Political Science Review* 64 (1970): 1033–53.

Savarkar, Vinayak Damodar. *Hindutva: Who Is a Hindu?* New Delhi: Bharatiya Sahitya Sadan, 1923.

Scheve, Kenneth and David Stasavage. "Religion and Preferences for Social Insurance." *Quarterly Journal of Political Science* 1, 3 (2006): 255–86.

Schwedler, Jillian. "Yemen's Aborted Opening." *Journal of Democracy* 13, 4 (October 2002): 48–55.

Schwedler, Jillian. "The Islah Party in Yemen," in Quintan Wiktorowicz, *Islamic Activism: A Social Movement Theory Approach*. Bloomington: Indiana University Press, 2004: 205–28.

Schwedler, Jillian. *Faith in Moderation*. Cambridge: Cambridge University Press, 2006.

Scott, James. "Corruption, Machine Politics, and Political Change." *American Political Science Review* 63, 4 (1969): 1142–58.

Scott, James. "Patron-Client Politics and Political Change in Southeast Asia." *American Political Science Review* 66, 1 (March 1972): 91–113.

Sekhon , Jasjeet. "The Neyman-Rubin Model of Causal Inference and Estimation via Matching Methods," in Janet Box-Steffensmeier, Henry Brady, and David Collier, eds. *The Oxford Handbook of Political Methodology*. Oxford: Oxford University Press, 2008: 271–99.

Sen, Amartya. "More Than 100 Million Women Are Missing." *The New York Review of Books* 37, 20 (1990).

Shah, Ghanshyam. "The BJP and Backwards Castes in Gujarat." *South Asian Bulletin* 14, 1 (1994).

Shefter, Martin. "Party and Patronage: Germany, England, and Italy." *Politics and Society* 7, 4 (1977): 403–51.

Sheth, D. L. "Profiles of Party Support in 1967." *Economic and Political Weekly* 6, 3/5 (January 1971): 275–88.

Simmons, Beth and Daniel Hopkins. "The Constraining Power of International Treaties: Theory and Methods." *American Political Science Review* 99, 4 (November 2005): 623–31.

Sivanandan, P. "Caste, Class and Economic Opportunity in Kerala." *Economic and Political Weekly* 14, 7/8 (February 1979): 475–80.

Snow, David and Robert Benford. "Framing Processes and Social Movements: An Overview and Assessment." *Annual Review of* Sociology 26 (2000): 611–39.

Snow, David A., E. Burke Rochford, Steven K. Worden, and Robert D. Benford. "Frame Alignment Processes, Micromobilization, and Movement Participation." *American Sociological Review* 51, 4 (August 1996): 464–81.

Snyder, Richard. "Scaling Down: The Subnational Comparative Method." *Studies in Comparative International Development* 36, 1 (Spring 2001): 93–110.

Springborg, Robert. "State-Society Relations in Egypt." *The Middle East Journal,* 45, 2 (Spring 1991): 232–49.

Srinivas, M. N. *Religion and Society among the Coorgs of South India.* Oxford: Clarendon Press, 1952.

Srinivas, M. N. "A Note on Sanskritization and Westernization." *Far Eastern Quarterly* 15 (1956): 481–96.

Stokes, Susan. *Cultures in Conflict.* Berkeley: University of California Press, 1995.

Stokes, Susan. "Perverse Accountability: A Formal Model of Machine Politics with Evidence from Argentina." *American Political Science Review* 99, 3 (2005): 315–25.

Stokes, Susan. "Pork, by Any Other Name…Building a Conceptual Scheme of Distributive Politics." Working paper, 2009.

Stokes, Susan. "The Opportunities and Limits of Field Experiments." *APSA-CP Newsletter* 21, 1 (Winter 2010).

Subramanian, S. "Examining the 'Creamy Layer' Principle." *Economic and Political Weekly* (November 11–17, 2006): 4643–5.

Sud, Nikita. *Liberalization, Hindu Nationalism, and the State.* Oxford: Oxford University Press, 2012.

Sundar, Nandini. "Adivasi vs. Vanvasi," in Satish Sabharwal and Mishurul Hasan, eds. *Assertive Religious Identities: India and Europe.* Delhi: Manohar, 2006: 357–90.

Swaminathan, Padmini, J. Jeyaranjan, R. Sreenivasan, and K. Jeyashree. "Tamil Nadu's Midday Meal Scheme: Where Assumed Benefits Score over Hard Data." *Economic and Political Weekly,* 39, 44 (October 30, 2004): 4811–21.

Teltumbde, Anand. "Hindutva, Dalits and the Neoliberal Order," in Anand Teltumbde, ed. *Hindutva and Dalits.* Delhi: Samya, 2005: 46–74.

Tessler, Mark. "The Origins of Popular Support for Islamist Movements," in John P. Entelis, ed. *Islam, Democracy and the State in North Africa.* Bloomington: Indiana University Press, 1997: 93–126.

Thachil, Tariq. "Neoliberalism's Two Faces in Asia." *Comparative Politics* 41, 4 (July 2009): 473–94.

Thachil, Tariq. "Elite Parties and Poor Voters: Theory and Evidence from India." *American Political Science Review,* 108, 2 (2014).

Thachil, Tariq and Emmanuel Teitelbaum. "Ethnic Parties and Public Spending in the Indian States." Draft manuscript, n.d.

Thakran, P. K. Michael. "Socio-Economic Factors in Educational Development: Case of Nineteenth Century Travancore." *Economic and Political Weekly* 19, 45 (November 10, 1984): 1913–28.

Tharamangalam, J. "The Perils of Social Development without Economic Growth: The Development Debacle of Kerala, India." *Bulletin of Concerned Asian Scholars* 30, 1 (1998).

Tibi, Bassam. "Why They Can't Be Democratic." *Journal of Democracy* 19, 3 (July 2008): 43–8.

Tillen, Louise. "Questioning Borders: Social Movements, Political Parties and the Creation of New States in India." *Pacific Affairs* 84, 1 (March 2011): 67–87.

Timmer, Peter. "The Road to Pro-poor Growth: The Indonesian Experience in Regional Perspective." *Bulletin of Indonesian Economic Studies* 40, 2 (2004): 177–207.

Tomsa, Dirk. *Party Politics and Democratization in Indonesia.* London: Routledge 2008.

Tomsa, Dirk. "The Party System after the Elections," in Edward Aspinall and Marcus Mietzner, eds. *Problems of Democratisation in Indonesia.* Singapore: ISEAS Press, 2010: 141–59.

Tomsa, Dirk. "Moderating Islamism in Indonesia." *Political Research Quarterly* 64, 1 (2011): 1–13.

Tomsa, Dirk. "What Type of Party? Southeast Asian Parties between Clientelism and Electoralism," in Dirk Tomsa and Andreas Ufen, eds. *Party Politics in Southeast Asia.* London: Routledge, 2012: 20–39.

Tomz, Michael, Jason Wittenberg, and Gary King. "CLARIFY: Software for Interpreting and Presenting Statistical Results, Version 2.0." (June 1 2001). Cambridge, MA: Harvard University, http://gking.harvard.edu.

Tsai, Lily. "Solidary Groups, Informal Accountability, and Local Public Goods Provision in Rural China." *American Political Science Review*, 101, 2 (May 2007): 355–72.

Tugal, Cihan. *Passive Revolution.* Stanford: Stanford University Press, 2009.

Ufen, Andreas. "Lipset and Rokkan in Southeast Asia," in Dirk Tomsa and Andreas Ufen, eds. *Party Politics in Southeast Asia.* London: Routledge, 2012: 40–61.

Van Cott, Donna. *From Movements to Parties in Latin America.* Cambridge: Cambridge University Press, 2005.

Van de Walle, Nicholas and Michael Bratton. "Neopatrimonial Regimes and Political Transitions in Africa." *World Politics* 46, 4 (July 1994): 453–89.

Van Hear, Nicholas. "The Socio-economic Impact of the Involuntary Mass Return to Yemen in 1990." *Journal of Refugee Studies* 7, 1 (1994): 18–38.

Vanaik, Achin. "Communalism and Our Foreign Policy." *Seminar* 374 (October 1990).

Varshney, Ashutosh. *Democracy, Development and the Countryside.* Cambridge: Cambridge University Press, 1999.

Varshney, Ashutosh. "Is India Becoming More Democratic?" *Journal of Asian Studies* 59, 1 (February 2000): 3–25.

Varshney, Ashutosh. *Ethnic Conflict and Civic Life.* New Haven: Yale University Press, 2002.

Wald, Kenneth, Dennis Owen, and Samuel Hill Jr. "Churches as Political Communities." *American Political Science Review* 82, 2 (June 1988): 531–48.

Wallace, Paul. "Introduction: India Shining Trumped by Poverty," in Ramashray Roy and Paul Wallace, eds. *India's 2004 Elections: Grass-roots and National Perspectives.* Sage: New Delhi, 2007: 1–9.

Wantchekon, Leonard. "Clientelism and Voting Behavior." *World Politics* 55, 3 (April 2003): 399–422.

Wedeen, Lisa. *Peripheral Visions.* Chicago: University of Chicago Press, 2008.

Weiner, Myron. *Party Building in a New Nation. The Indian National Congress.* Chicago: Chicago University Press, 1967.

Weiner, Myron. *The Indian Paradox.* New Delhi: Sage, 1989.

Weir, Shelagh. "A Clash of Fundamentalisms: Wahhabism in Yemen." *Middle East Report* 204 (July 2007): 22–3, 26.

Weitz-Shapiro, Rebecca. "What Wins Votes: Why Some Politicians Opt Out of Clientelism." *American Journal of Political Science*, 56, 3 (2012): 568–83.

Wickham, Carrie Rosefsky. *Mobilizing Islam*. New York: Columbia University Press, 2002.

Wiktorowicz, Quintan. *Islamic Activism: A Social Movement Theory Approach*. Bloomington: Indiana University Press, 2004.

Wilkinson, Steven. *Votes and Violence*. Cambridge: Cambridge University Press, 2004.

Williams, John. "Circumstantial Pragmatism: The Flexible Ideology of the Lebanese Hizbullah." *Journal of Middle Eastern Geopolitics* 2, 3 (2006): 37–49.

Wittenberg, Jason. *Crucibles of Political Loyalty*. Cambridge: Cambridge University Press, 2006.

Wittman, Donald. "Candidate Motivation: A Synthesis of Alternative Theories." *The American Political Science Review* 77, 1 (March 1983): 142–57.

Wood, Elisabeth. *Insurgent Collective Action and Civil War in El Salvador*. Cambridge: Cambridge University Press, 2003.

Yashar, Deborah. *Contesting Citizenship*. Cambridge: Cambridge University Press, 2005.

Zeliot, Eleanor. *From Untouchable to Dalit*. New Delhi: South Asia Books, 2005.

Zerinini, Jasmine. "The Marginalisation of the *Savarnas* in Uttar Pradesh," in Christophe Jaffrelot, and Sanjay Kumar, eds. *Rise of Plebians: The Changing Face of the Indian Legislative Assemblies*. New Delhi: Routledge, 2008: 27–64.

Media References

"ABVP to work for Harijans, tribals." *Organizer*, November 16, 1980, p. 15.

Ahmed, Sooror. "Giant-killer will be Jharkhand CM." *Rediff News*, November 14, 2000,

Arun, T.K. "See, hear and speak no evil, let evil prevail." *Economic Times*, March 21, 2002.

Bidwai, Praful. "End of social engineering." *Frontline*, 22, 26, December 17–30, 2005.

"BJP runs into OBC reality." *Statesman*, November 1999.

Chasin, Barbara and Richard Franke. "The Kerala difference." *The New York Review of Books* 38, 17 (October 24, 1991), available at www.nybooks.com/articles/3117.

Chatterjee, Partha. "Democracy and economic transformation in India." *Economic and Political Weekly*, April 19, 2008, pp. 53–62.

Chaudhuri, Kalyan. "The day of Jharkhand." *Frontline*, 17, 24, November 25–December 8, 2000.

"Congress did not do justice to Ambedkar: Advani." *Hindu*, April 14, 2009.

Daga, Mahesh. "Is the party over?" *Seminar*, 534, 2004.

Datar, Abhay. "A vote for secular politics." *Hindu*, May 20, 2004.

Deshpande, Rajeev. "A fine net widely cast." *Times of India*, October 24, 2005.

Dreze, Jean and Reetika Khera. "Water for the Leeward India." *Outlook*, March 24, 2014.

"Editorial: Chhattisgarh BJP leaders sulking with Shukla's inclusion." *The Statesmen*, March 16, 2004.

"Editorial: End of an idea." *Times of India*, December 8, 2005.

"Editorial: Shukla woos Raman, Sai feels no warmth." *Indian Express*, February 16, 2004.

"Flunking the test." *Times of India*, March 19, 2001.

Gatade, Subhash. "The ideological and institutional incorporation of Dalits into Hindutva maelstrom." *South Asia Composite Heritage*, February –April 2011, 1, 22, 18–20: http://www.sach.org.in/news_letter/issue22/feb_apr_11.pdf.

Ghimire, Yubaraj and N. K. Singh. "The Lotus Wars." *India Today*, May 15, 1992.

"Hindu-Dalit gap needs to be bridged," *Organizer*, January 3, 1988, p. 5.

Joshi, Poornima. "Strategems and spoils." *Caravan*, July 2013.

Khan, Atiq. "Kalyan Singh quits BJP." *Hindu*, January 21, 2009.

Khilnani, Sunil. "Retrieving the idea of India." *Hindu*, May 20, 2004.

Khosla, Shyam. "Significance of the BJP-BSP tie up in UP." *Organizer*, April 5, 1997.

Kumar, Sunil. "Fruits of Megalomania" *Seminar*, 2004: http://www.india-seminar.com/2004/534/534%20sunil%20kumar.htm.

Kumar, Vivek. "No Dalit equality in Sangh Parivar." *Pioneer*, November 6, 2000.

"Lakhs contribute to the Rs. 5 crore fund to protect dharma," *Organizer*, August 1, 1982, p. 4.

"MARG poll," *India Today*, May 31, 1996, p. 27.

Mathew, George. "Amartya Sen and the Kerala Model." *Hindu*, January 9, 2001.

Menon, Mukundan. "Mayawati deplores singling out Bangaru Laxman." March 27, 2001.

Mukhopadhyay, Nilanja. "Sangh clan's new plan." *Free Press Journal*, March 28, 1994.

Newman, Katherine and Sukhadeo Thorat. "Caste and Economic Discrimination." *Economic and Political Weekly* special issue, 42, 41 (October 13–19): 2007.

"No BJP strategy in 'defeat,'" *Hindustan Times*, December 13, 1993.

"Old caste system not all that bad: Sudarshan." *Hindustan Times*, January 28, 2006.

Parashar, Arpit. "One more party for the Dalits in Uttar Pradesh." *Tehelka*, May 4, 2011.

Pathak, Vikas. "RSS footprint shrinking." *Hindustan Times*, March 26, 2010.

Perry, Tom and Abdel Rahman Yousseff. "Egypt's Brotherhood turns to flour power." *Reuters*, June 13, 2013.

Raj, Udit. "A Hindu Rashtra? Sangh Parivar is daydreaming." *Indian Express*, December 31, 2002.

Rajagopalan, S. "A marriage of convenience." *Hindustan Times*, March 30, 1997.

Raman, P. "Growth pangs in the BJP." *Business Standard*, July 26, 1996.

Ramaswamy, Sushila. "Hedgewar and RSS-II." *Statesman*, June 24, 2003.

"RSS chief showers praise on Ambedkar." *The Free Press Journal*, October 3, 2006.

"RSS means Ready for Selfless Service." *Organizer*, June 22, 1980, p. 10.

"RSS, nationalism and Sanatana dharma: A historical view." *Organizer*, June 15, 1980, p. 8.

"RSS to educate swayamsevaks on Ambedkar's views." *Hindustan Times*, January 7, 2003.

"SBY benefiting from safety net programs." *Jakarta Post*, March 28, 2009.

"Service projects to touch one lakh during centenary." *Organizer*, March 26, 2006.

Rao, Parsa. "RSS involved in poll campaign to ensure Narendra Modi wins." *DNA*, June 9, 2014.

Sinha, Rakesh. "Sangh Parivar and the Dalits." *Times of India*, July 11, 1994.

Sonwalkar, Prasun. "Advani clarifies stand on 'swadeshi.'" *Times of India*, September 14, 1993.

Subrahmaniam, Vidya. "SIT: Modi tried to dilute the seriousness of riots situation." *The Hindu*, February 4, 2011.

Suchitra, M. "Undermining a fine system." *India Together*, January 2004.

Surendran, P. K. "Third Front May Emerge in Kerala." *Times of India* (January 8 1994).

"Tehelka tapes appear to be true: RSS." *Hindu*, March 17, 2001.

Tripathi, Purnima. "Once more, with hope." *Frontline*, 19, 9, April 27–May 10, 2002.

Tripathi, Purnima. "The great game." *Frontline*, 19, 10, May 11–24, 2002.

Venugopal, K. "CPM-SNDP ties hit new low." *Deccan Herald*, Bangalore, February 1, 2000.

Verghese, A.V. "Devaswom Bill draws flak." *Deccan Herald*, January 14, 1998.

Vishvanath, Rupa. "A textbook case of exclusion." *Indian Express*, July 13, 2012.

Vyas, Neena. "The BJP Riding Two Horses." *Hindu*, November 12, 2000.

Vyas, Neena. "BJP suspends Uma Bharati." *Hindu*, December 1, 2005.

"Wipe out caste barriers: RSS." *Deccan Chronicle*, December 13, 2005.

Yadav, Yogendra. "Radical shift in the social basis of political power." *The Hindu*, May 20, 2004a.

Yadav, Yogendra. "BJP's consolidation will be hard to break in Chhattisgarh." *The Hindu*, March 21, 2004b.

Yadav, Yogendra and Sanjay Kumar, "Understanding the Chhattisgarh vote." *The Hindu*, December 11, 2003.

Yadav, Yogendra and Sanjay Kumar. "Poor Man's Rainbow over Uttar Pradesh." *Indian Express*, May 17, 2007a.

Yadav, Yogendra and Sanjay Kumar. "Shaken to the core." *Indian Express*, May 18, 2007b.

Yadav, Yogendra and Sanjay Kumar. "BJP decline, Congress style." May 19, 2007c

Zaidi, Askari. "Battlefield of Chhattisgarh." *Hindustan Times*, November 23, 2003.

B. Cited Sangh Sources

Advani, Lal Krishna 1987 Presidential Address, from the complete collection of Bharatiya Janata Party papers. New Delhi: BJP Press, 2005.

"National Executive Resolution, 1985," Bharatiya Janata Party Press, 1985, p. 36. Bharatiya Janata Party 'Vision Document 2004'.

Presidential Speeches Part II,. New Delhi: Bharatiya Janata Party Press, 2005, pp. 97–113.

Seva Bharati, *Seva Disha* Annual Report, 1995.

Seva Bharati, *Seva Disha* Annual Report, 1997.

Seva Bharati, *Seva Disha* Annual Report, 2004.

Seva Bharati, *Seva Sadhana*. Organization Report, 2008.

Seva Bharati, Seva Disha Annual Report, 2009.

Seva Bharati Agra Mahanagar, *Annual Report*, published by Saraswati Shishu Mandir, Subhash Park, Agra.

Vajpayee, Atal. B. Address to BJP National Executive, Calcutta, 1985, published in *Presidential Speeches Part II*. New Delhi: Bharatiya Janata Party Press, 2005, p. 213.

Vanvasi Kalyan Ashram. *Van Bandhu* newsletter, November 2007.

Authored Articles from the Organizer *(Sangh Weekly):*

Ahmed Rashid Shervani, "A Warning to Caste Hindus." *Organizer*, June 1, 1980, p. 5.

Anand "Some Thoughts to Ponder for Our Harijan Brothers." *Organizer*, August 3, 1987.

M.V. Kamath, "The Brahmin Question in Tamil Nadu," *Organizer*, November 22, 1987.

Newspapers, news journals, and other primary sources consulted

Parliamentary Library Clippings Archives, New Delhi

> *The Hindu*
> *Hindustan Times*
> *Times of India*

Deccan Herald
Economic Times
Indian Express
Mumbai Free Press Journal
Pioneer
Telegraph (Calcutta)

Teen Murti Library Archives, New Delhi

Organizer (1980–2007)
India Today

Deshbandhu Press Archives, Raipur Chhattisgarh

Clippings on Chhattisgarh BJP and RSS, and Vanvasi Kalyan Ashram (Hindi and English).

BJP Party Office, New Delhi

BJP Party Manifestos, Presidential Speeches, and Executive Reports from complete collection of Bharatiya Janata Party papers. New Delhi: BJP Press, 2005.

Government Publications

Chhattisgarh State Government: chhattisgarh.nic.in/profile/corigin.htm.
Election Commission of India, *Statistical Reports on General Elections*, various issues, available at www.eci.gov.in.
Government of India, Home Ministry, Data on Communal Incidents, 1998–2004. Data collected from Rajya Sabha Starred Question No. 52, dated 26.07.2000, and Lok Sabha Starred Question No. 294, dated 21.12.2004 (collected by Indiastat online database).
Government of India, *Indian National Census* 1991, 2001, available at www.censusindia.net.
Government of India, National Commission for Scheduled Castes and Scheduled Tribes, *Annual Report on the Scheduled Castes and Scheduled Tribes for the Year* 2004, available at socialjustice.nic.in/schedule/ar-poa.pdf.
Government of India, *Handbook of Statistics on State Government Finances*, Reserve Bank of India, 2005–2006.
Government of India, *Budgets in Brief*, Ministry of Finance, various issues.
Government of India, *Economic Survey*, Ministry of Finance, 2011a.
Government of India, Planning Commission, *India Human Development Report*. Oxford: Oxford University Press, 2011b.
Government of Kerala, *Assembly Election Results*, Kerala Government Information Center, Thiruvananthapuram.
Government of Kerala, *Kerala Human Development Report*, released by State Planning Commission, 2005.
Government of Madhya Pradesh, *Niyogi Committee Report on Christian Missionary Activities*, 1956.
Government of Uttar Pradesh, *Uttar Pradesh: State Human Development Report* (2007).

D. Other Data Sources:

Arab Barometer Survey, 2006–2008 wave, accessed at www.arabbarometer.org.

Al Ahram Center for Political and Strategic Studies/Danish Egyptian Dialogue Institute, Egyptian Post-Election Survey, 2011.

Asian Barometer, 2005–2008 wave, accessed at www.asianbarometer.org.

Freedom and Justice Party, 2011 Election Program (accessed via website of Charles Kurzman, http://kurzman.unc.edu/).

Human Rights Watch, *Communalism as Political Strategy*, available at http://hrw.org/reports/2003/india0703/Gujarat-10.htm.

Human Rights Watch, *We Have No Orders to Save You*, 14, 3, April 2002, available at http://www.hrw.org/reports/2002/india/.

National Election Study, Lokniti, Center for the Study of Developing Society, 1967,

National Election Study, Lokniti, Center for the Study of Developing Society, 1996.

National Election Study, Lokniti, Center for the Study of Developing Society, 1999.

National Election Study, Lokniti, Center for the Study of Developing Society, 2004.

National Election Study, Lokniti, Center for the Study of Developing Society, 2009.

Gujarat State Election Survey, Lokniti, 2002.

Gujarat State Election Survey, Lokniti, 2012.

Planning Commission of India, *India Human Development Report*, Oxford: Oxford University Press, 2011.

Sewa Bharati, *Seva Disha 1995, 1997, 2004*, Bhopal.

Sewa Bharati, internal records collected by author in New Delhi, Raipur, Bilaspur, Thirvananthapuram.

United Nations Development Programme and Planning Commission of India, *National Human Development Report* 2001.

United Nations Development Programme, *Indonesia National Human Development Report*, 2004

United Nations Economic and Social Commission for Asia and the Pacific, *Easing the impact of subsidy reform: Indonesia's Bantuan Langsung Tunai cash transfer programme*, 2012.

USAID, "Situational Analysis Report of Agra City," December 2004.

Vanvasi Kalyan Ashram, internal records collected by author in Jashpurnagar, Chhattisgarh.

Varshney, Ashutosh and Steven Wilkinson, 2006-02-17, "Varshney-Wilkinson Dataset on Hindu-Muslim Violence in India, 1950–1995, Version 2," hdl: 1902.2/4342 Inter-university Consortium for Political and Social Research [Distributor].

Woodberry, Robert, Juan Carlos Esparza Ochoa, Reid Porter, and Xiaoyun Lu. "Conceptual Framework and Technical Innovations for Creating the Project on Religion and Economy Change Geo-Spatial Database." Project on Religion and Economic Change Working Paper #004. 2010.

World Bank, "Poverty and Social Safety Nets Building Block", in *Republic of Yemen: Comprehensive Development Review Phase I*, 2000.

World Values Survey, 2005 wave, accessed at www.worldvaluessurvey.org.

Index

Acemoglu, Daron, 3, 54
Adivasi, 6, 8, 9, 14, 23, 111
Advani, Lal Krishna, 60
age
  as a determinant of non-elite support for BJP
    (Chhattisgarh), 172, 174
AKP (Justice and Development Party), Turkey, 54
Al Nour Party, Egypt, 21, 240
al-Ahmar, Shaykh Abdallah, 241
al-Banna, Gamal, 20
al-Banna, Hassan, 19, 234
al-Hadi, Abd Rabbuh Mansur, 240
al-Zindani, Shaykh Abd al Majid, 242
Alianza Republicana Nacionalista, 4
All Cochin Pulaya Maha Sabha, 190
All India Anna Dravida Munnetra Kazhagam,
  268
All India Backward and Minority Communities
    Employees Federation (BAMCEF), 202
alternative explanations, 37
  coalitions, 72
  ethnic engineering, 65, 70
  Hindu-Muslim conflict, 62
  other strategic failures, 72
  preference for BJP, 96
  programmatic strategy, 58
  religious mobilization, 58
  voter support for communalism, 91
  voter support for liberalization, 91
Ambedkar, Bhimrao Ramji, 44
  conflict with Gandhi, 44
  conversion to Buddhism, 45
  Hindu nationalist appropriation of, 75

Arya Samaj, 38, 199
Assam, 136
associational membership
  as a determinant of elite support for BJP (all
    India), 84, 91, 96, 97, 99
  as a determinant of Indonesian support for
    PKS, 259
  as a determinant of Muslim or Christian
    support for BJP (all India), 95
  as a determinant of non-elite support for BJP
    (all India), 84, 91, 96, 97, 99
  as a determinant of non-elite support for BJP
    (Chhattisgarh), 173
  as a determinant of Yemeni support for
    Islamic parties, 247
Auyero, Javier, 25
Ayodhya mobilization, 60, 107, 215
Ayyankali, 190

Babri Masjid, 60, 61
Bahujan Samaj Party, 56, 65, 100, 201
  alliance with BJP in Uttar Pradesh, 217
  electoral strategy. See ethnic parties
  impact on service as an electoral strategy,
    184
  material reasons for non-elite support, 203,
    205
  politics of dignity, 205
  subaltern self-mobilization, 184
  symbolic reasons for non-elite support, 204
Bajrang Dal, 60
Bartels, Larry, 1, 79
Bastar, 164

Cambridge Studies in Comparative Politics

Beverly Silver, *Forces of Labor: Workers' Movements and Globalization since 1870*

Theda Skocpol, *Social Revolutions in the Modern World*

Dan Slater, *Ordering Power: Contentious Politics and Authoritarian Leviathans in Southeast Asia*

Regina Smyth, *Candidate Strategies and Electoral Competition in the Russian Federation: Democracy without Foundation*

Richard Snyder, *Politics after Neoliberalism: Reregulation in Mexico*

David Stark and László Bruszt, *Postsocialist Pathways: Transforming Politics and Property in East Central Europe*

Sven Steinmo, *The Evolution of Modern States: Sweden, Japan, and the United States*

Sven Steinmo, Kathleen Thelen, and Frank Longstreth, eds., *Structuring Politics: Historical Institutionalism in Comparative Analysis*

Susan C. Stokes, *Mandates and Democracy: Neoliberalism by Surprise in Latin America*

Susan C. Stokes, ed., *Public Support for Market Reforms in New Democracies*

Susan C. Stokes, Thad Hall, Marcelo Nazareno, and Valeria Brusco, *Brokers, Voters, and Clientelism: The Puzzle of Distributive Politics*

Duane Swank, *Global Capital, Political Institutions, and Policy Change in Developed Welfare States*

Sidney Tarrow, *Power in Movement: Social Movements and Contentious Politics, Revised and Updated 3rd Edition*

Tariq Thachil, *Elite Parties, Poor Voters: How Social Services Win Votes in India*

Kathleen Thelen, *How Institutions Evolve: The Political Economy of Skills in Germany, Britain, the United States, and Japan*

Kathleen Thelen, *Varieties of Liberalization and the New Politics of Social Solidarity*

Charles Tilly, *Trust and Rule*

Daniel Treisman, *The Architecture of Government: Rethinking Political Decentralization*

Guillermo Trejo, *Popular Movements in Autocracies: Religion, Repression, and Indigenous Collective Action in Mexico*

Lily Lee Tsai, *Accountability without Democracy: How Solidary Groups Provide Public Goods in Rural China*

Joshua Tucker, *Regional Economic Voting: Russia, Poland, Hungary, Slovakia and the Czech Republic, 1990–1999*

Ashutosh Varshney, *Democracy, Development, and the Countryside*

Jeremy M. Weinstein, *Inside Rebellion: The Politics of Insurgent Violence*

Stephen I. Wilkinson, *Votes and Violence: Electoral Competition and Ethnic Riots in India*

Jason Wittenberg, *Crucibles of Political Loyalty: Church Institutions and Electoral Continuity in Hungary*

Elisabeth J. Wood, *Forging Democracy from Below: Insurgent Transitions in South Africa and El Salvador*

Elisabeth J. Wood, *Insurgent Collective Action and Civil War in El Salvador*

41283682R00210

Made in the USA
Middletown, DE
08 March 2017